作者:保罗·J.克里斯托弗
　　　艾莉西亚·玛丽·史密斯
主译:方华文
译者:郭　雯　杜争鸣

英汉对照
Greatest Sports Heroes of all Times

50+1位 最负盛名的 体育明星

安徽科学技术出版社
Encouragement Press, LLC

U0595788

图书在版编目（CIP）数据

50+1位最闪耀的体育巨星 / （美）克里斯托弗，（美）
史密斯著；方华文，郭雯，杜争鸣译. -- 合肥：安徽
科学技术出版社，2009.06
　（50+1系列）
　ISBN 978-7-5337-4459-5

Ⅰ.①5… Ⅱ.①克… Ⅲ.①运动员－生平事迹－世
界 Ⅳ.①K815.47

中国版本图书馆CIP数据核字(2009)第095045号

50+1位最闪耀的体育巨星

（美）克里斯托弗　（美）史密斯 著　方华文　郭 雯　杜争鸣 译

出 版 人：黄和平
责任编辑：姚敏淑
封面设计：朱 婧
出版发行：安徽科学技术出版社(合肥市政务文化新区圣泉路1118号
　　　　　出版传媒广场,邮编：230071)
网　　址：www.ahstp.net
E - mail：yougoubu@sina.com
经　　销：新华书店
排　　版：安徽事达科技贸易有限公司
印　　刷：合肥瑞丰印务有限公司
开　　本：787×1092　1/16
印　　张：16
字　　数：440千
版　　次：2009年6月第1版　2022年1月第2次印刷
定　　价：46.00元

(本书如有印装质量问题,影响阅读,请向本社市场营销部调换)

译 者 序

他似凌空飞燕,将篮球一次次"塞入"篮中,姿势潇洒自如。欢呼声阵阵如潮,人群为之倾倒、陶醉。他叱咤国际球坛,以个人魅力感动了千千万万的人,拥有人数最多的球迷。他,名字叫乔丹,书写了篮球的神话!他是怎么成才的,怎么最终成为伟大的球星?

他像一个力大无穷的金刚,在拳坛"横扫千军如卷席",用一双拳头铸就了辉煌。他就是令人肃然起敬的阿里!他赢得人们的尊敬,不仅因为他技压群雄,掌握着"蝴蝶舞步","如蜜蜂般犀利蜇人",更因为他的"博爱":他反对越南战争,拒绝参加侵略军,并发表反战演说;他仗义疏财,拿出数百万美元救助弱势人群,还要求美国政府援助卢旺达难民,据估计有2200万灾民受到他直接或间接的救助。

他用一根球棒征服了球迷们的心,他所取得的伟大业绩成为美国棒球史上的一道丰碑。他不但征服了球迷,也赢得了电影明星玛丽莲·梦露的芳心,二人双双步入婚姻殿堂。他出身于平民,最终成为棒球界的"圣人"。他的名字叫狄马乔!

一个个矫健的身影活跃在运动场上,一双双眼睛在注视着他们所取得成就……随着赛事的起落,人们情不自禁地手舞足蹈、心驰神往:为一胜而振臂狂呼,为一败而伤心懊恼。这就是体育的魅力!尽管性别、年龄、职业、经历、兴趣甚至政见不同,但人们都关心体育,因为体育代表着人类的进取精神。无论胜利还是失败,它所追求的目标是全世界的团结、进步、和平和友谊。

"追星族"处处可见,有的追天姿国色的女影星或英俊的男星,

1

有的追满腹经纶的知识之星，有的则追力量和刚毅型的体育明星……有些"追星族"一提到自己喜爱的体育明星，就会兴奋起来，滔滔不绝，崇拜、激动之情溢于言表。其实，这些fans(粉丝)八成只是为明星的成就而倾倒。那么，体育明星的人生和梦想诸位知道多少呢?这本书通过一个个从"平凡"到"伟大"的故事，记载了一些世界顶级体育明星的人生经历以及他们如何把梦想变为现实的奋斗历程。

方华文

方华文简介

方华文，男，1955年6月生于西安，现任苏州大学外国语学院英语教授，著名学者、文学翻译家及翻译理论家，被联合国教科文组织国际译联誉为"the most productive literary translator in contemporary China"(中国当代最多产的文学翻译家，Babel.54:2,2008,145-158)。发表的著、译作品达1 000余万字，其中包括专著《20世纪中国翻译史》等，计200余万字;译著《雾都孤儿》《无名的裘德》《傲慢与偏见》《蝴蝶梦》《魂断英伦》《儿子与情人》《少年维特之烦恼》《红字》《从巅峰到低谷》《马丁·伊登》《套向月亮的绳索》《君主论》《社会契约论》以及改写本的《飘》《汤姆叔叔的小屋》《查特莱夫人的情人》《大卫·科波菲尔》《苔丝》《高老头》《三个火枪手》《悲惨世界》等;主编的译作包括《基督山伯爵》《红与黑》《简·爱》《汤姆·索亚历险记》《茶花女》《金银岛》《鲁滨孙漂流记》《巴黎圣母院》《莎士比亚戏剧故事集》《精神分析引论》《论法的精神》和《国富论》等;并主编了多部英汉对照读物。以上均为单行本著作，所发表文章不计在内。

Sports is one of the greatest highs there is — whether as a player or as an avid fan. Witness the spectacular rise in NASCAR, hockey, football and baseball attendance — college games alone have huge following and crazed fans. Who can not help but be fascinated by March Madness and its grip on the country each year?

Everyone has their favorite sport and everyone has their favorite sports heroes. But who are the best in the modern era in North America? How do you compare the exploits of a running back in football to the grace and finesse of a point guard in basketball or the rugged stamina of a soccer player?

The fact is that you probably cannot but we do know from research, our sports committee and a host of statistics and interviews that there are truly great, in fact, spectacularly talented athletes that deserve our attention and admiration.

Every sports fan who picks up this book will have opinions on who should and should not have been included. There is no doubt that many great names were left out, not because they are not worthy of mention but because the task was to come up with the 50 plus one greatest sports heroes. (Readers are invited to write us at michael@encouragementpress.com and let us know your opinions, one way or another. We would love to hear from you.)

Of course, our favorite sports heroes often are more than just athletes; they are people — active in their communities and the world at large. We have tried to show the full picture of each of our athletes — who they are, where they came from, what they accomplished and how they live their lives, both in and out of their chosen sports.

While our profiles of each athlete are short (by intention) we offer one or more resources where readers can learn more about their favorites — sometimes Websites, sometimes books or articles, but always informative and interesting.

Sit back, read and enjoy the 50 plus one Greatest Sports Heroes of All Times.

Paul J. Christopher
Alicia Marie Smith

Introduction

1

无论你是运动员，还是狂热的运动迷，体育总令人兴奋不已。虽然纳斯卡汽车协会、曲棍球、足球和棒球的兴起令无数观众着迷，但仅仅是大学比赛就已拥有无数追随者和疯狂的爱好者。谁能不为每年3月的赛事痴迷呢？

　　人人都有自己最爱的体育运动，也有自己喜爱的体坛英雄，但是谁是现代北美最佳风云人物？橄榄球跑卫功绩显著、篮球控球后卫沉着稳重、橄榄球队员精力充沛，怎样比较他们的优劣呢？

　　虽然不是人尽皆知，但是我们通过调查研究、体委及大量数据和访谈确定有很多伟大的、极具天赋的运动员值得我们关注和尊敬。

　　每位对体育痴迷的读者将从本书中认识他们。书中必定疏漏了很多伟大的名字，这并不是因为他们不值得一提，而是因为本书只着重介绍所列出的体坛巨星。

　　当然，这些最受欢迎的体坛英雄不仅仅是运动员，他们还活跃在各自的社会、甚至全球更广泛的领域。我们竭尽所能引领您进入所列出的体坛健儿的世界，包括他们的姓名、国籍、成就以及他们在体坛内外的生活。

　　请就座并欣赏我们精心为您准备的《50+1位最闪耀的体育巨星》吧。

保罗·J.克里斯托弗

艾莉西亚·玛丽·史密斯

Table of Contents

1

Table of Contents

目 录

2

Table of Contents

目　录

3

50+1位最闪耀的体育巨星

　　体育运动的终极目标在于追求人类健康、健美的发展，从而最大限度地激发人的潜能，以争取精神世界的健康自由，这种对提升勇气、信念、耐力、意志力品质的执著追求，往往会改善人的命运。书中这些体坛巨星的运动成就固然令人叹为观止，但从他们奋斗历程所提炼出的情感、态度和价值观，无疑会给我们许多思考和启迪……

Michael Jordan

Why He is Among the 50 plus one Greatest Sports Heroes

Former basketball star Magic Johnson seemed to say it all with these words:

"There's Michael Jordan and then there is the rest of us."

Jordan is considered by most — fans, players and experts alike — to be the greatest player in the history of the game. His athleticism was competitive, quick, powerful, artistic and graceful all at once, and he came to define the term superstar in the arena of professional basketball. During his career, Jordan was named an All–Star 14 times and he led his team to two separate National Basketball Association (NBA) championship three–peats. He has also been credited with gaining global recognition for the league through his fantastic playing abilities and his highly marketable charismatic personality. Jordan is hands–down one of the ultimate heroes ever to exist in the sports world.

On the Way Up

Michael Jeffrey Jordan was born on February 17, 1963 in Brooklyn, New York. He was the third son of James and Delores Jordan. He grew up in Wilmington, North Carolina with his four brothers and sisters. As a child, he played some football and basketball, but his greatest love was baseball, a passion that he shared with his father, James. Jordan started playing one–on–one pickup games against his older brother, Larry, and basketball soon moved into the number one spot in his heart as he tried again and again to beat his brother.

Jordan attended Emsley A. Laney High School in Wilmington. Although he got in trouble and was suspended various times during his freshman year and was cut from varsity basketball the following season due to an underdeveloped 5–foot 11–inch physique, he eventually became an excellent student and a star on the baseball, basketball and football teams. The summer between his sophomore and junior years, Jordan grew 4 inches and was even more dedicated to practicing his Michael Jordan skills. He finally made the varsity basketball team, averaging 25 points per game in both his junior and senior seasons. As a senior, Jordan was selected to the McDonald's All–American team and became the only high school player in history to average a triple–double with averages of 29.2 points, 11.6 rebounds and 10.1 assists.

After his super senior season, Jordan played for the University of North Carolina Tar Heels on a basketball scholarship. In 1982, he played somewhat below the radar as a freshman underneath upperclassmen stars, James Worthy and Sam Perkins, but he stepped into the spotlight at the end of the year during the NCAA Championship game against the Georgetown Hoyas and his future NBA rival, Patrick Ewing. Not only did Jordan score 16 points and pull down nine rebounds, but he also hit a 16–foot jump shot with 18 seconds left to carry the Tar Heels to a 63–62 victory. He was named the College Player of the Year by The Sporting News in 1983 and 1984, and received the Naismith and Wooden awards in 1984. The summer after his junior year, Jordan

+1. 迈克尔·乔丹

他为何入选《50+1位最闪耀的体育巨星》

昔日篮球明星埃尔文·约翰逊(魔术师约翰逊)似乎一语破的:"有了迈克尔·乔丹,才有了我们其余所有篮球运动员。"

乔丹被众多球迷、运动员及专家们称为篮球运动史上最伟大的球员。他是一位集好胜、快速、力量、艺术和优雅于一体的优秀运动员,是他重新定义了职业篮球领域超级明星的概念。乔丹在职业生涯中,曾14次荣获"全能明星"称号,并带领他的球队分别两次赢得美国全国篮球协会(NBA)"三连冠"。其精湛卓越的球技及非凡脱俗的个人魅力,也让全世界认识了他的球队。乔丹无疑是体坛中一颗永恒的璀璨之星。

成长之路

1963年2月17日,迈克尔·杰弗里·乔丹出生于纽约布鲁克林。他是詹姆斯和德罗拉的第3个孩子。乔丹和他的4个兄弟姐妹生长在北卡罗来纳州惠明顿市。孩提时的乔丹会踢足球、打篮球,但他的最爱是棒球,这是他和父亲詹姆斯共同的爱好。起初,乔丹跟他的哥哥莱瑞一起玩一对一的篮球"斗牛",后来,在他一次次地努力打败哥哥的过程中,篮球逐渐在他心中占据了第一位。

乔丹曾就读于惠明顿兰尼高中。虽然那时他坎坷多难,一年级时多次被停赛,且因那5英尺11英寸的矮个子被球篮校队排斥在接下来的赛事之外,但最终他还是成为棒球队、篮球队和足球队的优秀学生、卓越明星。在二、三年级之间的那个夏季,乔丹长了4英寸,他更加专心地练习球技。终于,他让校队在三、四年级赛季中每场比赛平均拿到25分。四年级时,乔丹入选麦当劳全美队,并成为历史上唯一获得三双场均为29.2分、11.6个篮板和10.1次助攻的高中生。

过了辉煌的第四学年后,乔丹获得北卡大学篮球奖学金并为该校球队效力。1982年,还是一年级的乔丹虽已初出茅庐,但在他之上还有高年级的詹姆斯·沃西及萨姆·帕金斯这样的明星们。然而,到年底的时候,他在北卡与佐治顿大学NCAA(全美大学生体育协会)决赛中就大出风头,未来的NBA对手帕特里克·尤因也认为此人不容小觑。乔丹不仅拿下了16分、抢了9个篮板,而且在最后的18秒内以16英尺处跳投为北卡大学赢得了63:62的胜利。在1983年和1984年,他被《体育新闻》评选为"年度最佳大学篮球球员",并获得1984年的奈史密斯奖和伍登奖。三年级的暑期过后,乔丹率领着以波比·奈特为主教练的

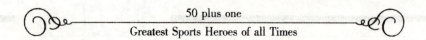
led the U.S. Men's Basketball Team, coached by Bobby Knight, to an Olympic gold medal in Los Angeles, California. Then, in the 1984 NBA Draft, he was selected as the third overall pick by the Chicago Bulls. He left school after that, but eventually graduated from North Carolina with a Bachelor of Arts degree in 1986.

Professional Career

The Bulls had only won 28 games in their last pre–Jordan season and it immediately became apparent that he was going to have a huge impact on the team. In his first NBA game, on October 26, 1984, he scored 16 points against the Washington Bullets, before scoring 40 or more points seven times and finishing his rookie season as one of the top scorers in the league with an average of 28.2 points per game. He also averaged 6.5 rebounds, 5.9 assists and 2.4 steals per game that year.

Jordan, who soon was nicknamed Air Jordan, established himself as one of the finest players in the league during his second season in the NBA, scoring 50 or more points eight times during the regular season and leading the league with a 37.1 points–per–game average. He also joined fellow legend Wilt Chamberlain to become one of only two players to score 3,000 points in a single season.

Jordan carried the Bulls into the playoffs every year, but the team did not make it all the way to the NBA Finals until the 1990–1991 season. The year before, the Bulls faced the Detroit Pistons in the Eastern Conference Finals and the Pistons employed what had become their usual game plan against Jordan's team: The Jordan Rules. Basically, they tried to force Jordan out of commission by double–and triple–teaming him every time he got the ball, stopping him from going to the baseline and hacking him whenever he drove to the basket. The Bulls lost to the Pistons in seven games during the 1990 Conference Finals, causing Jordan to agree to an offensive change by Coach Phil Jackson and Assistant Coach Tex Winter.

The Bulls began playing with a triangle offense, and this proved to be the jumpstart they needed to finish in first place for the first time in 16 years and to reach a franchise–record 61 wins in a single regular season. Jordan and his team went on to win their first NBA Championship ever in 1991 against Magic Johnson and the Los Angeles Lakers. They repeated their stellar performance over the next 2 years, defeating Clyde Drexler and the Portland Trailblazers in 1992 and Charles Barkley and the Phoenix Suns in 1993. During the six–game 1993 NBA Finals series, Jordan scored a finals–record average of 41 points per game and he became the first player in league history to win three consecutive finals MVPs.

In 1992, Jordan went to the summer Olympics again, this time as a member of the original Dream Team, which was the first Olympic team to include NBA players on its roster. Jordan averaged 12.7 points per game in Barcelona and won his second Olympic gold medal as the team swept through with a 6–0 record.

In October of 1993, Jordan announced he was going to retire, stating that he had simply lost the drive to play professional basketball. It was speculated that there were two main reasons for his early first retirement. One was that his father had been tragically killed by armed robbers in July of that same year, and the other was that the NBA had started an investigation into allegations that Jordan had illegally bet on league games, although all accusations against him were later cleared.

After retiring from the NBA, Jordan signed a minor league contract with the Chicago White Sox. He played as an outfielder for the Birmingham Barons, a White Sox farm team. Masses of

美国男子篮球队,在洛杉矶奥运会夺得了金牌。1984年,NBA选拔新秀时,他被芝加哥公牛队选为第3顺位。之后,他离开了学校,但在1986年获得了北卡大学文学士学位。

篮球职业生涯

公牛队在乔丹之前的赛季只赢得28场比赛,显而易见,他将在全队起到重要作用。1984年10月26日他在NBA中首次亮相,对抗华盛顿子弹队,并获得16分,之后,他7次获得40甚至40多分,他第一个赛季就以平均每场28.2分的成绩成为联盟的最高得分选手,同时荣获最佳新人称号。那年,他每次比赛平均6.5次篮板抢球,5.9次助攻,2.4次断球。

不久,"飞人乔丹"的昵称应运而生,在NBA第二赛季中他成为联盟最佳球员之一。在常规赛中,乔丹8次获得50分,甚至50多分,带领全队平均每场比赛拿到37.1分。同时,他与张伯伦一起成为仅有的两名单赛季得3000分的运动员。乔丹每年带领公牛队参加季后赛,但直到1990-1991年的赛季始终没有进入NBA决赛。在此之前,公牛队在东联盟决赛时遇见对手底特律活塞队,活塞队用上了他们的一贯策略来对付乔丹球队的"乔丹定律"。基本上只要乔丹拿到球,就有双人、三人包夹攻击,不让他接近端线,只要他投篮,就让他打手犯规。在1990年联盟决赛中,公牛队7次输给活塞队,乔丹不得不答应主教练菲尔·杰克逊和助理教练泰克斯·温特,来改变进攻主力。

公牛队开始进行三角进攻,这个改进是他们在16年里需要第一次首先完成的,也帮助他们在单赛季中创下了61次获胜的球队纪录。1991年,乔丹和他的公牛队在对埃尔文·约翰逊和洛杉矶湖人队比赛中获得了他们的第一个NBA冠军。随后的两年中,他们仍硕果累累:1992年击败了克莱德·德雷克斯勒和他所在的波特兰开拓者队;1993年他们打败了查尔斯·巴克利和他所在的凤凰城太阳队。在1993年NBA总决赛中,乔丹平均每场得41分,成为联盟历史上第一个连续3年获得NBA总决赛最有价值球员称号的运动员。

1992年,乔丹作为第一个吸纳NBA球员的国家队——梦之队的一员再次参加夏季奥运会。在巴塞罗那,乔丹平均每场得分27.2,第二次获得了奥运会金牌,使该队以6胜0负的战绩横扫对手。

1993年10月,乔丹宣布退役,宣称自己仅仅是失去了打职业篮球的动力。据推测,他这么早退役有两大原因:第一个是他父亲在这一年被持枪盗贼杀害的惨剧,另一原因是NBA开始调查并断言乔丹以联盟比赛非法赌博,不过所有指控最终都被澄清了。

乔丹从NBA退役后,与一个小联盟棒球队的芝加哥白袜队签约,身份是白袜子分队伯明翰男爵队的外场手。众多球迷蜂拥而至一睹他的崭新风采,但他的运球远不及投篮。

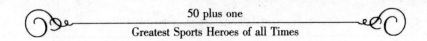

fans flocked to watch Jordan play his new game, but his batting was nowhere near as good as his shooting. After 127 games with the Barons, he finished with a. 202 batting average, three home runs, 51 runs batted in, six outfield assists, 11 errors and 114 strikeouts. Jordan switched to the Scottsdale Scorpions to play in the 1994 Arizona Fall League, where he maintained a .252 batting average.

Even though the Bulls had already erected a life-sized statue of Jordan in front of the United Center and retired his number, 23, he announced his return to the team on March 18, 1995 with probably the shortest ever press-release, which stated simply - I'm back. The very next day, he put on his new jersey No. 45, to finish out the rest of the regular season with the Bulls. They eventually lost to the Orlando Magic in that year's Eastern Conference Semifinals after Jordan had carried them to a 9-1 record in April. Nick Anderson of the Orlando Magic sparked the competitive spirit in Jordan once again after he stated that Jordan, "Didn't look like the old Michael Jordan."

Jordan began wearing his old No. 23, on a mission to prove that he was even better than before. In the 1995-96 season, he led the Bulls to finish 72-10, the best regular season record in the history of the NBA. He also topped the league in scoring with 30.4 points per game and carried his team all the way to their fourth NBA Championship victory against the Seattle SuperSonics. Jordan and the Bulls continued to dominate the league for the next 2 seasons and they became the first team in NBA history to repeat the feat of a three-peat. They defeated the Utah Jazz for both the 1997 and 1998 championship titles. In the 1998 Finals, Jordan was the top scorer in the series, averaging more than 30 points per game, including 45 in the sixth and final game. He earned his sixth Finals MVP, twice as many as any other player.

After this fantastic finale, Jordan retired from the NBA for a second time on January 13, 1999. He became President of Basketball Operations and part owner of the Washington Wizards in January of 2000, determined to turn the losing team into a winning one. After the team won a measly 19 games in the 2000-2001 season, a disappointed yet motivated Jordan started training again, eventually signing a 2-year contract with the Wizards in an effort to lead them to the playoffs. After the devastating attacks of September 11th, he announced that he would donate his entire season's salary to victims and their families. Even though Jordan was able to score his 30,000th career point on January 4, 2002 against the Bulls, the Wizards did not make it to post-season play. Jordan retired for a third and final time after his last game on April 16th, 2003.

Jordan retired with 32,292 points, making him the NBA's third all-time scorer behind Kareem Abdul-Jabbar and Karl Malone. He also finished with a career average 30.12 points per game, the best in NBA history. Jordan holds the NBA record for most seasons leading the league in scoring with 10 and he co-owns the league record with Wilt Chamberlain for most consecutive seasons as the NBA's top scorer with seven from the 1986-1987 season to the 1992-1993 season. He also holds the NBA record for most consecutive games scoring double digits with 842 and for most seasons leading the league in field goals made with 10 and attempted, also with 10. This is just a short list of all of the records that Jordan set during his career.

After Jordan retired for good, he received a plethora of awards honoring his tremendous presence in the NBA for so many years. In fact, during his final NBA game in Philadelphia, the opposing crowd forced Jordan's re - entry in the final minutes of the fourth quarter by repeatedly chanting,We want Mike! and they showered him with a more than 3-minute standing ovation at the end of the game. Even before that, at his last home game in Washington, U.S. Secretary of Defense Donald Rumsfeld presented Jordan with the American flag that had flown over the

在男爵队的127场比赛后，乔丹的最后成绩为平均运球拍击202,3次本垒打,51个打点,6次外场助攻,11次失误,114次三击未中而出局。乔丹又转入史考特蝎子队参加1994年亚历桑纳秋季联盟赛，并保持了252拍的平均运球率。

公牛队早已在联合中心前竖立了一座乔丹真人大小般的塑像，他的23号球衣也随之退役，然而，乔丹在1995年3月18日以最简短的新闻发布会形式宣布复出球坛，他仅说了一句:我回来了。 就在次日，他穿上了新的45号球衣，与公牛队一起做季赛的最后冲刺。这年4月乔丹率领公牛队获得9胜1负的战绩后，他们最终还是在东部联盟半决赛中输给了奥兰多魔术队。乔丹那不服输的精神再次被激发，只因魔术队尼克·安德森的一句话:"乔丹再也不是过去的迈克尔·乔丹了。"

乔丹重新穿上了他的23号球服，就想证明自己甚至比以往更出色。1995-1996赛季，他带领公牛队以72胜10负战绩告终，这是NBA有史以来的最佳常规赛成绩。他使联盟以每场30.4分的成绩排名第一，带领球队在对决西雅图超音速队中勇夺第四个NBA冠军。乔丹所在的公牛队在下两个赛季中继续保持联盟盟主位置，并成为NBA有史以来唯一蝉联三冠的球队。1997和1998年，他们两度打败犹他爵士队，荣获冠军头衔。1998年决赛中，乔丹得分最多，平均每场30多分，在第六场和决赛中都得过45分。他第六次获得了NBA总决赛最有价值球员称号，是其他运动员的两倍之多。

精彩的终场比赛结束后，1999年1月13日，乔丹第二次宣布从NBA退役。2000年1月他以合伙人和篮球事务主管的身份加盟华盛顿奇才队，决心让球队转败为胜。2000-2001赛季，该队仅赢了19场，乔丹化失望为动力，重新开始训练。最后，他与奇才队签订了两年合同，努力带领球队打入季后赛。9.11毁灭性袭击之后，他宣布将所有的季赛薪水捐给遇难者及其家属。2002年1月4日，乔丹在对公牛队的比赛中拿下了他职业生涯中第30000分，即便如此，奇才队还是没有进入季后赛。乔丹于2003年4月16日最后一场比赛后，第三次也是最后一次宣布退役。

乔丹退役时共得32292分，成为继卡里姆·阿卜杜勒·贾巴尔和卡尔·马龙后第三个得分王。他以NBA史上每场平均30.12分的最佳成绩结束了职业生涯。乔丹保持了多数NBA赛季纪录，10次带领联盟得最高分。他同张伯伦都是联盟最高分纪录保持者，并获NBA1986-1987、1992-1993年连续7个赛季得分王称号。乔丹保持了NBA纪录，连续双位数得分共842场，在NBA历史上获得10个赛季的最多的投中次数和投篮次数。这些仅是他职业生涯战绩的冰山一角。乔丹永久退役后，他因多年来在NBA的非凡表现获得了无数荣誉。其实，在费城NBA决赛中，对方观众不停地传来"我们要迈克!"的呼喊声使得乔丹在第四节比赛最后几分钟重新上场，比赛结束时，球迷起立并报以3分钟雷鸣般的掌声。

就在此之前，在华盛顿最后一次主场比赛中，美国国防部长拉姆斯菲尔德把"911"恐怖袭击纪念日当天悬挂在五角大厦的一面美国国旗，赠送给乔丹。在退役后的日子里，几乎每个NBA赛场都举行了欢送，芝加哥联合中心的球迷全体起立，欢呼鼓掌，面对如此经久不息的掌声，乔丹不得不打断他们，并发表即兴演讲。虽然乔丹从未效力过迈阿密热火队，但该队于2003年4月弃用23号球衣。此举更是令人难忘，因为这是该队

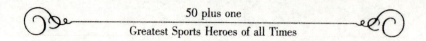
Pentagon on September 11th. In the days following his retirement, almost every NBA stadium held a tribute to him, and the crowd at Chicago's United Center gave him such a long, seemingly unending standing ovation that he was forced to interrupt it with an impromptu speech. Even though Jordan had never played for the Miami Heat, the team retired his No. 23 jersey in April of 2003. This act proved to be even more impressive because it was the first jersey ever to be retired by the team.

For a list of awards awarded to Michael Jordan, please visit
www.encouragementpress.com

About the Man Himself

Jordan has become one of the most marketed and most widely–recognized athletes in history. His face first popped up on a Wheaties cereal box in 1988, and he has worked as an influential spokesperson for such companies as Nike, Gatorade, Hanes, Nestle, McDonald's, Ball Park Franks, MCI and Rayovac. Nike developed a shoe in his honor, called the Air Jordan, and it became so popular that the corporation created a line of JORDAN athletic shoes and apparel. The brand has acquired endorsements not only from basketball players but from other athletes as well.

Throughout the years, Jordan has been involved in several restaurant ventures and has served on the corporate boards of Oakley and Divine InterVentures, most recently being made part–owner and the managing member of basketball operations of the Charlotte Bobcats. Besides appearing in numerous commercials for various products, he has also appeared on both the small and big screens, mostly in connection with cartoon characters. In 1991, he was featured in the NBC Saturday morning cartoon, ProStars, in which his character fought crime and helped children along with Gretzky and Bo Jackson. Jordan has also appeared with Bugs Bunny on more than one occasion. In 1993, he and the Looney Tunes character played basketball against a group of Martians in a Nike Super Bowl commercial, which inspired the making of the 1996 live action/ animated movie, Space Jam, also starring Jordan and his cartoon–bunny friend. The two have also appeared together in a few MCI commercials.

Besides working in the corporate and cartoon worlds, Jordan has also done his fair share of charity work. He remains an advocate of The Boys and Girls Clubs of America. In fact, Jordan, along with the Bulls franchise, built the James R. Jordan Boys and Girls Club and Family Life Center in 1996 to honor the memory of his father and to serve Chicago's West Side community. He also established the Jordan Family Institute at the University of North Carolina. The institute's projects provide training, research and technical assistance to professionals who believe that strong families are the basis of stable and caring communities. Jordan has also been involved with America's Promise, the United Negro College Fund, the Make–A–Wish Foundation and the Special Olympics.

Jordan married Juanita Vanoy in September of 1989. The couple lives in the Chicago area with their daughter and two sons. Jordan spends his free time with his family, working out, playing golf in celebrity charity tournaments and riding motorcycles. He has co–written several books, including Driven *From Within; For the Love of the Game: My Story; I Can't Accept Not Trying: Michael Jordan on the Pursuit of Excellence; and Rare Air: Michael on Michael.*

Although one of Jordan's books includes the line, "There is no such thing as a perfect basketball player...," he proved throughout his career that he was, and is, the most nearly perfect player to ever grace the sport. The power of Michael Jordan's name will surely never fade.

第一件永久退役的球衣。

关于乔丹

　　乔丹是有史以来最受青睐、最有名气的运动员。早在1988年,他的头像就第一次印在美国著名麦片食品包装盒上,他也是众多知名公司品牌代言人,比如耐克、佳得乐饮料、恒适服饰、雀巢、麦当劳、弗兰克斯热狗、MCI电信和雷特威。耐克公司推出的新鞋产品还以"飞人乔丹"命名,它的流行又让公司研制了乔丹系列品牌运动鞋和服饰。这个品牌得到了篮球以及其他领域运动员的认可。

　　随后,乔丹涉足餐饮业,与人创立了欧克莱运动眼镜品牌,并担任风险投资企业网络控股公司董事,近年来又成为夏洛特山猫队共有者兼主管。除了频繁出现在各种商业活动中,他还在大小荧屏上露面,主要是出演动画片。1991年他主演了NBA早间卡通片,在片中他与格雷兹基、博·杰克逊一起除暴安良、帮助儿童。乔丹还与兔八哥多次合作。1993年他与华纳家族卡通巨星一起在"耐克超级碗"商业广告中,与一群火星人比赛篮球,这激发了1996年拍摄《空中大灌篮》动画片的灵感,也是由乔丹和他的卡通兔朋友主演。他俩也共同出演了一些MCI电信广告。

　　乔丹除了参加公司事务及动画片演出外,还参与慈善义卖活动。他一直是"美国男孩女孩俱乐部"的代言人。1996年,他与公牛队共建"詹姆斯R·乔丹男孩女孩俱乐部和家庭生活中心",以纪念他的父亲,并为芝加哥西部社区服务。他还在北卡大学成立了"乔丹家庭学院",该学院课程为专业人员提供训练、研究和技术帮助,他们相信牢固的家庭是稳定而充满爱心的社会基础。乔丹还参与建立了美国黑人学院基金组织、"许愿基金会"和"特殊奥运会"。

　　1989年9月乔丹与朱安尼塔结婚,夫妻俩在芝加哥与一女二子共同生活。乔丹空闲时会与家人共度时光、参加名人慈善高尔夫球赛、骑摩托车。他与人合著了多本书籍,比如《来自内心》、《我所深爱的运动:我的故事》、《我一定要尝试:乔丹追求卓越之路》、《永恒的飞人:乔丹自述》。

　　虽然他有本书中这样写道:"不存在一个完美无缺的篮球运动员……",但是乔丹在整个职业生涯中就是这么一个人,他近乎完美,为篮球运动锦上添花。迈克尔·乔丹的名字将永载史册。

One

Hank Aaron

Why He is Among the 50 plus one Greatest Sports Heroes

Hank Aaron is best known as the home run king of major league baseball. He broke fellow legend Babe Ruth's career home run record despite having to endure many racist threats. Aaron kept on swinging and hitting eventually reaching a number so great (755) it remains a record unbroken even today. He set many other impressive records, a few of which still stand today. Aaron is a soft-spoken, well-rounded player whose skills were not fully appreciated until late in his career has earned his place as one of the 50 plus one greatest sports heroes of all times.

On the Way Up

Henry Louis Aaron was born on February 5, 1934 in Mobile, Alabama. He was the third of eight children born to Estella and Herbert Aaron. He and his brothers and sisters were raised in Toulminville, which was a village on the outer edge of Mobile. His younger brother, Tommie, would later join him in the major leagues and the two would become the first siblings to play together in a league championship series. Aaron attended Central High School for 2 years then moved to Josephine Allen Institute, a private high school to complete his senior high studies.

When Aaron was 14, Jackie Robinson and the Brooklyn Dodgers made their way through Mobile during spring training. After Aaron watched the legend play and listened to him speak in town, he knew that he also wanted to become a major league baseball player. Before he turned 15, he was playing shortstop and third base on a semi-pro team called the Pritchett Athletics. During his junior year in high school, he started playing for another semi-pro team, the Mobile Black Bears. The Bears played an exhibition game in 1951 against the Negro American League's Indianapolis Clowns. This was how Aaron got his first big break. He so impressed the Clowns' management that day and they immediately offered him a contract.

Even though his mother wanted him to go to college, Aaron signed with the Clowns and started playing shortstop for them in the spring of 1952. Although he batted using an odd cross-handed technique, he led the league with a. 467 average. It was not long before Aaron began attracting the attention of major league scouts, and halfway through his first season, the Boston Braves bought out his contract for $10,000.

For the remainder of the 1952 season, Aaron played on the Braves' farm team in Eau Claire, Wisconsin. He was named the Northern League's Rookie of the Year even though he had only played 87 games. In 1953, he became one of the first five black players in the South Atlantic League, and he was switched from shortstop to second base. Aaron played successfully in the face of Southern racism, leading the Jacksonville Tars to the Sally League pennant. He was voted Most Valuable Player as he led the league with a .362 batting average, 125 runs batted in (RBIs), 115 runs and 208 hits.

During the 1954 preseason, the Braves' starting left fielder, Bobby Thomson, broke his ankle. Aaron was named Thomson's replacement and began fulfilling his dream by playing in

汉克·阿伦

他为何入选《50+1位最闪耀的体育巨星》

　　汉克·阿伦是大名鼎鼎的美国职业棒球大联盟全垒打王牌选手。尽管要忍受各种种族歧视,他仍打破了棒球神话人物贝比·鲁斯的生涯全垒打纪录。阿伦继续挥打着球杆,最终获得755的高分,至今无人能破这个纪录。他还创造了其他令人难忘的世界纪录,有些至今仍保持着。阿伦说话慢条斯理,才华横溢,这些直到他职业生涯晚期才完全被人赏识,并在50+1位最闪耀的体坛英豪中赢得一席之地。

成长之路

　　1934年2月5日,亨利·路易斯·阿伦出生于阿拉巴马州莫比尔市。艾斯泰勒和赫伯特·阿伦共有8个孩子,汉克·阿伦排行老三。他与兄弟姐妹在莫比尔市郊外小村庄长大。他的弟弟汤米后来也加入了哥哥所在的大联盟,他们成为一起参加联盟冠军决赛的第一对兄弟。阿伦在中央高中学习了两年,后转学至私立高中,完成了他的高中学业。

　　当阿伦14岁时,杰基·罗宾森和他的布鲁克林道奇队在莫比尔市春季训练中一举成名。阿伦观看了这位传奇人物的比赛,并听了他在小镇发表的演说,他也想成为大联盟的棒球手。还不到15岁,他便在一个半职业性的普里切特球队做游击手和三垒手。中学三年级时,他开始在一个半职业的莫比尔黑熊队打棒球。1951年黑熊队和黑人美国联盟的印第安纳波利斯小丑队上演了一场表演赛。正是这场比赛给了阿伦一次绝佳机会。小丑队主管对他留下了深刻印象,并立刻跟他签约。

　　虽然他母亲希望他去读大学,阿伦却与小丑队签约并于1952年春季开始担任游击手。他虽用了一种奇特的十字手技术,但让联盟赢得467棒的平均打击率。不久,阿伦便引起了大联盟选秀人员的注意,在他第一个赛季中途,波士顿勇敢者队就以1万美元跟他签订了合同。

　　1952年余下的赛季中,阿伦为威斯康星州伊奥克莱尔的勇敢者队分队效力。虽然他就参加了87场比赛,他仍被评为"北方联盟年度新人"。1953年,他成为南大西洋联盟中首次出现的5位黑人球员中的一名,并从游击手转为二垒手。阿伦不顾南方种族歧视,最终获胜,带领捷克森维尔队进入突击联盟锦标赛。他率领联盟获得362棒的平均打击率,击球跑垒得分125,跑垒得分115,打点数208,这些成绩让他当选为"最具价值球员"。

　　1954年季前赛中,勇敢者队的左外场手波比·汤姆森跌断了脚踝。阿伦成了汤姆森的替补,实现了他在大联盟棒球赛季中比赛的梦想。

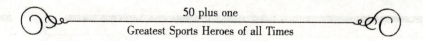
his first major league baseball season.

Professional Career

Aaron made his first major league appearance on April 13, 1954 in a game against the Cincinnati Reds. Although he went 0–5 against the Reds' pitcher, Joe Newhall, he got his first hit, a single, 2 days later against Vic Raschi, pitcher for the St. Louis Cardinals. And on April 23rd, again against Raschi, Aaron hit his first home run as a major league player. For the rest of that season, he maintained what would prove to be his lowest batting average until 1966 at .280, and he hit 13 home runs. Aaron broke his ankle on September 5th of that year, but was back the next season at right field, which is where he ended up playing for the majority of his career. After his rookie year, he would hit at least 20 home runs a season for the next 20 years and he hit 30 or more home runs in 15 of those seasons—a record that has yet to be broken.

From 1955–1967, Aaron, otherwise known as The Hammer or Hammerin' Hank, scored more than 100 runs per season. He led the Braves to a pennant victory over the St. Louis Cardinals in 1957 after hitting a home run in extra innings, and continued to carry them past the New York Yankees for a 4–3 win in the World Series. Aaron's contributions to that win included a .393 batting average with three home runs and seven RBIs. The Braves made it to the World Series again the following year with Aaron's .326 season batting average, 30 home runs and 95 RBIs, but this time the team fell to the Yankees after seven games.

On September 20, 1965, Aaron hit what was to be the last home run made by a Milwaukee Braves player at Milwaukee County Stadium. The following year, the team moved to Atlanta, Georgia and Aaron went right along with them. In 1969, the Braves won the first ever National League Championship Series, with Aaron hitting 44 home runs and bringing in 97 runs, although they eventually lost to the Mets in the playoffs.

On May 17, 1970, Aaron became the first player in league history to make both 3,000 career hits and more than 500 career home runs. At that point, fans and experts began speculating that he could one day break Babe Ruth's record of 714 career home runs, and this was the cause of heightened racial tension involving Aaron and his family. He hired a bodyguard in 1973 after receiving a number of death threats and his daughter, who at the time was student at Fisk University in Nashville, Tennessee, was the target of threatening phone calls and an unsuccessful kidnapping scheme. Despite the hateful distractions surrounding him, Aaron still managed to finish that season just two home runs shy of breaking Ruth's record.

In 1974, Braves' management decided to have Aaron sit out the first three games at Cincinnati so that he could break the home run record at home in Atlanta. Baseball's commissioner, Bowie Kuhn, did not like this decision and he demanded that Aaron play in the opening games. Aaron played two of the three games while tying Ruth's record, and on April 8, 1974 at Atlanta–Fulton County Stadium, he finally hit his 715th home run. The celebrated hit came in the fourth inning against a fastball thrown by the Los Angeles Dodgers' pitcher, Al Downing. A record 53,775 fans cheered Aaron on as he rounded the bases amidst a show of fireworks.

After that spectacular season, Aaron had had enough of the widely unsupportive locals and he returned to Milwaukee to play his final two major league seasons with the Brewers. In doing so, he helped the relatively new team establish the credibility it had been lacking since the popular Braves had departed from the city. On May 1, 1975, Aaron broke the league's all-time RBI record, and on July 20, 1976, he hit his final home run against the pitching of California Angels'

职业生涯

1954年4月13日与辛辛那提红人队的比赛中，阿伦首次在大联盟亮相。虽然他以0比5败给了红人队投手乔·纽赫，但两天后他与圣路易斯红雀队投手维克·瑞士奇的对决中，击中一球。4月23日，仍然是与瑞士奇的对抗中，阿伦以大联盟球员身份第一次本垒打。赛季的其他比赛中，他一直保持着自己最低的平均打击率，直到1966年达到了平均打击率280和13支本垒打。这一年的9月5日阿伦跌断了脚踝，但他回来参加了下一个赛季，并担当右外场球手，到结束职业生涯的大多数比赛中，他都在此位。第一年后的20年中，他每个赛季至少都有20支本垒打，其中15个赛季中都有过30或30多支本垒打——此纪录仍有待于被打破。

从1955年至1967年，阿伦或以"大槌兄"著称，或有"铁锤汉克"的昵称，他每个赛季跑垒得分都超过100。1957年与圣路易斯红雀队的加时赛中，他击中一个本垒打，带领勇敢者队获得锦标赛冠军，并在世界大赛中以4胜3负的成绩击败纽约扬基队。阿伦对此次胜利所作的贡献包括平均打击率393、3支本垒打、7个打点。第二年，勇敢者队以阿伦的平均打击率326、30支本垒打、95个打点，再次进入世界大赛，但这一次，该队在7场比赛后输给了扬基队。

1965年9月20日，阿伦在密尔沃基县露天体育场最后一次击中了密尔沃基勇敢者队员的本垒打。第二年，阿伦跟随该队移至佐治亚州亚特兰大市。1969年，勇敢者队以阿伦的44支本垒打和97个击球得分，第一次赢得了全国联盟冠军赛，但最终在季后赛中败给了大都会队。

1970年5月17日，阿伦成为了大联盟史上第一个获得3000支安打和500多支本垒打的棒球手。对于此成绩，球迷和专家开始设想他总有一天会打破贝比·鲁斯714支本垒打的纪录，这也加剧了阿伦和他家庭对种族关系的紧张感。1973年，当他收到许多死亡恐吓后，他雇佣一名保镖，当时在田纳西州纳什维尔费斯克大学读书的女儿，成为了恐吓电话和未遂绑架案的目标。虽然这些可恶的烦心事围绕着阿伦，他还是成功地完成了赛季，仅差两支本垒打就能打破鲁斯的纪录。

1974年，勇敢者队管理人员决定让阿伦在辛辛那提的前3场比赛中坐在一旁不参加，这样就能在亚特兰大主场赛中打破本垒打纪录。但是棒球理事鲍伊·库恩不喜欢这个决定，他要求阿伦在开赛中上场。阿伦在3场比赛中打了两场，并努力打破鲁斯的纪录，1974年4月8日，在亚特兰大富尔顿县露天大型运动场，他最终获得了715支本垒打的成绩。这著名的一击是他击中了洛杉矶道奇队投手阿尔·唐宁的一个快球。据记载，当阿伦环绕烟火表演场中起点线而行时，有53775名球迷为他欢呼。

那次公开赛季后，阿伦早已受够了当地的反对者，他重回密尔沃基参加了酿酒者队的最后两个大联盟赛季。他这么做，能帮助这支新队重建信誉，自从著名的勇敢者队远离这座城市后，它就一直缺乏可信度。1975年5月1日，阿伦打破了联盟一贯保持的打点数纪录，1976年7月20日，他在密尔沃基县露天体育场击败加州天使队投手迪克·德拉高获得了自己最后一个本垒打。1976年赛季终点时，阿伦退役，他获得755支本垒打，2297个打

Dick Drago at Milwaukee County Stadium.   Upon his retirement at the end of the 1976 season, Aaron had racked up 755 career home runs, 2,297 career RBIs, 6,856 career total bases and 1, 477 career extra base hits. All of these are records that remain unbroken to this day.

Aaron's No. 44, has been retired by both the Braves and the Brewers, and the Hank Aaron Award was established in 1999 to be given to the best hitters in the American and National leagues each year.   It was the first major award to be established by the league in more than 30 years, and was the first to be named in honor of a player who was still living at the time the award was introduced. Aaron has received many other honors for his athletic accomplishments, including being:

- Northern League's Rookie of the Year (1952)
- All–Star (1955–1975)
- National League Player of the Year, The Sporting News (1956 and 1963)
- Most Valuable Player, National League (1957)
- Golden Glove (1958–1960)
- Co–Player of the Month (May 1959)
- Player of the Month (June 1967)
- Lou Gehrig Memorial Award (1970)
- National Baseball Hall of Fame (1982)
- All–Century Team, Major League Baseball (1999)
- Number 5 out of the 100 Greatest Baseball Players, *The Sporting News* (1999)
- Twenty–one times to the All–Star roster (more times than any other player)

About the Man Himself

After Aaron retired, he moved back to Atlanta to serve in various business positions, including corporate vice president of community relations for Turner Broadcasting, a member of the TBS Board of Directors, vice president of business development for the Airport Network and as senior vice president of the Atlanta Braves. This position made him one of the first blacks to break into Major League Baseball's top–tier management. Since 2000, he has owned and operated a BMW dealership in Atlanta.

Aaron married Barbara Lucas in 1953. They had four children together, but divorced in 1971. He then married Billye Williams in 1973. The couple has one daughter. Aaron and Billye co–founded The Hank Aaron Chasing the Dream Foundation, which gives underprivileged children ages 9 to 12 the opportunity to follow their dreams in areas in which they have shown promise. He has been awarded numerous civic awards, including the Presidential Medal of Freedom, awarded to him in 2003 by President George Bush, and the Presidential Citizens Medal, bestowed upon him in 2001 by former President Bill Clinton.   Aaron cowrote several books, including his autobiography *I Had a Hammer: The Hank Aaron Story in collaboration with Lonnie Wheeler.* The book went on to become a best–seller. Other books written by Hank Aaron include *Aaron and Home Run: My Life in Pictures.*

Aaron may have been one of the most overlooked sports heroes during the era in which he played, but the memories of his accomplishments have continued to shine rather than fade throughout the years. The legend of Hank Aaron is awe–inspiring and only grows brighter with time.

点,垒打数为6856,非一垒安打数为1477。这些纪录至今仍无人打破。

阿伦的44号球衣被勇敢者队和酿酒者队封存,"汉克·阿伦奖"也于1999年成立,以此奖励每年美国和全国联盟中的最佳打击手。这个奖是联盟30多年以来创立的第一个大奖,也是第一个以当时仍然在世的运动员命名的奖项。阿伦还因他的运动成就获得了很多其他荣誉,包括:

"北方联盟年度新人"奖(1952年);
全明星(1955–1975年);
被《体育新闻》评为"年度全国联盟运动员"(1956和1963年);

全国联盟最具价值运动员(1957年);
金手套奖(1958–1960年);
每月共享球员(1959年5月);
每月最佳球员(1967年6月);
贾里格纪念奖(1970年);
全国棒球名人堂奖(1982年);
美国职棒大联盟世纪球队(1999年);
被《体育新闻》评为"百名最佳棒球运动员排名第五"(1999年);
21次上"全明星榜"(比任何球员都多)

关于此人

阿伦退役后,回到亚特兰大担任了很多商业职务,包括特纳广播公司公众关系部副部长、特纳广播公司董事会成员、机场网络商务部副部长、亚特兰大勇敢者队高级副总裁——这使他成为第一个担任大联盟职业棒球高层管理的黑人。从2000年起,他就拥有并经管宝马汽车特约经销处。

1953年,阿伦与巴巴拉·路卡斯结婚。他们共有4个孩子,但在1971年离婚。后于1973年与比丽叶·威廉姆斯结婚,生了一个女儿。他俩还共建了汉克·阿伦"追梦基金",帮助9至12岁贫困儿童在有前途的领域追逐他们的梦想。他一直多次获得"公民奖",包括2003年由布什总统颁发的"总统自由勋章"、2001年由前总统比尔·克林顿颁发的"总统国民勋章"。阿伦还合作出书,包括与鲁尼·惠勒合写的自传《我有把大锤:汉克·阿伦的故事》。这本书后来成为了畅销作品。其他书还有《阿伦与本垒:图片中的生活》。

在阿伦的运动年代,他可能是被忽视的体坛英雄之一,然而他的成就却永远辉煌、不会褪色。传奇之星汉克·阿伦折服众人,时间会让他更加璀璨夺目。

Two

Kareem Abdul–Jabbar

Why He is Among the 50 plus one Greatest Sports Heroes

He set the as–of–yet–unbroken record for the NBA's highest career point total. He won a record–making six NBA Most Valuable Player awards during the time that he starred on six NBA championship teams. In college, he played on three NCAA championship teams. When he retired, he was the all–time leader in nine NBA statistical categories. He is the basketball legend Kareem Abdul–Jabbar.

On The Way Up

Ferdinand Lewis Alcindor, Jr. was born on April 16, 1947 in Harlem, New York City. His parents, Ferdinand Lewis, Sr. and Cora were both tall, so it was no surprise when a 12 pound, 11 ounce and 221/2 inch Alcindor made his grand entrance into the world. In 1950, the family of three moved to Manhattan to escape Harlem's declining quality of life.

Alcindor attempted his first hook shot when he was 9 years old and even though he missed, the shot felt natural to him. By age 9, he had already grown to an impressive 5 feet, 8 inches tall. He grew rapidly and as a 6 foot, 8 inch eighth grader, Alcindor made the dunk shot look easy. But he was by no means finished growing, eventually reaching a height of 7 feet, 2 inches tall and weighing 267 pounds.

From 1962 to 1965, Alcindor played for the basketball team at his New York City high school, Power Memorial Academy. The star of the team, he led the way to three consecutive New York City Catholic championships and a 71–game winning streak, with a 95–6 overall record. As an individual, Alcindor was a 4–year letter winner and, from 1963 to 1965 was named All–City, All–American and Consensus All–American.

After his glory days at Power Memorial, Alcindor moved on to bigger and better things. In 1965, he chose to attend the University of California, Los Angeles (UCLA). During his time at the university, Alcindor converted from Catholicism to Islam and was renamed Kareem Abdul–Jabbar, which means noble, powerful servant. Khalifah Hamaas Abdul Khaalis, a former Nation of Islam leader and founder of the Washington D.C.–based Hanafi Madh–hab, performed the conversion.

Alcindor's new name would prove to be legendary, starting with his UCLA playing days. As Abdul–Jabbar, he became the guiding light of one of the best teams in college basketball history. The UCLA Bruins, coached by Hall of Famer John Wooden, won three NCAA titles back–to–back–to–back from 1967 to 1969. The team also hit a 3–year record of 88–2 and Abdul–Jabbar became the only player to be named the NCAA Tournament's Most Outstanding Player three times. He led the league with a .667 field goal percentage in 1967 and with a .635 field goal percentage in 1969. By the time he graduated from UCLA in 1969 with a B.A. in history, he had distinguished himself as the all–time leading Bruins scorer, with 2,325 points.

2

卡里姆·阿卜杜勒·贾巴尔

他为何入选《50+1位最闪耀的体育巨星》

他创造了一项至今无人打破的NBA职业生涯最高总分的纪录。他在6个NBA冠军球队担当主力时，曾6次获得NBA"最具价值球员"称号。大学期间，他3次参加了美国大学生篮球联赛冠军球队。他退役时，是前所未有的9项NBA数据统计首屈一指的纪录保持者。他就是篮球传奇名将卡里姆·阿卜杜勒·贾巴尔。

成长之路

1947年4月16日，刘易斯·奥辛道尔出生于纽约市黑人社区哈莱姆。他的父亲斐迪南·刘易斯和母亲科都很高，所以12磅11盎司22英寸的小奥辛道尔能步入巨人世界也不足为奇。1950年，一家三口为了脱离哈莱姆每况愈下的生活，搬到了曼哈顿。

9岁时，奥辛道尔第一次尝试了钩射投篮，虽然没投中，投篮却很自然。9岁的他已经是5英尺8英寸的大高个。他飞快地长高，当他是6英尺8英寸的八年级学生时，已能轻易地灌篮了。但他根本没停止生长，最终他身高达7英尺2英寸(2米18)，体重达267磅。

1962年至1965年，奥辛道尔参加了母校纽约市高中Power Memorial Academy篮球队。作为场上之星，他带领球队连续3次夺得了纽约市天主教学校比赛的冠军，并创造了连胜71场的辉煌战绩，该球队的总成绩为96胜6负。奥辛道尔连续4年被授予优秀运动员奖，1963年至1965年他获全城、全美最佳球员及全美新秀最佳阵容奖。

过了高中的鼎盛时期，奥辛道尔继续更大更好的事业。1965年，他前往加州大学洛杉矶分校就读。大学期间，奥辛道尔由信奉天主教改为信奉伊斯兰教，名字也改为卡里姆·阿卜杜勒·贾巴尔，意为"强大的英雄"。转教仪式由华盛顿特区前伊斯兰民族组织领袖、汉纳菲–马德布(Hanafi Madh–hab)宗教组织创立者Khalifah Hamaas Abdul Khaalis主持。

自从奥辛道尔开始在加州大学洛杉矶分校打球，他的新名字逐渐为人熟知。改名为阿卜杜勒·贾巴尔后，他成为了大学篮球史上最佳球队之一的领军人物。加州大学洛杉矶分校的熊队在名人堂约翰·伍登教练带领下，从1967年至1969年3次蝉联全美大学生篮球一级联赛冠军。该队还创下了3年88胜2负的纪录，阿卜杜勒·贾巴尔是唯一一次获得"全美大学生篮球一级联赛最杰出球员"称号的运动员。1967年他带领球队赢得平均667的投球命中率，1969年为平均635的投球命中率。1969年他毕业于加州大学洛杉矶分校，并获得历史文学士学位，成为熊队史无前例的得分高手，总分为2352分。

Professional Career

Abdul-Jabbar began his professional basketball career at a time when the two dominant centers in the NBA, Bill Russell and Wilt Chamberlain, were no longer the forceful threats that they had once been. Russell had actually just retired and Chamberlain was getting on in years. This paved the way for Abdul-Jabbar, who would bring more finesse and agility to the center position, which had otherwise been played mostly with the raw power of bigness.

After turning down a $1 million contract to play with the Harlem Globetrotters, Abdul-Jabbar was picked first by the Milwaukee Bucks in the 1969 NBA Draft. The team was only in its second playing season when he started, but by 1971, he had led the way to its sole NBA championship. During his first season, Abdul-Jabbar ranked second in the league in scoring with 28.8 points per game, and third in rebounding with 14.5 rebounds per game. He also came away with the NBA Rookie of the Year title. In 4 of his 6 years with the Bucks, Abdul-Jabbar averaged 30 or more points per game. He was named the NBA's Most Valuable Player in 1971-1972 and 1974.

When Abdul-Jabbar was traded to the Los Angeles Lakers for the 1975-1976 season it was the beginning of a beautiful thing. He would eventually lead the team to five NBA championships in 1980, 1982, 1985 and 1987-1988, and would clinch three more Most Valuable Player awards in 1976-1977 and 1980. Throughout his entire professional career, he was selected to play in 19 NBA All-Star Games and became the first player in NBA history to play 20 seasons. Abdul-Jabbar retired on June 28, 1989 and received standing ovations during all of the home and away games on his retirement tour. By the time he retired, he had set nine NBA statistical records, four of which have yet to be broken:
- Seasons played (20)
- Playoff scoring (5,762)
- MVP awards (6)
- Games played (1,560)
- Blocked shots (3,189)

Unbroken records include:
- Most career points in NBA history (38,387)
- Most career minutes played (57,446)
- Most career field goals attempted (28,307)
- Most career field goals made (15,837)

Abdul-Jabbar won some significant awards for his consistently smooth basketball skills, both during and after his career:
- Rookie of the Year (1970)
- Most Valuable Player (1971-1972, 1974, 1976-1977 and 1980)
- Finals Most Valuable Player (1971 and 1985)
- Sportsman of the Year, *Sports Illustrated* (1985)
- Naismith Memorial Basketball Hall of Fame (1995)
- One of the 50 Greatest Players in NBA History (1996)
- #7 in the Top 75 NBA Players of All Time, SLAM magazine (2003)

During his time on the professional basketball court, Abdul-Jabbar was no stranger to injuries. He committed a couple of aggressive acts that led to a broken hand, not once, but twice. At a pre-season game in 1974, after another player bumped him forcefully. He got so upset that he punched the basket support stanchion, thus breaking his hand. The injury caused him to miss the first 16 games of the season. Then, just 2 minutes into the opening game of the 1977-1978

◀ Kareem Abdul-Jabbar ▶

职业生涯

正当贾巴尔开始他的职业生涯之时，NBA的比尔·拉塞尔和威尔特·张伯伦已不再是昔日那令人敬畏的主力队员了。拉塞尔刚退役，张伯伦紧接着也将退役。这也为阿卜杜勒·贾巴尔做好了准备，让自己锻炼成为更有技术、更加灵活的主力队员，否则只得靠高个子蛮力才能打主力。阿卜杜勒·贾巴尔拒绝以一百万美金与哈莱姆亲善篮球队签署合同之后，他在1969年NBA选秀大会中第一次被密尔沃基雄鹿队选上。他参加时，该队才打第二个赛季，但在1971年，他带领该队获得了NBA冠军。阿卜杜勒·贾巴尔在第一个赛季中，以每场得分28.8在联盟中排名第二，以每场平均14.5个篮板球名列第三。他还获得了"NBA年度最佳新人奖"。在雄鹿队的6年中，阿卜杜勒·贾巴尔有4年都是每场比赛均分30甚至超过30。1971年、1972年和1974年，他都被评为"NBA最具价值球员"。

自从阿卜杜勒·贾巴尔转投洛杉矶湖人队参加1975-1976年赛季，出色战绩随之而来。1980年、1982年、1985年、1987年和1988年，他带领球队五度登顶NBA。1976年、1977年和1980年，他再获"最具价值球员奖"。在贾巴尔整个职业生涯中，他曾19次被选中参加NBA全明星赛，也是NBA史上首位打满20个赛季的球员。1989年6月28日，阿卜杜勒·贾巴尔退役，无论在主场还是其他退役巡回赛中，观众纷纷起立，向他鼓掌致敬。退役时，他创立了9项NBA第一的数据纪录，其中仍有四项有待打破，这些纪录包括：

参加的赛季(20)；

季后赛得分(5762)；

"最具价值球员"称号(6)；

参加的比赛(1560)；

盖帽次数(3189)；

未被打破的纪录包括：

NBA历史上最高得分(38387分)；

上场时间最多(57446分钟)；

投篮次数最多(28307次)；

投篮命中次数最多(15837次)

阿卜杜勒·贾巴尔以其一贯娴熟的球技获得了职业生涯中及退役后的多个重要奖项，包括：

年度新人奖(1970年)；

最具价值球员(1971-1972, 1974, 1976-1977 和 1980年)；

决赛最具价值球员(1971年和1985年)；

《体育画报》评为"年度体育人物"(1985年)；

入选奈史密斯篮球名人纪念堂(1995年)；

NBA史上50位最佳球员之一(1996年)；

美国职篮杂志评为"NBA史上最高75位球员排名第七"(2003年)

在职篮球场上受伤不足为奇。阿卜杜勒·贾巴尔在两次进攻中失误，导致不止一次，而是两次的手伤。1974季前赛中，一名球员重重地撞了他，他心中不快，便重捶了篮球支柱架，致使手受伤。这次受伤使他错过了赛季前16场比赛。就在1977-1978赛季开赛刚两分钟，由于密尔沃基雄鹿队的肯特·本森肘部撞击太重，贾巴尔就猛撞本森，导致自己下巴断裂，眼窝破裂。第二次受伤之后，阿卜杜勒·贾巴尔两个月都无法参赛。他的左眼

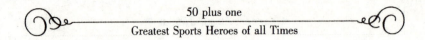
season Abdul–Jabbar punched Milwaukee's Kent Benson, breaking his jaw and shattering his eye socket, because Benson had hit him too hard with an elbow. Abdul–Jabbar could not play for 2 months after that second broken hand injury. And as a result of a scratched left cornea while on the basketball court, Abdul– Jabbar started wearing protective goggles to prevent additional injury to the eye.

All in all, Abdul–Jabbar contributed only greatness to the Lakers and the franchise repaid him for his efforts by retiring his jersey, No. 33 in 1989.

About the Man Himself

Following his retirement, Abdul–Jabbar tried to land an NBA coaching position. However, even though he had such an impact on the league as a player, he had also developed a reputation for being withdrawn and sullen, and had often rejected members of the media. It seems likely, then, that he has lost out on good coaching opportunities because of the negative reputation that he built up over the years. He began lobbying for a coaching position in 1995 and has since then worked as an assistant for the Los Angeles Clippers and the Seattle SuperSonics, the head coach for the 2002 Oklahoma Storm of the United States Basketball League and a scout for the New York Knicks. In September of 2005, Abdul–Jabbar rejoined the Lakers as a special assistant to Phil Jackson.

Since his days as an NBA player came to an end, Abdul–Jabbar has devoted much of his time and energy to being an international spokesperson. He has taught the game of basketball to children all over the world and has served as an ambassador of the American Goodwill. He has worked with Athletes and Entertainers for Kids to improve the lives of southern California's underprivileged youth. In 1989, the organization even started a program called *Kareem's Kids*, with the goal of encouraging young people to stay in school, out of gangs and away from drugs. Abdul–Jabbar has also spent a lot of time working with C.A.R.E to help in the fight against global poverty as well as with different literacy groups and RP International, an organization that is committed to finding a cure for blindness. For another project, he volunteered to be the coach for the Alchesay High School basketball team at Fort Apache's Indian Reservation in Arizona. He co–authored a book about his experiences there, called *A Season on the Reservation: My Soujourn with the White Mountain Apaches*. He has authored and co–authored several other books: *Black Profiles in Courage: A Legacy of African–American Achievement, Brothers in Arms, Giant Steps* and *Kareem*.

Besides his charity work, Abdul–Jabbar has also been in his share of movies and TV shows. Playing basketball in Los Angeles definitely had something to do with the start of his on–screen career. The movies in which he has had roles include: *Airplane!, Fletch, Game of Death, Slam Dunk Ernest* and *BASEketball*. He has also made appearances in various television sitcoms such as *Full House, Fresh Prince of Bel–Air* and *Scrubs*, and also in some television movies, including a version of Stephen King's *The Stand and The Vernon Johns Story*. On a more personal note, Abdul–Jabbar is father to two sons and two daughters with wife, Karen. They divorced in 1979.

Although he has accomplished a lot both on–screen and off since retiring from professional athletics, Kareem Abdul –Jabbar will always be remembered most for his awe –inspiring achievements on the basketball court.

角膜被划伤后,他开始在球场上戴护眼镜参赛,以免眼睛再次受伤。

　　总的来说,阿卜杜勒·贾巴尔为湖人队作出了巨大贡献,1989年球队把他的33号球衣永远保留了起来,作为对他努力的回报。

关于此人

　　退役后的阿卜杜勒·贾巴尔试图坐上NBA教练的位置。然而,虽然作为球员,他在联盟中极具影响力,但他却有着离群、阴郁的性格,还常常抵制媒体。看来就是这些年来的负面名声,使他错失良机,当不成教练。1995年他开始为教练职位游说沟通,从那以后,他成为洛杉矶快船队和西雅图超音速队的助理教练,并担任2002年美国篮球联盟俄克拉何马暴风队的主教练和纽约尼克斯队的选秀人员。2005年9月,阿卜杜勒·贾巴尔重返湖人队,担任菲尔·杰克逊的特别助理。

　　自从阿卜杜勒·贾巴尔的NBA生涯告终,他把大量的时间精力花在担当国际代言人上。他教全世界的儿童如何打篮球,并担任美国友好协会大使。他与"运动员、娱乐明星一切为儿童"组织一起工作,旨在改善南部加利福尼亚贫困孩子的生活。1989年,该组织开始了一项名为"卡里姆儿童"的计划,目的是鼓励年轻人在校学习,远离枪支、毒品。阿卜杜勒·贾巴尔还花了许多时间参与美国援外合作署的工作,与全球贫困作斗争;还参与了各种文化团体的工作,效力于"国际视网膜色素变性协会",一起为盲人寻找治疗方法。在其他工程中,他自愿担任亚利桑那州阿帕切印第安人居留地的艾尔切塞(Alchesay)高中篮球队教练。他的合著书籍《预定的赛季:我在白山阿帕切的所见所闻》,记载着那的经历。他的其他著作还包括:《勇往直前的黑人形象:美国黑人成就之遗产》、《武装的兄弟们》、《巨人的脚步》和《卡里姆》。

　　除了参加慈善活动外,阿卜杜勒·贾巴尔还在一些电影和电视中担任角色。在洛杉矶的篮球生涯使得贾巴尔有机会接触表演艺术。他出演的电影包括:《飞机!》、《弗莱切》、《死亡游戏》、《灌篮高手》和《棒篮小子》。他还在一些电视情景喜剧片中出演角色,比如:《全场满座》、《贝勒-艾尔区的王子》(Prince of Bel-Air)和《替补一线队员》(Scrubs),还有电视电影版史蒂芬·金的《看台》(The Stand)和《佛尔农·约翰斯的故事》(The Vernon Johns Story)。阿卜杜勒·贾巴尔的私生活更受关注,他与妻子卡伦育有两儿两女。1979年他们离婚了。

　　阿卜杜勒·贾巴尔退出运动职业生涯后,虽然在荧屏内外硕果累累,但为人们所记忆的仍是他在篮球场上令人敬畏的辉煌战绩。

Three

Muhammad Ali

Why He is Among the 50 plus one Greatest Sports Heroes

In 1999, *Sports Illustrated* named Muhammad Ali, Sportsman of the Century. Not Boxer of the Century. Sportsman of the Century. Not of the year. Not even of the decade. Of the century. He needs no further introduction. He is one of the greatest sports heroes in history. Period.

On the Way Up

Cassius Marcellus Clay, Jr. was born on January 17, 1942 in Louisville, Kentucky to Odessa Grady Clay and Cassius Marcellus Clay, Sr. His lifelong love affair with boxing came about completely by accident at age 12. It all started when his bicycle was stolen from in front of a department store. A very upset young Clay found a policeman, whom he would later come to know as Joe Elsby Martin, Sr., coach of the Louisville city boxing program. Clay proceeded to tell Martin what had happened and that he wanted to whup whoever had stolen his bike. Martin was quick to respond that Clay should learn to fight if he really intended to whup someone. The 89-pound boy showed up at Louisville's Columbia Gym the very next day. He started taking boxing lessons from Martin, who taught him the moves that would someday lead to his famous saying, "float like a butterfly, sting like a bee."

From that fateful day in 1954, Clay approached boxing with a more determined and committed attitude than most of the other young fighters. In fact, he did not work while he was a teenager, giving him that much more time to box and train. He was victorious in 100 out of 108 matches during his amateur career, winning six Kentucky Golden Gloves championships, two National Golden Gloves championships and two National Amateur Athletic Union titles before he even reached the age of 18. He also took home a light heavyweight gold medal from the 1960 Olympics held in Rome, just a few months after he turned 18. Martin contributed Clay's many early successes in part to his sassy yet hardworking attitude, which he said elevated Clay high above his opponents.

Professional Career

Throughout his professional boxing career, Clay never lost his sass. He was always running his mouth and even became dubbed The Louisville Lip. Not only did he constantly dog his opponents, but he also spoke in front of the media, which was rare in the days when managers usually talked on behalf of their fighters. Clay's big mouth certainly threw some fighters off of their game, as did his unorthodox heavyweight boxing style of relying on his reflexes and footwork rather than his hands to protect himself from getting hit in the face. Another fighting quirk that worked for Clay was that he focused on his opponents' heads, refusing to throw body punches. This way, he reduced the number of times he got hit simply because he could stay further away from the other fighters. And, of course, there was the Ali Shuffle, a move in which Clay would

穆罕默德·阿里

他为何入选《50+1位最闪耀的体育巨星》

1999年穆罕默德·阿里当选为《体育画报》"世纪最佳运动员"。不是"世纪拳击手",而是"世纪最佳运动员"。不是"年度",也不是"十年",而是"世纪"。用不着更多的介绍,他是运动史上叱咤风云的英雄之一。

成长之路

1942年1月17日,穆罕默德·阿里原名卡修斯·马塞勒斯·克莱,出生于肯塔基州路易斯维尔市,父亲是卡瑟斯·马塞勒斯·克莱,母亲是奥德婆·格莱迪·克莱。12岁那年的一次偶然机会让他接触到了终生热爱的拳击。他的自行车在一家百货商店门口被偷。小克莱十分沮丧,找到了警察,后来才知道这个警察叫乔·艾尔斯比·马丁,是路易斯维尔市拳击运动的教练。克莱继续告诉警察发生的事情,并声称要把偷车贼猛揍一顿。马丁很快回答他说,"要真想揍人,就该先学会打拳。"第二天,这个体重89磅的男孩就出现在了路易斯维尔市哥伦比亚体育馆。他开始跟马丁学习拳击,马丁教他的拳法可以概括成他日后的名言:"如蝴蝶般轻盈飞舞,也如蜜蜂般犀利蜇人"。

从1954年命中注定的这天起,克莱比其他拳击手更坚定、更专心地学习拳击。其实,青少年时期的阿里并没有工作,这样就有更多的时间练习拳击。在业余拳击生涯中,他赢得了108场比赛中的100场,6次获得肯塔基州金手套冠军,两次获得全国金手套冠军,还未满18岁,就两次荣获"全国业余体育联合奖"。1960年,刚满18岁后的几个月,他就把罗马奥运会上夺得的轻量级金牌带回了家乡。马丁在克莱早期成就中功不可没,某种程度上助长了克莱那狂妄但又刻苦的性格,让他远超对手。

职业生涯

克莱的整个拳击生涯中,尽显他的飞扬跋扈。他伶牙俐齿,常常咄咄逼人,还因此被封为"路易斯维尔的大嘴巴"。他不仅经常令他的对手很难招架,还常常当着媒体的面直接发表观点,这个在当时是很少见的,因为那个时候基本上都是经纪人代表拳击手与外界沟通。克莱的"大嘴巴"让一些对手败在唇枪舌剑上,在拳场上,他不用双手护脸,而是靠他那独特的重量级拳法,运用灵敏的应变能力和轻快敏捷的步法使自己远离对手攻击。克莱还有一个拳法就是集中打对手头部,不去重击对方身体。这样,他就减少了被击打的次数,原因很简单,因为他可以远离对手。当然还有阿里的"蝴蝶舞步",克莱快速移动脚步,来迷惑对手。

shuffle his feet really quickly in order to confuse his competitors.

Clay's distinctive and unusual style of fighting would eventually lead him to become one of, if not the best heavyweight boxers of all time. He won his first professional fight on October 29, 1960 in Louisville, and, from 1960–1963, his record was 190, with 15 knockouts. In 1964, Clay was the number one contender for Sonny Liston's title. Their fight took place in Miami on February 25th of that year. While the fighters were weighing in, Clay proclaimed for the first time what would later become his most famous quote. He said that he would "float like a butterfly and sting like a bee" and punctuated these witty words with, "Your eyes can't hit what your eyes can't see." He proved his proclamation right and the 7–1 odds wrong, forcing Liston to retire to his stool and not return for the seventh round. Thus, Clay became the heavyweight champion of the world.

The day after his victory, Clay announced that he had joined the Nation of Islam and changed his name to Cassius X. Soon after, Elijah Muhammad, the leader of the Nation, gave Clay his true Islamic name: Muhammad Ali. Amid negative national response, many journalists at that time refused to call Ali by his new name.

That same year, Ali failed the qualifying exam for the Armed Forces due to his below average writing and spelling abilities. But he was reclassified 1A in early 1966 when the exam was revised. However, because of his beliefs in the teachings of the Quran, Ali refused to serve in the army during the Vietnam War. As a result, he was all but banned from boxing in the United States and could only accept fights in other countries for most of 1966.

After a rematch defending his title against Liston, whom he knocked out in the seventh round, on May 25, 1965 in Lewiston, Maine and then defeating former champion Floyd Patterson in November of that same year, Ali defended his title another eight times. The force that eventually stopped him was not another fighter, but rather the Professional Boxing Commission, which took the championship title away from him near the end of 1967 because of his refusal to be drafted for the Vietnam War. The commission refused to let him fight professionally for more than 3 years, during which time Ali appealed his conviction and earned wages by speaking at rallies on college campuses that were against the war.

In 1970, a state senator helped Ali get his boxing license in Georgia, which led to his first return fight and win in October against Jerry Quarry. Soon after that fight, the New York State Supreme Court ruled that it had been unjust of the Professional Boxing Commission to deny Ali a boxing license.

The following year, on March 8th, Ali fought his first match against the undefeated champion, Joe Frazier, at Madison Square Garden. The fight was coined The Fight of the Century or more simply, The Fight. Even though Ali fought fearlessly, Frazier beat him in points, knocking him down with a hard left hook in the last round. However, a few years later, Ali beat Frazier in points at their 1974 rematch. He was on his way to another shot at the title.

This shot, a match that was hyped as The Rumble in the Jungle, would prove to be the most important one of Ali's career. The fight was against George Foreman and was one of the first matches to be promoted by Don King. It was set for October 30, 1974 in Kinshasha, Zaire. Proving many doubters wrong, Ali beat Foreman by knockout in the eighth round to regain the championship title.

In 1975, Ali converted from the Nation of Islam to orthodox Sunni Islam and won what many of his fans felt should have been his last fight before retirement. He fought Joe Frazier on October 1st in Quezon City, Philippines and won by TKO after 14 rounds, when Frazier's trainer refused to

　　即使克莱不是史上最好的重量级拳击手,他那与众不同的精湛技艺也使他成为史无前例的最佳重量级拳击手之一。1960年10月29日,在路易斯维尔,克莱赢得了他的首次职业拳赛冠军,从1960至1963年,他共获190场胜利,其中15次以击倒对手直接取胜。1964年,他成为索尼·利斯顿的头号竞争对手。同年2月25日,他们的拳王争霸赛在迈阿密举行。当他们称体重时,克莱当众说了一句话,这也成为他的日后最著名的名言。他说他要"像蝴蝶般轻盈飞舞,也要像蜜蜂般犀利蜇人",他又把这句诙谐妙语强调为"你捕捉不到视线范围以外的,便无法出拳"。克莱证明了此言正确无疑,他以7:1的悬殊比分,在第七回合轻松取胜,迫使利斯顿让出宝座。这样,克莱就获得了世界重量级拳王称号。

　　此次胜利之后,克莱向全世界宣布,他已经皈依伊斯兰教,并将自己的名字改为卡修斯。不久,伊斯兰民族组织领袖伊利贾·穆罕默德授予克莱一个真正的伊斯兰名字:穆罕默德·阿里。由于当时对少数民族的歧视,很多记者不愿意喊阿里的这个穆斯林名字。
同年,阿里因为拼写能力低于平均水平而没能通过参军考试。1966年初,考试进行修改后,阿里重新被定为一级水平。然而,由于阿里坚信《古兰经》教义,他在越南战争期间拒绝为军队效力。结果,美国很多州都吊销了阿里的拳击执照,1966年的绝大多数时间里,他只能参加国外的拳击比赛。

　　1965年5月25日,在缅因州刘易斯顿市,阿里再次迎战利斯顿,第七回合中把他击倒在地,首次卫冕成功。接下来的11月份比赛中,他击败了前拳王弗洛伊德·帕特森。阿里之后又8次卫冕成功。但最终让他备受打击的并不是什么拳击手,而是职业拳击委员会,1967年底,阿里的拳王桂冠被强制收回,就因为他拒绝参加越南战争。委员会禁止阿里参加职业拳赛长达3年多,在此期间,阿里在大学校园集会上发表演说,进行反战宣传,并挣了工资。

　　1970年,一位参议员帮助阿里恢复了佐治亚州的拳手资格,他重出江湖,10月份首战告捷,击败了杰瑞·高利。这场比赛不久之后,纽约州最高法院作出裁决,判定职业拳击委员会吊销阿里的拳击执照为不公正行为。

　　第二年的3月8日,在麦迪逊广场花园,阿里对抗卫冕冠军乔·弗雷泽。这次比赛被称作"世纪之战"或者简称为"对战"。虽然阿里毫不畏惧,弗雷泽还是在最后一个回合中以一记左勾拳把他击倒在地,最终以点数获胜。然而几年后,在1974年比赛中,阿里和弗雷泽再度重逢,这次,阿里以点数赢得了比赛。他又有机会冲击拳王称号。
　　随后的一场被称作"丛林大反攻"的比赛,给阿里职业生涯带来了重大转机。这次对手是乔治·福尔曼,也是著名经纪人唐·金组织的第一场比赛。比赛定于1974年10月30日,场地定在金沙萨。让许多人出乎意料的是,在第八回合中,阿里击倒对手,重新夺回了拳王金腰带。

　　1975年,阿里从伊斯兰民族组织转向逊尼派,并且赢得了众多拳击迷所认为的退役前最后一场比赛。10月1日在菲律宾奎松城的比赛中,阿里在第14回合以技术击倒把乔·弗雷泽打倒在地,弗雷泽的教练当即放弃,阿里夺冠。这次比赛被称作"马尼拉三重奏",

let him continue fighting. The fight, coined The Thrilla in Manila, became the fifth Ali match to be named Fight of the Year by Ring Magazine.

Ali held on to the championship title for 2 more years before losing by split decision to Olympic champion, Leon Spinks, on February 15, 1978 in Las Vegas. It was only the eighth professional fight of Spinks' young career, and the upset stunned Ali, motivating him to get back into the zone. Exactly 7 months later, on September 15th, Ali beat Spinks in a rematch set in New Orleans at the Superdome. This made him the first boxer to win the world heavyweight championship three times. On June 27th of the following year, he announced that he was retiring, and gave up the title.

Like so many other athletes in history, though, Ali could not seem to leave the sport he loved. He returned to challenge Larry Holmes for the WBC's version of the world heavyweight title on October 2, 1980. His goal was to set another record, this time as the first boxer to win the Heavyweight title four times. But it was not meant to be. Ali lost by TKO after 10 rounds because his trainer would not let him come out for the next round. After the fight, word got out that during an examination at the Mayo Clinic Ali had admitted that his hands were tingling and that his speech was slurred. The actual results of the exam showed that he had a hole in the membrane of his brain, a fact that Don King had hidden so that the fight could take place.

Ali finally retired permanently after he lost a 10-round unanimous decision to Trevor Berbick on December 11, 1980 in the Bahamas. He left the world of professional boxing with a career record of 56 wins (37 by knockout) and five losses.

About the Man Himself

After Ali's retirement, he underwent more medical studies and was diagnosed with Parkinson's syndrome in the early 1980s. For the next 2 decades, doctors argued about whether or not his symptoms had been caused by boxing and he was finally diagnosed with Pugilistic Parkinson's syndrome, a variation of the disease that plagues professional boxers due to receiving multiple blows to the head.

Even though Ali has a debilitating disorder, he has managed to accomplish so much since stepping out of the boxing ring more than 25 years ago. In practicing his Islamic duty of carrying out good deeds, he has donated millions of dollars to organizations and disadvantaged people of all religious denominations. He has also been involved in work that is both political and moral, traveling an average of 200 days each year in order to carry out this work. For example, he went to Iraq in 1990 to meet with Saddam Hussein and was able to negotiate the release of 15 hostages. He also asked the U.S. government to come to the aid of the refugees in Rwanda and to donate money to organizations that were trying to do just that. It has been estimated that Ali has helped to feed more than 22 million people who are afflicted by hunger.

On November 19, 2005, the doors of the $60 million non-profit Muhammad Ali Center opened in downtown Louisville. Not only does the center showcase Ali's boxing memorabilia, but it also promotes the themes of peace, respect, social responsibility and personal growth.

Over the years, Ali's charitable yet strong-willed heart and energetic personality have kept him in the spotlight. It seems as though organizations of all kinds consistently ask him to make special appearances. For example, he was asked to serve as a guest referee at the first-ever WrestleMania event in 1985, to light the flame at the 1996 Summer Olympics in Atlanta, Georgia and to greet runners at the Los Angeles Marathon start line every year.

也是阿里参加的比赛第五次被《拳击杂志》评为"年度之战"。

在接下来的两年多时间里,阿里一直卫冕冠军,直到1978年2月15日在拉斯维加斯爆了大冷门,阿里输给了年轻的奥运冠军里昂·斯平克斯。这是斯平克斯在其年轻的职业生涯中第八次参加职业拳赛,他出人意料地打晕了阿里,激发他重返拳场。9月15日,正好整整7个月后,在新奥尔良的超级穹顶体育馆,阿里与斯平克斯再次交锋,并击败了对手。这样,阿里成为世界上第一位获得重量级拳击三连冠的拳击手。第二年的6月27日,阿里宣布即将退役,放弃拳王称号。但是,与众多运动员一样,阿里似乎还是离不开他深爱的运动。1980年10月2日,世界拳击理事会世界重量级拳王争霸赛上,阿里向莱瑞·赫姆斯挑战。他的目标是再创纪录,成为第一个4次夺得重量级拳王称号的拳击手。然而,事与愿违。10个回合后,阿里被技术击倒,他的教练不让他在下个回合继续上场,就这样,阿里输了。这次比赛之后,有消息传出:阿里在梅奥诊所的一次体检中,确实查出双手抖动,话语含糊。这次检查确凿无疑,他的脑膜上有洞,唐·金隐瞒了这个事实,比赛才得以进行。

1980年12月11日,阿里在巴哈马的10回合的比赛中,毫无争议地输给了特雷沃·伯比克,在这之后,阿里正式告别拳坛。他留给世人的职业拳击生涯纪录为56胜(37次直接击倒获胜)5负。

关于此人

阿里退役后,他经受了更多医疗研究,并在80年代初被诊断为"帕金森综合征"。随后的20年中,医生对他的这个病是否由拳击引发,一直争论不休。最终,他被诊断为"拳击运动员帕金森综合征",是该病的一种变异,拳击手头部受过无数次重击,导致了这种病痛。

尽管阿里神经衰弱、神智紊乱,但自从退役后的25年以来,他一直努力做事。阿里履行伊斯兰教义,常行善事,把数百万美元捐给宗教组织及弱势人群。他还参加了兼具政治色彩和道德正义的工作,平均每年外出200天执行此类工作。比如,1990年他前往伊拉克与萨达姆·侯赛因会面,成功协商释放了15名人质。他还要求美国政府援助卢旺达难民,捐钱给一些组织来帮助难民。据估计,阿里曾救助过2200多万饱受饥荒之灾的人民。

2005年11月19日,耗资6000万美元的非赢利性"穆罕默德·阿里中心"在路易斯维尔城市商业区开业。它不仅展示了关于阿里的具有纪念意义的大事件,还宣扬了和平、尊重、社会责任和个人成长的主题思想。

多年来,阿里慈善、坚毅的品质和充满活力的个性,使他成为万人瞩目之星。似乎各种类型的组织都不断邀请他出席特别场合。比如,他在1985年唯一一次担当"摔跤迷活动"嘉宾裁判,1996年佐治亚州亚特兰大夏季奥运会上,他点燃了圣火,每年在洛杉矶马拉松比赛中,他都要站在起跑线上迎接选手们。

Four

Lisa Andersen

Why She is Among the 50 plus one Greatest Sports Heroes

Changing the game is the name of the game. And Lisa Andersen has most definitely changed the name of her game—surfing. Since she broke into the male–dominated sport, she has not only paved her own way, but also the way of current and future female surfers around the world. Her groundbreaking success and the courage it took to get her there place her right up there with the best of them.

On The Way Up

Lisa Andersen was born on March 8, 1969. At age 13 her family moved to Ormond Beach, Florida, where she traded in the baseball bat for a surfboard. She was the only female surfer in town when she first started surfing, but armed with a charismatic personality and rapidly developing skills, she slowly gained respect from the male surfers. Her parents, however, did not respect the sport of surfing or the fact that Andersen was so caught up in it. They threatened to put her on house arrest if she continued to concentrate on surfing rather than her education. In 1986, when she was 16–years old, Andersen left a note that promised she would become a world champion and ran away to Huntington Beach, California in order to train with the best surfers in the country. Practically homeless, she surfed every morning and waited tables part–time. She entered amateur competitions, winning 35 National Scholastic Surfing Association trophies in 8 months. She was also victorious in 1987 at the U.S. Championships at Sebastian Inlet in Florida.

Professional Career

After her 1987 championship win, Andersen turned pro at age 17 and finished 12th on the tour. That year she was voted Rookie of the Year. Her first professional wins did not come until 1990 in Australia and even then she was not a consistent surfer. Easily distracted by issues in her personal life, including relationship problems, she was unable to fully concentrate enough to turn her surfing skills into victories. She met Renato Hickel, head judge of the Association of Surfing Professionals in 1992 and became pregnant a short time later and they soon married. But the marriage quickly soured and ended not long after it had begun. Two weeks after the birth of her daughter, Erica, she was competing again. That year Lisa finished seventh in the women's world rankings. The birth of her daughter improved her perspective not only on how to deal with life, but also on how to handle surfing contests during a season.

In 1994, Andersen won her first World Championship Tour title, despite missing two late–season contests due to back pain. She went on to win the world title the next 3 years, making her the first surfer since Mark Richards to take home four championships consecutively. In between her first and last title win, Andersen was featured on the cover of the April 1996 issue of *Surfer* magazine. She was only the second woman in the magazine's 40–year history to get a spot on the

莉萨·安德森

她为何入选《50+1位最闪耀的体育巨星》

这项运动因她而改变。莉萨·安德森毫无疑问地改变了属于她的运动——冲浪。自从她闯入了男人的运动世界，她不仅为自己铺平了道路，也为现在和未来的全世界女性冲浪运动员铺平了道路。她创造的成功以及她勇往直前的勇气，让她站在了最佳运动员的巅峰。

成长之路

莉萨·安德森生于1969年3月8日。13岁那年，全家搬到了佛罗里达州奥蒙德海滩，在那里，她用一根棒球棒折价换了个新冲浪板。她开始冲浪运动时，还是小镇里唯一的女冲浪运动员，但她具有领袖气质，技术发展迅速，逐渐得到了男性冲浪运动员的尊重。然而她的父母并不看好冲浪运动，也不喜欢安德森对冲浪如此痴迷。父母威胁她，如果再不专心学习，只把精力放在冲浪上的话，他们就把她软禁在家。1986年，16岁的安德森留下一张纸条，许下承诺，说自己一定能成为世界冠军，为了与全国最优秀的运动员一起训练，她去了加利福尼亚州的亨廷顿海滩。她几乎无家可归，每天早上冲浪，兼职做餐厅服务员。她参加了业余比赛，在8个月内赢得全国学院冲浪协会35座奖杯。1987年在佛罗里达州塞瓦斯蒂安港举办的美国冠军锦标赛上，她也获得了胜利。

职业生涯

1987年夺冠后，安德森在17岁那年成为职业运动员，并在巡回赛中排名第12位。这一年，她被评为"年度新人"。直到1990年，她才在澳大利亚职业比赛中获得生平首次胜利，而且那个时候她还不是个意志坚定的冲浪运动员。她很容易被生活中的私事分散注意力，包括男女关系问题，她无法全神贯注地练习冲浪技术，常与冠军失之交臂。1992年，她认识了职业冲浪协会总裁判罗纳多·海格尔，很快，她便怀孕，两人结婚。但没过多久婚姻就以破裂告终。她生了女儿艾瑞可两周后，便重新参加了比赛。这一年，她在世界女子排名中名列第七。女儿的出世不仅改善了她的人生观，也使得赛季中的冲浪比赛更加得心应手。

1994年，尽管安德森由于背痛错过了两次后赛季比赛，她仍然获得了自己第一个"世界冠军巡回赛"冠军头衔。接下来的3年中，她继续夺得世界冠军，成为自马克·理查德兹以来，第一个把"四连冠"带回家的冲浪运动员。在她赢得第一个和最后一个冠军之间，她曾上了1996年4月期《冲浪者》杂志封面。她是该杂志40年以来，仅有的两位上过封面的女

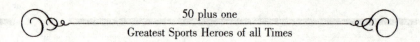

cover.

By the time her fourth world title rolled around in 1997, Andersen had gained the respect of male pro surfers everywhere—for herself and for women's surfing in general. This gave aspiring young female surfers the hope and motivation that they needed to go out and surf rather than to just watch the boys do it. By 1997, Andersen had also caused a spike in the surf market through her association with Roxy, the women's division of one of the surf clothing leaders, Quiksilver. The partnering started out as a sponsorship of Andersen by Quiksilver in 1992 and soon developed into something more. Andersen started helping to design women's board shorts.

Andersen retired in 1998 due to a recurring back injury. She stayed away from surfing for 18 months, concentrating on her family life instead. She bought a house in Ormond Beach and would only meet with the media for an occasional photo shoot. At the end of 1999, she announced that she was ready to compete again and she did exactly that a few months later. Andersen finished the 2000 season in fifth position after winning the Billabong Pro in Anglet, France. She missed the last two contests of that season because she was pregnant. She gave birth to her son in 2001.

For the second time in 2 years, Andersen went back to the pro tour, but ended the 2002 season in 15th place. She did not make the list of surfers qualified for the 2003 season. At that point, Andersen knew when to say that enough was enough and she ended her professional surfing career to pursue other avenues.

During her career as a pro surfer, Andersen racked up a total of 24 victories, 21 of which were in the World Championship Tour and three of which were in specialty events. The following is a complete listing of her wins:

2000: Billabong Pro (France)

1998: Typhoon Lagoon Surf Challenge (Specialty—USA)

1997: Quit Women's Classic (Australia), Grand Slam (Specialty—Australia), Marui Women's Pro (Japan), Kahlua U.S. Open of Women's (USA), Buondi Sintra Pro (Portugal), Expo 1998 Figueira 1997 (Portugal)

1996: Quiksilver Pro (Specialty—Indonesia), Rip Curl Women's Pro Saint Leu (Reunion Island), Billabong/CSI Pro (South Africa), Lacanau Women's Pro (France)

1995: Quit Women's Classic (Australia), OP Pro (USA), Gotcha Lacanau Pro (France)

1994: Reunion Pro (Reunion Island), U.S. Open (USA), Roxy Surfmasters (France)

1992: Quit Women's Classic (Australia), Lacanau Pro (France), Miyazaki Pro (Japan)

1991: Bounty Ice Cream Trophee (France)

1990: Bundaberg Rum Surfmasters (Australia), Quit Women's Pro (Australia)

About the Woman Herself

Since retiring from competition, Andersen has become the contest director for many of Roxy's events. She is also featured on Kelly Slater's Pro Surfer Play Station 2 video game. This makes sense since she is often compared to Slater, the six time men's world surfing champion. Their likenesses include their successful results, the way they manage their professional lives, they are both from Florida and they are the best paid, and most famous surfers worldwide within their own gender categories. Andersen was also the stunt double for Cameron Diaz during the surfing scenes in the movie *Charlie's Angels 2–Full Throttle*, during which she surfed the popular Pipeline reef in Oahu, Hawaii. Even though she is currently working with Warner Bros. on a movie about her life story, at 37, Lisa Andersen's life is far from over. Who knows what she will accomplish next.

性之一。

自从1997年安德森获得第四个世界冠军称号以后,各地男性职业冲浪运动员不仅对她表示尊重,也逐渐尊重整个女子冲浪运动。这给予有志的年轻女孩不少希望与鼓励,她们必须自己出去冲浪,而不只是观看男孩子冲浪。1997年,安德森成为著名滑板冲浪品牌Quiksilver女装Roxy旗下一员。这个合作始于1992年,Quiksilver公司力邀安德森做赞助,很快便有所发展。安德森开始帮助设计女式冲浪短裤。

由于背痛复发,安德森于1998年退役。离开冲浪运动的18个月里,她把精力放在了家庭上。她在奥蒙德海滩买了房子,偶尔被媒体拍到照片。1999年底,她宣布自己已准备好重新参赛,数月后,她真的参加了比赛。在法国昂格莱举行的职业冲浪比赛中夺冠后,她在2000年赛季中最终排名第五。她错过了那个赛季中最后两次比赛,因为她怀孕了。2001年,她生了一个儿子。

两年之中,安德森第二次参加职业巡回赛,但在2002赛季中仅排第15位。她没有资格选入2003赛季。对于这一点,安德森很清楚什么时候该说够了、到此为止,她结束了冲浪职业生涯,寻求其他出路。

在安德森的冲浪职业生涯中,共获得24次冠军,其中21次赢得世界冠军巡回赛,另外3次是在专业比赛中夺冠。以下是她全部获奖项目:

2000年:Billabong职业冲浪大赛(法国);

1998: Typhoon Lagoon 冲浪挑战赛 (美国专场)

1997: Quit 女子精英赛 (澳大利亚), 大满贯 (澳大利亚专场), 丸井 (Marui) 女子职业赛 (日本), Kahlua 美国女子公开赛(美国), Buondi Sintra 职业赛 (葡萄牙), 1998、1997年菲盖拉博览 (葡萄牙)

1996: Quiksilver 职业赛 (印尼), Rip Curl圣勒女子职业赛(留尼汪岛), Billabong/CSI 职业赛 (南非), Lacanau 女子职业赛 (法国)

1995: Quit 女子精英赛 (澳大利亚), OP 职业赛 (美国), Gotcha Lacanau 职业赛 (法国)

1994: 留尼汪职业赛(留尼汪岛), 美国公开赛 (美国), Roxy 冲浪名人赛(法国)

1992: Quit女子精英赛(澳大利亚), Lacanau 职业赛(法国), Miyazaki 职业赛(日本)

1991: Bounty 冰淇淋杯赛 (法国)

1990: Bundaberg Rum 冲浪名人赛 (澳大利亚), Quit 女子精英赛 (澳大利亚)

关于此人

安德森自从退出比赛,担任过许多Roxy大赛的指导。她还是凯利·史雷特职业冲浪游戏2台电子游戏中的主角,这合乎情理,因为她经常被比作史雷特,此人6次夺得男子世界冲浪比赛冠军。他们的相似之处包括辉煌的成绩、职业生活的处事方式、都来自佛罗里达州、都是薪水最高、在各自领域名气最响的世界级冲浪运动员。安德森还在卡梅隆·迪娅兹的电影《霹雳娇娃2:全速进攻》的冲浪镜头中担当替身,她在夏威夷瓦胡岛著名的波浪礁区完成了冲浪拍摄。虽然现年37岁的莉萨·安德森正与华纳兄弟公司合作拍摄一部关于她人生的电影,但她的人生却远不止这些。谁知道她接下来还会取得什么成就呢。

Eddie Arcaro

Why He is Among the 50 plus one Greatest Sports Heroes

Sports Illustrated once called Eddie Arcaro the most famous man to ride a horse since Paul Revere. And he was definitely famous for good reason: his ability to coax his mounts to the winner's circle was unprecedented. Described as a jockey with excellent hands and seat, he became the only rider to win twice the Triple Crown–the Kentucky Derby, the Preakness and the Belmont Stakes. In 1958, Arcaro was inducted into the National Museum of Racing and Hall of Fame, and he is now being inducted into this book as one of the 50 plus one greatest sports heroes.

On the Way Up

George Edward Arcaro was born on February 19, 1916 in Cincinnati, Ohio. He was the son of Italian immigrants and as a result of his father's frequent profession changes was raised in both Newport and Covington. His eventually settled down when his parents became owners of an Italian restaurant in Erlanger.

Arcaro began caddying golf at Highland Country Club in Fort Thomas, where someone suggested that he should try making it as a jockey because of his slender 5–foot–3–inch frame. Heeding the advice, he dropped out of school in 1930 to become an exercise boy at Latonia Race Course in Covington. He earned $20 per month with very little encouragement from the trainers.

Arcaro started jockeying the next year, riding his first race at age 15 on May 18, 1931 at Bainbridge Park near Cleveland. He rode illegally in a few other races at Latonia before hopping a freight train bound for Agua Caliente Racecourse in Tijuana, Mexico, where the rules were much more lax and age restrictions where not enforced. In January of 1932, after 45 initial losses, Arcaro finally won his first race aboard Eagle Bird at Agua Caliente.

When Arcaro turned 16, he returned to the United States as he was now of legal age to ride. He became the top apprentice jockey at the Fair Grounds Racecourse in New Orleans, Louisiana before moving to Chicago in 1934 and signing his first contract with Warren Wright, owner of Calumet Farm racing stable. He missed 3 months of riding due to a fall in June that left him with a fractured skull and a punctured lung. But that proved to be a minor glitch in what was to become a successful ride to the top of the jockeying world.

Professional Career

Throughout his career as an American Thoroughbred horse–racing jockey, Arcaro won five Kentucky Derbys, six Belmont Stakes, 10 J. Club Gold Cups, six Preakness Stakes, eight Suburban Handicaps and four Metropolitans. He would eventually become known as The Master, and also, more affectionately, as Banana Nose because of his big nose. Arcaro rode his horses in a distinctive manner because he sat almost perfectly still, and he popularized the practice of switching the whip back and forth during the home stretch. He rode the best mounts of that time

艾迪·阿卡罗

他为何入选《50+1位最闪耀的体育巨星》

《体育画报》曾把艾迪·阿卡罗称作继保罗·瑞佛之后最著名的赛马骑师。他的出名理所当然:他的成功离不开那空前绝妙的哄马本事。人们把阿卡罗形容成拥有超凡驾驭能力及优美坐姿的职业赛马骑师,他是唯一两次荣获三冠王的运动员,分别在肯塔基德比赛马会、普瑞克尼斯赛马会和贝尔蒙特赛马会上夺冠。1958年,阿卡罗入选国家赛马博物馆和名人堂,现在作为50+1位最闪耀的体育巨星中的一名,选入了本书。

成长之路

1916年2月19日乔治·爱德华·阿卡罗生于俄亥俄州辛辛那提市。他是意大利移民的孩子,那时他父亲的职业不停地在新港市和考文顿市中变动。最后终于在埃朗根市定居,他父母在当地开了一家意大利餐厅。

阿卡罗在福特托马斯的高地草场高尔夫俱乐部做球童时,有人因为他那5英尺3英寸的细长身材,建议他尝试去当职业赛马骑师。他没把这话当耳边风,1930年退学后,他开始在考文顿市的拉托尼亚赛马场作陪练。每月赚20美元,培训教练几乎从不给予他任何鼓励。

次年,阿卡罗便开始赛马,1931年5月18日,年仅15岁的他第一次在克利夫兰附近的班布里奇公园参加比赛。之后,他又陆续在拉托尼亚参加了一些非法比赛,直到他跳上一辆开往墨西哥蒂华纳市为阿瓜奔马赛赛场(Agua Caliente Racecourse)运东西的货运火车,那里的规则和年龄限制都要宽泛得多,而且不会强制执行。1932年1月,经过最初的45次失败后,阿卡罗终于在Agua Caliente骑着"老鹰"冠军马,取得首次胜利。

阿卡罗到了法定参赛年龄16岁时,重返美国。他成为路易斯安那州新奥尔良的Fair Grounds Racecourse赛马场上一颗闪耀的新星。1934年他移居芝加哥,并与卡拉麦赛马场场主沃伦·怀特签订了第一份合同。由于6月份他从马上摔落,导致颅骨断裂、肺部刺穿,3个月无法骑马。但这在他成为世界最佳职业赛马骑师的成功之路上,仅算是微小失误。

职业生涯

阿卡罗作为美国良种马职业赛马骑师,5次赢得肯塔基德比赛马会冠军、6次在贝尔蒙特赛马会夺冠、10次捧走美国马会金杯、获得6次普瑞克尼斯赛马会冠军、8次郊外让赛冠军和4次大都会冠军。他最终以"大师"闻名,或许那大大的"鹰钩鼻"更为出名。阿卡罗的坐姿与众不同,因为他基本上丝毫不动,他在终点直道上来回挥舞马鞭的习惯动作广为流传。那个时候他骑的都是最好的马,包括11匹名人堂冠军马,他给骑过的最好的一匹

period, including 11 Hall of Fame horses, and he named Kelso as the best horse that he rode during his career.

Arcaro's first Kentucky Derby victory came in 1938 while riding Lawring, and his first Triple Crown win took place in 1941 aboard Whirlaway. In 1940, he was the top money winner, and again in 1942 despite being suspended for 4 months after attempting to unseat another jockey. In 1945, Arcaro won his third Kentucky Derby while riding Hoop, Jr. and also his third Belmont aboard Pavot. He began riding for Calumet Farm again in 1948, starting out with Coaltown, but later deciding to ride with Citation after that horse's jockey, Albert Snider, disappeared during a hunting trip. Arcaro's decision led him to another Triple Crown victory, making him the only rider in history to win this prestigious race twice. When Citation defeated Coaltown in the Kentucky Derby, Arcaro gave half of his earnings to Snider's widow. He set a record that year with his winnings topping $1.6 million.

In 1950 and 1951, Arcaro won back-to-back Preaknesses aboard Hill Prince and Bold. The following year, he took the Kentucky Derby with Hill Gail as well as the Belmont with One Count. He then proceeded to break his own record with $1,859,591 in winnings. Due to severe bursitis in his arm, Arcaro rode his final race on November 18, 1961 when he was 45-years old. By then, he had compiled a total of 24,092 mounts with 4,779 wins, 807 seconds and 3,302 thirds. His record of 554 stakes wins lasted for 11 years. He was the leading money winner six times during his career (1940, 1942, 1948, 1950, 1952, and 1955) and set a record with his total career winnings, which amounted to $30,039,543.

Arcaro was presented with the George Woolf Memorial Jockey Award in 1940, and was inducted into the National Museum of Racing and Hall of Fame in 1958. His mounts won the Horse of the Year title eight times between 1941 and 1961.

About the Man Himself

After his retirement, Arcaro worked as a television commentator and racing expert for a short period before becoming a public relations officer for the Golden Nugget Casinos in Las Vegas, Nevada. He later retired to Miami, Florida, where he played golf on a daily basis, sometimes with a group of four other men that included Joe DiMaggio. Arcaro was married to his first wife, Ruth, for 50 years until she passed away in 1988. The couple had two children, Carolyn and Bob. A couple of years later he married his second wife, Vera. He wrote an autobiography called *I Ride To Win!* and another book called *The Art of Race Riding*. There were several games sold with Eddie's endorsement including the Eddie Arcaro Sweepstakes released in 1954. Arcaro died of liver cancer on November 14, 1997.

Just as Eddie Arcaro rode his way to a successful jockey career, so he has also ridden his way into the hearts of many for all time.

起名为"凯尔索"。

1938年阿卡罗首次骑着名叫"罗林"的竞赛马，获得肯塔基德比赛马会冠军，1941年他骑着"旋风"宝马首次获得三冠王。1940年，他成为最富的冠军，1942年，尽管他在一次马赛中摔下而停赛4个月，这一年他仍是最富的冠军。1945年，阿卡罗骑着"胡普"，第三次赢得肯塔基德比赛马会冠军，同时他靠"帕弗特"竞赛马，第三次在贝尔蒙特赛马会上获胜。1948年，他开始骑赛马"柯唐"再次效力于卡拉麦克马场，但自从赛马"西塔辛"的骑师阿尔伯特·斯尼德在一次打猎途中失踪后，阿卡罗开始骑"西塔辛"。此次决定让阿卡罗再次成为三冠王，也是有史以来唯一两次获此殊荣的骑师。"西塔辛"在肯塔基德比赛马会上胜过"柯唐"之后，阿卡罗把一半利润分给了斯尼德的遗孀。那一年，他创下了赢得160万美元的最高纪录。

1950年至1951年，他的"山王"和"勇士"宝马让他一次又一次地夺得普瑞克尼斯赛马会冠军。次年，他骑着"希尔·盖尔"在肯塔基德比赛马会上夺冠，同年，他名日"一下子"（One Count）的赛马为他赢得了贝尔蒙特赛马会的冠军。然后，他继续以185万9591美元的收益打破自己创下的纪录。由于患有严重的股囊炎，45岁的阿卡罗于1961年11月18日完成了最后一次比赛。到那时，他累计参加过24092次赛马比赛，其中4779次冠军，807次亚军，3302次季军。连续11年创下了554次有奖赛马会的冠军纪录。职业生涯中他6次成为最高金钱赢家（1940、1942、1948、1950、1952和1955年）并创下了整个职业生涯中共赢得3003万9543美元的纪录。

1940他被授予"乔治·沃尔夫职业赛马纪念奖"，1958年他入选国家赛马博物馆和名人堂。1941年至1961年，他的坐骑共获8次"年度宝马"称号。

关于此人
退役后的阿卡罗曾经短期做过电视解说员和赛马专家，后来担任内华达州拉斯维加斯金块赌场的公关主任。之后，他退居至佛罗里达州迈阿密，在那里他基本上每天都打高尔夫，有时还与包括乔·迪玛奇奥在内的其他4人一起打球。阿卡罗与第一任妻子路得婚龄长达50年之久，直到1988年路得去世。他们共有两个孩子：卡罗琳和鲍勃。两三年后，他与第二任妻子维拉结婚。他写过一本名为《赛马成就冠军》的自传，还写过一本《赛马艺术》。在经过阿卡罗批准后，有些游戏开始发行上市，比如1954年发行的"艾迪·阿卡罗赌马游戏"。1997年11月14日，阿卡罗死于肝癌。

阿卡罗靠骑马开辟了一条通往成功的职业生涯之路，这条路也始终通向世界人民之心。

Arthur Ashe

Why He is Among the 50 plus one Greatest Sports Heroes

Arthur Ashe was a successful professional tennis player, winning three Grand Slam titles and more than 800 victories during his career. What makes his achievements more spectacular is that he remains the only black male to win the singles title at Wimbledon, the U.S. Open or the Australian Open, and he is one of only two black men to take home a Grand Slam singles title. Ashe is also accredited with using his on-court success in ways that help bring about social change. In doing so, he has propelled himself to the top of history's most elite athletes.

On the Way Up

Arthur Robert Ashe, Jr. was born on July 10, 1943 in Richmond, Virginia. He was not athletically-inclined as a young boy, preferring instead to read and listen to music with his mother. However, he did show talent early on in the game of tennis. Because racial segregation laws were in effect in Richmond while Ashe was growing up, he was not allowed to play in junior tournaments there. Dr. Walter Johnson, a physician from Lynchburg, Virginia who coached female tennis legend Althea Gibson, eventually helped Ashe attend and complete high school at Sumner High in St. Louis, Missouri so that he could gain experience by participating in tennis competitions. In 1961, Johnson persuaded officials to let Ashe compete in the previously segregated U.S. Interscholastic tourney, which he ended up winning for his school.

By the time Ashe graduated at the top of his class from Sumner, his game had improved so much that the University of California, Los Angeles (UCLA) gave him a tennis scholarship. In 1963, he was the first African American ever to be selected to the U.S. Davis Cup team, and he won the U.S. Men's Hardcourt championships. Ashe became the leading player on the varsity team at UCLA, and won individual and team National College Athletic Association (NCAA) championships in 1965. He was an NCAA All-American from 1963–1965. Ashe also won the 1964 Johnston Award, given annually to the American tennis player who contributes the most to the growth of the sport while projecting good sportsmanship and character. He graduated from UCLA in 1966 with a B.A. in business administration.

Ashe served in the United States Army from 1966–1968, eventually reaching the rank of First Lieutenant. In order for him to keep his Davis Cup eligibility and acquire off-duty time so that he could play in major tournaments, he was forced to hold onto his amateur status during that time period.

In 1968, the United States Tennis Association altered tradition by turning the previously amateur U.S. Singles Championships at Forest Hills into the inaugural U.S. Open as well as holding a U.S. Amateur tournament at Longwood Cricket Club in Boston. Ashe was seeded first in the amateur event, and he ended up defeating teammate Bob Lutz 4–6, 6–3, 8–10, 6–0, 6–4. He went on to defeat pro Tom Okker 14–12, 5–7, 6–3, 3–6, 6–3 in the final round of the U.S. Open, despite the fact that he had been seeded fifth going into the competition. By winning both the U.S.

阿瑟·阿什

他为何入选《50+1位最闪耀的体育巨星》

阿瑟·阿什是一名成功的职业网球运动员,曾3次获得"大满贯"冠军,整个职业生涯中荣获过800多次胜利。更引人注目的是,他是唯一赢得温布尔登网球公开赛、美国公开赛、澳大利亚公开赛单打冠军的黑人运动员,也是仅有的两名捧回"大满贯"的黑人运动员中的一名。人们还认为他在球场上的成功帮助带来了社会变化。这样,他让自己跻身于史上最杰出运动员的行列之中。

成长之路

1943年7月10日,阿瑟·罗伯特·阿什出生于弗吉尼亚里士满。孩提时代的他并没有显露出多少运动员的迹象,反而更喜欢与母亲一起阅读或听音乐。但是,他很早就在网球运动上显现出了天赋。在阿什的成长期,种族隔离政策在里士满仍然生效,因此,他不能参加任何青少年锦标赛。最终,弗吉尼亚州林奇堡的内科医生沃特·约翰逊帮他进入密苏里州圣路易斯萨姆纳尔(Sumner)高中并完成学业,此人曾指导过女子网球传奇人物爱尔西亚·吉布森,阿什在他的帮助下,可以通过参加网球比赛获取经验。1961年,约翰逊说服有关当局,让阿什参加之前被禁止参赛的"美国校际比赛",他终于为学校赢得了冠军。

当阿什以名列前茅的成绩从Sumner毕业时,他的球技进展飞快,因此,他获得了加州大学洛杉矶分校的网球奖学金。1963年,他入选"戴维斯杯"美国队,成为前所未有的首位美国黑人队员,并获得"美国男子硬地锦标赛"冠军。阿什成为加州大学洛杉矶分校校队主力,1965年,他获得个人冠军,并带领球队赢得"全美大学生运动协会"(NCAA)大赛冠军。从1963年至1965年,他担任NCAA"全美明星队"队员。1964年,阿什还获得了"约翰斯顿"奖,每年此奖都会颁发给体育发展贡献卓著、具有运动家风格特色的美国网球运动员。1966年,他从加州大学洛杉矶分校毕业,获得"经济管理学"学士学位。

1966年至1968年,阿什曾效力于美国陆军,最后晋升为陆军中尉。为了保持在"戴维斯杯"美国队时的水平,能够参加业余大赛,他那时只能保持业余运动员的身份。

1968年,美国网球协会一改往日传统,把森林山的"美国业余单打冠军赛"转为"美国职业公开赛",同时,在波士顿长木乡村板球俱乐部举办"美国业余锦标赛"。阿什作为头号种子选手参加业余赛事,最终以4:6, 6:3, 8:10, 6:0, 6:4的成绩击败队友鲍勃·鲁茨。尽管阿什在美网职业公开赛中以第五的种子选手出场顺序参赛,他还是在最后一局中以14:12, 5:7, 6:3, 3:6, 6:3的成绩击败了职业网球运动员汤姆·欧柯。该年,他同时获得美国业余、职业公开赛的冠军,成为史无前例的双赢家。这是自1958年吉布森"森林山"夺冠后第一次

Amateur and Open championships that year, he became the only player ever to clinch both titles. It was the first major title victory made by an African American since Gibson's 1958 Forest Hills win as well as the first championship won by a U.S. male player since Tony Trabert's victory in 1955.

Ashe also helped the Davis Cup team win the Sterling Tub in 1968, their first one in 5 years. He won 11 consecutive singles in an effort to take the Cup from Australia, but ended up losing to Bill Bowrey. Ashe finished the season ranked No. 1 in the United States with 10 tournament wins out of 22 on a 72–10 match record.

Professional Career

Ashe turned pro in 1969. He was quick to realize that professional players were receiving prize money in amounts totally disproportionate to the rapidly growing popularity of tennis. He was one of the key players involved in forming what became known as the Association of Tennis Professionals (ATP), a major reason that today's best players are able to compete for such large winnings. Ashe would later be elected president of the association in 1974.

Also in 1969, Ashe was denied a visa by the South African government because of his skin color. The denial prevented him from competing in the South African Open, and spurred him to draw public attention to the country's apartheid policies. He called for South Africa to be expelled from the pro tennis circuit, a demand that was met by heavy support from a number of influential individuals and organizations.

After Ashe won the 1970 Australian Open championship and the 1973 South African Open doubles title, it appeared to many fans that he was spending more time on his causes than tennis. Realizing this, he began to devote more attention to his game and, in 1975 he achieved one of the finest accomplishments of his career by winning Wimbledon. He had been seeded sixth going into the competition and faced the defending champion, Jimmy Connors, in the final. Connors was a 10–to–1 favorite, but that did not seem to matter as Ashe took his opponent down 6–1, 6–1, 5–7, 6–4.

The Wimbledon win was the crowning moment of Ashe's career, and it was accompanied by an equally glowing season record. That year, 1975, he won 9 of 29 tournaments on a 108–23 match record, making him No. 1 in the United States and No. 4 in the world. In 1976, Ashe reached his career–high of No. 2 in the world rankings. He continued to play for several more years, but was forced into early retirement in 1980 after going through an unexpected heart surgery that year before.

By the time Ashe retired, he had reached the World Top Ten for a total of 12 years and the United States Top Ten for a total of 14. He was a Davis Cup team member in 1963, 1965–1970, 1975 and 1977–1978, and a captain for the team from 1966–1967 and in 1971. During his career, he won 33 singles and 18 doubles titles. The following is a listing of his Grand Slam performances:

· Australian Open (singles) Finalist (1966–1967 and 1971)
· U.S. Open (singles) Champion (1968)
· Australian Open (singles) Champion (1970)
· French Open (doubles) Finalist (1970)
· French Open (doubles) Champion (1971)
· Wimbledon (doubles) Finalist (1971)
· U.S. Open (singles) Finalist (1972)
· Wimbledon (singles) Champion (1975)

由美国黑人取得的胜利，也是继托尼·特拉博特1955年夺冠后第一次由美国男子运动员赢得的冠军称号。阿什还帮"戴维斯杯"美国队夺得1968年Sterling Tub大赛冠军，这是五年来他们第一次获胜。为了从澳大利亚捧回"戴维斯杯"，他全力以赴连续11次获得单打冠军，但最后输给比尔·鲍雷，以失败告终。此赛季后，阿什在美国排名第一，22次锦标赛上共获10次冠军，创下了72胜10负的纪录。

职业生涯

1969年阿什转为职业运动员。他很快便意识到职业运动员的过低奖金与网球快速流行度并不相称。于是他加入了创办国际职业网球协会的行列，才使如今的最佳运动员们赢得如此可观的收入。1974年，他被选为该协会的主席。

同样也是在1969年，阿什由于肤色问题被南非政府拒绝签证。因此，他被南非公开赛拒之门外，这件事促使他决心唤起民众对种族隔离政策的关注。他呼吁将南非从巡回赛中排除以示对种族隔离制度的抗议，很快阿什的提议得到网球圈内外很多名流和组织的支持。

阿什赢得1970年澳网公开赛冠军及1973年南非公开赛双打冠军后，很多球迷认为他在网球以外的事业上花的时间明显比网球本身多。意识到这一点后，阿什开始在网球上下更多工夫，1975年他获得了职业生涯中最辉煌的成就之———温布尔登网球公开赛冠军。他以第六位种子选手出场序进入比赛，并在决赛中遇到了卫冕冠军吉米·康纳斯。康纳斯十有八九稳操胜券，但这对阿什来说不算什么，他最终以6:1, 6:1, 5:7, 6:4的成绩击败对手。

温网夺冠标志着阿什在事业上登峰造极，同时伴随他的还有卓越的赛季纪录。就在1975年，他在29次锦标赛上9次夺冠，比赛纪录为108胜23负，美国排名第一、世界排名第四。1976年，阿什到达了他的事业巅峰，排名世界第二。他接着继续参赛几年，但是他在1979年接受了一次意想不到的心脏手术，迫使他在1980年提早退役。

到他退役时，已经连续12年世界排名前十，14年全美排名前十。1963年、1965-1970年、1975年、1977-1978年，他都是"戴维斯杯"美国队队员，1966-1967年及1971年，他担任该队队长。他在职业生涯中共获33次单打冠军、18次双打冠军。以下是他"大满贯"的比赛成绩：

·澳大利亚公开赛(单打)决赛选手(1966-1967年及1971年)
·美国公开赛(单打)冠军(1968年)
·澳大利亚公开赛(双打)冠军(1970年)
·法国公开赛(双打)决赛选手(1970年)
·法国公开赛(双打)决赛选手(1971年)
·温布尔登网球公开赛(双打)决赛选手(1971年)
·美国公开赛(单打)决赛选手(1972年)
·温布尔登网球公开赛(单打)冠军(1975年)

· Australian Open (doubles) Champion (1977)

During and after his career, Ashe was the recipient of numerous awards. Besides being inducted into the UCLA Sports, Virginia Sports, Eastern Tennis Association and U.S. Professional Tennis Association halls of fame, he was:

· Player of the Year, Association of Tennis Profiles (1975)
· International Tennis Hall of Fame (1985)
· Sportsman of the Year, *Sports Illustrated* (1992)
· Honored with a stadium dedicated in his name, where the U.S. Open is held
· United States Tennis Association (1997)

About the Man Himself

In 1969, while just beginning his professional tennis career, Ashe co-founded the National Junior Tennis League to provide disadvantaged young people with the opportunity to learn how to play tennis. Quite a few up-and-coming and/or prominent African American tennis stars have come out of the program, including James Blake and Serena and Venus Williams. In later years, Ashe would establish other tennis-and sports-related youth organizations, including the ABC Cities Tennis Program, the Athlete-Career Connection and the Safe Passage Foundation.

Ashe underwent a second heart surgery in 1983, but then rebounded into a life full of journalism, media and philanthropic achievements. Besides founding the above-named charity youth organizations, he worked as a commentator for HBO Sports and ABC Sports and a columnist for The Washington Post and Tennis magazine. He wrote a three--volume body of work entitled A Hard Road to Glory, which chronicled the progress made and obstacles overcome by African American athletes from 1619--1918. The work was published in 1988 and, after being adapted for television, it won an EMMY Award.

In 1988, while in the hospital for brain surgery, Ashe found out that he had contracted HIV through a tainted blood transfusion during one of his two heart surgeries. He and his wife, Jeanne Marie Moutoussamy, whom he had married in February of 1977, elected at first to keep the news private. Their decision was made mostly due to the desire to raise their only daughter in as normal an environment as possible.

In 1992, reports began to spread that USA Today had gotten wind of the information and was going to publish a story about Ashe's illness. On April 8th, he came forth with the news at a press conference before the newspaper could make its own headlines. He was greeted with much support from the public, which inspired him to found the Arthur Ashe Institute for Urban Health in an effort to address issues of inadequate health care delivery. Ashe died of AIDSrelated pneumonia 2 months later on February 6, 1993. Four months after his death, former President Bill Clinton presented Jeanne with Ashe's posthumous Presidential Medal of Freedom.

Ashe finished his memoir, *Days of Grace*, less than a week before his death. He wrote several other books having to do with tennis, including *Arthur Ashe: A Portrait in Motion*.

Arthur Ashe's pro tennis career and life ended prematurely but the accomplishments as ambassador of the sport of tennis and his dedication towards the betterment of society have formed a legacy make him one of the greatest athletes in history.

·澳大利亚公开赛(双打)冠军(1977年)

在整个职业生涯及退役后,阿什获得过无数荣誉称号。除了入选"加州大学洛杉矶分校名人堂"、"弗吉尼亚名人堂"、"东部网球联盟名人堂"和"美国职业网球协会名人堂"外,其他荣誉包括:

·被《网协概况》评为"年度体育人物"(1975年)
·国际网球名人堂(1985年)
·被《体育画报》评为"年度运动家"(1992年)
·美网公开赛曾使用过专门以他名字命名的露天体育场
·入选"美国网球协会"(1997年)

关于此人

1969年,就在阿什正式成为职业网球手时,他与人共同创建了"国家青少年网球联盟",为弱势群体提供了学习打网球的机会。相当一部分积极进取或卓越杰出的美国黑人网球明星都出自此联盟,包括詹姆斯·布莱克、塞瑞娜·威廉姆斯和维纳斯·威廉姆斯。随后几年,阿什又建立了其他网球组织或关于体育的青年组织,包括ABC城市网球计划、运动事业联合会和安全通道基金会。

1983年,阿什经受了第二次心脏手术,重新振作以后,他把生活的主要精力放在了新闻、媒体及慈善事业。除了成立上述列举的青少年慈善组织以外,他还担任美国家庭影院体育频道和ABC体育频道解说员,以及《华盛顿邮报》和《网球》杂志的专栏作者。他的著作包括一部三卷本的书《通往荣耀的艰辛之路》,记载了1619至1918年美国黑人取得的进步及克服的重重困难。此书出版于1988年,后拍摄成电视,获得了"艾美奖"。

1988年,阿什在医院接受脑部手术时获悉自己感染了HIV病毒,这肯定是在两次手术中的某次输血过程中感染的。起初,他与1977年2月成婚的妻子珍妮·玛莉·木图沙对此消息保持缄默。此决定主要出于对女儿能够在正常环境中成长的考虑。

1992年,有消息传播,说《今日美国》得到风声,并着手刊印关于阿什生病的报导。4月8日,在报纸还未刊登头版头条时,阿什在记者会上公开了病情。随即他得到了广泛的同情和支持,这也给予他莫大的鼓励,他创建了阿瑟·阿什城市健康学院,以解决健康保健供应不足的问题。两个月后的1993年2月6日,阿什死于艾滋病相关肺炎。他逝世后的4个月,美国前总统比尔·克林顿把"总统自由勋章"追颁给了珍妮。

就在逝世前不到一周,他完成了回忆录《优雅的日子》《days of grace》。他的作品还包括其他关于网球的书籍,比如《阿瑟·阿什:运动写真》。

阿瑟·阿什永远地结束了他的职网生涯、结束了他的生命,但是他是网球运动的重要代表,曾为改善社会呕心沥血,他留给世人的是那永载史册的光辉业绩。

Seven

Larry Bird

Why He is Among the 50 plus one Greatest Sports Heroes

On one occasion, Michael Jordan was asked what player, besides himself, he would pick to take a shot in a make–it–or–break–it game situation, and before the question could even be fully formed, he responded with two words: Larry Bird. That should say it all, as one basketball legend bows in respect to another. His aggressively intense and competitive playing abilities combined with his admirable team leadership skills have paved the way for Bird to be revered as one of history's top athletes.

On the Way Up

Larry Joe Bird was born on December 7, 1956 in West Baden, Indiana the fourth child of Georgia and Joe Bird. He was raised with four brothers and a sister in West Baden and the nearby town, French Lick, which is where his nickname the Hick from French Lick came from.

Bird soared to great heights by becoming Spring Valley High School's all –time scoring leader. He averaged 30 points and 17 rebounds per game during his senior year, and heroically scored 54 points and grabbed 38 rebounds during one particular game. Bird's skills brought fans of all ages to watch him play. At a time when French Lick had a total population of 2,059, it was amazing that fan attendance often reached 1,600, and that number spiked to about 4,000 when it came time for Bird's last home game in 1974.

After graduation, Bird started at Indiana University on a basketball scholarship, playing for the celebrated Hoosiers under head coach Bobby Knight. However, this arrangement was not meant to last and a homesick, overwhelmed Bird returned to French Lick. Finally, after attending a community college and working at odd and end jobs for a short period of time, Bird enrolled at Indiana State University (ISU) in 1975 and played for the Sycamores from 1976–1979. During that time, he led the team to an 81–13 record. In 1978, Bird was drafted into the NBA by the Boston Celtics as the sixth overall pick. He then returned to ISU to finish his senior year, which would become his best ever during college, leading the Sycamores to a 33–1 seasonal record. That year, Bird carried his team all the way to the NCAA championship game, but ended up losing to the Michigan State University Spartans who were led by Earvin Magic Johnson.

In honor of his awesome achievements at ISU, Bird was named The Sporting News College Player of the Year and won the Naismith and John R. Wooden awards as the top male college basketball player in 1979. He was also named The Sporting News All–America First Team in 1978 and 1979. Bird holds 30 ISU records, including most career points with 2,850, most career steals with 240 and most career rebounds with 1,247. He also scored in double figures in 93 out of 94 games, scored 40 or more points a total of 15 times and hit six triple doubles during his time as a Sycamore.

拉里·伯德

他为何入选《50+1位最闪耀的体育巨星》

有一次,当迈克尔·乔丹被问及除他自己以外,他会给哪个球员一个机会,去参加一场不成则败的比赛,问题话音未落,他就给出4个字:拉里·伯德。这足以说明,一代篮球传奇人物对另一球员是多么恭敬。伯德强烈的好胜心、精湛的球技,加上令人叹服的领袖才能,为他成为史上最佳运动员铺平了道路。

成长之路

1956年12月7日,拉里·乔·伯德生于印第安纳州西贝顿春谷,是母亲乔治亚和父亲乔·伯德的第四个孩子。他与4个兄弟、1个妹妹一起在西贝顿春谷和附近小镇弗兰奇利克长大,该地名就是他的昵称"希克"的由来。

伯德在春谷高中时就成绩显赫,一直是得分王。三年级时,他平均每场得分30、抢篮板17次,尤其在一次比赛中,他英勇地拿下54分,抢了38个篮板。伯德球技高超,各个年龄段的球迷都前来看他比赛。那时的弗兰奇利克小镇人口不过2059人,前去观看比赛的通常有1600人之多,1974年伯德在家乡最后一场比赛时,前往观赛的球迷达到了4000人。

高中毕业后,他获得印第安纳大学篮球奖学金,为鲍比·奈特主教练带领的著名的印第安纳州人队效力。但此次安排并没有持续多久,由于强烈的恋家情感,他回到了弗兰奇利克。最后,他进入了社区学院,同时兼打零工,不久后,在1975年他被印第安纳州立大学录取,从1976年至1979年一直在该校无花果队打球。这段时期内,他带领球队取得81胜13负的好成绩。1978年,伯德在波士顿凯尔特人队的选秀大会上被选为第六顺位,进入NBA。然后,他返回印第安纳州立大学完成最后一年的学业,这一年是他整个大学中最优秀的一年,因为他带领无花果队创下了33胜1负的纪录。此年,他带领该队进入了全美高等院校运动协会(NCAA)联赛的决赛,但却败给了魔术师约翰逊(埃尔文·约翰逊)带领的密歇根州立大学斯巴达人队。

为了庆祝伯德在印第安纳州立大学取得的卓越成就,他于1979年被《体育新闻》评为"年度最佳大学篮球球员"、赢得了年度最佳大学篮球球员的奈史密斯奖以及约翰·伍登奖。1978年和1979年,他被《体育新闻》评为"全美最佳第一阵容成员"。伯德保持着30项印第安纳州立大学纪录,包括最高得分2850分、最多抢断次数240次、最多篮板球次数1247次。担任无花果队队员时,他94场比赛中有93场得分为两位数,共15次得分40甚至超过40,6次砍下三双。

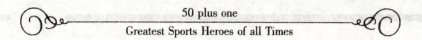
Professional Career

Before Bird appeared on the scene in Boston in 1979, the Celtics had not made it to the playoffs in two consecutive seasons. But that soon changed as Bird, later named NBA Rookie of the Year, took hold of the reigns, improving the team's subpar record of 29–53 the previous year to the league's then best record, 61–21. That first season, the team made it all the way to the conference finals, which was to be the beginning of the Celtics' 13 straight trips to the playoffs. And it was no coincidence that Bird played with Boston for exactly 13 seasons.

The next year, Bird, who played small forward and power forward, teamed up with Kevin McHale and Robert Parish. The threesome would form one of the best frontlines in the history of the NBA and would work together to do so for the 12 remaining years of Bird's career. That season, 1980–1981, he led his team to the NBA Finals, where they stomped out the Houston Rockets in six games to become the league champions.

In 1986, Bird continued to lead the way as the Celtic's finished the regular season with a 67–15 record and again beat the Houston Rockets in six games. He repeated the feat of being named the NBA MVP and the Finals MVP, averaging 24 points, 10 rebounds and 10 assists per game during the series. That was his third consecutive league regular season MVP award, making him the third player ever to reach that accomplishment.

In 1988, the Celtics lost to the Pistons in six games during the Eastern Conference Finals, and this probably had something to do with the fact that Bird was only able to play the first six games of the regular season before calling it quits to have surgery on both of his heels. He reappeared in 1989, but a combination of severe back pain and aging teammates hindered him from playing the same way he had in the old days. But that did not mean that Bird could not still perform. During his last 3 seasons with the Celtics, he averaged more than 20 points, 9 rebounds and 7 assists per game, shooting better than 45 percent from the field and leading his team to the playoffs each season.

As his back problems continued to get worse, Bird missed 22 games during the 1990–1991 season. It was discovered that he had a compressed nerve root in his back and despite undergoing surgery during the off–season to try to correct the condition the pain was relentless and proved to be unbearable. Bird missed 37 games during the 1991–1992 seasons and missed an easy lay–up at a crucial moment during the Eastern Conference Semifinals against the Cleveland Cavaliers. He ended up missing four games in the series because of his back pain and the Cavaliers beat the Celtics in seven games.

That summer, Bird, along with Johnson, Jordan and other NBA greats played for the United States basketball team in the 1992 Barcelona Olympics. Together, they were called the Dream Team because it was the first time in history that the U.S. had allowed professional basketball players to compete in the Olympic games. It was, of course, a cinch for the team to bring home the gold medal.

On August 18, 1992, Bird announced his retirement as a professional player. Bird finished his career with the following shooting percentages:

- 49.6 percent from the field
- 88.6 from the free throw line
- 37.6 from the three–point range

He played in 897 professional games, scoring a total of 21,791 points (24.3 points per game), including a career–high of 28.1 points per game in 1987. He was the league long–distance shootout winner from 1986–1988 and led the NBA in free throw shooting in 1984, 1986 and 1990.

职业生涯

1979年伯德登上波士顿赛场之前,凯尔特人队连续两个赛季都没有进入季后赛。但是伯德的到来很快改变了局面,当年他被评为"NBA年度最佳新人",在伯德的带领下,该队从去年低于联盟均分的29胜53负,转变为最佳纪录61胜21负。那个赛季,凯尔特人队直闯总决赛,开始了13次直入季后赛的旅程。伯德为波士顿恰好效力13年,这并非机缘巧合。

次年,伯德既打小前锋又打大前锋,他与凯文·麦克黑尔和罗伯特·帕里什组成铁三角,这也许是NBA历史上最好的组合,在他剩余的12年职业生涯中,这种合作关系一直继续保持着。1980-1981年的赛季,他带领球队进入了NBA决赛,该队在6场比赛中横扫劲敌休斯敦火箭队,夺得冠军。

1986年,伯德继续带领凯尔特人队,最终创下常规赛季67胜15负的比赛纪录,而且再次在六场比赛中击败休斯敦火箭队。他连续获得"NBA最具价值球员"称号和"总决赛最具价值球员"殊荣,平均每场比赛得分24分、10个篮板、10次助攻。这是他三次蝉联联盟常规赛季"最具价值球员"奖,成为有史以来第三位获此嘉奖的运动员。

1988年,凯尔特人队在东部联赛总决赛的6场比赛中输给了活塞队,这次失败可能与一件事情有关:伯德只能参加常规赛季前6场比赛,之后,由于接受双脚后跟手术,只好放弃比赛。1989年,他重出江湖,但严重的背痛和年老的队友们已成为他的障碍,使他无法像以前打球那么得心应手。然而,这些并不意味着伯德不能继续比赛了。他在凯尔特人队的最后3个赛季中,平均每场拿下20多分、9个篮板、7个助攻,投篮命中率超过45%,带领球队每个赛季都闯进季后赛。

由于伯德的背伤越来越糟糕,他在1990~1991年的赛季中错失22场比赛。虽然赛后他经受了严酷难熬的手术,好让背伤有所好转,但检查显示他的背部神经根受压损伤。1991~1992年赛季,伯德缺席了37场比赛,而且在与克里夫兰骑士队对决的东部联盟半决赛中,他在关键时刻连一个简单的篮下单手跳投得分都没拿到。伯德最终由于背痛错过4场比赛,因此,凯尔特人队在7场比赛中都败给了骑士队。

1992年巴塞罗那的夏季奥运会上,伯德与约翰逊,乔丹,还有NBA其他球星一起为美国篮球队效力。他们的队伍被叫做"梦之队",因为有史以来美国第一次允许职业篮球员参加奥运会。当然,对于该队来说,把金牌揽入囊中是完全没问题的。

1992年8月18日,伯德宣布告别职业生涯。以下是他职业生涯中的投篮命中率:
投篮命中率49.6 %
罚球命中率88.6%
三分球命中率37.6%
他参加了897场职业篮球比赛,总得分为21791分 (平均每场24.3分),包括1987年平均每场28.1分的最高纪录。1986年至1988年,他是联盟远射得分王,并且带领NBA队在1984年、1986年和1990年得到罚球得分机会。伯德退役后,他的33号球衣也永被弃用,同时,在

Besides having his jersey, No. 33, retired shortly after his retirement, Bird received many accolades during and after his 13–year professional career. These include:

- NBA Rookie of the Year (1980)
- All–NBA First Team (1980–1988)
- NBA All–Star 12 times (1980–1988 and 1990–1992)
- NBA All–Star Game Most Valuable Player (1982)
- NBA All–Defensive Second Team (1982–1984)
- NBA Most Valuable Player (1984–1986)
- Associated Press Male Athlete of the Year (1986)
- The Sporting News Man of the Year (1986)
- All–NBA Second Team (1990)
- NBA 50th Anniversary All–Time Team (1996)

About the Man Himself

Even though Bird was finished with professional basketball as a player, he remained a part of the NBA, first as an assistant in the Celtic's front office and then as the head coach of the Indiana Pacers. He did not have experience as a coach going in, but he managed to lead the Pacers to three consecutive Eastern Conference finals visits and a first–ever team trip to the 2000 NBA Finals. Bird was named NBA Coach of the Year for his outstanding leadership abilities during the 1997–1998 season. He resigned as head coach after the 2000 season, but returned to the Pacers in 2003 with his current role as President of Basketball Operations.

Bird is also involved in raising money for a variety of charity organizations like the Boys and Girls Club of Terre Haute, Indiana and the Daniel Marr Boys and Girls Club in Boston. In fact, in 1992, he made sure that all of the proceeds, totaling more than $1 million, from his glorious retirement ceremony were distributed amongst 25 Boston charity groups.

Off the court, Bird, has made appearances in three movies: Blue Chips, Space Jam and Celtic Pride. He has also served as commercial spokesperson for several companies.

Bird has written an autobiography called Drive: The Story of My Life and he is the co–author of several other books, including Bird Watching: On Playing and Coaching the Game I Love.

Bird's marriage to Janet Condra was very brief (1975–1976). He married Dinah Mattingly in 1989. He is the father of three children.

Whether it is in playing, coaching or presiding over the game of basketball, Larry Legend, as he is sometimes called, has managed to spread his wings and lead the way to fantastic personal and team victories throughout his lifetime. There is undoubtedly much more in store for Larry Bird, and the world will continue to watch and remember.

13年职业生涯中以及退役后,他获得了无数的荣誉称号,包括:
- ·NBA年度新人奖(1980年)
- ·NBA第一阵容队员(1980~1988年)
- ·12次获得NBA全明星(1980~1988年、1990~1992年)
- ·NBA 全明星赛最具价值球员(1982年)
- ·NBA第二防守阵容队员(1982~1984年)
- ·NBA 最具价值球员 (1984~1986年)
- ·入选美洲报联社"年度最佳男性运动员"(1986年)
- ·入选《体育新闻》"年度新闻人物"(1986年)
- ·NBA第二阵容队员(1990年)
- ·入选NBA 50周年大庆历史全明星阵容(1996年)

关于此人

  虽然伯德告别了职业篮球运动员的时代,但他仍然是NBA的一部分。首先,他担任凯尔特人队管理部门的助理,后来成为印第安纳步行者队主教练。起初,他并没有多少教练经验,但是他竭尽所能,连续三次带领步行者队挺进东部联盟决赛,并在2000年进入NBA总决赛。由于伯德在1997~1998赛季中的杰出领导才能,他获得了"NBA年度最佳教练"称号。2000年赛季后,他辞去了总教练的职务,但是2003年他以"篮球事务主席"的身份重返步行者队。

  伯德还积极为一些慈善机构筹款,包括印第安纳特雷·霍特"男孩女孩俱乐部"和波士顿丹尼尔·马尔"男孩女孩俱乐部"。其实,他在1992年,已确保把退役典礼中获得的100多万美元的钱分配给波士顿25个慈善团体。

  离开球场后,伯德还出演过3部电影:《蓝筹》、《空中大灌篮》和《凯尔特人的骄傲》。同时他还是几家公司的广告代言人。

  伯德写过一本自传:《奋力前进:我的生活》,还与人合写过几本书,包括《伯德观看比赛》、《当教练——我喜欢》。

  伯德曾与珍妮特·康德拉有过一次短暂的婚姻(1975~1976年)。1989年他与黛娜·马丁莉结,成为三个孩子的父亲。

  无论作为球员、教练还是篮球队总监,"拉里传奇"(昵称之一),充分发挥自己的才能,一生中创造了无数非凡的个人成就及球队冠军。毋庸置疑,拉里·伯德必将创造更多的辉煌,全世界都将拭目以待,永远铭记。

Eight

Bonnie Blair

Why She is Among the 50 plus one Greatest Sports Heroes

Bonnie Blair was one of the best female speed skaters of her time and remains one of the most decorated female Olympic athletes in history. During three separate Olympic games she won five gold medals and one bronze, setting several impressive world records along the way. Just as Blair became the first in several Olympic speed skating categories, so she is placed among the first ranks of the greatest sports legends.

On the Way Up

Bonnie Kathleen Blair was born on March 18, 1964 in Cornwall, New York to Charles and Eleanor Blair but she was raised in Champaign, Illinois. Her family was passionate about the sport of skating, so much so that on the day she was born, her father had taken five older siblings to a skating meet. They found out about her birth when the announcement of her arrival came over the public address system at the rink!

Blair started skating when she was only 2 years old and entered her first speed skating race at the age of 4. She developed her perfect technique at an early age and was able to maintain her composure unlike other skaters who lost precious time from random lapses in their own techniques.

Although four of her siblings speed skated, Blair was the only one who decided to pursue seriously the sport. After graduating from Champaign's Centennial High School, she moved to the Milwaukee area to train with the United States speed skating team. She made her first Olympic appearance at the Sarajevo Games in 1984 at age 19 and although she did not medal she showed the world her potential by finishing eighth in the 500-meter race.

Professional Career

Four years later at the 1988 Winter Olympics in Calgary, Alberta, Canada, Blair surpassed her previous performance at the Games by bringing home two medals. She captured the gold medal in the 500 meters while also setting a world record with her finish time of 39.10 seconds, and she took the bronze medal in the 1,000 meters. About 30 friends and family, dubbed the Blair Bunch, traveled to Calgary to cheer Bonnie on. With each Olympics she seemed to get even better and the Blair Bunch grew larger. Four years later, at the 1992 Games in Albertville, France, the Blair Bunch, now 45 supporters strong, watched Blair win two gold medals—one in the 500 meters and again in the 1,000 meters (which she finished in 1:21.90, just two hundredths of a second behind her closest competitor's time).

In 1994, just shy of her 30th birthday, Blair competed in the Winter Olympics in Lillehammer, Norway and again won gold medals in the 500 meters and the 1,000 meters to the delight of the now 60 Blair Bunch supporters. By winning two more gold medals, Blair became the most decorated Winter Games athlete in the history of the United States as well as the first female athlete to win five gold medals in any sport. Her third 500-meter gold also put her in the headlines

邦妮·布莱尔

她为何入选《50+1位最闪耀的体育巨星》

邦妮·布莱尔是当代最优秀的速度滑冰运动员之一，至今仍是最耀眼的奥运女运动员之一。在三次奥运会中，她获得五枚金牌、一枚铜牌，创造了永载史册的世界纪录。正因为布莱尔夺得了好几个奥运速滑冠军，她理所当然地跻身于体育传奇人物之列。

成长之路

1964年3月18日，邦妮·凯瑟琳·布莱尔生于纽约州康沃尔市，父亲是查尔斯·布莱尔，母亲是埃莉诺·布莱尔，但她却在伊利诺斯州尚贝恩市长大。她的家人非常热爱滑冰运动，以至于在她出生那天，父亲还将其他5个哥哥姐姐们带到了滑冰会。他们是通过溜冰场的公共广播才得知她出生的消息。

布莱尔年仅两岁就开始学习滑冰，4岁时参加了生平第一个速滑比赛。很小的时候，她就学会了精湛的技术，即使在前面小失误中耽误了时间，她仍能够保持冷静，这点不同于其他运动员。

虽然她四个哥哥姐姐都会速滑，但只有她一人决定要去认真追求这项运动。从尚贝恩百年高中毕业后，她迁居密尔沃基地区，参加了美国速滑队的训练。1984年，19岁的她首次亮相于萨拉热窝冬奥会赛场上，虽然她没有获奖，但她在500米比赛中排名第八的成绩，已向全世界证明了她的潜力。

职业生涯

4年后，在1988年加拿大卡尔加里冬奥会上，布莱尔超越了她以往的任何水平，夺得两枚奖牌。她不仅在500米决赛中赢得金牌，而且还创下了39.10秒的世界纪录，并获得1000米比赛季军。大约有30个亲朋好友组成了"布莱尔团队"，奔赴卡尔加里，庆贺布莱尔取得胜利。每次参加奥运会，她似乎一次比一次进步，"布莱尔团队"也逐渐壮大。4年后的1992年法国阿尔贝维尔冬奥会中，她的"布莱尔团队"已有45位支持者，他们亲眼看到布莱尔赢得了500米和1000米比赛的冠军（她的成绩是1:21.90，只比对手快0.02秒）。

1994年，即将步入30岁的布莱尔参加了在挪威利勒哈默尔举办的冬季奥运会，再次夺得500米和1000米的金牌，此时为她庆祝胜利的"布莱尔团队"已壮大到60人。这两次夺冠，让布莱尔成为美国历史上最耀眼的冬奥会之星，也是当时体育界第一个获得过5枚金牌的女性运动员。500米速滑3次夺冠，让她成为各大报纸头版头条上的体育之星，因为她

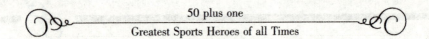
as the only athlete, man or woman, to win a gold medal in the same event at three consecutive Olympic Games. With a finish time of 39.25 seconds in the 500–meter race, she came in 0.36 seconds ahead of the second best time. Blair made history again when she finished the 1,000 meters in 1:18.74 with a 1.38–second margin that turned out to be the largest margin of victory ever in that event.

Shortly after the Lillehammer Games, Blair broke the 500–meter record for a second time on March 26, 1994. This time, she finished the event in 38.99 seconds, and in doing so, she became the first female skater to complete the 500 meters in less than 39 seconds. In February of 1995, Blair again broke the world record, finishing the 500 meters in 38.69 seconds. The following month, she set an American record when she completed the 1,000 meters in 1:18.05. That proved to be Blair's final opportunity to make history in skating because she retired after that race, on her 31st birthday, March 18, 1995.

Blair has been presented with numerous awards for her outstanding achievements during her speed skating career. She is the only U.S. Olympian to win gold medal in the same event in three consecutive Olympics. In 1992, she became only the second American (and third winter sports athlete) to win the Oscar Mathisen Award, a Norwegian award given annually to the world's best speed skater.

About the Woman Herself

Besides her obvious passion for the sport of speed skating, off the ice Blair was also a member of the 1989 Sundance Fruit Juicer Cycling Tour, riding with a team that included Connie Paraskevin Young, who won an Olympic bronze medal in 1988. Blair placed high in several sprint competitions, capturing the attention of the media at all of her races.

Blair also lends support to different charity groups through her organization, the Bonnie Blair Charitable Fund. For example, she teamed up with the NHL's Dallas Stars in 1997 to develop and carry out the Dallas Stars Bonnie Blair Golf Classic. Since its inception, the event has raised more than $342,000, which goes toward charities that fit the Dallas Star's Foundation's goal of helping and protecting children.

Blair is also on the board for United States Speed skating. She works as a motivational speaker for corporations and associations, and has written a book for children called *A Winning Edge*. Blair is married to four–time U.S. Olympic speed skater, Dave Cruikshank. They have two children.

Just as she attracted media attention throughout her skating days, Bonnie Blair will always be remembered for the way in which she carved out her world–class Olympic career.

是所有速滑运动员中唯一3次蝉联奥运冠军的选手。500米决赛中,她的最终成绩是39.25秒,比第二次的夺金成绩快了0.36秒。她在赛会上再次创造了1000米的世界纪录,最终成绩是1:18.74,创下了1.38秒最大幅度的差距。

　　就在里尔哈默冬奥会后不久,布莱尔于1994年3月26日再次改写了500米的世界纪录。她在这次赛会中的成绩是38.99秒,也因此成为首位39秒以内完成500米比赛的女性运动员。1995年2月,布莱尔再次创造世界纪录,这次成绩是38.69秒。3月,她以1:18.05的成绩创造了美国1000米比赛的新纪录。这也是布莱尔最后一次在滑冰史上写下的篇章,因为在1995年3月8日,也就是她31岁生日时,她退役了。
　　布莱尔在速滑史上硕果累累,奖项无数。她是唯一在相同赛会中蝉联3次奥运冠军的美国运动员。她成为仅有的第二位获得挪威奖项奥斯卡·马蒂森奖的美国人(也是第三位冬奥运动员),该奖项每年颁发给世界最佳速滑运动员。

关于此人

　　布莱尔对速滑运动的热情有目共睹,除此之外,她业余时曾是1989年Sundance Fruit Juicer Cycling Tour的成员,她参加的自行车队包括1988年奥运会铜牌得主康尼·帕拉斯科文·杨。在一系列的短道比赛中,布莱尔名列前茅,引起了媒体的广泛关注。

　　布莱尔还通过她的"邦妮·布莱尔慈善基金"支持各种慈善事业。例如,她在1997年与NHL达拉斯明星合作开发创办了"达拉斯明星邦妮·布莱尔高尔夫精英赛"。从创办初期开始,这项赛事共筹集到34万2000多美元,全部用在"达拉斯明星基金会"慈善事业上,旨在帮助和保护儿童。

　　同时,布莱尔也是美国速滑协会委员。她是一个动员演说者,积极呼吁团队协作,并为儿童写了一本名为《成功优势》的书。她嫁给了四次奥运速滑奖牌得主大卫·库鲁圣,两人育有两个孩子。
　　邦妮·布莱尔在速滑岁月中如此出类拔萃、惹人注目,在未来的日子里,人们也将一直记住她所开辟的世界级奥运之路。

Nine

Dick Butkus

Why He is Among the 50 plus one Greatest Sports Heroes

Dick Butkus is considered by many to be the best linebacker ever in the history of professional football. His playing style is described as being ferocious, intense, nasty and mean made him an effective team member of the Monsters of the Midway. Those traits combined with his strength and speed enabled him play in eight consecutive Pro Bowls and to be named NFL All–Pro seven times. Although his career was cut short because of injuries, Butkus proved during his nine seasons on the football field that he is worthy of being named one of the greatest sports heroes of all times.

On the Way Up

Richard Marvin Butkus was born on December 9, 1942 in Chicago, Illinois. He grew up in a big Lithuanian family on the city's South Side, and decided in fifth grade that he wanted to become a professional football player. It proved to be a decision, not just a dream as Butkus proceeded to pick and choose his schools, his summer jobs and his friends around his goal of making it to the pros. He went out of his way to attend Chicago Vocational High School so that he could play for Notre Dame graduate, Bernie O'Brien. In 1960, Butkus was named the Associated Press (AP) Prep–Football Player of the Year. He was an all–state fullback and was also successful on defense, having learned how to tackle a runner while stripping him of the ball at the same time.

Butkus played college football as a linebacker and center at the University of Illinois from 1962–1964. After the Fighting Illini suffered a losing 2–7 record during the 1962 season, he proceeded to lead them all the way to the 1964 Rose Bowl where they defeated the University of Washington Huskies 17–7 and finished with a No. 3 AP ranking. They also clinched the Big Ten Championship after Butkus made 145 tackles and caused 10 fumbles during that 1963 season. Throughout his career, he made 373 total tackles and established himself as the most unblockable linebacker in the history of college football.

Butkus received many awards for his collegiate playing days, both during and well after them. He is only one of two players to have had his uniform, No. 50, retired by Illinois, and he finished sixth and third, respectively, during the 1963 and 1964 Heisman Trophy balloting. In 1985, the Downtown Athletic Club of Orlando, Florida inaugurated the Butkus Award, a trophy that is given annually to the best college linebacker in the country. Other collegiate awards and honors Butkus has received includes:

- Consensus All–American (1963–1964)
- All–Big Ten (1962–1964)
- *Chicago Tribune* Silver Football as the Big Ten Most Valuable Player (1963)
- Player of the Year, American Football Coaches Association (1964)
- College Player of the Year, *Sporting News* (1964)
- College Football Hall of Fame (1983)

迪克·巴特肯

他为何入选《50+1位最闪耀的体育巨星》

迪克·巴特肯被众人称作职业橄榄球运动史上空前绝后的最佳中后卫。他以防守凶狠、速度快、进攻凶悍著称，这样的风格让他成为熊队极富影响力的队员。这种力量与速度的结合让他连续8次参加"职业碗"大赛，并7次获得国家橄榄球联盟全职业球员称号。尽管受伤缩短了巴特肯的职业生涯，但是他在9个赛季中证明了自己，当之无愧地成为出类拔萃的体坛英雄。

成长之路

1942年12月9日，理查德·马文·巴特肯生于伊利诺斯州芝加哥市。他从小在城市南边的一个立陶宛大家庭里长大，五年级时，他决定要成为一名职业橄榄球运动员。这是他的决心，而不仅仅是个梦想，巴特肯开始对学校、暑期工作和朋友都有选择性，只为一个目标——成为职业运动员。他特地到芝加哥本地职业高中读书，就为了效力于圣母大学毕业的波尼·奥布里恩教练。1960年，巴特肯被美联社评为"年度橄榄球预备队员"。他是一个全能后卫，也是成功的防守队员，他知道怎样与进攻者周旋、断球。

1962年至1964年，巴特肯在校队做中后卫，也是伊利诺斯大学校队的中锋。1962年赛季中Fighting Illini校队以2胜7负的成绩惨败，之后，他开始带领球队直奔1964年"玫瑰碗"美国大学美式橄榄球比赛，他们以17胜7负的成绩赢了华盛顿大学爱斯基摩犬队，最终排名第三。巴特肯在1963年赛季中，共有145次阻截擒抱、促使对方失球10次，他的球队最终赢得了十大联盟区冠军。在他的校队生涯中，共有373次阻截擒抱，让他成为大学橄榄球史上最所向披靡的中后卫。

巴特肯在大学期间及毕业后获得过无数奖项。在被伊利诺斯州退役的仅有的两件球衣中，他的50号是其中一件，并在1963年和1964年海斯曼奖杯票选中分获第六名和第三名。1985年，佛罗里达州奥兰多"市中心体育俱乐部"设立了巴特肯奖，此奖每年颁发给全美大学最优秀的中后卫。巴特肯获得的其他奖项和荣誉包括：

- 全美新秀最佳阵容奖 (1963~1964年)
- 入选十大联盟队 (1962~1964年)
- 被《芝加哥论坛报》评为"十大联盟最具价值球员" (1963年)
- 被"美国橄榄球教练员联合会"评为"年度运动员" (1964年)
- 被《体育新闻》评为"年度大学最佳球员" (1964年)
- 入选大学橄榄球名人堂 (1983年)
- 入选沃尔特·坎普世纪之队 (1990年)

- Walter Camp All–Century Team (1990)
- Rose Bowl Hall of Fame (1995)
- Sixth Best College Player Ever, *College Football News* (2000)

Professional Career

Butkus was signed as the first round draft pick by his hometown team, the Chicago Bears in 1965. He created an almost immediate improvement on the team, making a memorable debut in a game against the San Francisco 49ers with 11 unassisted tackles. Even though the Bears lost that game 52–24, the defense quickly began to shape up and they ended the season with a 9–5 record, a literal flip of their 5–9 record the year before. In 1965, the team also improved its total points yielded by 104, finishing the season with 275 points yielded. The Maestro of Mayhem, as fans affectionately called Butkus, led the Bears in tackles, pass interceptions and fumbles recovered during his rookie season.

His nickname was an indication that the 6 foot 3 inch, 245–pound Butkus was viewed as the leader of his team. For 8 consecutive years, he was the tackler for the Bears, averaging 120 tackles and 58 assists per season and he made a careerhigh 18 sacks in 1967. Butkus played in eight Pro Bowls in a row, from 1965–1972.

In 1970, Butkus suffered an injury to his right knee, and although he went through surgery, the injury never completely healed. Strong and brave, he was able to play on until the 1973 season, when the pain of his then multiple knee injuries had become too much for him to bear. In the fifth game of the season, against the Atlanta Falcons, Butkus was forced to take himself out of the game for the first time in his career. He endured several more weeks of pain before finally calling it quits and ending his days as a professional football player.

Upon retirement, Butkus had recovered an NFL–record 25 career fumbles, which currently puts him third on the all–time list. To put his ranking into perspective, Jim Marshall played 20 years and recovered 29 fumbles and Rickey Jackson played 15 years before recovering 28. During his 9–season career, Butkus also made a total of 1,020 tackles, 489 assists and 22 interceptions. Besides being named an NFL All–Pro seven times and having his No. 51 retired, he has received many honors for his Bear–playing years, including being:

- Pro Football Hall of Fame (1979)
- 75th Anniversary All–Time Team, NFL (2000)
- 70th Greatest Athlete of the 20th Century, ESPN
- Ninth Best Player in League History, *Sporting News*
- Fifth Best Player in League History, Associated Press

About the Man Himself

In 1975, Butkus filed a lawsuit against the Bears, stating that franchise members kept him on the field when they were fully aware that he should have had surgery on his knees. They reportedly denied him and other players the right to seek medical opinions other than those of the team doctor and gave him painkillers in generous doses so that he would remain active. The suit was eventually settled out of court, but it put a huge strain on Butkus' relationship with Bears' owner, George Halas, even though they had a lot in common: they had both been born and raised in Chicago as first–generation Americans and had both attended the University of Illinois.

A decade later Butkus signed to work as a WGN radio announcer for the team, along with first–year play–by–play man, Wayne Larrivee and former St. Louis Cardinals quarterback, Jim

·入选玫瑰碗名人堂(1995年)
·被《大学足球新闻》评为"第六位史上最佳大学球员"(2000年)

职业生涯

1965年巴特肯在家乡的芝加哥熊队第一轮选秀中脱颖而出,并与该队签约。很快,他在该队大有长进,与旧金山49人的比赛是他难以忘怀的首次亮相,这场比赛中他有11次无助攻阻截擒抱。虽然熊队以24:52的成绩输了这次比赛,但防守却迅速改善,这个赛季的最终成绩是9胜5负,正好和上个赛季的5胜9负颠了个个儿。1965年,该队比赛总分增长到104分,赛季结束后的总分是275分。巴特肯的球迷亲切称之为"爆发力大师"(Maestro of Mayhem),在他作为新人的赛季中,他带领球队成功擒抱、拦截传球、抢夺丢球。

巴特肯的昵称也显示出身高6英尺3英寸、体重245磅的他,是大家公认的领队人物。连续8年,他都是熊队的阻截队员,他平均每个赛季120次阻截,58次助攻,1967年他创造了职业生涯中擒倒对手的最多次数——18次。从1965年至1972年,巴特肯连续8次参加"职业碗"大赛。

1970年,巴特肯右膝盖受伤,虽然动过手术,但从未治愈。他坚毅勇敢的品质让他在1973年赛季重出江湖,那时,他膝盖的多处伤痛使他备受煎熬、疼痛不堪。那个赛季第五场对抗亚特兰大猎鹰队的比赛中,巴特肯第一次在职业赛中被迫出局。在放弃参赛和告别职业生涯之前,他又忍受了好几个星期的伤痛。

退役时的巴特肯刷新了美国国家橄榄球联盟的纪录,他创下了掉球25次的新纪录,目前一直排名第三。具体来说,吉姆·马歇尔在20年的职业生涯中掉球29次,瑞克·杰克逊15年里掉球28次。在9个赛季生涯中,巴特肯共有1020个阻截擒抱、489次助攻、22次拦截。巴特肯7次获得国家橄榄球联盟全职业球员称号,他的51号球衣也被退役,除此之外,为熊队效力的岁月中,他还获得过无数荣誉奖项,包括:
·入选职业橄榄球名人堂 (1979年)
·入选国家橄榄球联盟75周年全明星队 (2000年)
·被美国ESPN娱乐体育频道评为"20世纪第70位最佳运动员"
·被《体育新闻》评为"联盟历史上第九位最佳球员"
·被美联社评为"联盟历史上第五位最佳球员"

关于此人

1975年,巴特肯对熊队提起诉讼,起诉职业联盟会员在清楚知道他膝盖需要手术的情况下,仍强迫他上场比赛。据说,他和队友除了可以向队医求助,没有任何寻求其他医疗意见的权利,他只能靠服用大量止痛药来维持运动。最后,这个起诉私下解决了,可是巴特肯和熊队创始人乔治·哈拉斯的关系却变得格外紧张,虽然他们有很多相似之处:他们作为第一代在芝加哥出生、成长的美国人,都曾就读于伊利诺斯大学。

10年后,巴特肯为球队担当起WGN电台讲解员,一起工作的还有第一年实况报道解说员威尼·拉里维和圣路易斯红雀队前四分卫吉姆·哈特。他断断续续担任此职直到1994年,也是在这一年,熊队将他的球衣号码永久退役,当时的熊队已由乔治·哈拉斯的女儿

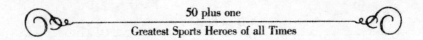

Hart. He would keep this position on and off until 1994, which was the same year that the Bears, then owned by the family of George Halas' daughter, Virginia McCaskey, retired his number. This ceremonious act signaled the end of the bitterness between Butkus and the Halas and McCaskey families.

Besides his WGN radio position, Butkus has also worked as a celebrity endorser and NFL radio and television announcer. In 2000, he was briefly named head coach of the Chicago Enforcers in the short-lived Extreme Football League (XFL). Although the announcement sold many tickets in the city, Butkus never actually coached a game because he had become the team's Director of Football Competition instead. In the end, it did not really matter since the XFL only lasted 1 season. In 2005, Butkus starred in an ESPN reality show called Bound for Glory –The Montour Spartans, in which he was the head coach of a struggling high school football team from McKees Rock, a suburb of Pittsburgh, Pennsylvania. He has also appeared in such movies as Necessary Roughness and *Any Given Sunday*, and as a regular character on such television series as *My Two Dads and Hang Time*.

When he is not acting, Butkus likes to golf. In the past, he has hosted a national golf tournament that raised money for the treatment of cystic fibrosis. He also formed a program called Mean and Clean in an effort to teach young athletes about the dangers of steroid abuse. Butkus has written and co-written a few books, including his autobiography, *Butkus: Flesh & Blood (How I Played the Game)*. He married his high school sweetheart, Ellen Essenhart, in 1963 and they had two sons and one daughter. Like father, like son Butkus' son Matt also played football and played on the University of Southern California's 1990 Rose Bowl-winning team.

Dick Butkus was regarded as possibly the meanest, fiercest and toughest linebacker to ever play football. A mastermind on the field and off, this tough-asnails Bear will forever be regarded as one of the greatest athletes of all times.

弗吉尼亚·麦克卡斯金继承。这个仪式化解了巴特肯与哈拉斯及麦克卡斯金家族的恩怨。

　　除了在WGN电台担任讲解员外，他还是名人背书人、国家橄榄球联盟广播台和电视台讲解员。2000年，他在极限橄榄球联盟XFL芝加哥执法者队担任短期的总教练。此消息一公布，全城售票火热，但是，巴特肯从未真正指导过一场比赛，因为他又转为橄榄球比赛理事。最后，他当不当教练也没有什么关系了，因为XFL只维持了一个赛季。2005年，巴特肯上了ESPN频道"奔向辉煌"(Bound for Glory –The Montour Spartans)的真人秀节目，在宾夕法尼亚州匹兹堡市的郊区，担任麦基斯·洛克(McKees Rock)高中一支勤奋的校队教练。

　　同时，他在一些电影中出演角色，比如《反败为胜》、《再战星期天》，在电视剧《我的两个爸爸》和《悬空瞬间》中扮演普通角色。

　　巴特肯演戏之余，喜欢打高尔夫球。以前，他曾组织过全国高尔夫锦标赛，筹款用于囊性纤维变性的治疗。他还创办了"简陋干净"(Mean and Clean)节目，旨在教育年轻运动员滥用类固醇会有哪些危害。巴特肯本人单独出书，也与人合作写书，包括自传《巴特肯：肉与血(我怎样打球)》》。1963年，他与高中女友艾伦·艾森哈特结婚，他们育有二子一女。有其父必有其子，他的儿子马特也打橄榄球，并参加了南加利福尼亚大学1990年"玫瑰碗"冠军队的比赛。

　　可能大家一致公认迪克·巴特肯是橄榄球史上空前绝后的凶狠、野蛮、暴力的中后卫。赛场内外的巴特肯是个极富才智的人，这个体壮如熊的运动员将永远是人们心目中的最佳球员。

Wilt Chamberlain

Why He is Among the 50 plus one Greatest Sports Heroes

Wilt Chamberlain's awesome scoring and rebounding skills quite literally changed the rules of NBA basketball. Besides his many other athletic accomplishments, the simple fact that he helped to shape the game so dramatically hints at why he is considered a larger than life sports hero, no pun intended.

On the Way Up

Wilton Norman Chamberlain was born on August 21, 1936 in Philadelphia. It must have been a shock to his parents, William and Olivia, when he reached his full height and weight of 7 feet, 1 inch and 275 pounds. William and Olivia were both only 5 feet, 8 inches tall. It is no wonder that Chamberlain eventually became known by his adoring fans as Wilt the Stilt, a nickname that he actually disliked. He was also dubbed the Big Dipper, which he preferred as it was a nickname bestowed upon him by friends.

Chamberlain did not always play basketball and did not develop an interest in the game until he was in his teens. Before that time, the Big Dipper was more like a little dipper, dipping into odd and end jobs in order to help his parents take care of himself and his 10 other siblings. By the age of 5, Chamberlain was delivering groceries and newspapers, washing windows and shoveling snow. He sold fruit, vegetables and junk and later formed his own painting and clean-up crews.

When Chamberlain started at Overbrook High School in 1951, his basketball career was ready to take off, especially during his junior and senior years. He led Overbrook to the City championship in 1954 and 1955 and was named an All-American in 1955. During one game against Roxborough High School, Chamberlain scored 90 points, 60 of which he scored in only a 10-minute span. His total high school point tallied an impressive 2,252, which was part of the reason he was the most sought-after high school recruit in the United States.

When Chamberlain started playing for the University of Kansas Jayhawks in 1957, he proved why he had been such a hot commodity right out of high school. He scored a total of 1,433 points and pulled down 877 rebounds, eventually carrying his teammates to the Big Seven championships in 1957 and 1958. He was the NCAA Tournament MVP in 1957, the Sporting News First Team All-American in 1958 and the First Team All-American in both 1957 and 1958. The university retired his jersey, No. 13, in 1998.

Despite his success, Chamberlain's awesome athletic abilities started to become a source of annoyance rather than joy for him. He was so good that he would either end up being double- or triple-teamed or waiting impatiently as the other team purposely held the ball for long periods of time. These schemes proved to be such a frustration for Chamberlain that he left the university in 1958 and toured with the Harlem Globetrotters for a short while until he was drafted into the NBA by the Philadelphia Warriors in 1959.

威尔特·张伯伦

他为何入选《50+1位最闪耀的体育巨星》

威尔特·张伯伦令人叹服的投篮得分及弹跳抢篮板的高超技巧，简直改变了NBA的篮球规则。且不说他的其他运动成就，光这个简单的事实——他帮助了篮球运动成形，就足以证明他是个"超越现实"(larger than life)的体育英雄，此话并非一语双关。

成长之路

1936年8月21日，威尔顿·诺曼·张伯伦生于费城。当他长成身高7英尺1英寸、体重275磅的青年时，他的父亲威廉和母亲奥莉花一定大为震惊。威廉和奥莉花两个人只不过5英尺8英寸的身高。难怪崇拜者们最后给他起了个昵称叫做"踩高跷的威尔特"，他个人比较讨厌这个名字。他还有个昵称叫做"大北斗"，他本人比较喜欢这个名字，因为是他的朋友给他起的。

张伯伦不常打篮球，对篮球也并没有多大兴趣，直到他十几岁时才显示出对篮球的爱好。在此之前，"大北斗"更像是"小勺子"，四处干零活，来帮助父母养活自己和其余10个兄弟姐妹。5岁时，张伯伦运货、送纸、洗窗、铲雪。他卖蔬菜、水果和旧货，后来成立了自己的油漆和清洁队。

1951年张伯伦开始就读于奥芬布卢克高中，此时他的篮球生涯也开始起步，尤其在他三、四年级阶段。1954年和1955年，他带领奥芬布卢克校队直冲城市冠军赛，并于1955年获得了"全美高中明星"的荣誉称号。在对抗罗布鲁高中的一场比赛中，张伯伦一人得分90分，其中60分是在短暂的10分钟内取得的。他在整个高中生涯中创造了令人难忘的2252的总分成绩，他为何成为全美最想寻求的新人？这高中纪录也是其中一个原因吧。

1957年，张伯伦开始效力于堪萨斯大学，证明了他为何刚从高中毕业就成为炙手可热的新人。他获得了1433的总分，抢下了877个篮板，带领全队挺进1957年和1958年的"七大联盟冠军赛"。1957年，他被评为"美国大学生篮球联赛最具价值球员"称号，1958年入选《体育新闻》全美第一阵容球员，1957年和1958年都入选了全美第一队。直到1998年，他的13号球衣才正式退役。

虽然张伯伦成功无数，他那精湛的球技却开始给他带来了烦恼，而并非快乐。他如此厉害，以至于要通过两三名球员一起拦阻，或者对方故意拖延持球时间，他的进攻才会被妨碍。这些战术使张伯伦大受阻挠、心灰意冷，终于在1958年离开了大学，并参加了哈林花式篮球队世界巡回赛，

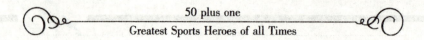

Professional Career

With only 2 years of college–level basketball under his belt, Chamberlain was ready for the big time. He would be involved in professional basketball for the next 16 years.

· Harlem Globetrotters (1958–1959), player
· NBA Philadelphia Warriors (1959–1962), player
· NBA San Francisco Warriors (1963–1964), player
· NBA Philadelphia 76ers (1964–1968), player
· NBA Los Angeles Lakers (1968–1973), player
· ABA San Diego Conquistadors (1973–1974), coach

Chamberlain shined so much more brightly than his fellow professional league players that NBA officials decided to change several of the rules in order to bring about some sense of fairness. These changes involved widening the lane and establishing offensive goaltending. They also banned the inbound pass over the backboard, the dunk from the foul line in a free–throw attempt and the alley–oop. It is easy to see, then, that the Big Dipper started making a name for himself early on in his professional career. His rookie year in the NBA with the Philadelphia Warriors was full of stellar achievements. He:

· Scored 53 points against Syracuse, March 14, 1960
· Scored 58 points against Detroit, January 25, 1960–single game record for most points by a rookie
· Scored 2,707 total points (37.6 points per game –seasonal record for most points by a rookie)
· Made 1,941 total rebounds (27 rebounds per game)–seasonal record for most rebounds by a rookie

It only took a couple of years for Chamberlain's accomplishments to be noticed nationally. The year 1962 ended up being a big one for him. While he was still with the Philadelphia Warriors, he set records in scoring, rebounding, minutes played and field goals:

· Single–game All–Star record for most points (42)
· Single–game record for most points (100), March 2, 1962 against New York
· Seasonal record for most minutes played (3,338 total, 41.7 per game)
· Seasonal record for most points (4,029)
· Seasonal record for most points per game (50.4)
· Seasonal record for field goals made (1,597)
· Seasonal record for field goals attempted (3,159)

As more years passed, Chamberlain kept getting better and better. He led two of his teams to the NBA championship title: the Philadelphia 76ers in 1967 and the Los Angeles Lakers in 1972. He also continued his record setting streak.

Of course, after setting such an admirable amount of records during his career in the NBA, it only followed suit that an equally admirable amount of honors would be bestowed upon him a long time after his exit from the world of professional basketball in 1973.

· NBA MVP (1960, 1966–1968)
· All–NBA First Team (1960–1962, 1964, 1966–1968)
· All–NBA Second Team (1963, 1965, 1972)
· All–Defensive First Team (1972–1973)
· NBA Finals MVP (1972)

不久后在1959年费城勇士队新秀选拔中入选了NBA。

职业生涯

张伯伦只拥有过两年的大学篮球经历，但他已经做好了登峰造极的准备。在接下来的16年里，他都以职业篮球运动员身份出场。

- 哈林花式篮球队(1958-1959年)，队员
- NBA费城勇士队(1959-1962年)，队员
- NBA旧金山勇士队(1963-1964年)，队员
- NBA 费城76人队 (1964-1968年)，队员
- NBA洛杉矶湖人队 (1968-1973年)，队员
- ABA圣迭戈征服者队(1973-1974年)，教练

张伯伦比职业联盟中的其他球员更加出色，以至于NBA管理者们决定改变一些规则，以便带来一丝公平的感觉。这些改变包括扩大罚球区、制定进攻干扰球。他们还规定禁止越过篮球架篮板掷界外球、禁止在罚球线处罚球出手后灌篮、禁止空中接力。

显而易见，这个"大北斗"早已在职业篮球场上出人头地。他在NBA费城勇士队第一年中成绩斐然。他：

- 于1960年3月14日对抗西拉克斯队中获得53 分
- 于1960年1月25日对抗底特律队中获得58分，成为单场比赛中得分最多的新人
- 获得2707的总分(每场平均37.6分，成为赛季纪录中得分最高的新人)
- 拿下1941个篮板 (每场平均27个篮板，成为赛季纪录中抢篮板最多的新人)

只用了两三年的时间，张伯伦的赫赫战功已引起全国关注。1962年对他来说是辉煌的一年。当他还在为费城勇士队效力时，他创下了投篮得分、抢下篮板球、上场时间和投中次数的纪录。

- 全明星赛单场得分最高纪录(42分)
- 1962年3月2日迎战纽约队中，单场比赛得分最高纪录 (100分)
- 赛季上场时间最多纪录(总共3338分钟，平均每场41.7分钟)
- 赛季得分最高纪录 (4029分)
- 赛季每场得分最高纪录(50.4分)
- 赛季投中次数最多纪录 (1597次)
- 赛季投篮次数最多纪录(3159次)

随着岁月流逝，张伯伦一直在进步。他带领球队两次赢得NBA冠军：一次是1967年带领费城76人队，另一次是1972年带领洛杉矶湖人队。他继续创造着连胜的纪录。

无独有偶，他也是在NBA生涯中创造了无数骄人成就后，直到1973年退役后，又过了相当长的一段时间，这些耀眼光环才戴在他的头上。

- NBA 最具价值球员 (1960年、1966-1968年)
- 入选 NBA最佳阵容第一队(1960-1962年、1964年、1966-1968年)
- 入选 NBA最佳阵容第二队(1963年、1965年、1972年)
- 入选最佳防守第一阵容(1972-1973年)
- NBA决赛最具价值球员 (1972年)

· Naismith Memorial Basketball Hall of Fame (1978)
· NBA 35th Anniversary All–Time Team (1980)
· NBA 50th Anniversary All–Time Team (1996)

Despite his awesome talent, tremendous achievements and inspiring honors, Chamberlain was often made fun of and looked down upon by onlookers, who expected more from him because he made everything look so easy or blamed him when his teams took a fall. On more than one occasion, he had been heard to say, "Nobody roots for Goliath."

About the Man Himself

Chamberlain was more than just a basketball legend. He was an all–around fantastic athlete. As a child, he dreamt of becoming a track and field Olympian. He was, in fact, a member of his high school's track team. During this time, he ran the 100–yard dash in 10.9 seconds, ran the 440 in 49.0 seconds, ran the 880 in 1:58.3, high jumped 6 feet 6 inches, long jumped 22 feet and threw the shot put 53 feet 4 inches. Also on the track and field team at the University of Kansas, Wilt Chamberlain Chamberlain won the high jump in the Big Eight track and field championships. He played volleyball and even founded and starred in a professional league, while also sponsoring a woman's track and a woman's volleyball team. Chamberlain's thirst for athletic involvement was not quenched easily. He participated in auto racing, tried out boxing and was even offered a professional football contract by the Kansas City Chiefs in 1966. After retirement, he ran a marathon in Hawaii and competed in a 50–mile race in Canada.

Chamberlain was also an intelligent man with varied interests, which was shown through his fluency in several languages besides English, including French, German, Italian and Spanish. Later in life, the Big Dipper went back to the little dipper ways of his youth and managed to bring in other forms of income even after retirement. A bit of an entrepreneur, he dabbled in race horses, owned his own nightclub in Harlem named Big Wilt's Small Paradise and appeared in television commercials. He even played a supporting role in the 1984 movie, Conan the Destroyer, starring Arnold Schwarzenegger. Chamberlain was a writer, too. He wrote four books, including *Wilt: Just Like Any Other 7–foot Black Millionaire Who Lives Next Door; A View from Above; Who's Running the Asylum? Inside the Insane World of Sports Today;* and a book about his house, which he dubbed Ursa Major.

Chamberlain, a lifelong bachelor, died of heart failure at his home on October 12, 1999. Upon his death, he gave $650,000 to the Kansas University Endowment Association. The donation provided four endowed funds in Chamberlain's name for scholarships, Kansas University men's and women's athletics and a Special Olympics clinic. Even today the legend of Wilt Chamberlain endures.

·入选奈史密斯篮球名人纪念堂(1978年)
·入选NBA 35周年大庆历史全明星阵容(1980年)
·入选NBA 50周年大庆历史全明星阵容(1996年)

张伯伦拥有令人敬畏的才华、无数丰功伟绩和鼓舞人心的荣誉，但是，旁观者总是过高寄予厚望，认为没有什么能难倒他，只要他没有达到，或让球队失败了，就会遭到嘲笑、鄙视、责骂。别人不止一次听见他说："没有人能铲除巨人。"

关于此人

张伯伦远不只是个篮球传奇人物。他是一个多才多艺的杰出运动员。孩提时的张伯伦梦想成为田径奥运会选手。实际上他是高中田径队队员。那时，他的百米短跑成绩是10.9秒，440米49.0秒，880米1分58.3秒，跳高成绩为6英尺6英寸，跳远成绩为22英尺，扔铅球为53英尺4英寸。张伯伦在堪萨斯大学田径队时，曾赢得八大联盟区田径大赛的跳高冠军。他也打排球，甚至建立并参加过一个职业联盟，还创办了女子田径队和女子排球队。张伯伦对体育运动的渴求从来没有停止过。他参加过赛车、试过拳击，而且在1966年堪萨斯城酋长曾邀请他签约职业足球。退役后，他参加了夏威夷的马拉松比赛和加拿大的50英里赛跑。

张伯伦人很聪明、兴趣广泛，除了英语，还会讲流利的法语、德语、意大利语和西班牙语。在下半生中，这个"大北斗"又变成了童年时期的小个子，在退役后还想方设法通过不同渠道来赚钱。他开始涉足商业，初试赛马业，并在哈林拥有自己的"大威尔特小天堂"夜总会，频频出现在电视广告中。1984年，他还在电影《毁灭者柯南》中出演配角，主角是阿诺德·施瓦辛格。张伯伦还是个作家。他写了4本书，包括《威尔特：就像任何一位邻家7英尺黑人百万富翁》；《从上往下看》；《谁在开疯人院？洞察如今疯狂的体育世界》；还有一本写的是他家，被他取名为《大熊星座》。

张伯伦终生未婚，1999年10月12日因心力衰竭死于家中。去世后，他的65万美元全部捐给了堪萨斯大学基金会。这些捐款以张伯伦的名义分别建立了四个基金会，包括奖学金、堪萨斯大学男子女子体育运动、特殊奥林匹克训练营。威尔特·张伯伦至今仍是不可思议的传奇人物。

Eleven

Jimmy Connors

Why He is Among the 50 plus one Greatest Sports Heroes

Jimmy Connors burst onto the professional tennis scene during an era when the sport was rising to prominence. With his charismatic personality, his aggressively exciting playing style and his famed rivalries with other players, Connors has been described as a key player in the high-profile development of the game. His hard work earned him five U.S. Open titles, an induction into the International Tennis Hall of Fame and a place as one of the 50 plus one greatest athletes of all times.

On the Way Up

James Scott Connors was born on September 2, 1952 in East St. Louis, Illinois. He was raised in the St. Louis suburb of Belleville, Illinois and reportedly began playing tennis when he was 2 years old. Connors learned the ins and outs of the game from his mother, Gloria Thompson Connors, who was a teaching pro, and his grandmother, Bertha Thompson. Growing up, he was smaller than many of his opponents, and his determination and toughness were instrumental in his success. When he was 8 years old, he played in his first U.S. Championship at the 1961 U.S. boys' 11 and under competition. Connors went on to play for the University of California, Los Angeles for 1 year, winning the 1971 NCAA singles title, before turning pro in July of 1972.

Professional Career

Connors won his first professional title during his rookie year at Jacksonville, Florida. However, he quickly began attracting the attention of the tennis world not so much because of his success but more so because of his highly competitive and outspoken nature and his willingness to put forth whatever amount of energy it took to win. Connors became known as the Brash Basher of Belleville because he would play to the crowd while at the same time verbally abusing his opponent or the umpire as a means of staying on top during competition. He also remained in the headlines when he began dating fellow tennis legend, Chris Evert, with whom he planned to marry in October of 1974 before the wedding was called off.

Throughout the early stages of his career, Connors vulgar behavior annoyed many tennis fans and officials alike. Besides his sometimes vulgar behavior on the court, he refused to play in the Davis Cup and he also made waves in 1972, when he refused to join the then new Association of Tennis Professionals (ATP). At the urging of his manager and promoter, Bill Riordan, Connors stayed out of the mainstream of professional tennis so that he could be the dominating force in a series of smaller tournaments.

Then, in 1974, Connors was banned from the French Open after signing a contract with Baltimore's World Team Tennis (WTT). All WTT players were prohibited from participating in the French Open because it conflicted with the tournament; Connors and Riordan sued the ATP and its president, Arthur Ashe, for a total of $10 million, complaining the ATP was restricting freedom

吉米·康纳斯

他为何入选《50+1位最闪耀的体育巨星》

吉米·康纳斯是在网球运动异军突起的年代开始登上职业网坛的。康纳斯具有独特的个人魅力、激情洋溢的作战风格以及有名的竞争对手,人们形容他是这项高度规范化发展运动的中流砥柱。他的努力为他赢得了五次美国网球公开赛,入选了"国际网球名人堂",也是50+1位最闪耀的体育巨星中不可或缺的一员。

成长之路

1952年9月2日,詹姆斯·斯哥特·康纳斯在伊利诺斯州东圣路易出生。他在贝尔维尔市东圣路易的郊区长大,据说两岁就开始打网球了。康纳斯从母亲葛罗莉亚·汤普森·康纳斯和外婆博莎·汤普森那儿了解到了网球运动的详细打法,他母亲是位网球培训教师。长大后,他比许多对手矮小,但他的雄心壮志和坚毅品质为他的成功推波助澜。1961年,年仅8岁的他第一次在"美国11岁以内男孩比赛"中夺得美国冠军。康纳斯为加州大学洛杉矶分校效力一年,赢得1971年全美大学生体育协会单打冠军,1972年正式成为职业球员。

职业生涯

在佛罗里达州杰克逊维尔,康纳斯第一次作为新人赢得了职业比赛。然而,他迅速引人注目的原因并不是由于他的成功,更多的是由于他超强的好胜心、直言不讳的本质,以及使出浑身解数夺冠的欲望。康纳斯开始以"贝尔维尔急躁的猛击者"著称,因为他会哗众取宠,同时会用言语辱骂对手或裁判,以此方法来控制局面。当他和网球传奇人物克里斯·埃弗特约会时也一直上头版头条,他原打算于1974年10月跟她结婚,后来婚礼又取消了。

康纳斯在职业生涯的人生舞台早期,他那低俗的行为惹恼了不少球迷和裁判员。除了球场上的一些低俗行为外,他拒绝参加戴维斯杯,1972年他还拒绝加入当时新建的职业网球协会(ATP),此举掀起波澜、引发争端。在他的经纪人和赞助人比尔·莱尔登的力劝下,康纳斯远离了职业网球的主流,以便能够在一系列小规模锦标赛上独占鳌头。

然而,在1974年,康纳斯与巴尔的摩世界网球团体(WTT)签约后却被禁止参加法国网球公开赛。所有世界网球团体的队员都被禁止参加法网公开赛,因为它与锦标赛相互矛盾;康纳斯和莱尔登一起控诉了职业网球协会和协会主席阿瑟·阿什,抱怨职网协会限制了在网球世界的自由权利,并索赔1000万美元。这起控诉最终庭外和解。这场纷争给康

in the tennis world. The suit was eventually settled out of court. The dispute cost Connors more than just a bad reputation. It turned out that the only tournament Jimmy did not win that year was the French Open (due to the banning). Sadly, his exclusion may have prevented him from being the first male player since Rod Laver to win all four Grand Slam titles in 1 year.

He again was the source of drama when he refused to participate in the Parade of Champions on the first day of the 1977 Wimbledon Centenary. The typically reserved fans displayed their displeasure with Connors by booing him when he made his way onto the court the following day.

Connors may have been outspoken in his manner of bucking tradition, but the term–all talk and no action–did not apply to him. His main strengths as a player were his killer double–handed backhand; his capacity for controlling points with his ground strokes; and his ability and willingness to run down balls in situations when most other players would have simply given up. These attributes led Connors to a fantastic career that spanned more than 2 decades.

The year 1974 was a tremendous one for Connors. He won 14 tournaments including his only Australian Open title, which he earned by beating Phil Dent in four sets during the final. He also won the first of his five U.S. Open titles and the first of his two Wimbledon singles titles after defeating Ken Rosewall in straight sets in the finals of both tournaments. Connors was ranked No. 1 in the world from July 29, 1974 until August 22, 1977 for a total of 160 consecutive weeks. He would own the World No.1 ranking for a combined 268 weeks throughout the entirety of his career.

In 1975, Connors came in second in the three Grand Slam events that he had swept the previous year. Ironically, he faced Ashe in the Wimbledon singles final, but ended up losing 1–6, 1–6, 7–5, 4–6. During that final, which was the second of his five Wimbledon final appearances, one of his fans roared out to him, "Come on, Jimmy!" Connors responded in the same cutting and loud manner as his fan by yelling, "I'm trying, for Christ's sake!"

Connor's famous rivalry with Bjorn Borg emerged in 1976, when the two met in the final of the U.S. Open. The win went to Connors as he saved four–set points in a tie–breaker in the third set and beat Borg 6–4, 3–6, 7–6, 6–4. In 1977, Connors and Borg faced off at the Wimbledon, but Connors lost in a five–set final. After getting under the skin of sponsors and tennis officials by snubbing his nose at the end–of–year Masters championships for the past 3 years, Connors finally decided to enter the competition in 1977. It was a wise decision as he ended up defeating Borg in the final for the title. The two rivals seemed to be volleying their wins and losses, as Borg beat Connors for the 1978 Wimbledon title, after which Connors crushed Borg in straight sets in the U. S. Open final to win 6–4, 6–2, 6–2. With that U.S. Open title, Connors became the first player to win the tournament on three different surfaces: grass in 1974, clay in 1976 and hard court in 1978.

During the rest of his career, Connors maintained noticeable rivalries with two, younger players, John McEnroe and Ivan Lendl. He faced McEnroe, the defending champion, in the Wimbledon final in 1982. Connors was three points away from losing when he rallied back in a fourth–set tie–breaker to win his second Wimbledon title in five sets. He also defeated Lendl in the 1982 and 1983 U.S. Open finals. McEnroe finally silenced Connors by beating him in straight sets 6–1, 6–1, 6–2 at the 1984 Wimbledon. Even though his opponent had badly beaten him, Connors remained as cocky and bold as ever. When asked after the competition if he would admit that McEnroe was a better player, he simply replied, "Never."

As Connors' career advanced, his on–court demeanor slowly mellowed out and he eventually grew into a respected, older player. In 1991, after playing only three tournament matches due to

纳斯带来的不仅是名誉扫地。结果,吉米唯一没有获胜的一次锦标赛就是法国网球公开赛(因为被禁)。很不幸的是,他被排斥在外,所以没有成为第一位一年之内荣获4次大满贯的男运动员,这个第一人成了罗德·拉沃。

1977年温布尔登百年纪念第一天,他拒绝参加冠军游行,再次成为戏剧性事件的主角。第二天,当康纳斯踏上赛场时,以往一贯沉默的球迷也对他嘘声一片,发泄不满。

康纳斯可能因其反叛的方式而直言不讳,但是光说不练并不适合他。他作为球员的杀手铜是双手反手击球、击落地球控制比分的能力,当大多数球员轻易放弃不可能接到的球时,他却表现出顽强的毅力追杀击球。这些优点及品质让康纳斯驰骋职业球场20年。

1974年对于康纳斯来说是丰收的一年。他赢得了14次锦标赛,包括唯一的一次澳大利亚网球公开赛冠军,在那次决赛中的四盘比赛里他击败了对手菲尔·邓特。同时,他赢得了美国公开赛五连冠的第一次冠军,此年也是他两次温网单打冠军的第一次夺冠,在这两次锦标赛中他都在决赛中直落盘数击败对手肯·罗斯沃尔。康纳斯从1974年7月29日至1977年8月22日以连续160周的纪录排名世界第一。在整个职业生涯中,他以总数268周排名世界第一。

1975年,他在3次大满贯赛事中获得第二,而去年却是夺冠。极为讽刺的是,他在温网单打决赛中遇到了阿什,但是比赛以1:6,1:6,7:5,4:6的失败成绩告终。那次决赛也是他五次参加温网决赛的第二次亮相,比赛中一名球迷冲他高喊:"加油,吉米!"康纳斯同样声嘶力竭地回答他:"我在努力,看在上帝的分上!"

康纳斯最著名的比赛出现在1976年,在美国公开赛决赛中,他遇到了对手比约恩·博格。在第三局中出现了平局决胜制(抢七局)时,康纳斯获胜并保住了第四局,最终以6:4,3:6,7:6,6:4的比分赢得了比赛。1977年,在温网比赛中,康纳斯再战博格,但是他在第五局决赛中失败了。康纳斯在过去三年的年底网球大师冠军赛中,他嗤之以鼻的态度激怒了赞助者和网球裁判们,1977年,康纳斯终于决定参加比赛了。参加比赛是他的明智选择,因为他在决赛中击败了博格,夺得桂冠。这两个对手似你追我赶、互拼输赢,博格于1978年击败康纳斯获得温网冠军,随后,康纳斯在美国公开赛的决赛中以直落三盘的6:4,6:2,6:2比分击败博格。这次获得美国公开赛冠军头衔后,康纳斯成为第一个在三种不同场地夺得锦标赛冠军的运动员:1974年草地赛、1976年红土场地赛和1978年硬地赛。

在康纳斯其余的职业生涯中,一直有两个值得注意的对手——年轻的约翰·麦肯罗和伊万·伦德尔。1982年的温网决赛中,他遇到了卫冕冠军麦肯罗。他在第四局决胜抢七的比赛中重整旗鼓,以三分优势赢得五次温网冠军的第二个冠军头衔。1982和1983年的美国网球公开赛的决赛中,他也击败了伦德尔。麦肯罗最终于1984年的温网锦标赛中以6:1,6:1,6:2的比分直落三盘,让康纳斯无话可说。虽然被对手打得惨败,康纳斯还是像以前那样趾高气扬、鲁莽无畏。当被问到输了比赛后是否会承认麦肯罗是更好的球员时,他只简单地回答:"绝不。"

随着康纳斯阅历增长,他的场上表现愈见老练成熟,逐步成长为一名备受尊重的老运动员。1991年,由于上个赛季左手腕受伤,他只能参加三次锦标赛,接受手术之后,他重

injury the previous season, he returned in 1991 after surgery on his left wrist, to play 14 tournaments and make it all the way to the semi–final of the U.S Open. When Connors finally retired in 1992, he had garnered a total of 109 men's singles titles –a record that remains unbroken today. He was ranked in the world's Top 10 for 16 straight years from 1973–1988 and took home 15 doubles titles. Connors won more matches than any other male professional player with a record of 1,337–285. He was named the ATP's Comeback Player of the Year in 1991; was inducted into the International Tennis Hall of Fame in 1998; and was awarded his own star on the St. Louis Walk of Fame in 2001.

The following is a list of Connors' major professional wins:
· Australian Open (singles) Champion (1974)
· Australian Open (singles) Finalist (1975)
· Italian Open (doubles) Finalist (1975)
· U.S. Open (singles) Champion (1974, 1976, 1978 and 1982–1983)
· U.S. Open (singles) Finalist (1975 and 1977)
· U.S. Open (doubles) Champion (1975)
· Wimbledon (singles) Champion (1974 and 1982)
· Wimbledon (singles) Finalist (1975,1977–1978 and 1984)
· Wimbledon (doubles) Champion (1973)

About the Man Himself

Connors has played on the ATP's Senior Circuit, which was dubbed Connors' Circuit because of his string of successful performances. He has participated in a variety of charity tennis events, including the Chris Evert Pro –Celebrity Tennis Classic and Pam Shriver's Charity Tennis Challenge. He earns a living as a motivational speaker and as a sports commentator for BBC Sport.

Connors married model Patti McGuire in 1980, and they have two children. He co–wrote several books, including *Don't Count Yourself Out: Staying Fit After 35* and *Jimmy Connors: How to Play Tougher Tennis*.

Along with his achievements in tennis, Jimmy Connors' never–give–up attitude and colorful competitive spirit have forever immortalized his name as one of the greatest athletes of all times.

回战场,参加了14次锦标赛,直奔美国网球公开赛的半决赛。康纳斯于1992年退役时,总共累积了109个男子单打冠军头衔——此项纪录至今未破。从1973年至1988年整整十六年他一直排在世界前十名,而且还赢得了15次双打冠军。康纳斯比其他任何男子职业球员赢得了更多的比赛,创下了1337胜285负的纪录。他被评为职业网球协会1991年度复出球员;1998年入选国际网球名人堂;2001年他在圣路易星光大道上拥有了属于自己的一颗星。

以下是康纳斯职业生涯中主要成就:
· 澳大利亚公开赛 (单打) 冠军 (1974年)
· 澳大利亚公开赛(单打) 决赛选手 (1975年)
· 意大利公开赛 (双打) 决赛选手 (1975年)
· 美国公开赛 (单打) 冠军 (1974年, 1976年, 1978年和 1982–1983年)
· 美国公开赛 (单打) 决赛选手 (1975年和1977年)
· 美国公开赛 (双打) 冠军 (1975年)
· 温布尔登(单打) 冠军(1974年和1982年)
· 温布尔登(单打) 决赛选手 (1975年,1977–1978年 和1984年)
· 温布尔登(双打) 冠军(1973年)

关于此人

康纳斯连续参加职业网球协会巡回赛,由于他一系列的成功,这个巡回赛被称作"康纳斯巡回赛"。他参加了很多慈善网球赛事,包括克里斯·埃弗特职业名人网球精英赛和帕姆·施赖弗慈善网球挑战赛。他当了动员演说者和BBC体育台解说员,以此谋生。

1980年康纳斯与模特帕蒂·马圭尔结婚,育有两个孩子。他与人合著的书籍包括《别漏数自己:35岁后保持健康》和《吉米·康纳斯:如何把网球打得更厉害》。

康纳斯的网球成就、永不言败的态度和有声有色的好斗精神,让人们永远记住了这位体坛名将。

Babe Didrikson (Zaharias)

Why She is Among the 50 plus one Greatest Sports Heroes

A young girl from Beaumont, Texas gained world fame in track and field and All–American status in basketball. She mastered tennis, played organized baseball and softball, was an expert diver, roller–skater and bowler. She won two gold medals and one silver medal, for track and field, in 1932 Olympics. She became a professional golfer and founding member of the LPGA. Much to the dismay of her competitors, Babe Didrikson excelled in every sport she tried. Her accomplishments during her short life earn her the admiration as one the Greatest Sports Heroes Of All Times.

On the Way Up

Mildred Ella Didriksen was born in Port Arthur, Texas the sixth of seven children of Norwegian immigrants Ole Nickolene and Hannah Marie (Olson) Didriksen. Babe later changed the spelling of her surname to Didrikson, to emphasize her Norwegian rather than Swedish ancestry. Ole Didriksen was a seaman and carpenter and Hannah was an accomplished skater in Norway. The family moved to Beaumont, Texas in 1914 after a hurricane destroyed Port Arthur.

An exuberant tomboy whose life was athletics, she was accomplished in just about every sport – basketball, track, golf, baseball, tennis, swimming, diving, boxing, volleyball, handball, bowling, billiards, skating and cycling. When asked if there was anything she did not play, she said "Yeah, dolls." Early on Babe knew which direction she wanted her life to take, "Before I was ever in my teens, I knew exactly what I wanted to be when I grew up. My goal was to be the greatest athlete that ever lived," she would say. It was reported that when Didrikson was a teenager she earned the nickname Babe by boys who were awed by her five Ruthian homers in a single game.

In February 1930, Colonel Melvorne J. McCombs of the Casualty Insurance Company recruited Didrikson to play for the company's Golden Cyclone basketball team in Dallas. She dropped out of high school in her junior year and went to work as a stenographer with the company with the understanding that she would have time to train and compete in athletics. During the next 3 years, 1930–1932, Didrikson was selected as an All–American women's basketball player and led the Golden Cyclones to the national championship in 1931. She often scored 30 or more points in an era when a cumulative team score of 20 points a game was considered respectable.

While working and playing ball in Dallas, she competed in other athletic events, including softball. Didrikson was an excellent pitcher and batted over .400 in the Dallas city league. Not surprising, however, her attention was turned to track and field and she became a member of the Golden Cyclone track team between 1930 and 1932, Didrikson held American, Olympic, or world records in five different track–and–field events. She stunned the athletic world on July 16, 1932, with her performance at the national amateur track meet for women in Evanston, Illinois. Didrikson

12

贝贝·迪德里克森
(扎哈里亚斯)

她为何入选《50+1位最闪耀的体育巨星》

　　一位来自得克萨斯州博蒙特的全能奇女子，在田径场上叱咤风云，在全美篮球运动中占有一席之地。她精通网球，参加组织性棒球和垒球比赛，是跳水能手、溜冰高手，还是板球投球手。1932年奥运会上，她获得了田径比赛的两枚金牌、一枚银牌。她是职业高尔夫球运动员，也是成立美国女子职业高尔夫巡回赛的成员之一。贝贝·迪德里克森总是让对手惊慌失措，她努力驰骋于各项体育运动。她短暂的一生中赢得无数令人赞叹的辉煌成就，不愧为50+1位最闪耀的体育巨星中的巾帼英雄。

成长之路

　　米尔德里德·埃拉·迪德里克森出生于得克萨斯州亚瑟港的一个挪威裔家庭，是7个子女中的第六个孩子。父亲叫欧莱·尼克龙·迪德里克森，母亲叫汉娜·玛丽·迪德里克森。后来贝贝把姓的拼法改了，以强调自己的挪威血统，而非瑞典血统。她的父亲是名水手也是木匠，母亲是挪威极具造诣的滑冰运动员。1914年，一场飓风毁了亚瑟港之后，她家就搬到了得克萨斯州的博蒙特市。

　　她是个精力旺盛的假小子，整个人生都是体育，她几乎精通体育的各个领域：篮球、田径、高尔夫球、棒球、网球、游泳、跳水、拳击、排球、手球、保龄球、弹子球、滑冰和自行车。当被问到有没有不会的项目时，她说："有，玩具娃娃。"很小的时候，贝贝就知道自己的人生目标，她曾说过，"我还不到十几岁时，就很清楚自己长大后想做什么。我的目标是成为有史以来最伟大的运动员。"据报道，迪德里克森十几岁时，在棒球领域中的惊人造诣已经比肩鼎鼎大名的棒球大王贝贝·鲁斯(Babe Ruth)，甚至创下了一场比赛打出5个本垒打的纪录，男孩们给她起了个"贝贝"的昵称。

　　1930年2月，伤亡保险公司的Melvorne J. McCombs上校聘请迪德里克森为公司在达拉斯市的金旋风篮球队效力。她于高中第三年退学，担任公司速记员，她知道这样会有时间训练参赛。随后的3年，从1930至1932年，迪德里克森被选为全美女子篮球队队员，并带领金旋风队闯入1931年的全国冠军赛。在那个年代，每场比赛累计得分20分已经相当不错，而她经常拿下30分，甚至更多。

　　在达拉斯工作、打球期间，她还参加了其他体育赛事，包括垒球。迪德里克森是个卓越的投球手，在达拉斯城市联盟的平均打击率超过了400。然而，不足为奇，迪德里克森的注意力转向了田径，1930年至1932年间，她成为金旋风田径队员，在5项不同的田径赛事中，她保持了美国、奥运会和世界纪录。1932年7月16日是她震惊体坛的日子，在伊利诺斯州伊云斯顿的"全国女子业余径赛运动会"上，她的表现一鸣惊人。迪德里

entered the meet as the sole member of the Golden Cyclone team and single–handedly won the national women's team championship by scoring 30 points. The Illinois Women's Athletic Club, which had more that 20 members, scored a combined 22 points to place second. In all, Didrikson won six gold medals and broke four world records in a single afternoon. Her performance was the most amazing feat by any individual, male or female, in the annals of track–and–field history. The outstanding performance at Evanston put Didrikson in the headlines of every sports page in the nation and made her one of the most prominent members of the United States Olympic team of 1932.

Babe qualified in five events for the 1932 Los Angeles Olympics but women were only allowed to compete in three events. She broke the world record and won the gold in the first women's Olympic javelin (143 feet, 4 inches) and set a world record in winning the first Olympic 80–meter hurdles (11.7 seconds), winning another gold medal. In the high jump, she and Jean Smiley both broke the world record at 5–foot–5+, but Smiley received the gold and Babe the silver when Babe was disqualified on a dubious ruling after her final jump. Babe also broke world records in the high jump and softball throw.

The consummate self–promoter always looking for a challenge, following the Olympics, she performed on the vaudeville circuit, traveled with a basketball team called Babe Didrikson's All–Americans and toured with the bearded House of David baseball team. She pitched at spring training for the St. Louis Cardinals, held golf ball driving exhibitions with Gene Sarazen, sang and ran on a treadmill in a one–woman vaudeville–type show and even challenged the winning horse of the Kentucky Derby to a foot race. Besides playing semi–pro basketball and softball, Babe had a brief stint as a successful harmonica–playing stage entertainer before taking up golf in the 1930's. At about this time Babe picked up a second nickname, the Texas Tomboy for her unwomanly activities.

She took her first golf lesson in 1931. In typical Babe fashion, she worked hard to become the best. When she first took up golf she would hit more than a 1,000 balls a day sometimes for 8 to 10 hours a day. The practice paid off, she won her first event in 1935, the River Crest Invitational in Forth Worth. Soon after winning the Texas Women's Amateur in 1935, the U.S. Golf Association ruled that for the best interest of the game, Babe was not an amateur because she had competed professionally in other sports. While Babe continued to golf–as well as play as many as 17 sets of tennis in one day and starring on the bowling lanes–it was not until 1943 that she was reinstated as an amateur.

In 1938 at the Los Angeles Open, Babe met George Zaharias, a 235–pound, wrestler who made his fortune as the Weeping Greek from Cripple Creek. They married 11 months later and Babe would change her name to Babe Didrikson Zaharias. George quit his career to manage Babe's career and golf became her focus. Traditionally an elite sport, it was an acceptable place for her to excel athletically.

When asked how she could regularly drive the ball some 250 yards though she weighed less than 145 pounds, she said, "You've got to loosen your girdle and let it rip." She ripped it far and straight enough, and putted well enough, that not only did she dominate women's golf, but also for 3 straight years (1945–1947) AP named her the Female Athlete of the Year. She would go on to win 55 amateur and professional events. She won the U.S. Women's Amateur tournament in 1946. Babe won an amazing 13 consecutive tournaments during 1946. The next year, she was the first American to win the British Amateur.

克森是金旋风队唯一参加运动会的队员,单枪匹马拿下30分,独揽全国女子队桂冠。伊利诺斯州女子体育俱乐部拥有20名成员,总共得分22分,排名第二。迪德里克森共揽6金,光一个下午就打破了4项世界纪录。她一个人就创下了不可思议的辉煌战绩,田径史上的男女运动员无人能及。在伊云斯顿的精彩表演让迪德里克森成为全国各大报纸体育版的头版头条人物,而且在1932年奥运会上,她是美国代表队的闪亮之星。

贝贝有资格参加五项比赛,但是妇女只允许参加3项比赛。她打破了世界纪录,在奥运会第一次的女子标枪比赛中夺得金牌(143英尺4英寸),赢得第一次奥运会80米跨栏赛跑冠军(11.7秒)并创造了世界纪录。在跳高方面,她与珍妮·斯麦莉都以5英尺±5的成绩打破了世界纪录,但是贝贝在最后一跳后的裁定却很有争议,最终并没有成为冠军,她拿了银牌,斯麦莉夺得金牌。贝贝在跳高和垒球比赛中也打破了世界纪录。

奥运会后,这位完美的自我炒作者总是寻找挑战,她参加了歌舞杂耍团的表演,与"贝贝·迪德里克森"的全美篮球队和戴维王蓄须棒球队一起旅游。她开始忙于圣路易红雀队的春季训练,与吉恩·萨拉森一起举办了高尔夫球表演赛,在女子单人歌舞杂耍秀上边踏水车边唱歌,甚至用竞走来挑战肯塔基德比赛马会的冠军马。除了是半职业篮球和垒球运动员外,在1930年正式从事高尔夫运动前的短时间里,贝贝曾是个成功的舞台和声表演者。差不多就在这个时期,贝贝有了第二个昵称:"德州假小子",因为她的言行举止实在不像女人。

1931年她上了高尔夫第一课。贝贝努力奋斗要做最出色的运动员,这是她的典型性格。刚开始打高尔夫时,她每天能打1000多个球,有时候一天练上8至10小时。苦尽甘来,1935年她第一次赢得了the River Crest Invitational in Forth Worth邀请赛。赢得1935年得克萨斯州女子业余比赛后不久,美国高尔夫球协会声明出于对大赛的考虑,取消贝贝的业余身份,因为她还参加了其他职业性的体育比赛。贝贝继续打高尔夫球,同时每天也打17局网球,在保龄球球道上也能一睹她的风采,直到1943年,她才重新恢复业余运动员的身份。

1938年洛杉矶公开赛上,贝贝认识了重达235磅的摔跤手乔治·扎哈里亚斯,使他以Weeping Greek from Cripple Creek的绰号发了财。11个月后他们结了婚,贝贝把名字改成了贝贝·迪德里克森·扎哈里亚斯。乔治放弃了自己的事业,成了贝贝"经纪人"支持她的工作,于是她把重心放在了高尔夫球上。这是一项传统的精英体育运动,对她来说是可以飞黄腾达、名声大噪的运动。

别人问她,她体重不足145磅,通常能挥动球杆打出250码的距离,是怎样办到的呢?她说,"你需要放下包袱、轻松上阵,不去管它。"她放下包袱,轻击球入穴,这不仅让她在女子高尔夫球场独占鳌头,而且让她连续3年(1945–1947年)获得美联社评出的"年度最佳女运动员"称号。她接着55次获得了业余和职业赛事的胜利。1946年她赢得了美国女子业余锦标赛冠军。1946年间,贝贝不可思议地13次蝉联锦标赛冠军。次年,她成为了赢得英国业余赛的第一个美国人。

Professional Career

She turned pro in the summer of 1947 after winning 17 of 18 tournaments.

After turning pro, she won 10 majors, including the U.S. Women's Open in 1948, 1950 and 1954. She lost only once in 7 years of competition. In 1948, Babe won her first U.S. Women's Open, the World Championship and the All–American Open. She continued her impressive performance on the LPGA Tour for the next several years. With Zaharias, Patty Berg and Fred Corcoran, she founded the Ladies Professional Golf Association in 1949.

Shortly after winning the inaugural Babe Zaharias Open in Beaumont in April 1953, Babe learned she had cancer. Surgeons removed the tumor and she went through a grueling cancer treatment. Just 14 weeks later, she was back on the LPGA tour and won the 1954 U.S. Open by a record 12 strokes.

Among the honors she received:
· Woman Athlete of the Year–Associated Press (1931, 1945, 1946, 1947, 1950, 1954)
· Greatest Woman Athlete of the First Half of the 20th Century–Associated Press (1950)
· LPGA Hall of Fame (1951)
· Bob Jones Award (1957)
· National Women's Hall of Fame (1976)
· U.S. Olympic Hall of Fame (1983)

A partial list of her 82 tournament wins during her 20–year career includes:
· All American Open, World Championship (1948)   · U.S. Women's Open (1948)
· World Championship, Eastern Open (1949)   · All American Open (1950)
· World Championship (1950)   · Miami Weathervane (1950)
· Western Open (1950)   · U.S. Women's Open (1950)
· All American Open (1951)   · World Championships (1951)
· Ponte Verde Open (1951)   · Tampa Open (1951)
· Fresno Open (1951)   · Texas Open (1951)
· Miami Weathervane Titleholders Championship (1952)
· Titleholders Championship (1952)
· Sarasota Open (1953)   · Babe Zaharias Open (1953)
· U.S. Women's Open (1954) · All American Open (1954)
· Sarasota Open (1954) · Serbin Open (1954)
· National Capital Open (1954) · Vane Trophy (1954)
· Tampa Open (1955) · Peach Blossom Classic (1955)

About the Woman Herself

In addition to being one of the most decorated and all–around athletes ever, Zaharias was a courageous groundbreaker who sought to tear down restricting social customs, which barred women from socially competing with men. Zaharias challenged this view. And no other woman has performed in so many different sports so well. She is arguably the greatest woman athlete of all time. A multi–talented athlete, Babe accomplished much during her years. In –between tournaments she appeared in the 1952 film Pat and Mike, playing a golfing competitor of Katharine Hepburn's character. She completed her autobiography: This Life I've Led was published in 1955. Sadly, in 1955 the cancer reappeared in her spine and she retired from sports permanently. On Sept. 27, 1956, Babe died of the disease in Galveston, Texas. She was 45. The Babe Zaharias Museum opened in Beaumont, Texas in 1976.

职业生涯

1947年,在18次锦标赛中赢得17次冠军之后,她正式成为职业运动员。

成为职业运动员后,她赢得了10次大赛,包括1948年、1950年和1954年的美国女子公开赛。在7年的比赛中,她只输过一次。1948年,贝贝第一次获得了美国女子公开赛冠军、世界冠军和全美公开赛冠军。接下来的几年时间里,她继续在美国女子职业高尔夫巡回赛中表现突出。1949年,她和扎哈里亚斯、帕蒂·伯格、弗雷德·科伦一起建立了女子职业高尔夫球协会。

1953年4月,贝贝在博蒙特市赢得以她命名的"贝贝·扎哈里亚斯公开赛"后不久,她知道自己得了癌症。手术除去了肿瘤,她经受了令人饱受折磨的癌症治疗。仅仅14周后,她又在美国女子职业高尔夫巡回赛中重出江湖,并且赢得了1954年美国公开赛,创下了12杆击球入洞的纪录。

她曾获得的荣誉有:
·被美联社评为"年度最佳女运动员" (1931年、1945年、1946年、1947年、1950年、1954年)
·被美联社评为"20世纪上半叶最优秀女运动员" (1950年)
·美国女子职业高尔夫巡回赛名人堂 (1951年)
·鲍勃·琼斯奖(1957年)
·全国女名人堂(1976年)
·美国奥林匹克名人堂(1983年)
以下是她20年运动生涯中82次锦标赛冠军的部分奖项,包括:
·全美公开赛,世界冠军 (1948年),·美国女子公开赛 (1948年)
·世界冠军,东部公开赛 (1949年),·全美公开赛(1950年)
·世界冠军 (1950年),·迈阿密风向标 (1950年)
·西部公开赛 (1950年),·美国女子公开赛 (1950年)
·全美公开赛(1951年),·世界冠军 (1951年)
·Ponte Verde 公开赛 (1951年),·坦帕公开赛 (1951年)
·弗雷斯诺公开赛 (1951年),·得克萨斯公开赛(1951年)
·迈阿密风向标卫冕冠军赛(1952年),·卫冕冠军 (1952年)
·萨拉索塔公开赛(1953年),·贝贝·扎哈里亚斯公开赛 (1953年)
·美国女子公开赛(1954年),·全美公开赛(1954年)
·萨拉索塔公开赛(1954年),·瑟宾公开赛(1954年)
·首都公开赛(1954年),·风向标杯 (1954年)
·坦帕公开赛(1955年),·桃花精英赛 (1955年)

关于此人

除了是一名最负盛名的全能运动员外,扎哈里亚斯还是一位勇敢无畏的开天辟地者,她试图摈弃社会中限制妇女与男人竞争的陈规陋习。扎哈里亚斯对那些观点提出挑战。没有其他妇女像她那样,能在各种体育领域都演绎得如此精彩。她享有空前绝后"最伟大女运动员"的美誉。贝贝是个多才多艺的运动员,拥有赫赫成功。在参加锦标赛期间,她出演了1952年的电影《帕特和麦克》,扮演了一名高尔夫球手,与凯瑟琳·赫本扮演的角色是竞争对手。1955年她完成了自传:《我所主导的这一生》。不幸的是,1955年癌症在她脊椎内复发,不得不永远退出体坛。1956年9月27日,贝贝在得州加尔维斯顿溘然辞世。终年45岁。1976年贝贝·扎哈里亚斯博物馆在得州博蒙特市正式开馆。

Thirteen

Joe DiMaggio

Why He is Among the 50 plus one Greatest Sports Heroes

Joe DiMaggio is considered by many to be the best baseball player in history. Not only did he possess a uniquely graceful athleticism, but he also strove to become better on a constant basis. During his career, DiMaggio led his major league team, the New York Yankees, to nine world championships and 10 American League (AL) pennants. He was inducted into the Hall of Fame in 1955 and was voted the Greatest Living Player in a 1969 Major League Baseball (MLB) fans poll. Through his accomplishments and his undying professionalism, DiMaggio has earned the right to sit amongst the greatest sports heroes of all time.

On the Way Up

Guiseppe Paolo DiMaggio, Jr. was born the fourth of eight children in Martinez, California. When he was 1-year old, his family moved to North Beach, an Italian neighborhood in San Francisco. His father, Guiseppe, was a fisherman and wanted DiMaggio and his four brothers to follow the same path. But DiMaggio had no interest in that kind of lifestyle and began playing baseball on the sandlot fields of San Francisco with two of his brothers, Vince and Dominic. At first, Guiseppe did not like his boys taking up baseball instead of fishing, calling them lazy and good for nothing. He eventually changed his mind, however when DiMaggio, Vince and Dominic all became successful players in the major leagues.

DiMaggio dropped out of San Francisco's Galileo High School by the time he was 16 and even though he tried his hand at odd and end jobs, including fishing, he spent most of him time playing baseball in a parking lot near Fisherman's Wharf. The first team he joined was sponsored by Rossi, a local olive-oil distributor. DiMaggio's two home runs helped the team win the championship. He received two baseballs and $16-worth of merchandise for his efforts.

In March of 1932, Vince made the cut for the San Francisco Seals, the city's minor league team. When a shortstop position opened up later that year, Vince recommended DiMaggio, who ended up playing in three games at the end of the season. In 1933, DiMaggio played his first full season with the Seals. He batted.340 with 160 runs batted in and 28 home runs, and it was soon apparent that he was not a shortstop but a great hitter and thrower, and soon his primary position became center field. During his first full season, DiMaggio attracted national attention with his 61-game hitting streak. Scouts came from all over the country to watch him play.

The Seals owner, Charlie Graham, traded DiMaggio to the New York Yankees in November of 1934. However, due to a knee injury, DiMaggio played with the Seals for one more year before leaving for New York. He ended that last season in the minor leagues with a flourish: a .398 batting average, 154 runs batted in (RBIs) and 34 home runs.

Professional Career

DiMaggio started playing for the Yankees in 1936, not a moment too soon as far as the team

13

乔·狄马乔

他为何入选《50+1位最闪耀的体育巨星》

　　乔·狄马乔是许多人公认的史上最出色的棒球运动员。他不仅拥有独特优美的运动风格，而且一直努力超越自我。在狄马乔的职业生涯中，他带领大联盟纽约扬基队夺得9个世界冠军和10次美国大联盟锦标赛冠军。1955年他入选名人堂，还被球迷评选为1969年美国职业棒球大联盟"当今在世的最伟大运动员"。狄马乔硕果累累、职业生涯永不褪色，他理所当然在50+1位最闪耀的体育巨星中占有一席之地。

成长之路

　　约瑟夫·保罗·狄马乔生于加利福尼亚州马丁内斯，在八个兄弟姐妹中排行老四。1岁时，他的家搬到了旧金山意裔移民居住区北滩。他的父亲约瑟夫是个渔夫，他想让狄马乔和四个兄弟子承父业。但是狄马乔对那样的生活并不感兴趣，于是，他开始在旧金山沙地上和他的两个兄弟文森和多米尼克一起打棒球。起初，约瑟夫不喜欢孩子们打棒球而不是捕鱼，说他们是懒惰的一无是处的饭桶。然而，他最终改变了看法，因为狄马乔、文森和多米尼克都成为大联盟里的成功球员。

　　狄马乔16岁时从旧金山伽利略高中退学，虽然他试着打零工，包括捕鱼，但他还是花了大量的时间在渔夫码头旁边的停车场打棒球。他参加的第一支球队是由当地一位名叫罗西的橄榄油批发商组建的。他的两个本垒打让球队获得了冠军。他的努力为他赢来了两只棒球和价值16美元的奖品。

　　1932年3月，文森入选该市的小联盟队旧金山海豹队。不久后球队公开招募游击手，文森推荐了刚在赛季末结束三场比赛的狄马乔。1933年，狄马乔首次在海豹队整个赛季中亮相。他的平均安打率为340,160个打点,28支本垒打,很快，大家有目共睹，他不只是个游击手，而是个优秀的击球手、投球手，不久后他就站在了中外野手的重要位置。狄马乔的第一个赛季中，他连续安打61场次的成绩在全国掀起了一阵旋风。全国各地的球探们都前去观看他的比赛。

　　1934年11月，海豹队老板查理·格雷厄姆把狄马乔换到了纽约扬基队。但是，由于膝盖受伤，狄马乔又为海豹队多效力了一年之后才去纽约。他在最后赛季给小联盟写下了精彩的一笔:平均398的打击率,154个打点,34支本垒打。

职业生涯

　　1936年狄马乔开始效力于扬基队，就该队而言，他本应来得更早。他带领球队获得四

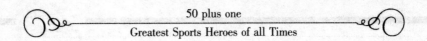
was concerned. After leading them to their first pennant in 4 years, he steered them to a World Series championship win over the New York Giants. Joltin' Joe, as he was sometimes called by fans, had definitely given the Yankees a jolt of DiMaggio magic, as they went on to win three more World Championships in a row from 1937–1939 against the Giants, the Chicago Cubs and the Cincinnati Reds.

DiMaggio, was also affectionately dubbed The Yankee Clipper. In 1937, he set a still-standing Yankee record for a right-handed hitter with 46 home runs, and in July of that year, he also set an MLB record with 15 home runs in a single month. He won the American League batting championship twice from 1939–1940, with .381 and .352 batting averages.

DiMaggio wowed the country with a 56–game hitting streak that lasted from May 15th until July 17th during the 1941 season, breaking the previous record of 44 that had been set by Willie Keeler more than 40 years before. While DiMaggio was in that amazing zone, he made 91 hits in 223 at bats for a .409 batting average. Ken Keltner, third baseman for the Cleveland Indians, ended the streak, but DiMaggio continued to hit successfully over the next 17 games. Also in 1941, DiMaggio carried the Yankees to yet another World Series win, this time against the Brooklyn Dodgers. That season, he had a .357 batting average with 125 RBIs and 30 home runs.

In February of 1943, DiMaggio enlisted in the United States Army, but like many other pro ballplayers who enlisted, he ended up spending most of his time in the United States playing baseball. He reached the rank of sergeant and served as a physical training instructor for the Air Force cadets until he was released from the Army in September of 1945. The following spring, the Yankees welcomed DiMaggio back with open arms. By the 1947 season, the Yankees were back to being the top dogs in the league and he again led the Yankees to the World Championship title against the Dodgers.

Despite suffering from a heel injury for most of the 1948 season, DiMaggio still managed to finish number one in the league with 39 home runs and 155 RBIs. The Yankees missed their chance at the playoffs 2 days before the end of the regular season, but redeemed themselves by bringing home the next three World Championship titles, beating the Dodgers in 1949, the Philadelphia Phillies in 1950 and the Giants in 1951.

DiMaggio retired at the end of the 1951 season, stating that due to aches and pains, he was no longer able to act as a productive force for the Yankees. Upon retirement, he was fifth in the league with 361 career home runs, and sixth with a .579 slugging percentage. DiMaggio played in 1,736 games during his career, finishing with a .325 batting average and 1,537 RBIs, and only striking out 369 times. He also played in 51 World Series games with a .271 batting average, 8 home runs and 30 RBIs. The Yankees retired his number in 1952.

年后的第一次锦标赛冠军,又率领球队击败纽约巨人队,夺得世界冠军联赛。狄马乔有时被球迷叫做"摇摆乔",他确实以神奇的魔力让扬基队震撼世人,1937至1939年,该队依次打败了巨人队、芝加哥小熊队和辛辛那提红人队,三次蝉联世界冠军。

狄马乔还有个昵称叫做"扬基快艇"。1937年,他以46支本垒打创下了右手打者的扬基纪录,至今无人能破,同年7月,他又创下了一个月内15支本垒打的职棒大联盟纪录。从1939年至1940年,他两次蝉联美国联盟打击率冠军,成绩分别为381和352。

1941年赛季,从5月15日至7月17日,狄马乔连续安打56场次,一鸣惊人、轰动全国,打破了40多年前威利·基勒创下的44场安打的纪录。狄马乔一举成名,他不可思议地创造了223个打数中91个安打、平均打击率为409的成绩。虽然克里夫兰印第安人队的三垒手肯·凯特纳改写了连续场次的纪录,但是狄马乔在未来的17年里继续谱写成功。还是在1941年,狄马乔率领扬基队击败布鲁克林道奇斯队,再次赢得世界冠军联赛。那个赛季中,他创造了平均357的打击率、125个打点数、30支本垒打的成绩。

1943年2月,狄马乔在美国陆军服兵役,但是与其他很多职业球手一样,当兵期间他把大量时间都花在打棒球上。后来,他晋升为陆军中士,1945年9月结束兵役前一直担任空军军校学员的体能训练指导。次年春天,扬基队热烈欢迎狄马乔归队。到了1947年的赛季,扬基队东山再起,成为联盟盟主,他再次带领球队击败道奇斯队,赢了世界冠军联赛。

1948年赛季的绝大多数时间内,狄马乔一直忍受着后跟伤痛,他竭尽所能保住联盟魁首位置,成绩为39支本垒打和155个打点数。常规赛季结束前两天,扬基队错过了季后赛,但是在随后的三年中,他们重振雄风,再度三次蝉联世界冠军,1949年击败道奇斯队、1950年击败费城费城人队、1951年击败巨人队。

1951年赛季季末,狄马乔退役,他宣称自己由于剧痛,无法再是为扬基队锦上添花的主力队员。退役时,他在职业生涯中本垒打为361支,排名联盟第五,平均长打率为579,排名联盟第六。整个职业生涯中,狄马乔参赛1736场,创下325的平均打击率,1537个打点数,只有369次三击不中而出局。他参加过51次世界冠军联赛,平均271的打击率、8支本垒打和30个打点。1952年扬基队退役了他的号码。

Fourteen

Dale Earnhardt

Why He is Among the 50 plus one Greatest Sports Heroes

Dale Earnhardt won virtually every major event and title that a NASCAR Winston Cup driver could obtain, including the Daytona 500. His fans loved him not only for these wins, but also for the way in which he arrived at victory--with an aggressive, determined style all his own. His car, No. 3, has been retired from NASCAR racing. This in itself points to the impact that Earnhardt had on the racing world and why he ranks among the best of the best in sports history.

On the Way Up

Ralph Dale Earnhardt was born on April 29, 1951 in Kannapolis, North Carolina. He grew up watching his father, Ralph Earnhardt, who was a NASCAR Sportsman Division champion, race stock cars throughout the Southeast. Naturally a fan of his father, young Earnhardt too became a fan of racing. But he did not want to settle for simply looking on from the stands with the rest of the crowd. He wanted the crowd to be watching him, cheering for him. He wanted to be a racer.

Earnhardt dropped out of school, never obtaining a high school degree. By the time he was 18, he held down jobs as a service station attendant and a mechanic to support himself, his first wife and the first of his four children. Besides working full-time, Earnhardt also managed to foster a driving career on weekends. He scavenged parts from the mechanic shop and junkyards to assemble and maintain his race cars.

In 1973, Earnhardt's father died of heart failure while working on his own vehicle. This tremendous loss was difficult for Earnhardt, but it made him even more focused on becoming a successful driver.

Professional Career

After a few years of driving on the NASCAR Sportsman Division circuit, Earnhardt made his Winston Cup debut at the World 600 in Charlotte in 1975, coming in 22nd. He drove intermittently on the Winston circuit a total of eight more times, until Rod Osterlund offered him a full-time spot behind the wheel for the 1979 Winston Cup Series. This was the greatest opportunity of Earnhardt's career.

The Intimidator, as he would soon be called by fans everywhere, proved that he was an aggressive driver to be reckoned with during his first two full-time racing seasons. In the 1979 season, he scored his first Winston Cup win at Bristol in only his 16th career start and drove to 11 Top 5 finishes. That year, Earnhardt ended up taking home the Rookie of the Year title after one of racing history's most competitive rookie wars. Then, in 1980, he beat a seasoned veteran for the NASCAR Winston Cup Series title, which made him the first driver to win the Rookie of the Year Award and the Winston Cup championship in consecutive years.

During the 1981 season, Osterlund sold his team, a move that caused Earnhardt to leave and finish the season driving for Richard Childress' team instead. By the time the year was over,

戴尔·厄恩哈特

他为何入选《50+1位最闪耀的体育巨星》

戴尔·厄恩哈特作为赛车手几乎赢遍了所有大型赛事,捧走了美国全国赛车协会(纳斯卡)温斯顿杯,包括戴通纳500英里大赛冠军。他的赛车迷们喜欢他不仅因为他的成功,还因为他力争胜利的态度让人崇拜——他勇于争先、意志顽强。他的冠军3号赛车已从纳斯卡赛车协会退役。这充分显示了厄恩哈特在赛车世界的重要影响力,他必然位居万古体坛最佳健儿之榜。

成长之路

1951年4月29日,拉尔夫·戴尔·厄恩哈特生于北卡罗莱那州坎那波利斯。成长过程中,他目睹纳斯卡运动员组冠军得主的父亲拉尔夫·厄恩哈特一次次参加车赛,驰骋于整个东南部。自然而然,作为父亲赛车迷的小厄恩哈特也开始着迷于赛车。但是他不想仅仅做个看台观众。他想让观众们注视他,为他欢呼。他想做赛车手。

厄恩哈特退学后,再也没拿过高中文凭。到了18岁,他当上了服务站助手和修理工,来养活自己和第一任妻子,还有他们的4个孩子。除了专职工作外,厄恩哈特还在周末发展赛车副业。他把修理店和废品站的零件清理干净,用来组装维修他的赛车。

1973年,厄恩哈特的父亲在驾驶自己的汽车时,因心力衰竭死亡。这个巨大的打击让厄恩哈特难以承受,但却促使他更加专心致志,下定决心成为一名成功的赛车手。

职业生涯

参加了几年的纳斯卡运动员组巡回赛后,厄恩哈特于1975年夏洛特市举办的世界600英里温斯顿杯大赛中首次登场,排名第22。他又陆续参加了8次温斯顿杯巡回赛,直到罗德·奥斯特兰德提供给他一个专职参赛机会,参加1979年温斯顿杯联赛。这给厄恩哈特的职业生涯带来了天大的机会。

"威吓者"是不久后赛车迷们给他起的外号,这个外号证明了他在头两个专职赛季中不好对付,是个不顾一切去夺胜利的车手。1979年赛季,他在布里斯托尔首次赢得温斯顿杯比赛,职业生涯中第16次参赛便在季末11名中排第五。这一年,厄恩哈特经过赛车史上最激烈的新人大战后,最终捧回了"年度新人"奖。随后的1980年,他打败了纳斯卡温斯顿杯联赛冠军的赛季老手,成为首位蝉联"年度新人"奖和温斯顿杯冠军得主。

1981年赛季中,奥斯特兰德卖了车队,此举迫使厄恩哈特离开,只好转投理查德·查尔里斯队结束赛季。年末,查尔里斯队发现厄恩哈特能够更好地驾驭赛车,在该队的强烈

Childress realized that Earnhardt was performing better than the teams' cars could handle and so at Childress' urging, The Intimidator accepted a deal to drive for a more established team and a wealthier sponsor. He drove for Bud Moore's team and Wrangler for the 1982 and 1983 seasons. During that time, Earnhardt won three races and finished 12th and eighth in points.

After Childress' team made major improvements to their cars, Earnhardt rejoined the team for the 1984 season. He would continue driving for Richard Childress Racing (RCR) until the end of his career, almost 20 years later. The Man in Black, so named for his black No. 3 car, raced most of his final season in 2000 as a dual camp driver. He raced not only for RCR, but also for his own team, Dale Earnhardt, Inc. (DEI). This team included his son, Dale Earnhardt, Jr., as well as other drivers.

Throughout his career, Earnhardt won a total of 76 races. He had 428 Top 10 finishes and 22 poles. His key successes are listed here:

· Seven NASCAR Winston Cup titles to tie Richard Petty's record (1980, 1986–1987, 1990–1991 and 1993–1994)

· Won the 1998 Daytona 500

· Only three–time winner of The Winston (1987, 1990 and 1993)

· The only six–time winner of the Busch Clash (1980, 1986, 1988, 1991, 1993 and 1995)

· Won four IROC championships (1990, 1995, 1999 and 2000)

· 12–time winner of the 125–mile qualifying race at Daytona, including 10 straight wins from 1990–1999

As a result of his many outstanding performances during his racing career, Earnhardt received these awards and honors:

· Rookie of the Year Award (1979)

· National Motorsport Press Association's Driver of the Year Award (1980, 1986–1987, 1990 and 1994)

· ESPY's Driver of the Decade Award (1990s)

· Most Popular Driver Award (2001)

· Named one of NASCAR's 50 Greatest Drivers, along with his father, Ralph Earnhardt (1998)

· American Driver of the Year (1987, 1994)

· First American to receive AUTOSPORTS Gregor Grant Award

· 2006 International Motorsports Hall of Fame Inductee

Earnhardt's racing career came to an abrupt end on February 18, 2001 at the Daytona 500. He was driving behind the two other qualifying DEI team members, including his son. Many of his fans and NASCAR analysts believe that Earnhardt was trying to hold an interference position at 3rd in order to allow one of his other two teammates to take the lead so that the DEI team would end up in the top three positions. But something caused Earnhardt's car to spin out of control on the very last turn of the very last lap. It crashed into a wall and another car at nearly 200 miles per hour, most likely killing Earnhardt on impact. He was officially pronounced dead after being transported to a nearby hospital, attended by his wife and son. Dale Earnhardt was the first driver ever to be killed while racing in the Daytona 500. Such a tragic end to such a tremendously successful career and life will make Earnhardt's name last forever in the hearts and minds of racing and sports fans of all kinds.

About the Man Himself

Although much of Earnhardt's life revolved around racing, he also led a full life when away

要求下,"威吓者"同意为这个更有组织性的车队、为更富裕的创办人效力。1982年和1983年的赛季,厄恩哈特分别为巴德摩尔车队和"牧马人"队效力。在那期间,他赢得三场比赛,季末成绩排名分别为第十二和第八。

查尔里斯队大大改进赛车后,厄恩哈特重新入队参加1984年赛季。在此后将近20年的时间里,直到职业生涯结束,他一直为理查德·查尔里斯赛车队(RCR)效力。他的"黑衣人"冠军3号车参加了2000年最后赛季的大多数双程营地比赛。他不仅为理查德·查尔里斯赛车队,也为自己的戴尔·厄恩哈特车队效力。该队成员包括他的儿子小戴尔·厄恩哈特和其他车手。

厄恩哈特整个职业生涯中共赢得76场比赛。428次排名前十,22次杆位。以下是主要获奖成绩:

· 7次获得纳斯卡温斯顿杯奖项,追平了理查德·佩蒂的纪录 (1980、1986-87、1990-1991和 1993-1994年)
· 1998年戴通纳500英里冠军
· 唯一3次赢得温斯顿冠军的赛车手 (1987、1990 和 1993年)
· 唯一6次赢得Busch Clash冠军的赛车手 (1980、1986、1988、1991、1993和 1995年)
· 4次赢得国际汽车锦标赛冠军(1990、1995、1999 和 2000年)
· 12次在戴通纳赢得125英里排位赛,包括1990-1999年十次蝉联冠军

厄恩哈特在赛车生涯中成绩显著,获得无数荣誉与奖项:
· 年度新人奖 (1979年)
· 获得全国汽车体育新闻联社"年度赛车手"奖(1980、1986-1987、1990和1994年)
· 评为"年度卓越体育表现奖"之"时代最佳赛车手奖"(90年代)
· 最受欢迎车手奖 (2001年)
· 与父亲拉尔夫·厄恩哈特一起入选"纳斯卡50位最优秀车手"(1998年)
· 美国年度赛车手(1987、1994年)
· 首位获得"汽车运动葛瑞格·格兰特奖"的美国人
· 入选 2006年国际汽车运动名人堂

2001年2月18日,在戴通纳500英里大赛中,厄恩哈特意外丧生,他的赛车生涯戛然而止。在排位赛中,他紧跟其他两名戴尔·厄恩哈特队员,包括他的儿子。许多赛车迷及纳斯卡分析者认为厄恩哈特想占领第三位阻挡其他对手的威胁,来帮助两名队友的其中一人夺冠,这样他们队就会占据前三名。但是,在最后一圈距离终点不远的转弯处,他的车突然失控。车正面撞到墙上,另一辆时速200英里的车差点在冲撞中压死他。他在儿子和妻子的陪同下被送到了附近医院,不久就被正式宣布死亡。戴尔·厄恩哈特是第一个在戴通纳500英里车赛中意外死亡的车手。如此成功的职业生涯就在这个噩耗中结束,所有赛车迷和体育迷们都会把厄恩哈特的名字铭记于心,他永远活在人们心中。

关于此人

虽然厄恩哈特的生活重心是赛车,但赛场以外的人生依然精彩。他结过三次婚,育有

from the track. He married three times and had four children. He and his third wife, Therese, were married in 1982. Earnhardt enjoyed spending time with his family at his farm in Mooresville, North Carolina, and he also hunted, fished and attended charity events.

The Dale Earnhardt Foundation was established after his death to continue his lifelong dedication to education, children and the environment/wildlife preservation. Up to seven education scholarships or grants of up to $7,000 each are given away every year through The Legend Leadership Award program. This award recognizes and encourages original, creative and innovative solutions for society – and community –based problems. The Foundation also gives away 21 educational grants or scholarships to Boys and Girls Clubs.

Feed the Children is a program that has distributed more than 200 tons of food to 10, 000 plus children and families in 16 of the states where Earnhardt raced. Another program, Youth Homes, donates special E–Wheeler tricycles to children and youth homes and gives Christmas gifts to all young patients confined to some cancer treatment centers for the holiday.

The foundation has established the Dale Earnhardt Forest (DHF) program to help replenish the tree canopy in areas that have been drastically damaged by drought or natural disaster. It also chooses specific middle schools to become Living Classrooms for the DHF, providing them with environmental software, trees and Earth Science curriculum lesson plans. Yet another way the Dale Earnhardt Foundation gives back to the environment is by either planting a tree in honor of someone or giving a Dale Earnhardt E Tree seedling kit to everyone who makes a donation of $10. The foundation also provides a grant to support 58,000 acres of Louisiana Wetlands to help recover earthen dams that supply habitat for more than 900 types of animals and plants.

All that Dale Earnhardt accomplished during his lifetime and all that the foundation provides in his absence will ensure that his name will always be remembered.

四个孩子。1982年他和第三任妻子德瑞莎喜结连理。在北卡罗莱那州摩斯维尔市的农场，厄恩哈特享受着与家人共度的时光。他还打猎、钓鱼、参加慈善活动。

他逝世后，戴尔·厄恩哈特基金会成立，以此延续他的人生，为教育、儿童和环境及野生动物保护作出贡献。共有七项每项价值7000美元的教育奖学金、助学金每年都通过"传奇领导奖"的活动分发出去。这个奖项承认并鼓励原创的、富有创造力和新精神的方法来解决社会和社团问题。基金会还为"男孩女孩俱乐部"分发了21项助学金、奖学金。

"喂养儿童"的活动已为厄恩哈特比赛过的全美16个地区10000多名儿童和家庭分发了200多吨食物。另一个名为"青春之家"的活动为儿童和青年家庭捐赠特殊的电动三轮轮椅车，并为禁闭在癌症治疗中心的年轻病人们赠送圣诞节礼物。

基金会还成立了"戴尔·厄恩哈特森林计划"，帮助那些遭受旱灾或其他自然灾害的地区大面积地植树造林。它还选择特别的中学作为"戴尔·厄恩哈特森林计划"的活动教室，为它们提供有关环保的软件、树木及地球科学课程计划。戴尔·厄恩哈特基金会为恢复环境所做的另一种贡献就是为植一棵树的人，或者给每个捐款10美元的人发戴尔·厄恩哈特树木籽苗工具包。基金会还为58000英亩的路易斯安那州湿地拨款，重新修建现有的大坝，给900多种动植物提供栖息生长之地。

戴尔·厄恩哈特一生中成就无数，去世后他的基金会又贡献巨大，他的名字一定会流芳百世。

Fifteen

Chris Evert

Why She is Among the 50 plus one Greatest Sports Heroes

She retired in 1989, but Chris Evert continues to hold the record for the highest winning percentage in the history of both men's and women's professional tennis. That awe-inspiring achievement is the umbrella under which all of her many other athletic accomplishments sit. And the umbrella combined with everything it protects for the world to remember is what makes Evert one of the most elite athletes of all time.

On the Way Up

Christine Marie Evert was born on December 21, 1954 in Fort Lauderdale, Florida. Christine was the second of five children born to parents, Jim and Colette. She grew up in a family of five tennis-playing children, but only she and her younger sister, Jean, would end up making it to the pros. Her father, Jim, was a professional tennis player and instructor and at age 5 he began giving her lessons on the city's clay courts. Evert developed her famous two-handed backhand out of necessity as a youngster because she was too small and did not have the strength to swing it one-handed. As an eighth grader in 1969, she was named one of Sports Illustrated's Faces in the Crowd because of her national rank of No. 1 in girls' 14 and under tennis.

In 1970, Evert entered a small tournament in North Carolina and defeated the then No. 1-ranked female tennis player in the world, Margaret Court, who had just completed her singles Grand Slam. The 7-6, 7-6 upset by the 15-year-old Evert made everyone sit up and take notice. The following year, at 16, she was the youngest player ever to reach the U.S. Open at Forest Hills. Although she eventually lost to Billie Jean King, who became the champion, Evert steadfastly defeated four seasoned pros in a row: Edna Buding, Mary Ann Eisel, 5th-seeded Francoise Durr and Lesley Hunt.

In between tournaments, Evert attended classes at St. Thomas Aquinas High School in Fort Lauderdale. In order to keep her amateur status, she refused to accept any prize money that she earned from the tournaments. In 1973, the same year that she graduated from high school, Evert turned pro.

Professional Career

Evert was known as Little Miss Icicle and The Ice Maiden due to her ability to remain calm under pressure. She always acted in a composed manner, never questioned line calls and was able to steer away from errors even in the most difficult game situations. Her poised demeanor and cool attitude played an important part in her success because it tended to instill fear into her opponents. Her other strengths were her two-handed backhand and her unstoppable baseline game.

Starting with the French Open and the Wimbledon in 1974, she won 18 Grand Slam singles titles during her career and for an open era record of 13 straight years, she took home a minimum

克里斯·埃弗特

她为何入选《50+1位最闪耀的体育巨星》

即使到1989年退役，克里斯·埃弗特在男女职业网坛中仍然保持着史上最高成功率的纪录。她那令人敬畏、不可思议的成就仿佛一把撑开的大伞，收揽着其他的累累硕果。这把伞保护着世人所记住的一切，那就是埃弗特是历史上最出类拔萃的运动员之一。

成长之路

1954年12月21日，克莉丝蒂娜·玛丽·埃弗特出生于佛罗里达州劳德代尔堡。克莉丝蒂娜是吉姆和克莱特5个孩子中的老二。她的家庭中5个孩子都打网球，但只有她和她妹妹珍妮后来成为了职业球员。她父亲吉姆是个职业网球运动员和教练，在她5岁时，他便在该城的红土场地教她打球。埃弗特在很小的时候就练习她著名的双手反手球，对于这个年龄并没有必要，因为她太小了，根本还没力气单手挥拍。1969年，还在上八年级的她已入选《体育画报之芸芸众生》，因为她在14岁以内女孩网球比赛中名列第一。

1970年，埃弗特参加了北卡罗莱那州的小型锦标赛，击败了当时女子世界排名第一的玛格丽特·考特，考特刚结束单打大满贯。7:6,7:6的成绩让对手意外而郁闷，15岁的埃弗特让全场观众站起来，她开始备受关注。次年，16岁的她作为有史以来最年轻的选手参加了森林山美国公开赛。虽然埃弗特最终输给了冠军比莉·珍妮·金，她连续4个赛季毫不动摇地击败职业选手：埃德娜·巴丁，玛丽·安·埃塞尔，5号种子选手弗朗科伊斯·杜尔和蕾丝莉·亨特。

锦标赛期间，埃弗特参加了劳德代尔堡的圣托马斯阿奎纳高中的课程。为了保持业余选手的地位，她拒绝接受从锦标赛赢得的各种奖金。1973年，埃弗特高中毕业，就在同年，她成为职业网球手。

职业生涯

埃弗特以"冰小姐"、"冰皇后"著称，因为她面对压力时，能够沉着冷静。她镇定自若，从不在意被邀请出场的方式，即使在最困难的比赛情形下也能驾轻就熟，避免错误。她冷静的外表、镇定的风度在她成功中起了重要作用，给对手造成畏惧心理。她的其他强项包括双手反手球和不可阻挡的底线球。

从1974年的法国公开赛和温布尔登公开赛开始，她陆续赢得18次单打大满贯，而且开天辟地的创下了从1974至1986年整整13年的纪录：每年至少捧回一次大满贯。另一项

of one Grand Slam title annually from 1974–1986. In another impressive feat, Evert made it to at least the semifinals in 52 out of the 56 Grand Slam events that she entered. In fact, between the ages of 16 and 32, she only lost once during the pre–semifinals of a Grand Slam event and that loss happened at Wimbledon in 1983 after a bout with food poisoning. Evert was ranked No. 1 in the world from 1975–1977 and from 1980–81, and was in the World Top 10 for 17 years. In the U.S., she was ranked No. 1 from 1974–1978 and in 1981, and was the first female player since Alice Marble in the late 1930s to make the No. 1 spot 5 years in a row. Evert was also in the U.S. Top 10 for 19 years, which beat Billie Jean King's record by one.

Evert took part in two of the most famous female rivalries of the open era, one being between her and Australia's Evonne Goolagong and the other being between her and Martina Navratilova. Evert and Goolagong first played each other during the 1972 Wimbledon semifinals and their rivalry would continue until Goolagong's retirement in 1983. Evert came out with a 21–12 record against Goolagong. Her rivalry with Navratilova was friendlier in nature, and encompassed 80 matches from 1973–1988. Possibly the two most triumphant victories of Evert's career took place at the 1985 and 1986 French Open finals in Paris, when she beat Navratilova 6–3, 6–7, 4–7, 7–5 and 2–6, 6–3, 6–3, respectively. Although Navratilova boasted a 43–37 record over Evert, it was a hard fought victory.

Evert matched or broke many records during her career:

· During the 1974 season she won 16 out of 24 tournaments and finished with a 103–7 record.

· The only female player besides Court and King to win more than 100 matches in a single season.

· She set an open era record in 1974 with a 55–match winning streak, which was later broken by Navratilova in 1984.

· In 1976, Evert became the first woman in professional tennis to reach $1 million in career prize money.

· The first player to win more than 1,000 singles matches, which she did in 1984.

· Victorious in 157 tournaments throughout her career, places her second among both male and female players for this record category.

· Won six out of eight U.S. Open singles titles from 1975–1982, making her the only female player to win that title on both clay and hard courts.

· Holds the career record for most singles wins (101) at the U.S. Open.

· Won a total of seven French Open singles titles, putting her at the top of that record category as well.

· Holds the record for 125 consecutive matches on one surface, clay, throughout an almost 6–year period between August of 1973 and May of 1979.

Evert retired in 1989 after losing a quarterfinal match to Zina Garrison at the U.S. Open. She bid adieu to the sport with the same grace and dignity with which she had entered, leaving a .900 winning percentage, achieved with a 1,309–146 record. This percentage remains the best ever in professional tennis.

A list of Evert's professional wins and the honors bestowed on her is available at *www.encouragementpress.com*.

About the Woman Herself

Evert was married to John Lloyd, an English pro player, for 8 years until they divorced in 1987. The following year, she married ex–Olympic skier, Andy Mill, with whom she has three

令人难忘的成绩就是56场大满贯赛事中,至少参加过52场半决赛。事实上,她在16岁至32岁的这段时间里,只在一次大满贯赛事的半决赛预赛中失败过,那是在1983年的温网赛事中,由于食物中毒导致失败。1975年至1977年、1980年至1981年,埃弗特排名世界第一,连续17年名列世界前十名。在美国,从1974年至1978年和1981年,她都是第一名,也是自30年代末艾丽丝·马贝尔后首位5年蝉联第一的女运动员。她还连续19年位居美国前十,以一年的优势超越了比莉·珍妮·金创下的纪录。

埃弗特遇到了职业生涯中最著名的两次激烈竞争,一次是与澳大利亚的艾弗尼·古拉岗之间的较量,另一次是与马蒂娜·纳芙拉蒂诺娃之间的对抗。1972年的温网半决赛中,她和古拉岗第一次交锋,她俩的比赛一直延续到1983年古拉岗退役。埃弗特最终以21胜12负的成绩赢了古拉岗。她与纳芙拉蒂诺娃之间的竞争本质上更友好,从1973年至1988年总共包含了80场比赛。 埃弗特职业生涯中获得的最大胜利当属1985年和1986年在巴黎举行的法国公开赛中,她分别以6:3, 6:7, 4:7, 7:5和2:6, 6:3, 6:3的比分战胜了纳芙拉蒂诺娃。虽然纳芙拉蒂诺娃最终以43胜37负的成绩超过了埃弗特,但是胜利实属不易。

埃弗特职业生涯中参赛无数,也打破了许多纪录:
· 1974年赛季中,她在24次锦标赛中赢了16次,最终成绩为103胜7负。
· 除了古特和金外,仅有的一位一个赛季中赢得100场比赛的女运动员
· 1974年她第一次创造了连续55次夺冠的纪录,1984年被纳芙拉蒂诺娃打破。
· 1976年,埃弗特成为第一个获得100万美元职业生涯奖金的女性职业网球手
· 第一位赢得1000次单打比赛的运动员,她于1984年创造了此纪录。
· 职业生涯中共获157次锦标赛冠军,在男女记录项目中排名第二。
· 1975年至1982年,八次美国公开赛单打比赛中赢得六次冠军,成为赢得红土场地赛及硬地赛的唯一女运动员。
· 获得美国公开赛单打冠军最多的纪录保持者(101次)
· 共赢得7次法国公开赛单打冠军,也让她成为最高纪录保持者
· 从1973年8月至1979年5月,几乎六年的时间内,一直保持了红土场地赛中蝉联125次冠军的纪录。
美国公开赛的四分之一决赛中埃弗特输给了兹娜·加里森后,她于1989年退役。她同样以刚出道时那种优雅端庄的举止告别了体坛,留下了平均900的胜率和1309胜146负的纪录。这项胜率至今在职业网坛中仍岿然不动。
埃弗特职业生涯中获得的冠军及荣誉可通过www.encouragementpress.com查阅。

关于此人
埃弗特嫁给了英国职业运动员约翰·洛伊德,婚姻维持了8年,1987年两人离婚。次年,她嫁给了前奥林匹克滑雪运动员安迪·米尔,两人育有3个儿子。自从退役后,埃弗特

sons. Since her retirement, Evert and her husband have been very active in raising money both for her own organization, Chris Evert Charities, and for other groups, including the Special Olympics, March of Dimes, Martina Navratilova Youth Foundation, Red Cross, Elton John AIDS Foundation and U.S. Olympic Ski Team.

The first fundraiser for Chris Evert Charities was the Chris Evert Pro–Celebrity Tennis Classic and was held in Boca Raton, Florida. By the time the 16th annual Chris Evert Pro–Celebrity Tennis Classic rolled through in 2005, the organization had raised a total of $14 million, which have been distributed to various programs in need throughout Florida.

Evert has also been asked to serve as a member of numerous boards, including but not limited to; the Ounce of Prevention Fund of Florida, the Make–A–Wish Foundation of South Florida, the Florida Sports Foundation, Save the Children, the American AIDS Association, the Women's Sports Foundation, the International Tennis Hall of Fame and the National Committee to Prevent Child Abuse. Evert also served as the president for the WTA for 9 years until August of 1992.

Evert has been honored many times for her charity work. In May of 1993, she was presented with the March of Dimes Lifetime Achievement Award for her superior commitment to excellence in both her professional and her personal lives. In 1991, the Palm Beach County Convention & Visitors Bureau honored her with the Providencia Award for her contributions to the international image of the county's tourism. Evert was also named one of the Nine Women of the Year by Glamour magazine in 1990 for her remarkable commitment to social causes.

Evert co–authored a book with her then husband, John, called Lloyd on Lloyd (1986). Evert also co–wrote an autobiography called Chrissie: *My Own Story (1982)*. Her television appearances include: *Wimbledon, the Movie (2004)*, and the mini–series, *A Century of Women (1994)*.

Her ability to hide her true feelings may have brought her success on the tennis court, but opening up and showing the world her warm heart is what has brought her success in many other aspects of life. Chris Evert serves as an inspiration to us all.

和丈夫积极投身于慈善团体的筹款，包括她的克里斯·埃弗特慈善基金会、特殊奥林匹克、分积角累会、马蒂娜·纳芙拉蒂诺娃青年基金会、红十字、埃尔顿·约翰艾滋病基金和美国奥林匹克滑雪队。

　　第一个为克里斯·埃弗特慈善基金会募捐的是克里斯·埃弗特职业名人网球精英组织，活动在佛罗里达州波卡瑞顿举行。到2005年第16年度克里斯·埃弗特职业名人网球精英组织举办活动时，已筹集到1400万美元，分发到佛罗里达州各项需要资金的活动中。

　　埃弗特还应邀作为许多协会的成员，包括：盎司预防基金、南佛罗里达州许愿基金会、佛罗里达体育基金会、救助儿童基金会、美国艾滋病协会、女子体育基金会、国际网球名人堂和美国联邦防止虐待儿童委员会。埃弗特还在女子网球协会担任了9年主席，直到1992年。

　　埃弗特因对慈善事业的贡献多次获得奖项。1993年5月，由于她在职业生涯及个人生活中的卓越贡献，获得了"分积角累会终生成就奖"。1991年，棕榈滩县旅游局为她颁发了超前奖(Providencia Award)，以此褒扬她为该县旅游业树立的国际形象。1990年她因为社会事业作出的巨大贡献而被《魅力》杂志评为"年度九大杰出女性"之一。

　　埃弗特与前任丈夫约翰合写了一本名为《Lloyd on Lloyd》的书(1986)。埃弗特还合著了一本自传《克里斯：我自己的故事》(1982)。她的荧屏亮相包括：电影《温布尔登》(2004)，电视连续剧《女人的世纪》(1994)。

　　她善于隐藏真实情感的本领，让她可以叱咤网坛，但是坦诚真挚而充满热情的爱心成就了她生活中的许多其他领域。克里斯·埃弗特鼓舞着我们每一个人。

Sixteen

George Foreman

Why He is Among the 50 plus one Greatest Sports Heroes

The formidable George Foreman stepped out of the ring for the last time almost 10 years ago, but many boxing fans still consider him a Top 10 heavyweight favorite. He is, in fact, considered to be one of the greatest heavyweight fighters in the sport's history, winning the world championship twice and being inducted into the International Boxing Hall of Fame. Perhaps one of the most astonishing feats of Foreman's career was when he broke the record for being the oldest fighter to win the world heavyweight crown. It took a lot for him to achieve such a successful career and it took a lot for him to leave the sport he loved, but it did not take a lot for Foreman to be chosen as one of the top sports legends of all time.

On the Way Up

George Edward Foreman was born on January 10, 1949 in Marshall, Texas. He was the third youngest of four boys and three girls. As a youth, Foreman frequently got into trouble–mugging people by holding them upside–down by their feet, and getting into numerous fights. It was only when he finally joined the Job Corps and was introduced to boxing did he find direction in his life. In 1968, at the age of 19, Foreman won the National Amateur Athletic Union heavyweight championship and a heavyweight gold medal at the Olympic Games in Mexico City. Although his amateur career was proving to be a success, it provided only a hint of what was to come.

Professional Career

The year after his two big wins, Foreman turned pro, winning his first fight against Donald Walheim with a three–round knockout. He fought 13 fights during his debut year and won all of them, 11 by knockout. For the next 3 years, Foreman would remain undefeated, and on January 22, 1973, he fought world heavyweight champion Joe Frazier in Kingston, Jamaica. Foreman won solidly, knocking his opponent out in the second round, and took the title of world champion of heavyweight boxing. The fight was the very first transmission of HBO Boxing and the call made by broadcaster Howard Cosell, "Down goes Frazier! Down goes Frazier! Down goes Frazier! " is still one of the most unforgettable sports calls in history.

Foreman successfully defended his title against Jose Roman, the Puerto Rican Heavyweight champion, in Tokyo. The fight was over in 50 seconds, making it the quickest ever world Heavyweight championship challenge. Then, in 1974 in Caracas, Venezuela, Foreman retained the title by defeating Ken Norton with a second round knock out. This was a huge victory since Norton had beaten Muhammad Ali the year before.

Foreman suffered his first loss of his then 5–year career–the loss of the championship title in a match against Muhammad Ali. The fight, called The Rumble in the Jungle, took place on October 30, 1974 in Kinshasha, Zaire. Ali's Rope–a–dope boxing technique had its desired effect and Foreman was knocked out in the eighth round.

乔治·福尔曼

他为何入选《50+1位最闪耀的体育巨星》

"魔鬼"乔治·福尔曼差不多十年前就退出拳坛了，但是许多拳击迷至今仍追捧他为前十位最受喜爱的重量级拳击手。实际上，他堪称体坛历史上最出色的重量级拳王之一，两次赢得世界冠军，并入选国际拳击名人堂。可能福尔曼职业生涯中最震惊世人的便是他打破了世界纪录，成为夺得重量级桂冠的最年长的拳王。福尔曼呕心沥血、苦尽甘来，终于成就非凡，他离开自己深爱的运动也很不容易，但是，他却轻而易举地入选了50+1位最闪耀的体育巨星。

成长之路

1949年1月10日，乔治·爱德华·福尔曼生于得克萨斯州马歇尔。他有四个兄弟、三个姐妹，弟兄中排行老三。年少时的福尔曼经常制造事端、抢劫斗殴，把别人头朝下脚朝上倒着挟持。直到他最后参加了职业训练团，开始涉及拳击后，才找到生活的方向。1968年，19岁的福尔曼获得美国业余体育联盟重量级冠军，并在墨西哥城奥运会中夺得金牌。虽然他的业余生涯是成功的，这只为即将到来的时刻做了铺垫。

职业生涯

两次大获全胜的第二年，福尔曼转为职业拳击手，随即在第三回合击倒对手唐纳德·沃尔海姆，职业生涯首战告捷。首次登上职业拳坛的那一年，他共打了13次，每次都取胜，11次击倒对手。随后的三年，福尔曼战无不胜，1973年1月22日，他在牙买加金斯敦迎战重量级世界冠军乔·弗雷泽。福尔曼出手稳健利落，在第二回合中击倒对手，赢得比赛，摘下了重量级世界冠军的桂冠。这是HBO电视台第一次播放拳击赛事，广播员赫伍德·考塞尔激动的喊声"弗雷泽倒了！"至今仍是体育史上最令人难忘的声音之一。

福尔曼在东京与波多黎各重量级冠军乔西·罗曼的比赛中，卫冕成功。结束比赛只用了50秒，堪称重量级世界拳王争霸赛有史以来最快的一场。1974年在委内瑞拉加拉加斯的比赛中，福尔曼于第二回合击倒对手肯·诺顿，再次卫冕成功。此次成功意义非凡，因为诺顿刚在去年打败了穆罕默德·阿里。

福尔曼在前五年职业生涯中遭遇的头一次失败，是在与穆罕默德·阿里的拳王争霸赛中。1974年10月30日在扎伊尔金沙萨举行的这场经典之赛叫做"丛林大反攻"。阿里"以逸待劳"的技巧出奇制胜，福尔曼在第八回合被击倒在地。

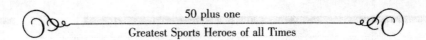
Foreman did not fight the following year, but he returned to boxing in 1976 for a fight in Las Vegas against Ron Lyle. Ring Magazine called it The Fight of the Year as both men fought brutally, knocking each other down multiple times until they were so exhausted that it was just a matter of one having enough energy left to knock the other out. Foreman proved to be the stronger fighter, knocking Lyle out in the fifth round. To finish 1976, Foreman fought and knocked out Frazier in a rematch in five rounds, Scott Ledoux in three rounds and Dino Dennis in four rounds.

In 1977, Foreman's career took a dramatic turn. He knocked out Pedro Agosto in four rounds in Pensacola, Florida and then lost a 12-round decision to Jimmy Young in Puerto Rico. After that fight, Foreman suffered from severe heat exhaustion and heatstroke while in his dressing room. He claimed that he had a near death experience and had been in total despair, causing him to ask God for guidance. Foreman said that he could sense God asking him to change his lifestyle, and so he became a born-again Christian. He retired from boxing and became an ordained minister of a Texan church, committing all of his time and energy to his family and parishioners as well as opening up the George Foreman Youth Development Community Center in Houston.

But boxing had not seen the last of Foreman. He made a surprise comeback 10 years later, in 1987, with the purpose of raising money for his youth center and to prove that people could still reach their goals even after hitting the big 40. Foreman won five fights that year, and nine the following year. His biggest upset in 1988 was against the former world light heavyweight and cruiserweight champion,Dwight Muhammad Qawi, whom he knocked out in seven rounds.

Over the next few years, Foreman continued to win, finally competing in one of his dream fights in 1991, when he challenged world heavyweight champion Evander Holyfield for the title during a match aired on Pay-Per-View. Ring Magazine named round 7 of that fight the Round of the Year. Even though Foreman lost the decision, he was happy to have shown that a 40+ year-old boxer could still go the full 12 rounds. He got his next shot at the world title just three fights later. He went up against Tommy Morrison for the vacant WBO championship, but again lost after 12 rounds by decision.

On November 5, 1994 in Las Vegas, Nevada, he challenged Michael Moorer for the International Boxing Federation (IBF) and the World Boxing Association (WBA) titles. This time, Foreman was victorious, knocking out Moorer in the 10th round despite losing on all scorecards in the earlier rounds. He broke two records with this win. The first was that at 45 years of age, he became the oldest fighter in history to win the world heavyweight title. The second record was that since 20 years had passed since he had lost his first world title, he was now the fighter with the most time between one world championship streak and the next.

Only a short while passed before the WBA title was taken away from Foreman due to his refusal to fight Tony Tucker, who was his mandatory opponent. Soon after this, Foreman beat Axel Schulz by a 12-round majority decision in order to keep his IBF title. However, controversy surrounded the verdict, causing the IBF to call for an immediate rematch in Germany. Foreman was then stripped of the IBF title because he refused to go to the other country to fight.

In 1996 and 1997, Foreman beat both Crawford Grimsley and Lou Savarese by a 12-round decision, respectively. Then, the World Boxing Council announced that they were going to give the winner of the upcoming fight between Foreman and Shannon Briggs a shot at the title against Lennox Lewis. Briggs ended up winning a questionable 12-round split decision after which Foreman announced his retirement.

Foreman made an attempt to fight a comeback bout in 1999, but it was canceled, and then he announced in February of 2004 that he was training for one last return fight, but his wife

第二年，福尔曼没有参赛，但是1976年他重归拳坛，在拉斯维加斯迎战罗恩·莱尔。《拳击》杂志称之为"年度之战"，因为比赛血腥残忍，双方互击，倒地无数，最后两人都筋疲力尽，只要留有余力的拳手击倒另一方就能获胜。福尔曼稍胜一筹，在第五回合把莱尔击倒在地。为了给1976年的比赛画上圆满句号，福尔曼再次迎战弗雷泽，五回合击倒对手；与斯哥特·勒杜比赛中，三回合击倒对手；对抗迪诺·丹尼斯的比赛中，四回合击倒对手。

1977年，福尔曼的职业生涯有了戏剧性转变。在佛罗里达州潘萨寇拉的比赛中，他在四回合中击倒佩德罗·阿格斯托，后来，在波多黎各与吉米·杨的决战中，他在第十二回合输给了对手。此次比赛之后，福尔曼在更衣室里突发严重的热衰竭和中暑症状。他宣称自己差点接近死神，几乎绝望中，他请求上帝帮助。福尔曼说他能感觉到上帝让自己改变生活方式，然后他重生为基督徒。他退出拳坛，当上了德州教堂的牧师，把所有精力和时间都放在了他的家庭和教区居民上，同时在休斯敦开办了乔治·福尔曼青年发展社区中心。

但是福尔曼对拳击并非就此告别。10年后的1987年，他奇迹般的复出，目的是为了给他的青年中心筹款，也为了向世人证明即使步入40岁，人们还是能够实现理想的。那年，福尔曼五次获胜，次年又九次夺冠。最大的意外就是他于1988年对抗前世界轻重量级及次重量级拳王德怀特·穆罕默德·沃的比赛中，以七回合击倒对手获胜。

随后的几年，福尔曼继续赢得比赛，终于在1991年参加了他的梦想之战，他挑战了世界重量级拳王伊万德·霍利菲尔德，此次比赛通过PPV付费台播放。《拳击》杂志称比赛的第七回合为"年度回合"。虽然福尔曼输了比赛，他仍然很高兴，因为他展示了自己作为40多岁的拳手依旧能打满12回合。又经过三次比赛后，他再次获得了称霸世界拳坛的机会。他与汤米·莫里森争夺空缺的世界拳击组织拳王称号，但12回合后再次失败。

1994年11月5日，在内华达州拉斯维加斯，他向迈克尔·摩尔挑战"国际拳击联合会"及"世界拳击协会"的拳王称号。这次，福尔曼赢了，他在第十回合击倒了摩尔，尽管之前的所有回合的记分卡上他都是落后。这次比赛让他打破了两项纪录。第一项是45岁的年龄让他成为史上最年长的世界重量级拳王。第二项是自从第一次输掉世界拳王头衔后已经过了20年，这是拳击手两度称霸世界冠军跨度最长的时间。

没过多久，福尔曼的"世界拳击协会"拳王称号就被取消了，因为他拒绝和强制委派的对手托尼·塔尼比赛。很快，福尔曼为保住"国际拳击联合会"拳王称号，他在12回合比赛中以多数判决击败了阿克塞尔·舒尔茨。然而，裁定很有争议，国际拳击联合会呼吁立刻在德国重新比赛。福尔曼的"国际拳击联合会"拳王称号又被剥夺，因为他拒绝去外国比赛。

1996年和1997年，福尔曼在12回合比赛中分别击败了克劳佛·格力姆斯力和卢·萨瓦雷斯。随后，世界拳击理事会宣布将给福尔曼和仙农·布里格斯一次机会，让他俩比赛决出冠军，以挑战伦诺克斯·刘易斯的拳王称号。布里格斯最终以颇受争议的12回合判定胜出，之后，福尔曼宣布退役。

1999年，福尔曼试图重出江湖，再次作战，但是比赛被取消，他又在2004年2月宣称自己正为复出的最后一战训练，但他妻子很快阻止了他。就这样，"大乔治"(有时人们这样

stopped him short. So, Big George, as he was sometimes called, ended his career with only 6 losses and a hefty 76 wins, 68 by knockout.

In June of 2003, Foreman was inducted into the International Boxing Hall of Fame while also being named boxing's ninth greatest puncher of all time by *Ring Magazine* that same year.

About the Man Himself

Foreman and his wife, Joan, have five sons and five daughters. One of his daughters, Freeda, is a former competitor in women's boxing. Foreman named all of his sons George Edward, and one of his daughters is named Georgette. Supposedly, he said that the purpose of naming all his son's after himself was so that they, unlike he, would know who their father was from the very beginning.

Besides leading a full life with his family, Foreman keeps busy with charity work, donating time and money to many organizations. In 1991, he donated $100,000 to the AIDS Foundation Houston and subsequently won the 1992 Humanitarian Award at the Annual Conference on AIDS in America. Foreman's donation was the largest single donation given to the foundation during its then 10-year history and was also one of the largest donations given by an individual at a national level. He received an honorary doctorate in 1998 from the Houston Graduate School of Theology for his charity work involving children.

Foreman, who was known in his early boxing days as being standoffish to the media, has since changed his ways and has become a friendly entrepreneur. He has appeared on countless Meineke Muffler ads and loves signing autographs, which he has plenty of opportunities to do while on worldwide tours to promote the George Foreman Lean Mean Grilling Machine. It is interesting to note that his grilling machine contracts have brought in more money than his boxing career ever did, and Foreman has also hinted, probably jokingly, that he is more famous for his grill than for his boxing. In 1993, he starred in a sitcom on ABC called George, but the show did not do well and the plug was pulled on it shortly after it had begun.

Foreman is the co-author of numerous books, including multiple grilling books, a children's book called *Let George Do It!* and his autobiography, *By George: The Autobiography of George Foreman.*

Transforming himself from a mean championship fighter into an embraceable champion both in and out of the boxing ring, not to mention naming all of his sons after himself, George Foreman has ensured that the world will never forget his name.

叫他)结束了职业生涯,只输过6次,76次大获全胜,其中68次击倒对手。

2003年6月,福尔曼入选"国际拳击名人堂",同年还被《拳击》杂志选为"拳坛史上排名第九的最伟大拳击手"。

关于此人

福尔曼和妻子共有五个儿子和五个女儿。其中一个女儿弗瑞达曾是女子拳击手。福尔曼给所有的儿子起名为乔治·爱德华,给一个女儿起名为乔治特。他说他给所有儿子以他的名字起名,可能是因为他不想让孩子们跟他一样,他希望他们一开始就知道父亲是谁。

福尔曼与家人过着充实的生活,此外,他还忙于慈善事业,在很多慈善团体上奉献了大量的时间和金钱。1991年,他为休斯敦艾滋病基金会捐赠10万美元,1992年在美国艾滋病年会中获得"人道主义奖"。福尔曼是当时10年历史中为基金会个人捐款最多的人,也是全国范围中捐款最多的个人之一。1998年,他因为慈善事业,包括对儿童慈善事业的贡献而获得休斯敦技术研究生院颁发的荣誉奖项。

福尔曼在早年拳击生涯中,给大众的感觉有点冷漠,现在已经改变了态度,成为一名平易近人的企业家。他多次登上Meineke Muffler商业广告,喜欢签名活动,他在全国巡回宣传乔治·福尔曼过滤油烧烤机时,会有很多机会签名。有趣的是,他的烧烤机订单为他赚来的钱比拳击还要多, 福尔曼可能一直开玩笑地说, 他的烧烤机比拳击更让他出名。1993年,他参演了ABC电视台《乔治》的情景剧,但是并不成功,还没开始多久,就停止了。

福尔曼还与人合著了不少书籍,包括许多关于烧烤的书,一本《让乔治来做!》的儿童书,他还写了自传《乔治·福尔曼自传》。

拳坛内外他从一个平庸的拳击手变成一个受人拥戴的拳王,更不必说他用自己名字给儿子们起名,乔治·福尔曼早已在世人心中树立了威信,人们将永远铭记这位英雄。

Seventeen

Red Grange

Why He is Among the 50 plus one Greatest Sports Heroes

Red Grange is widely accepted as the player who brought fame to professional football, legitimatizing it in a world that had previously focused on the college aspect of the sport. He led his team to two NFL championships and was inducted into two football halls of fame. Today, Grange is often referred to as the Babe Ruth of Football, a title that merits a spot among the greatest sports heroes.

On the Way Up

Harold Edward Grange was born on June 13, 1903 in Forksville, Pennsylvania. His mother died when he was 5 years old, and shortly after that, his father moved the family to Wheaton, Illinois. Grange, who was nicknamed Red for his fiery red hair, attended Wheaton Community High School and was a star athlete on the baseball, basketball, football and track and field teams. He lettered in each of the four sports every year, earning a total of 16 letters. Although he was a phenomenal all-around sportsman, Grange shined the brightest on the football field. During his junior year, he scored 36 touchdowns and led his team to an undefeated season. His father reportedly would give him a quarter each time he scored, and by the time he graduated, Grange had scored a total of 74 touchdowns. He was a very popular recruit out of high school, and in 1923 he chose to go to the University of Illinois at Urbana-Champaign. At first, he only wanted to play baseball and run track, and had to be talked into playing football by his Zeta Psi fraternity brothers.

Grange scored three touchdowns against Nebraska in his first game. He soon became ranked among the best college players, but that would change on October 18, 1924 after a game against Michigan, a team that had been undefeated for 3 years. Grange started by scoring a 95-yard touchdown on the opening kickoff and then, in the first 12 minutes, he scored three more touchdowns in three runs totaling 167 yards. His four touchdowns equaled the number of yards Michigan had given up during the 2 previous seasons combined. Needless to say, Illinois won 39-14. After the game, sportswriter, Grantland Rice, gave Grange the nickname The Galloping Ghost because of his elusive ways on the field. The *Chicago Tribune* published an article that included this line about Grange's performance: "They knew he was coming; they saw him start; he made no secret of his direction; he was in their midst, and he was gone! "

By the time the Michigan game was over, (or perhaps even as it was being played), Grange went from being considered a great player to being put high up on a pedestal as a legend. That year, he ran for 723 yards and scored 12 touchdowns in seven games, guiding his teammates to an undefeated season as the national champions. People from all over the country wanted to watch Grange play. By the time his final game rolled around in 1925, 72,657 fans made their way to Ohio State to get a glimpse of his legendary skills. The day after that game, he signed with the Chicago Bears amidst the negative reaction from Illinois head coach, Bob Zuppke, and numerous

瑞德·格朗奇

他为何入选《50+1位最闪耀的体育巨星》

    大众一致公认瑞德·格朗奇为职业橄榄球普及全球起了推波助澜的作用，而在这之前，它只是学院热衷的体育运动。他带领球队两次夺得国家橄榄球联盟冠军，入选两个橄榄球名人堂。如今，格朗奇常与贝贝·鲁斯相提并论，堪称"橄榄球坛的贝贝·鲁斯"，这个称号足以证明他在体坛中的英雄地位。

成长之路

    1903年6月13日，哈罗德·爱德华·格朗奇生于宾夕法尼亚州福克斯维尔市。他五岁时，母亲就去世了，不久以后，他父亲把家搬到了伊利诺斯州惠顿。格朗奇因一头红发得了个昵称叫"红毛"，他就读于惠顿社区高中，在棒球、篮球、橄榄球和田径校队中都是明星。他每年都因四项运动的优秀成绩而被授予校名首字母奖品，总共获得过16次。格朗奇无疑是个全能运动员，但他最擅长的还是橄榄球。他在第三年，36次触地得分，带领球队在整个赛季处于不败之地。据报道，每次只要得分，他父亲就给他两毛五分钱，到毕业时，格朗奇总共74次触地得分。高中毕业后，他成了非常抢手的新人，1923年他选择就读于伊利诺斯大学香槟分校。起初，他只想参加棒球队和田径队，还得靠兄弟会的杰塔·帕西说服他去参加橄榄球队。

    格朗奇在第一次对抗内布拉斯加大学的比赛中获得三个触地得分。很快他便在最佳大学生运动员中名列前茅，但是形势在1924年10月18日突然转变，他们遇到了卫冕三年的冠军密歇根队。格朗奇在开场比赛中就以95码触地得分，随后的12分钟内，他总共以167码的距离三次持球跑进攻，三次触地得分。他的四次触地得分的码数与密歇根队前两个赛季输掉的总数持平。不用说，伊利诺斯队以39胜14负成绩取胜。比赛结束后，体育运动专栏作家格兰特兰·赖斯称格朗奇为"高速魔鬼"，因为他在球场上无人能及。《芝加哥论坛报》杂志发表了一篇文章，有一句话这样写道："他们知道他要冲上来了；看见他开球了；他直奔目的地；他在他们之中；然后他就不见了！"

    与密歇根队比赛结束后，(甚至可能就在进行时)，格朗奇从之前的优秀球员荣升为偶像级的传奇人物。那一年，持球跑的距离为723码，7场比赛中共12次触地得分，率领全队成为所向披靡的赛季全国冠军。来自全国各地的观众都希望一睹格朗奇的球场风采。1925年，又是他决赛的时候，来自俄亥俄州的72657名球迷纷纷前来观赏他的精湛球艺。比赛后第二天，他就与芝加哥熊队签约，此举招来伊利诺斯队总教练鲍勃·祖佩克和无数队员的斥责。

other collegiate football figures.

In an era when football scores were much lower than they are today, Grange's college game performances were almost unbelievable. During his career, he scored 31 touchdowns and gained 3,367 yards running. Grange was named an All–American all 3 years that he played for Illinois, and in 1924 he became the first Chicago Tribune Silver Football Award winner as the Big Ten MVP. He appeared on the cover of *TIME* magazine's October 5, 1925 issue. University of Illinois an retired his No. 77, that same year.

Professional Career

The contract that Grange and his manager, C.C. Pyle, initially signed with the Bears stated that he agreed to play in a 19–game barnstorming tour in exchange for a salary and a share of the gate receipts, which ended up totaling $100,000. This was incredible during a time when average league salaries were not even $100 per game. The tour lasted 67 days and is said to be the defining period in professional football when it became validated all around the country as a sport worthy of watching. Grange was the most influential figure during this period, showing college football fans that paid professional athletes could definitely get the job done, too. In fact, a crowd of only 7,500 showed up to watch the Bears' last pre–Grange game, while a whopping 36,000 braved a snowstorm and packed into what is now known as Wrigley Field to witness his first game ever as a professional player.

Some of the games on the tour did not attract nearly as many fans as that first one, but others drew even more. When the Bears played New York and Los Angeles, the attendance numbers added up to more than 65,000 fans per game. Grange played in 17 of the games, missing only two due to injury. He returned home to Wheaton once the tour came to an end on January 31, 1926. He and Pyle then bid to buy a piece of the Bears franchise, but player/manager George Halas rejected their offer. That same year, the two attempted to form their own league, which they called the American Football League, and had Grange playing with the New York Yankees. The league only lasted a year, and then the Yankees joined the NFL. However, Grange severely injured his knee in the third game of the 1927 season, and ended up missing all of the following season as well. After the injury, he lost some of his dashing abilities as a running back and was never able to fully retrieve them.

Grange rejoined the Bears in 1929. Even though his role on the team morphed into being more of a defensive back than a running back, he still managed to lead them to two major victories in consecutive seasons. The first win came in 1932 after the Bears finished tied for first place with the Portsmouth Spartans. It was the first tie in the history of the NFL, leading league officials to schedule an additional regular–season game to serve as a tie–breaker and determine which team would be honored as the league champion. On December 18th, the Bears defeated the Spartans 9–0. Grange scored the winning touchdown on a two–yard pass from teammate and fellow legend, Bronko Nagurski.

The second major victory took place in 1933 in the NFL's first ever championship game. The Bears beat the New York Giants 23–21 after Grange made a touchdownsaving tackle near the end of the fourth quarter to preserve their tight lead. Two years later, after the 1934 season, Grange retired from professional football.

在那个年代，橄榄球记分比现在低得多，格朗奇在大学校队的表现实在不可思议。在那段时期，他31次触地得分，持球跑码数为3367码。他为伊利诺斯队效力的整整3年中一直获得"全美大学明星"称号，1924年，他成为首位获得《芝加哥论坛报》Chicago Tribune Silver Football Award "十大联盟最具价值球员"称号的运动员。他还上了1925年10月5日一期的《时代》杂志封面。同年，伊利诺斯大学退役了他的号码77。

职业生涯

格朗奇及经纪人派尔最初与熊队签订的合同上声明，他同意参加19场的巡回赛，以此换取薪水和部分门票费，最终所得共计10万美元。这实在令人难以置信，因为那时联盟每场比赛薪水还不到100美元。此次巡回赛持续了67天，据说是为职业橄榄球借风造势，把该项运动在全国范围内合法化，使之值得观赏。格朗奇是那时最有影响力的人物，也向大学橄榄球迷证明了带薪职业球员肯定也能干好。实际上，只有7500人到场观看格朗奇职业生涯前在熊队的最后一场比赛，但是却有36000人冒着暴风雪前往今天著名的威格力球场观看他职业生涯的第一次比赛。

虽然有几场巡回赛到场人数没有第一场多，但是其他比赛的到场人数远远超过第一次。当熊队对抗纽约队和洛杉矶队时，每场观众人数增至65000多。格朗奇参加了17场比赛，由于受伤仅错过两场。1926年1月31日，巡回赛接近尾声时，他回了惠顿老家。他和派尔企图购买熊队分队的股份，但被运动员兼经纪人的乔治·哈拉斯拒绝了。同年，两人试着组建了自己的联盟，称之为"美国橄榄球联盟"，格朗奇以队员身份参加了与纽约扬基队的比赛。联盟只维持了一年，扬基队加入了国家橄榄球联盟。然而，1927年赛季的第三场比赛中，格朗奇膝盖严重受伤，最后错过了赛季的所有其他赛事。受伤后，作为跑锋的他缺少了冲击力，而且再也不能完全恢复了。

1929年格朗奇重新进入熊队。虽然他更多的担当后卫而非跑锋，他仍然成功地带领球队蝉联两个赛季的大赢家。第一个胜利是在1932年，熊队与普兹茅斯斯巴达人队平局加赛后夺冠。这是国家橄榄球联盟史上第一次平局，联盟负责人不得不再安排一场常规赛季比赛，破除平局来决定谁将联盟冠军收入囊中。12月18日，熊队以9:0的比分轻取斯巴达人队。格朗奇在队友球星布朗克·纳古尔斯基的两码传球的帮助下，拿下了决胜的触地得分。

第二次胜利是在1933年国家橄榄球联盟前所未有的第一次冠军赛中获得。格朗奇在第四节将近结束时，他擒抱对手、持球触地得分挽救了比赛，最终以23比21险胜纽约巨人队，保住了冠军位子。两年后，过了1934年的赛季，格朗奇退出了职业橄榄球坛。

Eighteen

Wayne Gretzky

Why He is Among the 50 plus one Greatest Sports Heroes

Wayne Gretzky was the top scorer during hockey history's highest scoring period. It is easy then to believe that he holds virtually every offensive record in the National Hockey League (NHL) for both regular– and post–season play. He was a driving force in the capture of four Stanley Cup championships and three Canada Cup tournament titles, and is widely accepted as the individual player who has had the most impact on hockey's popularity, especially in the United States. A gracious and valiant leader, Gretzky has earned his rightful place among the greatest heroes in sports history.

On the Way Up

Wayne Douglas Gretzky was born on January 26, 1961 in Brantford, Ontario, Canada. He was the oldest of five children born to Walter and Phyllis Gretzky. Walter, a former hockey player himself, taught Wayne how to play hockey on a rink in their backyard. As a 6–year old, he scored a goal while playing on a 10 and under team. When he was 10, he played in the Brantford Atom league and finished the 85–game season with 378 goals and 120 assists. The following year, he scored 517 points.

As a 16–year old, the Sault Ste. Marie Greyhounds selected Gretzky third in the 1977 annual midget draft. During what would prove to be his only full year of major junior hockey, he scored six goals in his debut appearance before eventually recording totals of 70–112–182 and winning the Ontario Hockey Association Rookie of the Year Award. In 1978, Gretzky carried Team Canada to a bronze medal in the World Junior Championship, leading the tournament with 17 points in six games.

Professional Career

On June 13, 1978, Gretzky began his professional career by signing with the Indianapolis Racers of the World Hockey Association (WHA). He was sold to the Edmonton Oilers on November 2nd that same year after playing only eight games with the Racers. On January 5, 1979, Gretzky fulfilled his childhood dream by centering the WHA All–Star Team line with Gordie Howe, who had been his idol as a youngster. He finished the season with 110 points and was named Rookie of the Year by the WHA after helping the Oilers to reach the ranking of first overall in the league.

The WHA folded in 1979, and the Oilers moved to the NHL, bringing Gretzky along with them. The team lost its debut league appearance against the Chicago Blackhawks, but Gretzky was able to make his first NHL point, an assist on Kevin Lowe's goal at 9:49 in the first period. Four nights and two games later, he scored his first NHL goal on a power play at 18:51 in the third period. Gretzky completed his rookie season in the league with a record of 51–86–137 and won the first of his nine straight Hart Trophies as the NHL's Most Valuable Player.

韦恩·格雷兹基

他为何入选《50+1位最闪耀的体育巨星》

韦恩·格雷兹基是曲棍球最高得分史上首屈一指的得分王。那个时候，他能够保持美国曲棍球联盟常规赛和季后赛的进攻得分纪录，实在不可思议。他英勇神猛，4次捧得斯坦利冠军杯，3次获得加拿大锦标赛奖杯，他为普及曲棍球运动立下了汗马功劳，尤其在美国。格雷兹基有着优雅而勇敢的领袖风范，他当然是体坛风云人物之一。

成长之路

1961年1月26日，韦恩·道格拉斯·格雷兹基出生于加拿大安大略省布兰特福德市。他是沃特和菲丽丝5个孩子中的老大。沃特本来也是曲棍球运动员，他在后院的冰球场上教韦恩打球。韦恩6岁时，在10岁以内儿童队打进了一球。10岁的他便为布兰特福德原子联盟效力，结束85场比赛的赛季时，他进球378个，助攻120个。次年，他得到总分为517分。

16岁时，他被Sault Ste. Marie Greyhounds选为1977年度小型选秀会第三名。这一年只是他曲棍球运动的青少年鼎盛期，作为新秀，初登球场，就进了6个球，最终创下了70-112-182的总分纪录，被评为"安大略曲棍球协会年度新人"。1978年，格雷兹基率领加拿大队在世界青少年冠军赛中夺得铜牌，在锦标赛的六场比赛中积分17分。

职业生涯

1978年6月13日，格雷兹基与世界曲棍球协会的印第安纳赛车曲棍球队签约，开始了他的职业生涯。11月2日，他仅参加了8场比赛就转给埃德蒙顿油工队。1979年1月5日，格雷兹基与他少年时的偶像高迪·郝威一起被选为世界曲棍球协会全明星队的中线，实现了自己童年时期的梦想。赛季结束时，他获得110的总分，为油工队排名联盟第一助一臂之力，被世界曲棍球协会评为"年度新人"。

1979年世界曲棍球协会倒闭，油工队转至国家冰上曲棍球联盟，格雷兹基随队而去。该队在首次联盟亮相中不敌芝加哥黑鹰队，但格雷兹基成功地帮助球队取得国家冰上曲棍球联盟中的第一分，第一场比赛9分49秒之时，他为凯文罗威助攻进球得分。四夜两次比赛之后，他在第三场比赛的18分51秒之时，以一记重击射门得分，拿下了自己进入国家曲棍球联盟以来的第一分。格雷兹基以51-86-137的纪录结束了新秀赛季，第一次获得哈特杯"国家冰上曲棍球联盟最具价值球员"称号，他曾连续九次获此殊荣。

Gretzky averaged close to 192 points per season for the next 8 years. During that period he broke an impressive number of records. For example, in the 1981–1982 season, he scored 50 goals in the Oilers' first 39 games and then proceeded to set an all–time record by finishing the regular season with 92 goals. In the 1983–1984 season, Gretzky managed a 51–game point–scoring streak; and he set an all–time single season scoring record for the playoffs with 47 points the following year. He finished the 1985–1986 season by setting the all–time regular season record with 215 points.

Gretzky, nicknamed The Great One, guided the Oilers to the finals five times, and to the Stanley Cup four times. The team lost the Cup to the New York Islanders in the 1982–1983 season, but went on to defeat the Islanders the following year; the Philadelphia Flyers in 1984–1985 and 1986–1987 seasons; and the Boston Bruins in the 1987–1988 season. Gretzky was also a key member on the Team Canada crews that captured the Canada Cup in 1984, 1987 and 1991.

On August 9, 1988, the Oilers traded Gretzky and two of his teammates to the Los Angeles Kings for three future first–round draft picks and $15 million. By 1991, the team became the only Southern California franchise to play at home in front of sold–out crowds for a whole season and Wayne Gretzky was the catalyst.

In Gretzky's first season with the Kings, their 42–31–7 record was the most improved in the NHL. They placed second in the Smythe Division and Gretzky finished second in league scoring with 168 points. The next season, he became the NHL's all–time leading scorer when he surpassed Gordie Howe's 1,850–point total on October 15, 1989 at Edmonton.

On April 28, 1992, the Kings fell to the Oilers in a six–game opening round playoff series. After that, Gretzky would not play for more than 8 months due to suffering a herniated thoracic disc. Defying speculation he would not be able to play again, he rejoined the Kings for his 1,000th career game on January 6, 1993. That year, he played in 45 games and finished with a 16–49–65 record, leading his team to their first ever Stanley Cup finals. Although the Kings lost to the Montreal Canadians in five games, Gretzky extinguished any lingering doubts about his post–injury playing abilities by scoring 40 points in 24 postseason games.

On March 23, 1994, Gretzky scored his 802nd goal, surpassing Howe's record as the league's all–time leading goal–scorer. At the end of the season, he was presented with the Lester Patrick Trophy for his outstanding service to hockey in the United States. Gretzky finished the 1994–1995 season as the top Kings scorer for the sixth time in seven seasons, and then was traded to the St. Louis Blues.

From February to July of 1996, Gretzky led the Blues in scoring with 102 points. He also registered 23 goals and 79 assists while bringing the team to within one goal of the Western Conference finals. He signed as a free agent with the New York Rangers on July 12, 1996, and then proceeded to pull off a 15–game scoring streak in the first playing month. He made 97 points as the leading scorer for the Rangers, and tied the team's single season record for assists by a center when he topped the league with 72 assists.

Gretzky played for Canada in the 1998 Olympic Games in Nagano, Japan while leading the league again with 67 assists, and also hit his 1,851 career assist–yet another record to Gretzky's credit. Gretzky retired from the NHL on April 18, 1999. By that time he owned or shared 61 NHL records: 40 for regular season, 15 for Stanley Cup playoffs and six for All–Star Game. In 1,487 career games, he made a record 894 goals, 1,963 assists, 2,857 points and 50 hat tricks. His total for regular season and playoff games is a still–standing record of 3,239 points.

In 2000, at the NHL All–Star Game in Toronto, every member club officially retired Gretzky's jersey No. 99. Gretzky has been honored with numerous awards both during and after his career

　　随后的八年中,格雷兹基几乎每个赛季均分都达192分。那段岁月中,他不断创造着辉煌的纪录。例如,1981至1982赛季,他在油工队头39场比赛中有50次射门得分,接着又创了常规赛季总共92次射门得分的空前纪录。1983至1984赛季,格雷兹基在51次比赛中一直连续得分;次年,他创造了单季季后赛中夺得47分的空前纪录。1985至1986赛季,他总共拿下215分,创造了史无前例的常规赛季得分纪录。

　　格雷兹基昵称为"伟大冰球手",率领油工队五次进入决赛,四次将斯坦利杯收入囊中。该队于1982-1983赛季输给了纽约岛民队,没能捧回金杯,但于次年击败了岛民队;1984-1985赛季和1986-1987赛季赢得了费城飞人队;1987-88赛季打败了波士顿棕熊队。格雷兹基也是加拿大队的主力队员,该队在1984、1987和1991年都赢得了冠军,捧得加拿大杯。

　　1988年8月9日,油工队以未来三次首轮选秀新人和1500万美元为交换条件,将格雷兹基和另两名队友换到了洛杉矶帝王队。到了1991年,该队成为加利福尼亚南部在整个赛季主场比赛中都能预售完门票的唯一转让会员队,当然,韦恩·格雷兹基起了不小的推动作用。

　　格雷兹基在帝王队的第一个赛季中,该队就以42-31-7的成绩成为国家曲棍球联盟中进步最大的球队。他们夺得了Smythe分区第二名,格雷兹基以168的总分在联盟中排名第二。下一个赛季,他成为国家曲棍球联盟中空前绝后的得分王,超过了1989年10月15日高迪·郝威在埃德蒙顿创下的1850总分纪录。

　　1992年4月28日,帝王队在季后赛的六场开赛中输给了油工队。之后,格雷兹基由于严重的胸椎间盘突出,无法参赛达八个多月之久。为了打破再也不能参赛的传言,1993年1月6日,他东山再起,重入帝王队参加了职业生涯中第1000次比赛。这一年,他参加了45次比赛,获得16-49-65的成绩,带领球队第一次闯入斯坦利杯决赛。虽然帝王队最终在五场比赛中输给了蒙特利尔加拿大人队,但是格雷兹基在24场季后赛中获得40分,就足以打破之前对他运动能力的猜疑流言。

　　1994年3月23日,格雷兹基第802次射门得分,超过了联盟得分王郝威创造的得分纪录。赛季末,他因为美国曲棍球运动作出的杰出贡献而获得莱斯特·帕特里克奖杯。1994-1995赛季结束时,是格雷兹基七次获得帝王队赛季得分王称号的第六次,那时,他又转至圣路易布鲁斯队。

　　从1996年2月至7月,格雷兹基带领布鲁斯队取得102分。他创下了23个射门得分和79次助攻的成绩,终于率领球队冲向唯一目标,即挺进西部总决赛。1996年7月12日,他与纽约游骑兵曲棍球队签约成为自由人,紧接着,在头一个月比赛中连续赢得15次得分记录。他成为游骑兵队得分王,获得97分,作为中线,他以72次助攻位居联盟榜首,这与该队单赛季助攻纪录持平。

　　1998年日本长野奥运会中,格雷兹基为加拿大队效力,同时再次率领联盟赢得67次助攻,达到了职业生涯的1851次助攻,这又是格雷兹基创造的纪录。1999年4月18日,格雷兹基退出国家冰上曲棍球联盟。到此为止,他已拥有或享有61项国家冰上曲棍球联盟记录:40项常规赛季纪录,15项斯坦利杯季后赛纪录和6项全明星比赛纪录。在1487次比赛中,他射门得分894次,助攻1963次,得分2857分,50次在同一场比赛中连续三次得分。他创下了常规赛和季后赛3239分的总分纪录,至今仍然无人能打破。

　　2000年,在多伦多国家曲棍球联盟全明星比赛中,每位正式会员都参加了格雷兹基99号球衣退役仪式。格雷兹基职业生涯中及退役后获得了无数奖项,包括:

including:
- Hart Trophy as the NHL's Most Valuable Player (1980–1987 and 1989)
- Lady Byng Memorial Trophy as the NHL's Most Gentlemanly Player (1980, 1991–1992, 1994 and 1999)
- Second All–Star Team (1980, 1988–1990, 1994 and 1997–1998)
- First All–Star Team (1981–1987 and 1991)
- Art Ross Trophy as the NHL's Scoring Champion (1981–1987, 1990–1991 and 1994)
- Lester B. Pearson Award as the NHL's Outstanding Player (1982–1985 and 1987)
- NHL Plus/Minus Award (1982, 1984–1985 and 1987)
- NHL All–Star Game Most Valuable Player (1983, 1989 and 1999)
- Conn Smythe Trophy as the NHL's Playoff Most Valuable Player (1985 and 1988)
- Chrysler–Dodge/NHL Performer of the Year (1985–1987)
- Lester Patrick Trophy for outstanding service to hockey in the United States (1994)
- Voted No. 1 out of the 50 Greatest Hockey Players in NHL History, *The Hockey News* (1997)
- Hockey Hall of Fame (1999)
- Fifth Greatest Athlete of the 20th Century, ESPN (1999)

About the Man Himself

In 2002, Gretzky served as the executive director of Team Canada's Olympic hockey team during the Winter Olympics in Salt Lake City, Utah. He led them all the way to the nation's first hockey gold medal in 50 years. He was awarded with the Olympic Order, which is the highest honor given by the International Olympic Committee. He served as Team Canada's executive director again for the 2004 World Cup of Hockey and the 2006 Winter Olympics in Turin, Italy. The team failed to medal in 2006 as they were eliminated in the quarterfinals. In 2005, Gretzky signed a multi–year contract as head coach for the Phoenix Coyotes.

From his playing years until now, Gretzky has been a spokesperson for such companies as Anheuser–Busch, Pepsi–Cola Canada, McDonald's Canada, Ford and Bill Blass. There is a Wayne Gretzky clothing line at Hudson's Bay Co., and McFarlane Toys has created Wayne Gretzky figurines while Sony Computer Entertainment America Inc. has developed a PlayStation2 video game featuring Gretzky. He also owns a restaurant in Toronto that bears his name.

Gretzky established the Wayne Gretzky Foundation in order to give underprivileged children in North America an opportunity to play hockey. So far, the foundation has spearheaded two successful hockey equipment drives, and it raised more than $120,000 at the first Golf Classic in 2004. Besides his own organization, Gretzky also donates his time to other charities, including the Ronald McDonald Children's Charities in Canada and Right to Play.

Gretzky married actress Janet Jones in July of 1988. They have three sons and two daughters, and live in California. Gretzky has co–written a few books, including *Gretzky: From Backyard Rink to the Stanley Cup* and *Gretzky: An Autobiography*.

The Great One's achievements on and off the ice make him one of most influential individuals ever to play the game of hockey and one of the greatest athletes of all times.

· 哈特杯"国家曲棍球联盟最具价值球员"称号 (1980–1987和1989年)
· 宾尼夫人纪念奖"国家曲棍球联盟最具价值球员"称号(1980, 1991–1992, 1994 和1999年
· 入选全明星第二阵容队(1980, 1988–1990, 1994和1997–1998年)
· 入选全明星第一阵容队(1981–1987 和 1991年)
· 阿特·罗斯奖"国家曲棍球联盟得分冠军"称号(1981–1987, 1990–1991 和1994年)
· 莱斯特·B·皮尔森奖"国家曲棍球联盟杰出运动员"称号(1982–1985 和 1987年)
· 国家曲棍球联盟Plus/Minus Award奖(1982, 1984–1985 和1987年)
· 国家曲棍球联盟全明星赛最具价值球员 (1983, 1989 和 1999年)
· 康恩·斯迈思奖"国家曲棍球联盟季后赛最具价值球员"称号(1985 和 1988年)
· 克莱斯勒·道奇/国家曲棍球联盟年度表现奖(1985–1987年)
· 美国曲棍球运动杰出贡献莱斯特·帕特里克奖(1994年)
· 《曲棍球新闻》中评选为国家曲棍球联盟史上50位最伟大曲棍球员第一名(1997年)
· 曲棍球名人堂(1999年)
· 被体育电视频道评为"20世纪最伟大运动员第五名" (1999年)

关于此人

　　2002年,格雷兹基在犹他盐湖城冬奥会中担任加拿大奥林匹克队执行总裁。他率领球队取得50年以来国家队的第一枚金牌。他被授予奥林匹克勋章,这是国际奥林匹克组委会颁发的最高荣誉。2004年曲棍球世界杯赛和2006年意大利都灵冬奥会中,他再次担任加拿大队执行总裁。2006年,该队没有获得奖牌,因为在四分之一决赛中遭淘汰。2005年,格雷兹基与凤凰城野狼队签下多年合同,担任该队总教练。

　　从参赛至今,格雷兹基还担任一些公司的代言人,比如安豪泽·布施公司、加拿大百事可乐公司、福特公司和比尔·布拉斯公司。在哈得逊湾公司还有韦·格雷兹基服装生产线,麦克法兰玩具公司出产了韦恩·格雷兹基的小塑像,索尼电脑娱乐美国公司还开发出格雷兹基为原型的家庭电脑游戏机。在多伦多他开了一家"韦恩·格雷兹基"饭店。

　　格雷兹基创立了韦恩·格雷兹基基金会,为北美贫困儿童进行曲棍球运动提供了机会。迄今为止,该基金会已经成功准备了两套曲棍球设备器材,并为2004年第一届高尔夫精英赛筹款超过12万美元。格雷兹基除了自己的基金会外,还投身于其他慈善事业,包括加拿大麦当劳叔叔之家儿童慈善基金会和"运动机会"组织。

　　1988年7月,格雷兹基与演员珍妮特·琼斯结婚。他们在加利福尼亚与三儿两女共同生活。格雷兹基与人合写了一些书,包括《格雷兹基:从后院冰球场到捧回斯坦利杯》和《格雷兹基自传》。

　　"伟大冰球手"在赛场内外取得的成就,让他成为曲棍球球坛中最富影响力的球员之一,也是50+1位最闪耀的体育巨星中的一名明星。

Nineteen

Eric Heiden

Why He is Among the 50 plus one Greatest Sports Heroes

Speed skater Eric Arthur Heiden was the first athlete ever to take home five, count them, five gold medals in individual events from a single Olympic Games. Before that, he won multiple World Sprint and All–Around Speed Skating titles. He is now a member of three separate halls of fame. These are only some of the reasons why Heiden deserves to be hailed as a greatest sports hero.

On the Way Up

Eric Arthur Heiden was born on June 15, 1958 in Madison, Wisconsin. Growing up in a middle–class family, he played other sports, including soccer and hockey. By the time he was 14 he decided to devote his time and attention to speed skating and trained 5 hours every day all–year–round. Even in summer or on warmer winter days when there was no ice, Heiden would practice in the basement, skating in his socks on a large sheet of plastic. His sister, Beth, also a speed skater, won a bronze medal in the women's 3,000–meter race during the 1980 Olympics.

Heiden began competing in pack–style skating and won the National Indoor and Outdoor Championships as a midget. He took home his first medal in metric skating after finishing third in a 1975 race. His commitment to the sport began to pay off when at the Innsbruck, Austria Olympics in 1976 he finished seventh in the 1,500–meter race and 19th in the 5,000–meter race. One year later he swept the 1977 World Junior Overall, Senior Overall and Sprint championships at the age of 18. As if that was not amazing enough, Heiden repeated the sweep three times, making him the sprint and overall champion for 4 straight years from 1977–1980. At the 1979 competitions, he set a record of 14:43.11 in the 10,000–meter race and, in 1980 he set two world records in the 1,000–meter race with 1:13.60 and the 1,500–meter race with 1:54.79.

Professional Career

Even though Heiden's name was famous by the end of the 1970s in speed–skating loving countries like Norway and the Netherlands, he was nowhere near as wellknown in the United States. That came to an abrupt end in 1980, not only because of his fourth sweep of the sprint and overall world championship titles, but also because of his astonishing performance at that year's Olympics in February at Lake Placid, New York. Rising to new heights since his debut appearance at the Olympics 4 years earlier, Heiden clinched a total of five gold medals in five individual events: the 500–meter, 1,000–meter, 1,500–meter, 5,000–meter and 10,000–meter races. This was an unprecedented achievement in the history of the Olympic Games.

Heiden did not just win gold medals during his 9 days of competition. He set four Olympic records in the 1,000 meters, 1,500 meters and 5,000 meters and also set two world records in the

埃里克·海登

他为何入选《50+1位最闪耀的体育巨星》

埃里克·阿瑟·海登是唯一一位在一届奥运会中独揽5枚个人赛事金牌的速滑运动员。在此之前，他获得过无数世界短距离速滑锦标赛和速滑全能比赛的奖牌。如今，他是3个名人堂成员。这也只能说明他傲视体坛群雄的一些原因。

成长之路

1958年6月15日，埃里克·阿瑟·海登出生于威斯康星州麦迪森市。在中产阶级家庭长大的他，还常常进行其他体育运动，比如足球和曲棍球。14岁时，他决定把时间和精力都花在速滑运动上，年复一年，日复一日，天天都练习5个小时。即使是在夏天或没有冰冻的稍暖和的冬日，海登也会穿着短裤，在地下室一大片塑料板上练习。他的妹妹贝丝也是速滑运动员，她在1980年奥运会女子3000米比赛中获得一枚铜牌。

海登开始参加速滑比赛，年纪轻轻就获得了全国室内和户外冠军赛大奖。1975年米制赛结束后，他排名第三，第一次赢得了奖牌。终于，付出初显回报，1976年奥地利因斯布鲁克奥运会中，他在1500米比赛中位居第七，5000米比赛中排名第十九。一年后，18岁的他在1977年世界青少年全能赛、青年全能赛和短距离速滑冠军赛中横扫对手。海登接连三次横扫对手，这还不足为奇，他从1977至1980年整整四年蝉联短距离和全能冠军。1979年比赛中，他创下了1万米14:43.11的纪录，1980年他创造了两项世界纪录，分别是1000米1:13.60的成绩和1500米1:54.79的成绩。

职业生涯

虽然到了70年代末，海登的名字在喜爱速滑运动的挪威和荷兰是家喻户晓，但都不及在美国的知名度。1980年他一鸣惊人，不仅四次包揽短距离和全能世界冠军，而且在2月份纽约普莱西德湖奥运会中表现出色、令人叹服。在奥运会的首次亮相海登更上一层楼，他在五项个人赛事中包揽了全部金牌：500米、1000米、1500米、5000米和10000米。这是奥运会史无前例的辉煌成就。

海登在九天的比赛中不仅获得了金牌。他创造了四项奥运会纪录，包括1000米、1500米、5000米，并创造了两项世界纪录，包括500米38.03秒的成绩，500米是他的最弱项，还有

500–meter race, his weakest event, with 38.03 seconds and in the 10,000–meter race with 14:28.13. Perhaps even more impressive was that the night before the 10,000–meter event, Heiden stayed up to watch the U.S. Olympic hockey team defeat the Soviet Union and ended up oversleeping. He had to rush to the speedskating rink for his race. Despite waking up late and eating a non–breakfast of champions that only consisted of a couple of slices of bread, Heiden was still able to beat the previous world record by 6.20 seconds for his fifth gold medal. He retired from speedskating immediately following this fabulous five medal feat.

For his awesome accomplishments in the sport both leading up to and during the 1980 Olympics, Heiden was:

· James E. Sullivan Award (1980)

· UPI International Athlete of the Year (1980)

· United States Olympic Committee Sportsman of the Year (1979 and 1980)

· U.S. Olympic Hall of Fame (1983)

· Speedskating Hall of Fame (1989)

· Winter Olympian of the Century, Associated Press (1999)

· Voted 63rd among the Top 100 Greatest Athletes of the 20th Century, ESPN SportsCenter (1999)

· Won the Oscar Mathisen Award four times in a row from 1977 until 1980. (He is the only skater who has won the award four times)

· Remained at top place of the Adelskalender for an astounding 1,495 days

About the Man Himself

Like many other speed skaters, Heiden trained as a cyclist during the off–season. After he retired from skating, he became one of the leading cyclists in the United States for the better half of a decade. While generating public interest in the sport, he made the 1980 U.S. Olympic cycling road team as an alternate, won the 1985 U.S. Professional Road Cycling Championship, finished first in the Hot Spot Sprints at the 1985 Tour of Italy and, in 1986, was a member of the first U.S. team to compete in the Tour de France.

Unlike many other Olympic and professional athletes, Heiden preferred to remain obscure and chose not to accept many of the endorsement deals he was offered, including a chance to be on the Kellogg's Corn Flakes box. However, he did team up with 7–Eleven because it sponsored the U.S. men's cycling team, Schwinn because they gave the team bicycles and Descent apparel because they manufactured speed skating and cycling suits.

Heiden's endorsement money helped him stay debt–free while he attended medical school at Stanford University in California. He became an orthopedic surgeon and an assistant professor of orthopedic surgery at the University of California, Davis. Heiden was the doctor for the U.S. Speedskating team during the Salt Lake City Olympics in 2002 when he treated Apolo Anton Ohno's cut after the skater's well–known crash. He also served as team doctor for the Sacramento Kings and the Sacramento Monarchs.

Heiden, along with his wife, Karen, and his daughter and son, will relocate from Sacramento to Utah in of the summer of 2006 when he and Dr. Massimo Testa move their medical practices to The Orthopedic Specialty Hospital. As a result of the move, the two doctors will be able to work closely with the national governing organizations of cycling, skiing, speedskating and snowboarding.

10000米14:28.13的成绩。 可能更令人难忘的是10000米决赛前夜，海登熬夜观看了美国奥林匹克曲棍球队对抗苏联队的比赛，结果睡过头了。他不得不跑到速滑赛场参加比赛。尽管晚起床，早饭几乎没吃，就吃了几片面包，海登还是打破了前世界纪录，快了6.20秒，赢得了第五块金牌。包揽五枚金牌后，很快他就退役了。

1980年奥运会前后体育生涯中，海登取得许多令人敬佩的成绩，包括：
· 詹姆斯沙利文奖(1980年)
· UPI 年度国际运动员 (1980年)
· 被美国奥组委评为"年度体育人物" (1979 和1980年)
· 入选美国奥林匹克名人堂 (1983年)
· 速滑名人堂 (1989年)
· 被美联社评为"世纪冬奥运动员"(1999年)
· 被体育运动中心评选为"20世纪100位最伟大运动员第63名"(1999年)
· 1977至1980年连续四次获得奥斯卡·马西森奖 (他是唯一四次获得此奖的滑冰运动员)
· 1495天都保持Adelskalender独占鳌头之势，令人震惊。

关于此人

跟许多速滑运动员一样，海登业余时还参加了自行车训练。结束速滑生涯后，他引领了美国五年的自行车运动。他表现出对体育的广泛兴趣，担当了1980年奥运会自行车公路赛的车队候补选手，赢了1985年美国职业自行车公路冠军赛，1985年环意大利公路自行车赛中，获得了"热点追逐赛"第一名，1986年，他作为美国第一支自行车队队员，参加了环法自行车赛。

与其他奥运会和职业运动员不同，海登更喜欢低调处世，别人邀请他签约一些商业合同，他也不全盘接受，包括有一次上"家乐氏玉米片"包装盒的机会。然而，他与7-11连锁便利店合作，因为能够资助"思汶"美国男子自行车队，提供自行车；为迪森特提供服装，比如生产速滑装和自行车赛服。

海登的背书金帮他免费进入加利福尼亚斯坦福大学医学院读书。他成为整形外科医生，也是加州大学戴维斯分校整形外科副教授。海登担任了美国速滑队队医，2002年盐湖城奥运会曾发生过一次著名的撞击，速滑名将阿波罗·安东·奥诺就是由海登为他做的手术。同时，他也是萨克拉门托帝王队和萨克拉门托天王队的队医。

2006年夏天，海登携带妻子和一儿一女又重新从萨克拉门托搬到了犹他，因为他和医生马西摩·太斯塔把医疗实践转到了整形专科医院。这次搬家可以让两位医生密切联系国家自行车、滑雪、速滑等团体。

Twenty

Bobby Hull

Why He is Among the 50 plus one Greatest Sports Heroes

Bobby Hull became famous as a professional hockey player not only because of his lightning–quick speed in everything from his skating to his backhand shot, but also because he was instrumental in the establishment of the World Hockey Association and to the successful mixing of talented European players into the world of North American professional hockey. He is a member of the Hockey Hall of Fame for a reason, and that reason is, quite simply, that he ranks among the greatest athletes of all time.

On the Way Up

Robert Marvin Hull was born on January 3, 1939 in Pointe Anne, Ontario, Canada and he grew up on a farm near Belleville, about 2 hours away from Toronto. His parents gave him his first pair of skates the Christmas before his fourth birthday and his sisters took him out on the frozen Bay of Quinte to teach him how to skate, later swearing that they could not keep up with him by the end of the day.

Hull quickly made his way up through the minor hockey leagues and was signed by the Chicago Blackhawks, which is why he later dropped out of St. Catherines Collegiate School. The team put him on the Ontario Hockey Association's (OHA) Galt Black Hawks when he was 15 and he played in a few games before the franchise moved him up to the main junior affiliate, the St. Catherines Teepees of the OHA. During the 1956–1957 season, Hull scored 16 points in 13 playoff matches for the Teepees, which was enough to get him shot up to the pros the following year.

Professional Career

Hull made his National Hockey League (NHL) debut at the age of 18 in the 1957–1958 season. That year, he scored 47 points in 70 games and was the runner–up for the Calder Trophy, awarded annually to the league's outstanding rookie. The following year, he scored 50 points, but the 1959–1960 season was when he really began to shine, scoring a league–high of 39 goals and 81 points. Hull was also a very fast skater, having been clocked at 28.3 mph while with the puck and almost 30 mph without it.

Just as the Blackhawks saw a rise in its fan–base as a direct result of the arrival of Hull and his teammate, Stan Mikita, so the team also experienced its own revival. The franchise had not made it to the playoffs in 11 out of the 12 seasons before Hull began playing with them, but he led them all the way to a Stanley Cup at the end of the 1960–1961 season, scoring 14 points in 12 post–season games. The championship was the team's third ever and also the first that they had captured since 1938. They have yet to win another Stanley Cup.

Hull, along with Stan Mikita, became famous for developing the curved hockey stick, which caused the puck to take off at a greater velocity and to move in different ways, similar to a curve

波比·荷尔

他为何入选《50+1位最闪耀的体育巨星》

波比·荷尔能成为举世闻名的职业曲棍球运动员，不仅因为他在冰上闪电般的滑速和反手击球，还因为他为创建世界曲棍球协会立下了汗马功劳，成功引进了才华横溢的欧洲运动健儿，为北美职业曲棍球事业锦上添花。他成为曲棍球名人堂成员的原因也很简单，那就是他是体育史上名列前茅的最伟大运动员之一。

成长之路

1939年1月3日，罗伯特·马文·荷尔出生于加拿大安大略的Pointe Anne，在离多伦多两小时车程的贝而维尔附近农场长大。他的父母在他4岁生日之前的那个圣诞节送给了他第一双溜冰鞋，他姐姐们带他到结冰的昆特湾，教他如何溜冰，这天快过去，他发誓她们会赶不上他。

荷尔很快便从小型曲棍球联盟脱颖而出，并与芝加哥黑鹰队签订合同，这也是他后来为何离开St. Catherines Collegiate School的原因。15岁时，该队让他在安大略曲棍球协会的高特黑鹰队出场比赛，在分会将他转至主要的青少年分会——安大略St. Catherines Teepees of the OHA之前，他还参加过一些比赛。1956–1957赛季，荷尔在13场延长夺标赛中为印第安帐篷队赢得16分，这个成绩足以让他在第二年进入职业生涯。

职业生涯

18岁的荷尔在国家曲棍球联盟的初次登场是1957–1958年的赛季。那一年，他在70场比赛中拿下47分，并获得了哥特纪念奖第二名，此奖每年颁发给联盟杰出新人。次年，他拿下50分，但是1959–1960年的赛季才是他一鸣惊人的时候，创下了联盟最高纪录：39个射门得分，和81分的总分。荷尔滑冰速度极快，曾经创下过带球滑28.3英里/小时的纪录，如果不带球滑，速度高达30英里/小时。

黑鹰队也意识到随着荷尔与队友斯坦·米其塔人气升高，各自球迷也增多，该队自己内部成员就出现了竞争。荷尔效力于分会之前，分会在12次赛季中，有11次都没有参加常规赛季后的夺标决赛，但是荷尔于1960–1961赛季末带领球队直闯斯坦利杯决赛，在12场季后赛中获得14分。该队共获得3次冠军，这次是自从1938年以来的第一次夺冠。他们还要再次赢得斯坦利杯。

荷尔和斯坦·米其塔因开发了打冰球的曲棍而闻名，曲棍能使冰球以更快的速度朝不同方向移动，这与棒球曲球同理。荷尔已有令人敬畏的超强射门能力（他击球速度达

ball in baseball. Hull, who already had an intimidating and powerful shot, (his slap hot was timed at 118.3 mph; his wrist shot at 105 mph; and his backhand shot at 96 mph) was able to use the curved stick to his full advantage, instilling fear into many of the league's goalies.

In 1962, Hull became the third player in NHL history to score 50 goals in a single season. Two years after that, despite missing nine games due to injury, he scored 39 goals and helped the Blackhawks again reach the Stanley Cup finals, which they ended up losing to Montreal. In the 1965–1966 season Hull became one of the first players to score more than 50 goals and set a league record with 54. After he scored his monumental 51st goal, the fans honored him with a 7–minute standing ovation.

Hull broke his own record again when he scored 58 goals during the 1968–1969 season. And in 1972, he played the best post–season of his entire career, scoring 11 goals and 25 points in 18 games. He carried the Blackhawks once again to the Stanley Cup finals, but they lost to the Montreal Canadiens after letting their lead slip away from them late in the seventh game. Hull had reached the 50–goal mark for the fifth time that season and many fans and experts of the sport raved that he was playing the most well rounded hockey of his career.

In an unexpected twist, Hull jumped to the newly formed World Hockey Association (WHA) in 1972 to play for the Winnipeg Jets. He made big news several months later by signing a 10–year $2.75 million contract with a $1 million signing bonus, making it the first $1 million contract in the history of the game. Hull's leap from the NHL to the WHA resulted in higher salaries for professional hockey players in general and legitimized the NHL's new rival. Because the NHL saw him as a traitor, they did not allow him to participate on behalf of Canada in the 1972 Summit Series against the Soviet Union. By the time Hull had moved over to the WHA, he had scored 604 goals, coming in second as the NHL's all–time scorer.

While with the Jets, he earned the nickname Golden Jet and became part of one of the best forward lines worldwide when he teamed up with Anders Hedberg and Ulf Nilsson, who were both from Sweden. Together, the three set numerous scoring records and during his first 4 years with the Jets, Hull scored a total of 234 goals. Once again he broke the professional record for most goals in a single season with 77 in 1975. Earlier that season, he finally got the opportunity to play against the Soviet Union during the second Canada–USSR series, even though the WHA team lost 4 games to 1, with three ties.

Hull was one of the driving forces behind the Jets when they won the Avco Cup in 1976 and 1978–1979. Before the 1976–1977 season, he was selected to play for the Canadian team in the first ever Canada Cup tournament, which showcased the best hockey players from all over the world. Hull contributed greatly to Canada's eventual victory.

In 1979, the WHA collapsed, which resulted in the Jets joining the NHL. Hull played with the team for 18 games during the 1979–1980 season before being traded to the Hartford Whalers. He retired at the end of that season after scoring a career total of 610 goals in 1,063 regular–season games.

118.3英里/小时；腕射达105英里/小时；反手速度达96英里/小时），使用曲棍可以使他的优点全面施展，对联盟的守门员造成了不小的威慑力。

1962年，荷尔单赛季射门得分50次，成为国家曲棍球联盟有史以来的第三高手。两年后，尽管由于受伤错过9次比赛，他仍然创下了39次射门得分，帮助黑鹰队再次闯进斯坦利杯决赛，最终却输给了蒙特利尔队。1965-1966年赛季，荷尔成为首次射门得分超过50个的高手之一，创造了54次射门得分的联盟纪录。在他第51次射门得分的历史时刻，球迷起立为他喝彩长达7分钟。

1968-1969年赛季，荷尔以58次射门得分打破了自己创下的纪录。1972年，他创造了整个职业生涯中季后赛的最佳成绩，11次射门得分，18场比赛得分25分。他再一次率领黑鹰队进入斯坦利杯决赛，但是在第七场比赛快结束时，他们最前面的队员却滑倒到一边，最终输给了蒙特利尔加拿大人队。这个赛季中荷尔第五次获得他第50个射门得分，许多球迷和体育专家称赞这是他职业生涯中最完美的射门。

1972年的一次出乎意料的转机，让荷尔转到了新成立的世界曲棍球协会，为温尼伯喷射机队效力。几个月后，一个特大新闻不胫而走：他签订了10年275万美元的合同，附加100万美元奖金，也是曲棍球运动史上第一份签订100万奖金的合同。荷尔从国家曲棍球联盟跳槽至世界曲棍球协会，比其他职业曲棍球运动员拿到更多薪水，正式成为国家曲棍球联盟的新对手。国家曲棍球联盟把他当做叛徒，并禁止他代表加拿大队参加1972年对抗苏联队的高级联赛。那时，荷尔已经转到世界曲棍球协会，总共604次射门得分，位居第二，与国家曲棍球最高纪录持平。

在为喷射机队效力时，他有个昵称叫"金喷射机"，他与两位瑞典运动员安德斯·海德贝格和沃夫·尼尔森合作时，成为全球最佳锋线组合。他们三个一起创造了无数得分纪录，荷尔在喷射机队前四年中，总共234次射门得分。1975年他创下了77次射门得分的纪录，再次打破了单赛季职业比赛进球纪录。这个赛季早期，他获得了第二届加拿大对阵苏联的机会，虽然世界曲棍球协会的球队最后输了四场，赢了一场，三场平局。

1976年、1978-1979年，喷射机队赢得了Avco Cup杯，荷尔功不可没。1976-1977年赛季之前，他入选加拿大队，参加唯一一次加拿大杯锦标赛，来自全球的最出色曲棍球运动员都会在比赛中亮相。荷尔为加拿大队最终获胜立下了汗马功劳。

1979年，世界曲棍球协会解散，喷射机队只好加入国家曲棍球联盟。1979-1980赛季，荷尔为球队效力参加了18次比赛，之后他转至哈佛捕鲸人。赛季结束时，他宣布退役，整个职业生涯的1063次常规赛中共有610次射门得分。

Twenty-one

Duke Kahanamoku

Why He is Among the 50 plus one Greatest Sports Heroes

Duke Kahanamoku won six medals and set several world records during his successful Olympic swimming career. Even more so than his swimming medals, Kahanamoku is best known for the gigantic strides that he made in another aquatic sport: surfing. Though he surfed during an era when the sport was not yet a competitive one, he is best known by athletes and fans worldwide as the father of modern surfing–in part because of his skills and because he traveled the world teaching others about Hawaii's secret sport. To be called the father of a sport is why the Big Kahuna is recognized as a 50 plus one greatest sports heroes.

On the Way Up

Duke Paoa Kahinu Mokoe Hulikohola Kahanamoku was born on August 24,1890 in Honolulu, Hawaii. Most people knew him simply as Duke or The Duke, although his close island friends called him Paoa. He has also been called Hawaiian Ambassador of Aloha and The Big Kahuna. Although many assume that Kahanamoku was a real duke because of his name, this was not the case. In actuality, he was named after his father, who, like some other boys at that time, had been named after the Duke of Edinburgh following an official visit to Hawaii.

Kahanamoku, whose father was a policeman, came from one of the last traditional Hawaiian families. Following ancient custom, his father and uncle baptized him when he was a young boy by taking him out in an outrigger canoe and throwing him into the ocean surf. Kahanamoku, along with his sister and five brothers, was encouraged to enjoy the water and to never be afraid of it. Thus began a lifetime affair between Kahanamoku and the sports of canoeing, swimming and surfing.

When he was young, Kahanamoku preferred using a traditional surfboard, constructed to look and perform like the ancient Hawaiian olo boards. The 16–foot, 114–pound board was made of koa tree wood and did not have a skeg (the fin on the rear bottom of the surfboard used for steering and stability). Later in his career, Kahanamoku started using smaller surfboards, but he preferred boards that were made of wood.

In 1910, top Australian swimmers visited Hawaii and Kahanamoku took the opportunity to study their skillful maneuvers in order to improve his own swimming abilities. He perfected his stoke and gained speed by developing the flutter kick in place of the scissor kick. He called it The Hawaiian Crawl–it later became known as The American Crawl. Soon, others began to notice the immense improvements in Kahanamoku's swimming. Bill Rawlins, an island attorney tried to put the spotlight on Kahanamoku's talent, but in order to obtain official sanction for swimming records, an athlete had to be a member of a recognized club. So, in 1911, Kahanamoku and his friends started their own club, Hui Nalu (Club of the Waves) and sent in the times from his performance at an amateur swim meet on August 11th of that year in Honolulu Harbor. With 55.4 seconds, Duke had broken the existing 90–meter freestyle world record by 4.6 seconds and had

杜克·卡哈纳莫库

杜克·卡哈纳莫库在他成功的奥运会游泳运动生涯中，获得过6枚奖牌，并创造了几项世界纪录。除了游泳运动获得奖牌外，卡哈纳莫库最著名的是他发明的另一项大步驰骋于水上的运动：冲浪。虽然那个时代冲浪还不是比赛运动，但是全世界的运动员和运动迷们把他称作"现代冲浪之父"，此称号得来原因有二，一是他精湛的技术，二是他周游世界，教别人这个夏威夷神奇运动。被称作运动之父，恰能说明"大卡哈纳"为何在50+1位最闪耀的体育巨星榜上有名。

成长之路

1890年8月24日，杜克·卡哈纳莫库出生于夏威夷火奴鲁鲁。大多数人只知道他叫杜克或者"公爵"，虽然他的亲密岛友们叫他Paoa。别人还把他叫做"阿罗哈夏威夷大使"或者"大卡哈纳"。由于他名字的缘故，有些人以为卡哈纳莫库真的是公爵，然而他并非公爵。实际上，他是以父亲的名字命名，他父亲和当时其他男孩一样，在爱丁堡公爵访问夏威夷之后，都用了这个名字。

卡哈纳莫库的父亲是警察，卡哈纳莫库出生于最后一个传统夏威夷家庭。按照古代风俗，他的父亲和叔叔把小卡哈纳莫库带到独木舟上进行洗礼仪式，把他扔进海浪里。卡哈纳莫库和他的姐姐还有五个兄弟，都被鼓励要喜欢水而不是惧怕水。就这样，卡哈纳莫库这一生开始与船只、游泳和冲浪打交道。

卡哈纳莫库年轻时，更喜欢用传统冲浪板，它的构造看上去和用起来都像古代夏威夷欧罗板。这种16英尺，114磅重的板是由柯亚树木制成，没有尾鳍(装在冲浪板底用来控制方向和稳定性的)。后来，卡哈纳莫库开始用小一点的冲浪板，但是他比较喜欢木制的。

1910年，澳大利亚名列前茅的游泳运动员访问夏威夷，卡哈纳莫库抓住机会学习他们的精湛技术，来提高自己的游泳技能。他不断完善泳式，用浅打水代替剪式打腿动作来提高速度。他称之为"夏威夷爬泳"，很快便以"美国爬泳"著称。不久，大家开始注意到卡哈纳莫库的游泳技术取得长足进步。当地律师比尔·罗林斯想让卡哈纳莫库的才能闻名于世，但是如果要使游泳纪录获得正式认可，运动员必须是正式俱乐部成员。因此，1911年，卡哈纳莫库和他的朋友成立了自己的俱乐部，名叫Hui Nalu(波浪俱乐部)，并参加了8月11日火奴鲁鲁港举办的业余游泳运动会的几项赛事。杜克90米自由泳的成绩是55.4秒，以4.6秒的优势打破了世界纪录，还打破了200米自由泳的世界纪录，并且与46米自由泳纪录持平。

also broken the 200–meter freestyle record and tied the 46–meter freestyle record. The Amateur Athletic Union (AAU) was in such a state of shock by Kahanamoku's record–breaking times that they would refuse to recognize his accomplishments until years after the fact.

After the AAU's disappointing rejection, Kahanamoku's supporters decided that they would just have to raise funds in order to send him and another Hawaiian swimmer to travel to the U.S. mainland to compete. In 1912, Kahanamoku qualified for the U.S. Olympic swimming team after breaking the record for the 200–meter freestyle in his trial heat for the 4 x 200–meter relay.

Professional Career

Kahanamoku's six –medal Olympic career started with the 1912 Games in Stockholm, Sweden. Almost 22–years old, he won a gold medal and set a world record in the 100–meter freestyle and a team silver medal in the 200–meter relay. Eight years later, he traveled to Antwerp, Belgium to compete in the 1920 Olympics. There, he captured another gold medal and, finishing in 60.4 seconds, he broke his own world record in the 100–meter freestyle. That year, he also won a team gold medal and set a world record in the 4 x 100–meter freestyle relay. In 1924, Kahanamoku took home a silver medal for the 100–meter freestyle at the Paris, France Olympic Games and, at the Los Angeles Olympics in 1932, he won a bronze medal as an alternate on the men's water polo team.

In between his Olympic performances, Kahanamoku traveled to Australia, the United States and other countries to give swimming and surfing exhibitions. The 1916 Olympics were canceled due to World War I, and Kahanamoku went to work with the American Red Cross in order to train volunteers in the basics of water lifesaving. He also conducted a nationwide tour with a team of American watersport champions in an effort to raise money for the Red Cross. Kahanamoku made it clear that, in doing this, he had an ulterior motive: he wanted to demonstrate the art of surfing at any beach that had an appropriate amount of surf. He worked hard in trying to achieve this goal, especially on the East Coast and particularly in New Jersey.

On June 14, 1925, Kahanamoku was living in Newport Beach, California when he and a group of other surfers rescued 12 out of 29 men from a fishing boat that had flipped over in heavy surf while trying to enter the harbor. Kahanamoku was able to save eight of the 12 fishermen single–handedly, while two other surfers saved the remaining four. Due to his efficient and quick use of a surfboard, many lifeguards today keep rescue surfboards on hand.

About the Man Himself

While living in California, Kahanamoku began a Hollywood career as an extra and character actor in about 30 silent and talkie films with stars the likes of John Wayne. These films include Lord Jim in 1925, the Mascot serial, *The Isle of Sunken Gold* in 1927 and *Mister Roberts* in 1955.

After his final Olympics in 1932, Kahanamoku ran a Union Oil Company gas station in Waikiki and another in Honolulu for a couple of years and then, in 1936, he was elected Sheriff for the City and County of Honolulu. The position was mainly a ceremonial one. After serving as Sheriff for 28 years, Kahanamoku retired and was named the Official Greeter for Honolulu, a position that called on him to welcome dignitaries and celebrities.

Since he was a young boy, anyone who met him could see that he embodied Hawaii's spirit of aloha. The following message was printed on the back of his personal business card:

In Hawaii we greet friends, loved ones or strangers with Aloha, which means with love. Aloha is the key word to the universal spirit of real hospitality. Try meeting or leaving people with Aloha.

业余体育联合会对于卡哈纳莫库打破纪录的成绩感到震惊，尽管取得了成就，但此后他们一直不承认他的成绩。

业余体育联合会令人失望的举动让卡哈纳莫库的支持者们决定筹集资金，把他和另一名夏威夷游泳运动员送到美国大陆去比赛。1912年，卡哈纳莫库在4×200米接力赛预赛中打破了200米自由泳纪录之后，被批准加入美国奥林匹克游泳队。

职业生涯

卡哈纳莫库六次奥运会奖牌的职业生涯始于1912年在瑞典斯德哥尔摩举办的奥运会。22岁左右，他就获得了100米自由泳冠军并打破了世界纪录，他的游泳队还获得200米接力赛亚军。八年后，他参加了比利时安特卫普奥运会。他以60.4秒的成绩获得100米自由泳金牌，并打破了自己创造的世界纪录。这一年，他们队也赢得了冠军，并创下了4×100米接力赛的世界纪录。1924年法国巴黎举办的奥运会上，卡哈纳莫库获得100米自由泳亚军，1932年洛杉矶奥运会中，他作为候补队员参加了男子水球比赛，为该队赢得一枚铜牌。

在奥运会期间，卡哈纳莫库去了澳大利亚、美国和其他国家，进行游泳和冲浪表演。

由于第一次世界大战，1916年奥运会被取消，卡哈纳莫库加入美国红十字会工作，教志愿者基本的水上救生。他还组织了全国巡回活动，与一群奥运会水上运动冠军得主们一起为红十字会筹款。卡哈纳莫库此举显然是别有用心的：他想证明冲浪运动在任何海边都可获得一席之地。他为实现这个目标而努力工作，尤其在东海岸和新泽西地区。

1925年6月14日，卡哈纳莫库正住在加利福尼亚的纽波特海滩，那天有一艘渔船正要进入港湾，却被一个大浪突然掀翻，他与另几名冲浪运动员救下了29人中的12人。卡哈纳莫库单枪匹马成功救出12个渔民中的8人，另两名冲浪运动员救下了其余4人。由于他及时有效的使用冲浪板，如今许多救生员身边都带着冲浪救生板。

关于此人

住在加州时，卡哈纳莫库开始了好莱坞电影生涯，他与约翰·韦恩一样作为临时或性格演员，出演了约30部无声和有声电影。电影包括1925年的《吉姆老爷》、1927年的《沉没金岛》和1955年的《罗伯茨先生》。

1932年最后一次参加奥运会后，卡哈纳莫库在威基基和火奴鲁鲁都经营着联合石油公司的加油站，几年后，他于1936年被选为火奴鲁鲁城县治安长官。这只是个名誉职位。当了28年的治安长官后，卡哈纳莫库退役，并命名为火奴鲁鲁官方迎宾员，请他来接待贵宾和名人。

自从少年时代，人们就能看见他体现着夏威夷"阿罗哈"精神。以下是印在他的商业名片反面的一段话：

在夏威夷我们本着"阿罗哈"爱的精神，问候朋友、爱人或者陌生人。"阿罗哈"是全世界热情好客精神的关键词。试着用"阿罗哈"去迎接人们或者与人分别。你将被他们所做

You will be surprised by their reaction. I believe it, and it is my creed. Aloha to you.

His quiet and caring strength combined with his athletic accomplishments made Kahanamoku one of the most famed and adored people in the history of Hawaii.

Kahanamoku died on January 22, 1968, leaving behind Nadine, his wife of 27 years. However, his legend continues through the work of the Outrigger Duke Kahanamoku Foundation, established in February of 1986. The foundation is a result of two preceding foundations: the Duke Kahanamoku Foundation and the Outrigger Foundation. The first foundation was formed in 1963 by Kahanamoku's friends with the goal of immortalizing his name and helping young people in areas of swimming and surfing. The second foundation was established in 1981 by the Outrigger Canoe Club to make a formal program of grants for sports' participants.

The goals of the Outrigger Duke Kahanamoku Foundation is to remember Kahanamoku by helping Hawaiian athletes participate in athletic competitions and to further athletes' educations in the hopes that they will follow in the footsteps of Kahanamoku and become upstanding, productive people.

Kahanamoku received various honors both during and after his living years. He was the first athlete ever to be inducted into both the Swimming Hall of Fame and the Surfing Hall of Fame. In 1999, he was named the Century's Most Influential Surfer by *Surfer* magazine, which also placed his picture on the cover of its annual collector's edition. The Duke Kahanamoku Invitational Surfing Championship and numerous other events are held at Sunset Beach in Oahu, Hawaii. Showcasing his major influence on surfing, one of Kahanamoku's early surfboards, with his name across the bow, is on exhibit at the Bishop Museum in Honolulu.

Kahanamoku is honored in Australia as well. The board he used on that special day in 1914 is held by the Freshwater Surf Club and there is also a statue of him on the headland at Freshwater Beach. He is recognized in the Citizens Savings Hall of Fame Athletic Museum, and other museums and memorials worldwide, including California, Florida and New York.

With his successful and long-running Olympic career, his quiet ownership of the beginnings of modern surfing and his ambassadorship of aloha, Duke Kahanamoku will forever live in the hearts of many.

出的反应而惊讶。我相信它,而且它是我的信念。向你致以"阿罗哈"的问候。

卡哈纳莫库默默地体现着他的爱心,他的体育成就连同关爱精神,让他成为夏威夷历史上最负盛名、最受崇拜的名人之一。

卡哈纳莫库于1968年1月22日逝世,离开了与他携手共度27载的妻子娜丁。然而,他的传奇故事通过1986年2月成立的奥瑞格杜克·卡哈纳莫库基金会仍然继续着。这个基金会归结于先前的两个基金会:杜克·卡哈纳莫库基金会和奥瑞格基金会。第一个是1963年卡哈纳莫库的朋友们建立的,旨在纪念他并帮助在游泳和冲浪运动领域的年轻人们。第二个是在1981年由奥瑞格独木舟俱乐部成立的,旨在建立正规活动以承认体育参赛者的合法性。

奥瑞格杜克·卡哈纳莫库基金会目的是通过帮助夏威夷运动员们参加比赛,来纪念卡哈纳莫库,并希望进一步教育运动员沿着卡哈纳莫库的足迹,把自己培养成为正直而多才的人。

卡哈纳莫库生前及身后都获得了无数荣誉。他是史上第一个同时入选游泳运动名人堂和冲浪运动名人堂的运动员。1999年,他被《冲浪》杂志评为"世纪最具影响力冲浪运动员",并将他的照片登上了年度收藏版的封面。杜克·卡哈纳莫库冲浪冠军邀请赛和其他许多赛事纷纷在夏威夷瓦胡岛夕阳海滨举办。为了展示卡哈纳莫库为冲浪运动带来的重大影响,他早期的带有姓名的弓形冲浪板陈列在火奴鲁鲁主教博物馆里。

卡哈纳莫库在澳大利亚同样广受尊重。1914年他使用过的冲浪板陈列在淡水冲浪俱乐部里,在淡水海滩角还有他的一尊塑像。他入选了Citizens Savings体育名人堂博物馆,还被选入加利福尼亚、佛罗里达和纽约的博物馆和纪念馆。

卡哈纳莫库拥有成功而漫长的奥林匹克生涯,他是现代冲浪运动的创始人,是"阿罗哈"精神的传播大使,这些贡献将永远铭记在人们心中。

Twenty-Two

Karch Kiraly

Why He is Among the 50 plus one Greatest Sports Heroes

Karch Kiraly has been dubbed the Michael Jordan of volleyball. In the course of his career, he has collected three Olympic gold medals, more tournament wins than any other volleyballer, and more than $3 million in earnings (again a record). This would be remarkable enough, but his gold medals were won in both the indoor and outdoor versions of the sport (the only American to win both). Add to this the fact that his career spans 4 decades, that he has won at least one tournament in 24 of 27 seasons played, and that he has continued playing volleyball, successfully, into his mid–40s, and it is clear that Kiraly, generally regarded as the greatest player of the 20th century–a claim confirmed by the International Volleyball Federation (FIVB)–merits a place in the list of the world's greatest athletes.

On the Way Up

Charles Frederick (Karch) Kiraly was born on November 3, 1960 in Jackson, Michigan–his parents having fled to the USA from Hungary after the failed 1956 revolution. The family eventually settled in Santa Barbara, California. Kiraly began playing volleyball at age six, learning the game from his father, László, who had played the sport in the Hungarian Junior National team. By the time the boy was 11, father and son were entering beach volleyball competitions as partners. Kiraly earned his A and AA rating on the beach at 15, and his AAA rating at 17.

At Santa Barbara High school, he led the volleyball team to an undefeated senior season and the Southern California Championships. He was named the high school's MVP. During his school years, he also played for the U.S. Junior National team, whom he helped win the Paci.c Rim Tournament in 1978 and 1979, again as MVP.

After high school, Kiraly attended UCLA, where he led the Bruins to three national titles in 1979, 1981, and 1982, including two undefeated seasons (the team's record was 123–5 in his 4 years at the school). At UCLA he was coached by Hall of Famer Al Scales, he also made his first appearances for the Senior National Team. In 1983, Kiraly gained a Bachelor's Degree in Pre-Med, Biochemistry. Nine years later, he was inducted into the UCLA Hall of Fame, and his jersey was retired.

Professional Career

Upon leaving college, Kiraly became a fixture of the U.S. National Team throughout the 1980s as a combination setter/hitter. In 1984 and 1988, he was pivotal in Team USA's Olympic gold medal victory. He was the youngest player in the 1984 team, where he also won the FIVB sportsmanship award. After the 1984 Olympics, he went on to complete volleyball's triple crown with the 1985 World Cup (MVP) and the 1986 World Championships. To round it all off, he was the team captain and MVP in the 1988 Olympic victory.

Kiraly retired from the national team after the 1988 Olympics. He moved to Italy, where he

卡奇·基拉伊

他为何入选《50+1位最闪耀的体育巨星》

卡奇·基拉伊拥有排球界迈克尔·乔丹之美誉。在他的职业生涯中,他将3枚奥运金牌揽入囊中,赢得了比其他排球运动员都多的锦标赛冠军,赚了300多万美元(又是一项纪录)。除了这些荣誉外,他还获得了室内室外比赛的双料冠军(唯一赢得两枚金牌的美国人)。40载的运动生涯中,他在27个赛季的24次比赛中至少赢得一次锦标赛,他继续打排球,战绩斐然,直到40岁以后。显而易见,被国际排联誉为"20世纪最伟大球员"的基拉伊在世界50+1位最闪耀的体育巨星中拥有一席之地。

成长之路

1960年11月3日,卡奇·基拉伊出生于密歇根州杰克逊县——他的父母在1956年革命失败后从匈牙利逃亡至美国。他们家终于在加州圣塔巴巴拉定居。基拉伊六岁开始打排球,向他父亲拉兹罗讨教,他父亲曾效力于匈牙利国家青年队。基拉伊11岁时,父子俩作为搭档一起参加了沙滩排球赛。15岁时,基拉伊就赢得了沙滩排球A、AA等级,17岁时获得AAA等级。

就读于圣塔巴巴拉高中时,他带领球队闯入战无不胜的第三个赛季,并赢得南部加州冠军。他被誉为高中最具价值球员。在高中期间,他也为美国青年国家队效力,帮助该队赢得1978年和1979年泛太平洋锦标赛冠军,再次被评为最具价值球员。

高中毕业后,基拉伊进入加州大学洛杉矶分校,分别于1979年、1981年和1982年为熊队赢得三次全国冠军头衔,包括两次卫冕赛季(该队在他就读的四年中获得123胜5负的成绩)。在加州大学洛杉矶分校时,他的教练是入选名人堂的阿尔·斯盖尔,并首次亮相于国家青年队。1983年,基拉伊获得生物化学医学预科的学士学位。九年后,他入选加州大学洛杉矶分校名人堂,他的队服也随之退役。

职业生涯

大学毕业时,基拉伊在整个80年代一直拥有美国国家队二传手和扣球手的双重身份。1984年和1988年,他是美国队赢得奥运金牌的中流砥柱。他是1984年国家队中最年轻的运动员,并获得国际排联运动精神奖。1984年奥运会后,他继续争夺三连冠的后两个桂冠,即1985年的世界杯(获得最具价值球员称号)及1986年世界冠军。让结局更为圆满的是,他在1988年夺冠的奥运会中担当了国家队队长,并成为最具价值球员。

1988年奥运会后,基拉伊退出国家队。他侨居意大利,为Il Messaggero of Ravenna队效

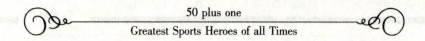
played for Il Messaggero of Ravenna (1990–1992), who won the 1991 World Championship (with Kiraly again MVP). Upon returning to the U.S., he started playing beach volleyball full–time, sporting his trademark pink cap, which he has worn in every competition since 1992. Over the years, he has amassed a record 148 professional beach volleyball titles, smashing the previous record of 139 (in the process, he has made it to at least the semi.nals in more than 80 percent of the tournaments that he has entered). At the age of 36, Kiraly partnered with Kent Steffes to win the inaugural Olympic Games beach volleyball tournament in 1996 at Atlanta.

Even in his mid–40's Kiraly continues to compete against far younger players on the Beach Volleyball circuit. He is the oldest pro player to win a Pro Beach tournament (at 41, 42, 43 and 44 years of age), and the oldest to compete at the highest level of the sport.

Since partnering with Mike Lambert, his career has undergone a renaissance. The two were named the 2004 AVP Team of the Year after capturing three titles. His most recent win was in August 2005, where he and Lambert won the AVP tournament in Huntington Beach, California (win number 148). His stats for 2005 show just how much of a force he still is, finishing fourth on the tour in both kills and digs. In 2006, he began partnering with Larry Witt.

To what can we attribute this extraordinary success? According to Kiraly, all that he has tried to do is be a well–rounded, consistent player. He is renowned for his overall volleyball skill and intense concentration, displaying a legendary ability to shut out the world during games. He is hard–driven and fiercely competitive, but never displays petty or mean–spirited behavior. He has an uncanny ability to make impossible plays possible, and turn a match to his team's advantage. Of course, volleyball is a team game, and Kiraly's complete dedication to playing superb volleyball has always proved to be an inspiration to his teammates who, looking to him as an example, have been encouraged to perform at their best.

Kiraly was inducted into the Volleyball Hall of Fame in 2001. The many other accolades that he has won during his long and storied career include:

Beach
- AVP Best Offensive Player (1990, 1993, 1994)
- AVP Most Valuable Player (1990, 1992–1995, 1998)
- AVP Sportsman of the Year (1995, 1997, 1998)
- Olympic Gold Medal (1996)
- AVP Miller Lite Cup Champion (1996)
- AVP Comeback Player of the Year (1997)
- King of the Beach (1997)
- AVP Most Inspirational (1998)
- AVP Sportsman of the Year (1999)
- AVP Most Inspirational (1999)
- AVP Most Valuable Player (1999)
- AVP Best Defensive Player (2002)
- AVP Special Achievement (2002)

Indoor
- MVP State (CIF) (1978)
- MVP Paci.c Rim Tournament (1979)
- U.S. Junior National Team (1977–1979)

力(1990-1992年),该队赢得1991年世界冠军(基拉伊再次获得"最具价值球员"之荣誉)。重返美国时,他成为全职沙滩排球队员,从此戴着他那标志性的粉色球帽驰骋于每一个球场,直到1992年。 这些年来,他创下了参加148次职业沙滩排球赛的纪录,超过了之前139次比赛的纪录(其中,他参加的锦标赛中至少有80%是进入半决赛的)。36岁时,基拉伊在1996年亚特兰大奥运会沙滩排球锦标赛上与肯特·斯特福携手,夺得首次冠军。

即使步入四十岁后,基拉伊仍然在沙滩排球巡回赛中与比自己年轻得多的选手们较量。他是赢得职业沙滩锦标赛的最年长的职业球员(41岁、42岁、43岁和44岁时),也是参加最高级别体育赛事的最年长运动员。

自从与迈克·兰博合作以来,他的事业再次如日中天。他俩将三次桂冠揽入囊中后,被誉为"2004年度职业沙滩排球队"。最近的一次胜利是在2005年8月,他与兰博在加州亨廷顿海滩赢得了职业沙滩排球锦标赛(第148次胜利)。2005年的亮相向世人显示了他还有多少力量,最终在巡回赛的kills and digs中位居第四。2006年,他开始与搭档莱瑞·惠特合作。

什么能够解释这次非凡的胜利?根据基拉伊自己所言,他所能做到的就是努力成为一名完美而坚毅的运动员。他以全面精湛的球技和聚精会神的态度而闻名,向世界展示了他那传奇般的能力。他具有超常的能力,可以使不可能胜利的比赛变成可能,能使球队在一场比赛中发挥优势、转败为胜。当然,排球是一种团队比赛,基拉伊竭尽所能奉献最佳水平,这也使他队友深受鼓舞,他们会以他为榜样,发挥自己最佳水平。

2001年基拉伊入选排球名人堂。在漫长而著名的职业生涯中,他还荣获其他表彰,包括:

沙滩
- 职业沙滩排球赛最佳进攻队员 (1990, 1993, 1994)
- 职业沙滩排球赛最具价值球员 (1990, 1992–1995, 1998)
- 职业沙滩排球赛年度体育人物 (1995, 1997, 1998)
- 奥运会金牌 (1996)
- 职业沙滩排球赛Miller Lite 冠军杯 (1996)
- 职业沙滩排球赛年度最佳复出运动员 (1997)
- 沙滩之王 (1997)
- 职业沙滩排球赛最励志奖 (1998)
- 职业沙滩排球赛年度体育人物(1999)
- 职业沙滩排球赛最励志奖(1999)
- 职业沙滩排球赛最具价值球员(1999)
- 职业沙滩排球赛最佳防守队员(2002)
- 职业沙滩排球赛特殊成就奖(2002)

室内
- 最具价值球员 (CIF) (1978)
- 泛太平洋锦标赛最具价值球员 (1979)
- 美国国家青年队 (1977–1979)

- NORCECA Championships (Silver) (1981)
- MVP USVBA National Tournament (1982)
- MVP World Championship (1982)
- NORCECA (Gold) (1983)
- Olympic Gold Medal (1984)
- World Cup (Gold) (1985)
- NORCECA Championships (Gold) (1985)
- World Championships (Gold) (1986)
- Pan American Games (Gold) (1987)
- NORCECA Championship (Silver) (1987)
- Savin Cup (Gold).(1987)
- Olympic Gold Medal (1988)
- Club World Championship (1991)

About the Man Himself

Kiraly resides in San Clemente, California with his wife, Janna, and two sons, Kristian and Kory. He is an accomplished author, and acts as a contributing editor to several volleyball publications. When not playing, Kiraly also serves as a color commentator on TV. His hobbies include spending time with his family, camping and photography. Among his favorite athletes are Al Oerter and Carl Lewis—two superlative athletes who won gold medals in four consecutive Olympics and exemplify greatness over time. We can certainly extend such sustained greatness to Karch Kiraly, who by rights should be called not the Michael Jordan of volleyball, but the Karch Kiraly of volleyball—which is praise enough, indeed.

- 中北美以及加勒比排球协会冠军赛 (亚军) (1981)
- USVBA 国家锦标赛最具价值球员 (1982)
- 世界冠军赛最具价值球员 (1982)
- 中北美以及加勒比排球协会 (冠军) (1983)
- 奥运会金牌 (1984)
- 世界杯(金牌) (1985)
- 中北美以及加勒比排球协会冠军赛 (金牌) (1985)
- 世界冠军赛 (金牌) (1986)
- 泛美运动会(金牌) (1987)
- 中北美以及加勒比排球协会冠军赛 (亚军) (1987)
- Savin杯 (冠军)(1987)
- 奥运会金牌 (1988)
- 俱乐部世界冠军杯 (1991)

关于此人

基拉伊与妻子佳娜和两个儿子克里斯第安、科瑞定居至圣瑰市。他是个极有造诣的作家,也是个极有建树的排球出版物编辑。不再参赛时,基拉伊还担任电视解说员。他喜爱和家人共度时光,爱好野营、摄影。他最喜欢的运动员是阿尔·奥特和卡尔·刘易斯——这两位超级运动员曾4次蝉联奥运冠军,是世世代代的伟人榜样。我们当然可以把这种伟大扩大到卡奇·基拉伊身上,他不应被叫做"排球界的迈克尔·乔丹",而理应被誉为"排球界的卡奇·基拉伊"——实为荣耀之至。

Twenty-Three

Vince Lombardi

Why He is Among the 50 plus one Greatest Sports Heroes

During his coaching career, Vince Lombardi led his pro football team to six division titles, five NFL championships and two Super Bowl victories. His tremendous success made him so popular that Richard Nixon is said to have considered him as a running mate for the 1968 presidential election before realizing that he was a Kennedy Democrat. Lombardi's success has also made him a member of several sports halls of fame and has caused the renaming of the Super Bowl trophy in his honor. A man who receives such accolades must be included among sports histories finest.

On the Way Up

Vincent Thomas Lombardi was born on June 11, 1913 in Brooklyn, New York. He was the oldest of Henry and Matilda's five children and was raised in the Sheepshead Bay area of southern Brooklyn. He attended a preparatory seminary for 2 years before transferring to St. Francis Preparatory High School, where he was a standout fullback on the football team.

Lombardi accepted a scholarship in 1933 to Fordham University in New York City. After playing on the freshman football team his first year, he was brought up to play guard on the varsity team by Coach "Sleepy" Jim Crowley. The offensive line that Lombardi joined was dubbed the Seven Blocks of Granite and it contributed greatly to the team's fantastic run of 25 straight wins, not allowing the opposing teams to score a single point on several occasions. Lombardi graduated cum laude from Fordham in 1937 with a business major.

Following graduation, Lombardi worked at a .nance company and played semipro football with the Wilmington Clippers of Delaware while also attending night classes at Fordham's law school. This lasted for 2 years until, in 1939; he was offered a teaching and coaching job at St. Cecilia High School in Englewood, New Jersey. Lombardi taught algebra, chemistry, Latin and physics and coached thebaseball, basketball and football teams as well.

In 1940, Lombardi married Marie Planitz, and he eventually left the high school in 1947 to coach Fordham's freshman football team for a year. The next year, he served as an assistant coach for the varsity team. In 1949, Lombardi accepted an offer to manage the varsity defensive line for the United States Military Academy of West Point. He worked long hours with Coach Earl "Colonel Red" Blaik, who taught him even more about being an effective leader, including such strategies as employing only clear-cut plays, holding out for perfect execution and behaving respectfully on the field.

Professional Career

Lombardi accepted an assistant coaching offer with the New York Giants in 1954, thus beginning his soon-to-be legendary career as a professional football coach. He was in charge of the team's offensive strategy, and by his third season, the Giants had gone from scoring the lowest

文斯·隆巴迪

他为何入选《50+1位最闪耀的体育巨星》

在文斯·隆巴迪的职业橄榄球教练生涯中,他带领球队赢得6个分区赛头衔,5个美国职业橄榄球大联盟冠军和两个"超级碗"。巨大的成功使他大受欢迎,据说理查德·尼克松认为他是自己1968年美国总统竞选伙伴,但是后来得知他是肯尼迪民主党派的支持者。由于隆巴迪战果累累,他入选了不少体育名人堂,并以他的名义重设了超级碗隆巴迪奖杯。拥有这么多荣誉的人理应在体育名人榜上有名。

成长之路

1913年6月11日,文斯·托马斯·隆巴迪出生于纽约布鲁克林。他的父亲亨利和母亲马蒂尔娜共有5个孩子,他排行老大,生长于布鲁克林南部的羊头湾小区。他先在一所预科学校就读两年,随后进入圣弗朗西斯预备高中,并担任橄榄球队出色的进攻后卫。

1933年隆巴迪获得奖学金,就读于纽约市的福德汉姆大学。参加了第一年的新生橄榄球队后,他被教练吉姆·克罗利培养成为校队后卫。隆巴迪加入的攻击线是著名的"七座岩队"(Seven Blocks of Granite),它为该队25次蝉联冠军立下了汗马功劳,好多次对手都无机可乘、得不到一分。1937年,隆巴迪以优等学业成绩毕业于福德汉姆大学,获得商务专业学位。

大学毕业后,隆巴迪在一家金融公司工作,并参加了特拉华州威尔明顿快艇半职业橄榄球队,晚上还在福德汉姆大学法学院上夜校。两年后的1939年,他受聘于新泽西英格伍德市的圣西西利亚高中,既教书又做教练。隆巴迪教代数、化学、拉丁文和物理,还担任棒球队、篮球队和橄榄球队的教练。

1940年,隆巴迪与玛丽·布拉尼兹结婚,1947年离开高中,担任福德汉姆大学新生橄榄球队教练一年。次年,他担任校队副教练。1949年,隆巴迪管理起美国西点军校校队防守线。他与厄尔·布雷克教练数小时地工作,厄尔教给他的远不止如何做个有用的领导者,包括一些策略,比如只接管明确的比赛,坚持完美的技术,在赛场上行为举止要受人尊重。

职业生涯

1954年,隆巴迪应邀担任纽约巨人队副教练,他传奇般的职业橄榄球教练生涯即将开始。他负责该队的进攻战术,但在第三个赛季,巨人队以全联盟最差成绩3胜9负而无缘冠军。1956年该队战胜芝加哥熊队的主要原因之一就是隆巴迪把弗兰克·吉福特从防守

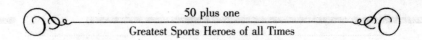
amount of points in the league with a lowly 3–9 record to being champions. One of the major reasons that the team was able to beat the Chicago Bears for the title in 1956 was that Lombardi had switched Frank Gifford from defense to offense as a pass–option player. This proved to be a tremendous change for the Giants, who did not have a losing season during the entire 5–year period that Lombardi was with them. It also proved to be career altering for Gifford as an individual because he was nominated as a halfback on the All–Pro Team for each of those 5 years as well.

In January of 1959, Lombardi made the move to Green Bay, Wisconsin after accepting a 5–year contract as general manager and head coach of the Packers. The team had come away from the previous season with only a single win and one tie to its name. Lombardi looked at his new job as a challenge and a good way to prove that his coaching skills were as good as he knew they could be. He did not mess around, either. He started immediately, holding the first of what would become his notorious training camps. The camps were intense, grueling and punishing in nature, showing that Lombardi expected, in fact demanded, total dedication and effort from his players. He told them that while dancing was a contact sport, football was indeed a hitting sport.

Lombardi's military–style of coaching immediately had a positive effect on the team, leading them to a 7–5 record in 1959. The next season, the Packers were Western Conference champions. Although they ended up losing the NFL championship game 17–13 to the Philadelphia Eagles, they made it up the following year by defeating the New York Giants 37–0 for the title. In 1962, Lombardi again led the way to the championship game and the Packers won 16–7, ripping the title away from the Giants for the second straight year.

During his years as the Packers' head coach, Lombardi converted Paul Hornung from quarterback to a full–time halfback, running a play for him in which offensive linemen swept to the outside and blocked downfield. Lombardi had originally developed that play for Gifford when he was with the Giants and it would eventually become known as both the Packer Power Sweep and the Green Bay Sweep. Lombardi was also famous for his constant development of new plays and game strategies. He once changed his players' jersey numbers right before a game in order to confuse another legendary football figure, George "Papa Bear" Hallas, coach of the Chicago Bears.

With his hard–working and demanding leadership, Lombardi guided the Packers to a total of six Western Conference titles from 1960–1962 and 1965–1967, five NFL championships from 1961–1962 and 1965–1967, and the first two Super Bowls in history from 1966–1967. The team's three–consecutive NFL championship victories remain unprecedented in the league even today. Lombardi retired after 9 years as head coach following the 1967 season, leaving the Packers with a 98–30–4 record. He kept his position as general manager of the team, though.

Lombardi was not truly ready to give up coaching and he accepted a position as head coach with the Washington Redskins in 1969. That year, he guided the team in breaking its 14–season losing streak. The season was Lombardi's final one and he finished with a career head coaching record of 105–35–6, having never experienced a losing record.

Throughout the years, Lombardi's competitive spirit, dedicated manner and winning record have earned him numerous awards and honors, including the moment when the Super Bowl Trophy was renamed the Vince Lombardi Super Bowl Trophy in 1971. In honor of Lombardi, the Rotary Club, in 1970, created the Rotary Lombardi Award for outstanding college offensive or defensive linemen. Some of the other honors that he has received are:

·Coach of the Year Award, NFL (1959)
·Man of the Decade Award, NFL (1960s)

队员换成了进攻队员，作为传球手。这对巨人队来说是一次巨大的变动，隆巴迪担任教练的整整五年，该队都没有输过任何一次赛季。这对吉福特本人来说也意味着职业生涯的变化，因为他在整个5年中一直担当全职业队的半卫。

1959年1月，隆巴迪定居威斯康星州绿湾，与包装工队签订5年合同，担任总经理和总教练。该队上个赛季只赢了一次，还有一次平局。隆巴迪把新工作看成一个挑战，也是证明他自认不错的教练才能的绝好机会。他也确实没有浪费时间。他立刻着手开始了第一个远近闻名的训练营。这个训练营训练强度大、把人折磨得筋疲力尽，根本就是体罚，显示了隆巴迪的期望，实际上是他的要求，他要求队员要有献身精神、努力拼搏。他告诉他们，舞蹈是交际运动，而橄榄球是一种攻击运动。

隆巴迪军事化训练很快见效，让球队在1959年以7胜5负的成绩获胜。下个赛季，包装工队成为西部联盟冠军。虽然与费城老鹰队的对决中以13:17的成绩告负而无缘美国职业橄榄球大联盟冠军，但第二年，他们以37:0的成绩击败纽约巨人队，赢得桂冠。1962年，隆巴迪再次带领球队直闯冠军赛，包装工队以16:7获胜，连续两年从巨人队手里夺回冠军头衔。

在担任包装工队总教练的岁月中，隆巴迪把保尔赫农从四分卫调成全职半卫，进攻线卫外线阵并阻挡前冲。隆巴迪最早是在巨人队时训练吉福特这个位置，最终以"包装工队强侧跑阵"和"绿湾强侧跑阵"而出名。隆巴迪还以坚持培养新人和制定比赛策略而闻名于世。有一次，就在比赛前的片刻，他变动了队员球服号，使另一位传奇人物——芝加哥熊队教练"熊爸爸"乔治·哈拉斯搞不清状况。

隆巴迪工作努力、要求严格，他引领包装工队在1960-1962和1965-1967年间共六次夺得西部联盟的胜利，1961-1962和1965-1967年间5次夺得美国职业橄榄球大联盟冠军，1966-1967年，有史以来首度获得两个超级碗。该队3次蝉联美国职业橄榄球大联盟冠军的纪录是史无前例的，至今在联盟中无人能打破。隆巴迪1967年赛季结束后就告别了9年的总教练生涯，包装工队最终成绩是98-30-4。但是他仍保留着该队总经理职位。

隆巴迪并没有真正准备好放弃教练工作，1969年他担任了华盛顿红人队总教练。那年，他带领球队打破了连输14个赛季的厄运。那是隆巴迪的最后一个赛季，他以105-35-6的成绩结束了自己的总教练生涯，从未有过失败的纪录。

这些年来，隆巴迪的竞争精神、奉献精神和赫赫战功让他获得不少荣誉和奖励，包括1971年超级碗奖杯重新以他名字命名为"文斯·隆巴迪超级碗杯"。为了纪念隆巴迪，1970年，扶轮社为奖励杰出的大学进攻线卫和防守线卫而制定了"扶轮社隆巴迪奖"。他还获得了以下荣誉：
·美国职业橄榄球大联盟年度教练奖 (1959)
·美国职业橄榄球大联盟"时代最佳人物奖" (60年代)

·Fordham University Hall of Fame charter member induction (1970)
·Professional Football Hall of Fame induction (1971)
·Green Bay Packers Hall of Fame induction (1975)
·Coach of the Century Award, ESPN (2000)

About the Man Himself

The reason that Lombardi was unable to continue on as head coach for the Redskins was that he was diagnosed with intestinal cancer in June of 1970. The cancer was discovered late and it had already spread from his colon to his liver, peritoneum and lymph nodes. Lombardi died less than 3 months later on September 3, 1970. He was survived by his wife of 30 years, Marie, his son and his daughter. More than 3,500 people attended Lombardi's funeral at St. Patrick's Cathedral in New York City. Football players cried in plain sight and President Nixon sent Marie a telegram of condolence that was signed—The People.

Vince Lombardi, Jr. has written many books about his father, including *The Lombardi Rules* and *What it Takes to Be #1: Vince Lombardi on Leadership*.

Lombardi starred in the motivational film *Second Effort*, which is still viewed by sales teams around the world. Vince Lombardi was known for saying, "Winning isn't everything, it's the only thing." This captured his undyingly fierce competitive attitude toward the sport of football, and his name will undoubtedly live on forever with as much, if not more, intensity.

·入选福德汉姆大学名人堂创始会员 (1970)
·入选职业橄榄球名人堂 (1971)
·入选绿湾包装工队名人堂 (1975)
·被美国体育娱乐频道评为"世纪教练" (2000)

关于此人

隆巴迪无法继续担任红人队总教练的原因是因为1970年6月他被诊断出患有肠癌。癌症被发现时已是晚期，早已从结肠扩散到肝脏、腹膜和淋巴结。之后不到3个月，1970年的9月3日，隆巴迪永远地离开了人世。他继续活在家人心中，包括结婚30年的妻子玛丽和一双儿女。3500多人参加了在纽约市圣派屈克天主大教堂举行的葬礼。橄榄球运动员们毫不掩饰地痛哭流泪，尼克松总统给玛丽发来一封署名为"人民"的慰问电报。

文斯·隆巴迪的儿子写了不少关于父亲的书籍，包括《隆巴迪规则》和《怎样成为第一：文斯·隆巴迪的领导观》。

隆巴迪曾出演励志电影《第二次努力》，至今仍受全球销售团队青睐。文斯·隆巴迪有句至理名言："胜利不是一切，而是唯一。"这显示了他对橄榄球运动执著强烈的好胜态度，毋庸置疑，他的大名将永远铭记在人们心中。

Twenty-four

Mickey Mantle

Why He is Among the 50 plus one Greatest Sports Heroes

Plagued by injuries throughout his professional baseball career, Mickey Mantle was still able to accomplish so much that he is still considered by many fans and experts alike to be one of the best players in history. He led his team to seven World Championships with his awesome home run–hitting abilities, and to this day, owns several World Series records. One of his home runs is listed in the Guinness Book of World Records as the longest home run ever measured. Mantle's powerful hard–hitting ways have blasted him right to the top of the list as one of the greatest athletes of all times.

On the Way Up

Mickey Charles Mantle was born on October 20, 1931 in Spavinaw, Oklahoma, but he grew up in Commerce. He was the oldest son of Elvin "Mutt" and Lovell Mantle. Micky had three brothers and a sister. From the time that he was able to swing a bat, his father, Mutt, a retired semi–pro player, and his grandfather, Charlie, would pitch to him after school each day. He began working at the nearby lead mines during the summers, which enabled him to build up his strength. One position that he held was known as the screen ape, and it called for him to use a sledgehammer to smash large rocks into small stones until he was unable to hold the hammer any longer. Being a screen ape, as well as doing a variety of farm chores, most certainly played a part in the development of Mantle's strong arms, forearms, shoulders and wrists.

Mantle attended Commerce High School, where he excelled at baseball, football and basketball. One day, during football practice, a teammate accidentally kicked him in the left shin. The wound developed into osteomyelitis, a chronic bone infection, which became so bad that doctors recommended amputation of his leg. At the urging of Mantle's mother, Mutt drove him the 175 miles to Oklahoma City so that he could be seen by doctors at the Crippled Children's Hospital. At the hospital, he was treated and cured with the then–new drug, penicillin, thus saving his leg from being amputated. The bout with osteomyelitis would render Mickey unfit for military duty.

After recovering from his injury, 16–year old Mantle started playing shortstop with a local semi–pro team called the Baxter Springs Whiz Kids even though it was a general rule that players had to be 18 before being considered for the team. In 1948, he caught the attention of a New York Yankees scout, Tom Greenwade, when he hit one righty and one lefty home run into a river that was a considerable distance beyond the ballpark's fences. Greenwade was eager to sign Mantle right away, but Mantle was only 16 so he promised to come back and sign him with the Yankees on his graduation day the following year. True to his word, on May 16, 1949, Mantle signed to a minor league contract with the Yankees' Class D team in Independence, Kansas. In the press release that announced Mantle's signing,Greenwade reportedly said that Mantle was the best prospect that he had ever seen.

米奇·曼托

他为何入选《50+1位最闪耀的体育巨星》

作为棒球运动员,米奇·曼托整个职业生涯都遭受着受伤之苦,但他仍然努力取得巨大成就,被众多球迷和专家们公认为史上最佳运动员之一。他以出色的本垒打帮助球队将七个世界冠军奖杯收入囊中,至今仍拥有不少世界联赛纪录。其中一个本垒打列入了吉尼斯世界纪录,因为是最长距离的本垒打。曼托强有力的重击打方式让他荣登50+1位史上绝顶运动员榜。

成长之路

米奇·查尔斯·曼托于1931年10月20日出生于俄克拉何马州斯帕维诺,但是他生长在克马斯。他是艾尔文·马特和罗微尔·曼托的大儿子。米奇有3个弟弟、一个妹妹。当他能够挥动球棒时,退役的半职业运动员父亲马特和祖父查理每天在他放学后帮他练习棒球轮击。每年暑假他便在附近铅矿打工,这样能增大力量。其中有一种工作是作为screen ape ,这需要他用大锤把大块岩石打碎成小石块,直到再也没有力气握住大锤为止。他不仅要做screen ape,还干农场杂活,很多工作都能帮他练就强壮的上膊、前臂、肩膀和手腕。

曼托就读于克马斯高中时,他在棒球、橄榄球和篮球方面表现突出。有一天,在练习橄榄球时,一位队友不小心踢伤了他的左胫。这次受伤引发了骨髓炎,这是慢性骨病,非常严重,医生都劝他截肢。在曼托母亲的催促下,马特带着儿子驾车至175英里以外的俄克拉何马市,这样就能在伤残儿童医院看病。在医院,他接收了当时最新药物青霉素的治疗,这才保住他的腿免受截肢。骨髓炎病症发作让米奇无法服兵役。

受伤康复后,16岁的曼托开始担当游击手,效力于当地半职业球队Baxter Springs Whiz Kids队,虽然有规定说球员必须年满18岁方可入队。1948年,他引起了纽约扬基队球探汤姆·格林卫德的注意,因为他用左右手击中本垒打,而且距离棒球场围栏甚远。格林卫德迫切想跟曼托签约,但是曼托只有16岁,因此他答应明年毕业那天回来签约扬基队。1949年5月16日,曼托兑现了承诺,他与堪萨斯独立城扬基D级队的小联盟签约。在宣布曼托签约的新闻发布会上,格林卫德宣称曼托是他见过的最有前途的运动员。

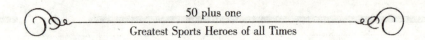

Mantle's Independence team won the Kansas –Oklahoma –Missouri Championship that summer, after which he moved to Joplin, Missouri to play for the Yankees' Class C team. Then, in 1951, Mantle got his chance to participate in spring training with the Yankees in Arizona. Mantle's speed, along with his continuously far–reaching home runs, prompted the manager, Casey Stengel, to convince the Yankee's management to bring him up to the major leagues that season. Mantle was the first player in Yankees' history to jump directly from Class C to the majors.

Professional Career

During Mantle's rookie year, 1951, the Yankees switched him from shortstop to the outfield. He hit a slump and was sent down to the team's farm club in Kansas City, Missouri before returning to the majors for good near the end of the season. He finished with a .297 batting average and 13 home runs in 96 games.

That year, the Yankees faced the New York Giants in the World Series. Mantle was playing right field during the second game and he ran over to center in an effort to help DiMaggio after the Giants' Willie May hit a pop fly. But his spikes got caught in a drain cover when he made an abrupt stop in order to avoid colliding with his teammate. Injuring his right knee, Mantle fell to the ground and had to be carried off of the field on a stretcher. It was the first of many injuries that would trouble him throughout his professional career. Other injuries include: a hip infection in 1961, a torn thigh muscle in 1962 and a broken bone in his left foot in 1963.

Despite playing through what seemed to be a constant state of injury, Mantle played more games, with 2,401, and had more at–bats, with 8,102, as a Yankee than any other player. During his 14 years with the team, he made 12 World Series appearances from 1951–1953, from 1955–1958 and from 1960–1964. Mantle, also known as The Commerce Comet, played on seven World Championship teams. The Yankees defeated the Brooklyn Dodgers for the title from 1952–1953 and in 1956. They were also victorious against the Giants in 1951 and 1962, the Milwaukee Braves in 1958 and the Cincinnati Reds in 1961. Although Mantle set a career World Series record of 54 strikeouts, he also set five others that are still in place today: 18 home runs, 42 runs, 40 RBIs, 43 bases on balls and 123 total bases.

In 1956, Mantle won Major League Baseball's Triple Crown, leading the league with a .353 batting average, 52 home runs and 130 runs batted in (RBIs). During his career, The Mick hit 536 home runs, which was the third highest upon his retirement and still the most ever by a switch–hitter. On April 17, 1953, he hit a 565–foot home run at Washington's Griffith Stadium. This is the run that is listed in the Guinness Book of World Records as the longest home run ever measured. The book also states that Mantle's 643 –foot home run hit, which took place on September 10, 1960 at Tiger Stadium in Detroit, Michigan, is the longest home run measured– mathematically after the fact. However, he also reportedly hit a 656–foot home run during an exhibition game in 1951 at the University of Southern California. As the story goes, the ball left the University's Bovard Field and then proceeded to cross an adjacent football field.

Mantle hit his last home run on September 20, 1968 and he retired from professional baseball on March 1, 1969. His No. 7 was retired by the Yankees on June 8th of that same year, and Mickey Mantle Day is September 9th. Among other honors, Mantle was:
- All–Star (1952–1965 and 1967–1968)
- Most Valuable Player, American League (1956–1957 and 1962)
- Sports Broadcasters Association Award (1957)
- Gold Glove (1962)

曼托的独立城队在那年夏天赢得堪萨斯—俄克拉何马—密苏里冠军,之后他迁至密苏里贾柏林,效力于扬基C级队。1951年,曼托有机会在亚利桑那参加扬基队的春季训练。曼托的速度和他频繁的远距离本垒打促使经理凯塞·斯登杰尔(Casey Stengel)说服扬基队管理层,在下个赛季把他带入大联盟。曼托成了扬基队历史上第一个直接从C级跳到大联盟的队员。

职业生涯

1951年,曼托作为新秀的第一年,扬基队把他从游击手换成外场手。他一度萎靡不振,被派送到该队在密苏里堪萨斯城的农场俱乐部,之后在将近赛季末时才重返大联盟。在96场比赛中,他最终成绩为297打击率、13个本垒打。

那年,扬基队在世界联赛中遇到纽约巨人队。曼托在第二场比赛中担任右外野手,巨人队威利·梅击中一个高飞球后,他迅速跑到中外野帮助狄马乔。但是他的钉鞋在排水沟处卡住了,他只好突然停下,避免与队友相撞。曼托右膝受伤,他摔倒在地,被担架抬出比赛场地。这是他众多受伤经历中的头一次,伤痛困扰着他整个职业生涯。其他受伤情况包括:1961年髋部感染,1962年大腿肌肉拉伤,1963年左脚骨裂。

尽管一直伤痕累累,曼托作为扬基队员仍不断参加更多的比赛,多达2401场,创下了更多的打数,达8102,其他运动员无人能比。为该队效力的14年里,他分别于1951-1953年间、1955-1958年间和1960-1964年间,在12次世界联赛中亮相。曼托还以"克马斯彗星"著称,他曾7次效力于世界冠军队。扬基队于1952-1953年和1956年战胜布鲁克林道奇队夺冠。该队分别于1951、1952年战胜巨人队;1958年战胜密尔沃基勇敢者队;1961年战胜辛辛那提红人队。曼托在世界联赛中不仅创下了54次三振出局纪录,他还创造了保持至今的其他5项纪录:18个本垒打,42次跑垒得分,40个打点,43个四坏球上垒和123个垒打数。

1956年,曼托是职棒大联盟三冠王,他率领联盟获得平均353打击率,52个本垒打,130个打点。在他职业生涯中,"米克"击中536个本垒打,这是他快退役时的第三个最高纪录,也是双手皆打的运动员的最高纪录。1953年4月17日,他在华盛顿格里菲斯露天体育场创造了距离565英尺的本垒打。这是有史以来距离最长的本垒打,被列入了吉尼斯世界纪录。这本书还纪录了1960年9月10日,曼托在密歇根底特律老虎露天体育场创下的距离643英尺的本垒打,这是精确测量的最长距离。而且,据说1951年他在南加州大学表演赛中曾打出距离656英尺的本垒打,有传言说球从大学Bovard体育场一直打到了相邻的足球场上。

1968年9月20日,曼托击中了职业赛场上最后一个本垒打后,于1969年3月1日退役。同年6月8日,他的7号球衣也正式退役,"米奇·曼托日"定于9月9日。曼托获得的荣誉还包括:
· 全明星 (1952-1965,1967-1968年)
· 美国联盟最具价值球员 (1956-1957年和1962年)
· 体育广播电视联盟奖(1957年)
· 金手套 (1962年)

·Triple Crow (1956)
·AL Slugging Leader (1955–1956, 1961–1962)
·AL Runs Scored Leader (1954, 1956–1958, 1960–1961)
·National Baseball Hall of Fame (1974)
·Longest official home run (565 feet) April 17, 1953

About the Man Himself

Mantle married Merlyn Johnson in December of 1951. The couple had four sons. The third son, Billy, would die the year before Mantle from complications relating to Hodgkin's disease. The disease ran in the family as his father and one of his uncles both died from it in 1952, and another uncle in 1947. This proved to be a primary reason for the way in which Mantle carried out his personal life. He became known as a partier and a womanizer, living life to what he thought was the fullest at the time because the prospect of an early death was a constant presence in the back of his mind.

Mantle wrote and co–wrote several books, including The Mickey Mantle Story; The Quality of Courage; All My Octobers: My Memories of Twelve World Series When the Yankees Ruled Baseball; and his autobiography, The Mick. He also released an autobiographical documentary film called Mickey Mantle: The American Dream Comes to Life.

After retirement, Mantle became a broadcaster for New York's Sports Channel and he managed various businesses, including a few clothing stores and restaurants. His restaurant, Mickey Mantle's Restaurant and Sports Bar, opened in 1988 and is one of New York City's most popular dining spots.

In 1983, Mantle started working in public relations at the Claridge Hotel and Casino in Atlantic City, New Jersey. This led to his banishment from baseball by the league's commissioner, Bowie Kuhn. The next commissioner, Peter Ueberroth, reinstated Mantle into the sport in 1985.

In January of 1994, Mantle entered the Betty Ford Center in Rancho Mirage, California and went through a month–long program for alcohol abuse rehabilitation. Mantle turned this experience into a public service message by speaking out to children about the negative effects of drug and alcohol abuse.

Mantle underwent liver transplant surgery the following summer at Baylor University Hospital in Dallas, Texas, after he developed liver cancer. Later that summer, doctors discovered that the cancer had traveled to Mantle's lungs and he was readmitted to the hospital only to find out that it had spread to more parts of his body as well. Mantle died at the hospital on August 13, 1995. In honor of the legend Yankee, September 9th has been designated Mickey Mantle Day.

Before he died, Mantle established the Mickey Mantle Foundation in an effort to make people aware of the importance of organ donation. His wish was to eliminate completely the loss or quality of life resulting from the unavailability of organs and tissue for transplantation. After Mantle's death, his family continued the foundation to try and make his dream come true.

While Mickey Mantle's hard–hitting ways on and off the baseball field have earned him nothing but respect from fans and experts of the sport. He will go down in history as an athlete to be remembered.

·三冠王 (1956年)
·美联长打王 (1955–1956, 1961–1962年)
·美联跑垒得分王 (1954, 1956–1958, 1960–1961年)
·入选国家棒球名人堂 (1974年)
·1953年4月17日,最长距离本垒打 (565 英尺),

关于此人

1951年曼托与玛琳·约翰逊结婚。他们有4个儿子。老三比利因霍奇金病比曼托早逝一年。这个疾病有家族遗传,曼托父亲和一个叔叔都于1952年死于此病,另外一个叔叔是在1947年去世的。这也能够解释曼托私生活方式。他是有名的社交人物、追求女色,他认为这样的生活是最充实的,因为在他脑海深处,一直提醒他的就是随时都会英年早逝。

曼托自己写书,也与人合著,包括《米奇·曼托的故事》《勇气》《我的所有十月:扬基棒球队的十二次世界联赛回忆录》,还有自传《米克》。他还发行了一部自传电影《米奇·曼托:美国梦实现于生活中》。

退役后,曼托成为纽约体育台的播音员,他还管理很多生意,包括一些服装店和餐饮店。他的曼托餐厅和体育酒吧于1988年开张,成为纽约市最著名的餐饮场所之一。

1983年,曼托开始在克拉瑞奇饭店和新泽西亚特兰大市卡西诺做起公关。这导致联盟主任Bowie Kuhn将他从棒球联盟开除的后果。下任领导彼得·伍伊贝罗斯(Peter Ueberroth)于1985年重新恢复了曼托在联盟的身份。

1994年1月, 曼托进入加州幻象牧场的贝蒂福特中心进行一个月的酒精滥用者康复治疗。曼托把这次经历作为公共演说内容,告诫儿童关于毒品和酒精滥用的副作用。

次年夏天,曼托发现患有肝癌后,在德州达拉斯贝勒大学医院接受肝移植手术。夏末,医生发现癌细胞已扩散到曼托肺部,他再入院时,被查出癌细胞扩散到了更多部位。1995年8月13日,曼托在医院逝世。为了纪念这位扬基传奇英雄,9月9日被定为"米奇·曼托日"。曼托去世前,他成立了米奇·曼托基金会来唤醒人们对于器官捐赠重要性的认识。他的愿望是完全消除由于无法获得器官和移植器官而遭受的痛苦甚至丧命。曼托死后,他的家人继续管理着基金会,努力实现他的梦想。

米奇·曼托在棒球赛场内外惊人的力量为他带来了球迷和体育专家的尊重和爱戴。他将成为名垂青史的运动员。

Twenty-five

George Mikan

Why He is Among the 50 plus one Greatest Sports Heroes

George Mikan played in an era long before supersized was the thing to be, but that does not stop many fans and experts from saying that he was professional basketball's first real superstar and dominant big man. He was just plain big and so effective that he set rule changes in motion during both his college and professional playing days. An athlete with such influence over the game he played can only be described as one of the best there ever was. Mikan was without a doubt one of the best there ever was and therefore, is considered one the greatest sports athletes of all times.

On the Way Up

George Lawrence Mikan, Jr. was born on June 18, 1924 in Joliet, Illinois. He was one of three boys and they all worked in the family restaurant after school every day. When Mikan was young, he loved and excelled at playing the piano, hoping to become a concert pianist when he grew up. Surprisingly, what he did not really excel at was basketball and when he was 13, he broke his leg during a game. While he attended Joliet Catholic High School for a year in 1937, the basketball coach actually discouraged Mikan from playing because of his poor eyesight. The next year, he transferred to Chicago's Quigley Seminary, which was 35 miles away from his home. The long commute guaranteed that Mikan could not join the basketball team.

But whether it was because of Mikan's size at 6 feet, 10 inches and 245 pounds or something else entirely, it seems that he was destined to play the game of basketball. When he enrolled at DePaul University in 1941, he landed a spot on the team and soon became a force with which to be reckoned. In 1945, he was the top scorer for DePaul, averaging 23.3 points per game and with 120 points in three games. Under coach Ray Meyer, he led the team to the National Invitational Tournament championship against Ohio's Bowling Green State University.

Throughout his 4 years there, Mikan's teams compiled a total record of 81–17 and Mikan himself scored a total of 1,870 points (19.1 points per game). This made him the best scorer in DePaul's history upon his graduation and he still ranks among the school's top five in scoring all these years later. His record of 53 points in one game against the University of Rhode Island has yet to be broken by another DePaul player. On the other end of the spectrum, the NCAA established a rule prohibiting defensive goaltending due to Mikan's overwhelming talent for rejecting shots. He was a 4-year letter winner and was named The Sporting News First Team All-America in 1944 and 1945.

Professional Career

Mikan's professional playing days began in the 1946–1947 season when he was drafted by the Chicago American Gears of the National Basketball League (NBL). That year, he continued his championship-winning ways and guided the Gears to the NBL title. The following year, Mikan was

乔治·迈肯

他为何入选《50+1位最闪耀的体育巨星》

乔治·迈肯的时代还没到超级身高主宰一切的时代，但是这并不能阻止球迷和专家把他认定为职业篮球史上第一位超级巨星、主宰比赛的大高个。他只是一般的高个子，但是他战斗力太强，以至于大学比赛和职业生涯中的运动规则都被迫改变。一个运动员能有如此大的影响力，成为最优秀运动员之一当然也无可厚非。迈肯毫无疑问地成为有史以来最佳运动员之一，也是公认的50+1位最闪耀的体坛英豪之一。

成长之路

乔治·劳伦斯·迈肯于1924年6月18日出生于伊利诺斯州乔利矣特。家里共3个儿子，他们每天放学后都帮家里开的饭店工作。孩提时的迈肯喜欢弹钢琴而且弹得很出色，他希望长大后成为音乐会钢琴演奏家。奇怪的是，他不是很擅长打篮球，13岁时，他在一次比赛中还跌断了腿。1937年他进入乔利埃特天主教高中就读一年，由于他视力不好，篮球队教练使迈肯灰心丧气，不让他打球。第二年，他转学到离家35英里的芝加哥奎格莱高等中学。这次远距离的变动意味着迈肯不可能加入篮球队。

但无论是因为身高6英尺10英寸、体重245磅，还是别的什么原因，迈肯似乎注定要打篮球。1941年当他在迪保罗大学注册入学时，他加入篮球队，很快成为大家寄予厚望的主力。1945年，他成为迪保罗队得分王，每场比赛平均得23.3分，3场比赛平均得120分。在教练瑞梅尔指导下，他率领球队闯进全国冠军邀请赛，对抗俄亥俄鲍灵格林州立大学队。

大学四年，迈肯队累积纪录为81胜17负，他本人总共得分1870分（每场平均19.1分）。毕业时，他成为迪保罗大学前所未有的得分王，随后的这些年间，他仍然在全校五大得分王排名中榜上有名。在与罗德岛大学的一次比赛中，他拿下53分，该纪录后来被另一名迪保罗队员打破。另一方面，由于迈肯阻止投篮的超级才能，美国大学篮球联赛制定了干扰球规则，禁止防守干扰投篮得分。他4年获得校名首字母殊荣，于1944年和1945年荣获《体育新闻》"全美大学最佳阵容第一队队员"称号。

职业生涯

迈肯的职业生涯始于1946-1947赛季，那一年他是美国篮球联盟芝加哥美国齿轮队的选秀新人。他仍继续着自己冠军赢球方式，带领齿轮队闯入美国篮球联盟赛。次年，迈

chosen by the Minneapolis Lakers in a dispersal draft. The team joined the Basketball Association of America (BAA) in 1948 and won another championship title under Mikan's lead. Then, in 1949, the BAA became the familiar NBA of today. Mikan was such a powerful presence in the league at that point that the sign outside of New York City's Madison Square Garden once read before a game: George Mikan vs. Knicks.

Judging from the impact that Mikan had on the NBA early on, the sign truly said it all. Just like during his college days, his awesome playing abilities caused officials to modify or develop new rules. The NBA found it necessary to double the width of the free throw lane, partly because Mikan was just too big for the existing parameters. Then, in one game, the Fort Wayne Pistons used slowdown tactics against him and scored only 19 points to beat the Lakers' 18 points, making it the lowest-scoring game in NBA history. This was too much for league of.cials, who thereafter decided to institute the 24-second shot clock.

Mikan went on to play with the Lakers for 6 full seasons in the NBA, bringing the team four additional championships in 1950 and from 1952-1954. In his 9 seasons as a professional player, he scored 11,764 points (22.6 points per game), which was the league's top career points total when he retired. Mikan led the various leagues in scoring six times from 1946-1952, including a career-high of 28.4 points per game in 1951. He also led the NBA in rebounding average in 1952 with 13.5 rebounds per game as well as in rebounding in 1953 with 1,007 (14.4 rebounds per game). Mikan was one of the league leaders in free throw attempts every year, with a career total of 4,597. The round-rimmed eyeglasses that he wore became a familiar and famous fixture to fans and fellow players and he was sometimes called Harold Lloyd of Basketball because of them.

Mikan retired from professional basketball after the 1953-1954 season, after which he made a short-lived, 37-game return to the Lakers in the 1955-1956 season. Then he called it quits for real. Mikan's record of scoring the highest percentage of a team's points in a single game has yet to be touched, let alone broken. The 83.3 percentage came from the infamous low-scoring Lakers vs. Pistons game when Mikan scored 15 of his team's meager 18 points. He also owns the second-highest percentage of a team's points in a single game and that came in 1952, during a game against Rochester when Mikan scored 61 of the Lakers' 91 points, a 67.0 percentage.

The honors for Mikan's tremendous contributions to the Lakers in particular and the NBA as a whole started rolling in during his years as a player. The stream continued long after he had left the game, making it uncertain whether it will ever stop. Awards Mikan has received include:

· All-NBL First Team (1947 and 1948)
· NBL Most Valuable Player (1948)
· All-BAA First Team (1949)
· Greatest Player in the First Half-Century, Associated Press (1950)
· NBA Champion (1950, 1952-1954)
· All-NBA First Team (1950-1954)
· NBA All-Star (1951-1954)
· NBA All-Star Game Most Valuable Player (1953)
· Naismith Memorial Basketball Hall of Fame (1959)
· Basketball Hall of Fame (1959)
· NBA 25th Anniversary All-Time Team (1970)
· NBA 35th Anniversary All-Time Team (1980)
· NBA 50th Anniversary All-Time Team (1996)
· One of 50 Greatest Players in NBA History (1996)

肯在选秀会中被明尼阿波利斯湖人队选中。该队于1948年加入美国篮球协会,在迈肯的率领下再次摘下桂冠。1949年,美国篮球协会就成为如今著名的NBA(国家篮球协会)。迈肯在联盟中是不可或缺的核心人物,以至于在一次比赛前夕,纽约市麦迪逊花园广场的大幅广告牌上写道:乔治·迈肯对抗尼克斯队。

从迈肯早年在NBA影响力可以判断,那个牌子写的都是事实。就像他在大学时代表现一样,他惊人的才能不得不让有关人员调整或制定新规则。NBA国家篮球协会认为有必要把罚球区扩大了一倍,有部分原因是因为迈肯太高大,融不进当时的界限范围。随后,在一次比赛中,韦恩堡活塞队用放慢节奏的战术来对付他,结果总分只拿下19分,以19:18的成绩赢了湖人队,这是NBA史上最低分数的一次比赛。联盟官员实在无法忍受,他们随后决定设置24秒必须投篮的时限钟。

迈肯在NBA国家篮球协会继续为湖人队整整效力6个赛季,1950年和1952-1954年间又为球队赢得四次冠军。在他作为职业球员的第九个赛季,他总共得分11764分(平均每场比赛22.6分),到他退役时,这个记录一直是联盟最高职业生涯得分。1946-1952年间,迈肯六次成为联盟得分王,包括1951年平均每场职业生涯最高的28.4分。他还带领NBA于1952年获得场均13.5个篮板球的纪录,1953年的总纪录为1007个(场均14.4个)。迈肯每年都是联盟中罚球次数最多者,职业生涯中共有4597次。球迷和队友分外熟悉他那著名的标志性圆框眼镜,有时候大家称他为"篮球界的Harold Lloyd"(Harold Lloyd是一位很有名的电影明星)。

1953-1954赛季后迈肯退出职业篮球生涯,之后,他又短暂地出现在1955-1956赛季的37场比赛中,然后才正式退役。迈肯单场比赛个人得分占球队总得分最高比例的纪录至今无人能及,更别说有谁能打破了。在湖人队对抗活塞队的最低得分场次的那场比赛中,迈肯得到了湖人队18分中的15分:达到83.3%。迈肯同样保持着第二高的纪录,67.0%:在1952年对阵罗彻斯特队(国王队前身)时,他得到了湖人队91分中的61分。

迈肯为湖人队作出的巨大贡献和对整个NBA的贡献,让许多荣誉纷至沓来。即使他退役后,这些荣誉和奖励仍然不断,仿佛永无止境,它们包括:
·入选全美篮球联盟第一阵容 (1947和1948年)
·美篮联盟最具价值球员 (1948年)
·入选全美篮球协会第一阵容 (1949年)
·被美联社评为"20世纪上半叶最伟大球员" (1950年)
·NBA 冠军 (1950, 1952-1954年)
·入选NBA全明星第一阵容 (1950-1954年)
·NBA 全明星 (1951-1954年)
·NBA 全明星赛最具价值球员 (1953年)
·入选奈史密斯篮球名人纪念堂 (1959年)
·入选篮球名人堂 (1959年)
·入选NBA25周年纪念最佳阵容 (1970年)
·入选NBA35周年纪念最佳阵容 (1980年)
·入选NBA50周年纪念最佳阵容 (1996年)
·NBA史上50位最佳球员之一 (1996年)

About the Man Himself

In 1956, around the time that Mikan said his true good–byes to professional basketball as a player, he ran as the Republican candidate for the 3rd congressional district of Minnesota. He lost to the incumbent Democrat Congressman. In 1958, Mikan coached the Lakers for a short while and later became the first commissioner of the first American Basketball Association (ABA). He introduced the 3–point line to the ABA as well as the league's distinctive red, white and blue basketball.

Mikan wrote an autobiography that came out in 1952. It was called *Mr. Basketball:George Mikan's Own Story*. He also co–wrote another book that came out more than 40 years later called Unstoppable: The Story of George Mikan, the First NBA Superstar.

As a result of his struggle with diabetes, Mikan's right leg was amputated below the knee in March of 2000. The following year, the Minnesota Timberwolves showed their respect and admiration for him by erecting his statue in the lobby of the Target Center in Minneapolis. A few years later, on June 1, 2005, Mikan died in Scottsdale, Arizona due to complications from diabetes and other issues. Shaquille O'Neal of the Los Angeles Lakers offered to pay for his funeral, and Mikan's family accepted.

Up until the time that Mikan died, he had been receiving only about $1,400 per month in pension from the NBA. That amount was less than the amount he was required to pay to live in an assisted living facility, and it seemed strange to many people that although he was considered one of the greatest NBA players in history, he received such a paltry amount in comparison to today's NBA stars. And he was not the only one. So, without meaning to, Mikan caught the attention of the media even in death. Since then, many sports commentators have voiced their belief that active players should demand an increase in pensions for former players, especially for players who were active long before today's era of the supersized contract.

George Mikan was larger than life and the impact he has after his death ensure that his name will forever remain in the hearts of sports fans everywhere.

关于此人

1956年,就在迈肯真正与职业篮球生涯说再见时,他参加了明尼苏达第三议会区的共和党候选人竞选。他败给了领先的民主党议会委员。1958年,迈肯短暂地出任湖人队教练,之后成为第一个美国篮球协会的第一任行政长官。他向美国篮球协会引入了三分球,并提出使用与众不同的红、白、蓝三色球。

迈肯写了本自传,并于1952年出版。该书名为《篮球先生:乔治·迈肯自己的故事》。他还与人合写了一本40多年后才出版的书:《永不停止:乔治·迈肯——第一位NBA超级巨星的故事》。

在与糖尿病对抗后,2000年3月迈肯右腿膝盖以下被截肢。次年,明尼苏达森林狼队为了表示对他的尊敬和爱戴,在明尼阿波利斯标靶中心大厅里竖立了他的雕像。几年后,2005年6月1日,迈肯由于糖尿病和其他器官组织并发症,在亚利桑那州斯科特斯戴尔与世长辞。洛杉矶湖人队的沙奎尔·奥尼尔要求为他的葬礼出资,迈肯的家人最终答应了。

直到迈肯去世时,一直拿着NBA发的微薄的养老金,每月只有1400美元。这个数目还不够他花在支援性住宅设施上,而且在很多人看来奇怪的是,虽然他是NBA元老级人物之一,但与如今NBA明星相比,他却得到如此微薄的养老金,而且受此待遇的不只他一人。因此,迈肯自然而然地成为媒体关注的焦点,甚至在他死后。从那时起,很多体育评论员纷纷发表见解,认为现在的运动员应该要求为老运动员们提高养老金额,尤其该为那些早于如今超级巨星时代的打井者们。

乔治·迈肯是位传奇人物,他去世后仍具影响力,他的姓名将铭记在全球球迷的心中,永不消逝。

Twenty-six

Stan Mikita

Why He is Among the 50 plus one Greatest Sports Heroes

Upon his retirement from the National Hockey League (NHL) in 1980, Stan "Stosh" Mikita was the all-time leader in games played, assists made and points scored for his team. One of the biggest achievements of his career was when he captured three major trophies in 1 year and then repeated that feat the following year. Throughout the 1960s, Mikita was one of the top players in the NHL and he helped lead his team to a Stanley Cup Championship after a 23-year drought. All of these accomplishments and more put Mikita at the top of his game while he was a player, and they have now put him amongst the top of history's greatest sports heroes.

On the Way Up

Stanislaus Gvoth was born on May 20, 1940 in Sokolce, Czechoslovakia. Stan immigrated with his aunt and uncle to Saint Catharines, Ontario, Canada after a new regime was installed in Czechoslovakia by the Communist Russians in 1948, and just as the Iron Curtain was closed. Makita was adopted by his aunt and uncle Gvoth and Americanized his first name to Stanley and changed his last name to Mikita, which was the surname of his aunt and uncle. Some of his childhood was difficult because he did not speak English and was often the recipient of other children's insults. However, he learned the language soon enough after being brought back down to kindergarten for 3 weeks before he returned to his third-grade class.

Before moving to Canada, Mikita had no idea what the game of hockey was. Even though he did not own a pair of skates, he responded to an advertisement in the local newspaper about a Canadian Legion little league hockey program. He became an instant lover of the game and began skating at the arena in St. Catharines whenever he had the chance.

In 1956, Mikita began playing with an Ontario Hockey Association (OHA) junior hockey team, the Teepees, which was an affiliate of the Chicago Blackhawks. He played with the team for 3 seasons, finishing with 47 points during his rookie year, 78 points during his second year and 97 points during his third and final year. That last year, Mikita led the OHA in points as well as assists (59), and he scored 38 goals, leading him to the Most Valuable Player award. He was drafted by the Blackhawks although he did not realize until years later that his being drafted meant he could only play for Chicago if he ever ended up in professional hockey. And end up in professional hockey he did. He performed in his first NHL trial in 1958 with the Blackhawks and became a regular with the franchise the following year.

Professional Career

Mikita was a center for the Blackhawks throughout his entire career, which spanned 3 decades, from 1959-1980. He was a part of the famous Scooter Line with Ken Wharram and Abe McDonald and later Doug Mohns. Mikita stood at only 5 feet, 9 inches and weighed only 169 pounds, but he was never intimidated by hockey's tough physical aspects. In fact, nicknamed Le

斯坦·米其塔

他为何入选《50+1位最闪耀的体育巨星》

斯坦·米其塔从全国冰上曲棍球联盟退役前,一直是球队里的核心人物:助攻者和得分王。他职业生涯中最大的成功之一就是一年里连捧3个大奖杯,次年也是如此。整个19世纪60年代,米其塔都是全国冰球联盟中最出色运动员之一,带领他的球队捧回久违了23年的斯坦利冠军杯。米其塔取得的所有成就都让他成为冰球领域的佼佼者,也让他荣膺50+1位最闪耀的体育巨星中的一名。

成长之路

1940年5月20日,斯坦斯洛斯·格弗斯出生于捷克斯洛伐克。1948年前苏联统治捷克斯洛伐克,"铁幕"也随之结束,他与姑姑、姑父移民至加拿大安大略省圣凯瑟琳斯市。米其塔是由姑姑和姑父格弗斯收养的,并把名字改为具有美国特色的斯坦利,把姓改成了米其塔,这是他姑姑和姑父的姓氏。由于不讲英语,他的童年生活总有些麻烦,他一直是其他孩子羞辱的对象。然而,他被重新送往幼儿园3个星期,迅速学习了英语,然后再重返三年级。

移民加拿大之前,米其塔根本不知道什么是冰球。他没有溜冰鞋,但是给当地报纸上刊登的加拿大退伍军人协会冰球小联盟招募广告写了回信。他立刻喜欢上了这个运动,只要一有机会,他就在圣凯瑟琳斯的竞技场内练习滑冰。

1956年,米其塔开始效力于安大略冰球协会青少年队——帐蓬队,它是芝加哥黑鹰队的前身。他在球队打了3个赛季,第一年得分为47分,第二年得分为78分,最后一年97分。在最后一年里,米其塔帮助安大略冰球协会得分并助攻得分(59分),他单枪匹马拿下38分,获得最具价值球员奖。他参加了黑鹰队选秀大会,虽然过了些年才入选,这意味着他一旦成为职业曲棍球手,就能为芝加哥效力。最终他被选为职业运动员。1958年,他第一次在全国冰上曲棍球联盟选拔赛中亮相于黑鹰队,第二年他成为分会正式队员。

职业生涯

米其塔在职业生涯中一直担任黑鹰队的中锋,整整30年,从1959年至1980年。他与Ken Wharram、Abe McDonald组成了著名的Scooter Line,后来是与Doug Mohns组合。米其塔身高只有5英尺9英寸,体重169磅,但是他从来没有被曲棍球严酷的体能要求而吓倒。事实上,他有个昵称叫"小恶魔",在联盟早期赛季的岁月中,他是经常犯规被罚的队

Petit Diable, or the Little Devil, he was often among the league's most–penalized players during his early seasons, something of which he was not particularly proud in later years. What made Mikita clean up his game was when his then 4–year old daughter asked him why he had sat on the other side of the ice all by himself and away from his teammates during one game that she had been allowed to stay up and watch on television. She wanted to know whether or not Mikita liked the other players. He tried to explain what a penalty was to her and decided to cut down on his penalty minutes after that episode. In the 1967–1968 season, his penalty minutes dropped from more than 100 down to a mere 12. That was the year that he became the first player to win the Art Ross, Hart Memorial and Lady Byng Memorial (for sportsmanlike conduct) trophies all in 1 season. He duplicated this accomplishment the very next year as well.

In 1961, Mikita and the Blackhawks broke the franchise's 23–year losing spree by winning the Stanley Cup Championship. That started what would be the best decade of Mikita's career. He was very effective at scoring and led the NHL in points from 1963–1965. He was also named Most Valuable Player twice and an NHL All–Star eight times, six times on the First Team and two times on the Second Team.

During the 1960s, Mikita scored an average of one point per game, but his productivity level had shrunk by the mid–1970s due to consistent lower–back injuries. When he retired in 1980, he was the all–time leading scorer with 541 goals and was the Blackhawks' all–time leader in three categories with 1,394 games played, 926 assists made and 1,467 points scored. He also had the secondhighest career–scoring total in the entire NHL upon retirement.

After suffering a concussion, Mikita designed a helmet according to his own specifications to protect his head. He turned this into a successful business as the Stan Makita helmet gained in popularity with amateur and pro skaters during the 1970s.

Interestingly, during his time on the ice, he discovered that a curved blade helped the puck to slide and dip in way similar to a fastball. Mikita was the first Czechoslovakian–born player in the NHL and, on October 19, 1980, he became the first player in Blackhawks history to have his jersey, No. 21, retired. He was inducted into the Hockey Hall of Fame in 1983 and into the Slovak Hockey Hall of Fame in 2002.

During his many years with the Blackhawks, Mikita acquired these awards:
· Art Ross Trophy (1964–1965 and 1967–1968)
· First All–Star Team Center (1962–1968)
· Second All–Star Team Center (1965, 1970)
· Hart Memorial Trophy (1967–1968)
· Lester B. Pearson Trophy (1976)
· Lady Byng Trophy (1967–1968)
· Hockey Hall of Fame (1983)

About the Man Himself

Along with maintaining a family life with his wife and children, Mikita also lends much of his time and energy to different charitable organizations. One of his major contributions began in 1973, when he established the Stan Mikita Hockey School for the Hearing Impaired, for which he raised money by hosting charity hockey games. As one of the co–founders of the American Hearing Impaired Hockey Association, he managed the school for more than 30 years and was awarded the Lester Patrick Trophy by the NHL for his outstanding service to United States hockey. He has also served on the Chicago Blackhawk Alumni Association's Board of Directors.

员之一,这是他后期生涯中尤其不值得自豪的事情。让米其塔重整旗鼓的是他那四岁的女儿。有一次女儿被允许熬夜看电视比赛,她后来问父亲,为什么他一个人坐在冰场另一边,而其他队友都在比赛。她想知道米其塔是否跟其他队员一样。他试着向她解释什么是处罚,也决定今后减少处罚分钟。1967-1968赛季,他的处罚时间从100分钟减少到只有12分钟。那一年他成为第一位在一个赛季中捧回阿瑟·罗斯杯、哈特纪念杯和宾尼夫人纪念奖杯(每年颁给表现最佳的后卫)的人。次年,他再次捧回同样的奖杯。

1961年,米其塔协助黑鹰队捧回了久违23年的斯坦利冠军杯。这也是米其塔职业生涯巅峰时刻的到来。他非常擅长进攻得分,率领全国冰球联盟从1963到1965年连续得分。他两次被评为最具价值球员,8次评为全国冰球联盟全明星,6次入选第一阵容队,两次入选第二阵容队。

在整个60年代,米其塔场均得分1分,但是他的水平从70年代中期开始有所下降,因为受到下背部疼痛困扰。1980年退役时,他一直是得分王,共进球541个,也一直是黑鹰队三项王,分别为最多比赛次数:1349次,最多助攻次数:926次,最高得分数:1467分。到退役为止,他还创造了全国冰球联盟职业生涯总得分第二高分。

米其塔遭受脑震荡后,他根据自己头部特征设计了头盔来保护头部免受伤害。他把这个发明发展成为成功的事业,"斯坦·米其塔头盔"风靡70年代,在业余和职业运动员中广受欢迎。

他在冰上打曲棍球时,发现一个有趣的现象:弯曲的冰刀可以帮助冰球滑动、倾斜,就像棒球手投出的快球。米其塔是全国冰上曲棍球联盟中第一位捷克斯洛伐克运动员,1980年10月19日,他的21号球衣退役,这是黑鹰队史上第一位退役球衣的队员。1983年他入选曲棍球名人堂,2002年入选斯洛伐克曲棍球名人堂。

米其塔在黑鹰队的职业生涯中,获得以下殊荣:
· 阿瑟·罗斯杯(1964-1965、1967-1968)
· 第一全明星队中锋 (1962-1968)
· 第二全明星队中锋(1965, 1970)
· 哈特纪念杯(1967-1968)
· 莱斯特·B·皮尔森杯(1976)
· 宾尼夫人纪念奖杯(1967-1968)
· 曲棍球名人堂 (1983)

关于此人

米其塔与妻子孩子共度家庭生活,他还把很多时间和精力投入各种公益活动中。他的主要贡献之一开始于1973年,他为听力障碍儿童建立了斯坦·米其塔曲棍球学校,通过举办曲棍球慈善赛筹集资金。作为美国听力障碍曲棍球协会成立者之一,他管理学校30多年,由于对美国曲棍球事业的杰出贡献,他被全国冰上曲棍球联盟授予莱斯特·帕特里克杯。他同时担任芝加哥黑鹰校友协会董事长。

Twenty-seven

Joe Montana

Why He is Among the 50 plus one Greatest Sports Heroes

Joe Montana led his NFL team to four Super Bowl victories in the span of a single decade. The Pro Football Hall of Famer became known as a come–from–behind quarterback for he pulled together his team for 31 fourth quarter comebacks throughout his professional career. With his many accomplishments on the field, though, Montana did not have to come from behind in order to be considered one of sports history's greatest legends.

On the Way Up

Joseph Clifford Montana, Jr. was born on June 11, 1956 in New Eagle, Pennsylvania. An only child, he starred on the baseball, basketball and football teams at Ringgold High School. In football, he started for 2 seasons and won the Parade All–American honors his senior year. Also during his senior year, he led his basketball team to the league championship and served as the class vice president.

After graduation, Montana attended the University of Notre Dame in Indiana, where he began earning his career–long reputation as a come–from–behind quarterback. In 1977, he guided the football team to the national title and 2 years later, he was selected by the San Francisco 49ers in the third round of the 1979 NFL Draft.

Professional Career

Montana did not become a starter for the 49ers until late in his second year, but by 1981 he was the top dog on offense. That season, he guided the team to a 13–3 record, the NFC title and a Super Bowl victory. Montana, also known as Joe Cool and The Comeback Kid, was instrumental in The Catch, a famous play that occurred during the NFC championship game against the Dallas Cowboys. While three opposing players were closing in on him with 51 seconds left in the game, he launched the football to Dwight Clark, who was waiting in the end zone. The six–yard touchdown pass gave the 49ers the slight edge they needed to beat the Cowboys 28–27. The team went on to defeat the Cincinnati Bengals 26–21 for the Super Bowl title.

In the 1984 season, Montana again brought the 49ers to the Super Bowl, this time against the Miami Dolphins. Although his rival, Dan Marino, had just broken an NFL record by throwing for 48 touchdowns, Montana proceeded to overshadow Marino's accomplishment by passing for 331 yards and three touchdowns. The 49ers ended up winning 38–16.

Montana underwent back surgery in 1986 after he ruptured a disc while throwing a pass during the season opener. Even though his doctors had suggested that he should consider quitting football for health reasons, he returned to the game 2 months later and threw three touchdown passes to Jerry Rice. However, Montana suffered an injury at the end of the season as well. This time, the helmet of New York Giants' noseguard, Jim Burt, ended up jammed under Montana's chin. Montana was forced out of the playoff game, which turned out to be a 49–3 loss for the

乔·蒙塔纳

他为何入选《50+1位最闪耀的体育巨星》

乔·蒙塔纳仅在10年内就带领国家橄榄球联盟球队赢得4个"超级碗"。职业橄榄球名人堂以拥有"后发制人"的四分卫运动员而著名,因为他在职业生涯中为球队创造了31个第四节的大逆转。蒙塔纳在球场上取得了许多成就,理应成为万古体坛中最出色的传奇健儿之一。

成长之路

1956年6月11日,约瑟夫·克里福特·蒙塔纳出生于宾夕法尼亚州纽英格尔市。少年时代,他已在Ringgold高中的棒球队、篮球队和橄榄球队中亮相。在橄榄球队,他参加了两个赛季,在高三时赢得Parade全美奖。同样在高三那年,他率领篮球队闯入联盟冠军赛,并担任年级学生会副主席。

毕业后,蒙塔纳进入印第安纳州圣母大学,开始了他著名的"后发制人"四分卫职业生涯。1977年,他带领球队进入全国大赛,两年后,他在1979年国家橄榄球联盟第三轮选秀大会中被选入旧金山49人队。

职业生涯

蒙塔纳直到第二年下半年才在49人队亮相,但是到了1981年,他成为最佳进攻者。那个赛季,他率领球队取得13胜3负的成绩,赢得国家橄榄球协会冠军和"超级碗"。蒙塔纳还有"乔酷"和"打不倒的小子"的昵称,他在与达拉斯牛仔队争夺国家橄榄球协会冠军的著名比赛中,成为接球"工具"。在最后51秒时,他在3名防守球员围堵的情况下,将球传给在另一端等待的德怀特·克拉克。这个6码距离的触地得分让49人队以微弱的优势险胜牛仔队,比分为28:27。该队接着以26:21的比分战胜辛辛那提猛虎队,捧得"超级碗"。

1984年赛季中,蒙塔纳再次带领49人队夺得"超级碗",这次是战胜迈阿密海豚队。虽然蒙塔纳的对手丹·马里诺曾以48码触地得分打破国家橄榄球联盟纪录,他却以码数为331码的3个触地得分的成绩盖过了马里诺的风头。49人队以38:16的比分获胜。

1986年,蒙塔纳在赛季开赛时的一个传球导致背骨破裂,不得不接受背部手术。虽然医生建议他为健康考虑,放弃橄榄球事业,他仍然于两个月后复出,3次触地得分,传球给杰瑞·赖斯。然而,蒙塔纳在赛季末再次受伤。这次,纽约巨人队边卫吉姆波特的头盔压伤了蒙塔纳的下巴。蒙塔纳被迫退出季后赛,导致49人队以3:49的成绩失败告终。

49ers.

In what was becoming a trend, Montana led the 49ers to another Super Bowl victory in the 1988 season. The team beat the Dolphins 20–16 after Montana completed 23 of 36 passes for two touchdowns and 357 yards, which was a Super Bowl record. The following season, he guided the 49ers to a 14–2 season and earned his fourth and final Super Bowl ring. During the postseason, San Francisco won each of its three games by 28, 27 and 45 points while Montana completed 78 percent of his passes for 800 yards, 11 touchdowns and no interceptions. In the Super Bowl itself, the 49ers defeated the Denver Broncos 55–10, and Montana completed 22 of 29 passes for 297 yards and a Super Bowl–record five touchdowns.

Montana missed the 1991 season due to an elbow injury, and further complications forced him to sit out all of the 1992 season except for the final game. He had missed 31 straight games, but came back with a vengeance, showcasing his comeback skills against the Detroit Lions. In the second half, Montana completed 15 of 21 passes for 126 yards and two touchdowns, carrying San Francisco to a 24–6 victory over the Lions.

The 49ers traded Montana to the Kansas City Chiefs in 1993, and he led his new team to the playoffs for 2 straight seasons before retiring in 1995. Upon his retirement, he ranked fourth in each of these categories: career passing yardage with 40,551 yards, attempts with 5,391 and passing touchdowns with 273. He also ranked third in career completions with 3,409 and second with a career passer rating of 92.3.

During his career, Montana led the NFC in passing five times, in 1981, 1984–1985, 1987 and 1989. He won the NFL's passing title in 1987 and 1989 and, in 1994, became only the fifth quarterback in the league's history to pass for more than 40,000 career yards. Montana also set an NFL record with his six 300–yard passing performances in postseason games, and he set career playoff records for attempts, completions, touchdowns and yards gained passing and he led his teams to the playoffs 11 times.

Of course, Montana, whose No. 16 was retired by the 49ers, has received a vast amount of honors and awards over the years. Besides being named All–NFL three times and All–NFC five times as well as being selected to eight Pro Bowls, one of the most interesting of honors came in 1993, when the small town of Ismay, Montana changed its name to Joe for the entire football season. Montana has also been:

· Super Bowl Most Valuable Player, NFL (1981, 1984 and 1989)
· Co–Comeback Player of the Year, PW (1986)
· Offensive Player of the Year, Associated Press (1989)
· Most Valuable Player, NFC (1989)
· Most Valuable Player, NFL (1989–1990)
· Most Valuable Player, Associated Press (1989–1990)
· All–Decade Team (1980s)
· Sportsman of the Year, *Sports Illustrated* (1990)
· Super Bowl Silver Anniversary Team
· NFL 75th Anniversary All–Time Team
· Pro Football Hall of Fame (2000)

蒙塔纳率领49人队在1988年赛季中捧得"超级碗",这已是趋势所向。在36个传球中,蒙塔纳完成了23个传球,并两次触地得分,码数为357码,该队以20:16的比分战胜海豚队,赢得超级碗。下个赛季中,他带领球队取得14胜2负的成绩,捧回他第四个,也是最后一个超级碗。在季后赛中,旧金山49人队以28、27和45分赢得3场比赛,其中,78%的传球都是蒙塔纳完成的,11个毫无拦截的触地得分,码数为800码。在"超级碗"比赛中,49人队以55:10的成绩击败丹佛野马队,蒙塔纳在29个传球中成功传球22个,创造了码数为297码的5个触地得分的"超级碗"纪录。

由于肘部受伤,蒙塔纳错过了1991年赛季,更痛苦的并发症让他不得不在1992年整个赛季都坐观比赛,除了在最后的决赛中上场。他连续错失31场比赛,但是最终"王者归来",重整旗鼓,给底特律雄狮队来了个下马威。在第二节中,蒙塔纳拿下21个传球中15个成功传球,2个触地得分,码数为126码,让旧金山队以24:6的比分战胜雄狮队。

1993年,49人队把蒙塔纳换到堪萨斯城首长队,1995年退役前,他率领新球队连续两个赛季都进入了季后赛。他退役时,在以下各项都排名第四:职业生涯码数40551码,传球5391个,273个触地得分。他完成了职业生涯中3409次传球,排名第三;传球成功率为92.3%,位居第二。

蒙塔纳在国家橄榄球协会的职业生涯中,分别于1981年、1984–1985年、1987年和1989年五次传球达阵。他在1987年、1989年和1994年成为国家橄榄球联盟传球王,这是联盟史上第五个传球码数超过40000码的四分卫。蒙塔纳还在季后赛中,创了6次300码传球的国家橄榄球联盟纪录,他还创下了传球次数、传球成功率、触地得分、传球码数的季后赛纪录,而且他带领球队11次闯进季后赛。

当然,蒙塔纳的16号球衣也被49人队退役,他整个职业生涯中获得无数荣誉和奖项。他3次入选国家橄榄球联盟全明星阵容队、5次入选国家橄榄球协会全明星阵容队、8次被选入"职业碗"比赛,但最有意思的奖项是在1993年获得的,蒙塔纳在伊斯美小镇比赛时,把小镇的名字改成了乔,整整比赛了一个赛季。他的其他荣誉称号包括:
·国家橄榄球联盟"超级碗"最具价值球员(1981、1984、1989年)
·PW "年度东山再起球员"之一(1986年)
·被美联社评为"年度进攻球员"(1989年)
·国家橄榄球协会"最具价值球员" (1989年)
·国家橄榄球联盟"最具价值球员"(1989–1990年)
·被美联社评为"最具价值球员" (1989–1990年)
·时代全明星阵容队 (80年代)
·被《体育画报》评为"年度体育人物"(1990年)
·入选超级碗25周年全明星队
·入选国家橄榄球联盟75周年全明星队
·入选职业橄榄球名人堂(2000年)

Twenty-eight

Bronko Nagurski

Why He is Among the 50 plus one Greatest Sports Heroes

With his aggressively physical, yet all–around talented game, many football fans still consider Bronislau "Bronko" Nagurski to be the best player of all time. He carried his professional team to three NFL championships as well as several division titles and was enshrined as a charter member of the Professional Football Hall of Fame. Ernie Nevers once said that "tackling Bronko was like trying to stop a freight train running downhill," but the greatest thing about Nagurski was that he never crashed. After leaving football Nagurski became a successful wrestler before finishing out his quiet life after retirement as one of his town's most respected citizens. He has most definitely earned his spot among history's leading athletes.

On the Way Up

Bronislau Nagurski was born on November 3, 1908 in Rainy River, Ontario, Canada to parents from the Polish Ukraine. He grew up on his family's farm in Minnesota, near the Canadian border. Nagurski ran 4 miles to school and back each day. Nagurski, who had five siblings, was an athlete at heart and loved wrestling and boxing when he was a teenager. He attended high school in International Falls and Bemidji, both towns of Minnesota. A popular story was repeated over and over again by the media about how Nagurski was supposedly discovered by the man who would become his college football coach. The coach had become lost while on a recruiting trip and asked a strong, young farmer for directions. That farmer, who turned out to be Nagurski who was plowing the field without a horse, pointed the man in the right direction--one-handedly, with his mud plow.

That story might not be completely accurate, but what is accurate is that Nagurski proved himself as a dominating player during college. He went to the University of Minnesota from 1926–1930 and was a member of the Gophers' football team. He was an All–American from 1927–1929 and became the first college athlete in the history of the United States to be honored as an All–American at two positions, fullback and tackle, in the same year. With Nagurski, the Gophers held a record of 18–4–2 and they won the Big Ten title in 1927. The team was 6–2 in both 1928 and 1929, losing the four games by just five points. In 1930, George Halas signed him to the Chicago Bears.

Professional Career

In an era when most tackles weighed between 175 and 190 pounds, at 6 feet, 2 inches and 225 pounds, Nagurski was one of the biggest guys out on the field. He was known for his bull–like running, but was also extremely effective at blocking and tackling. Needless to say, he made spectacular things happen on both the offensive and defensive end as a fullback and defensive tackler. Nagurski has been called the complete player. During his time in Chicago, Nagurski proved that he was truly one of the original Monsters of the Midway. In a story that is most likely

布罗科·纳戈斯基

他为何入选《50+1位最闪耀的体育巨星》

布罗科·纳戈斯基出色的战斗力及其多才多艺,被众多橄榄球迷称颂为历史上最佳球员。除了赢得区冠军头衔以外,他还率领球队3次赢得国家橄榄球联盟冠军,并被选为职业橄榄球名人堂创始会员。厄尼·内弗斯基曾说过:"阻截布罗科,就像阻截一辆从山上冲下来的货运列车。"但是纳戈斯基最了不起的是他从未"撞车"。离开橄榄球赛场后,纳戈斯基并没有很快开始退役后的平静生活,而成为一名成功的摔跤手,他是家乡最受尊重的市民之一。毋庸置疑,他已在万古体坛中享有一席之地。

成长之路

1908年11月3日,布罗科·纳戈斯基出生在加拿大安大略,是波兰与乌克兰混血儿。在加拿大边界附近的明尼苏达有他家的农场,他就在此生长。纳戈斯基每天上学来回要跑4英里。纳戈斯基有五个兄弟姐妹,年少时的他是个不折不扣的运动员,喜欢摔跤运动和拳击。他高中就读于国际瀑布和本明吉,这两个地方都是明尼苏达州的市镇。有一个故事被媒体广泛流传,经久不衰,故事关于纳戈斯基是如何被他大学橄榄球队教练发现的。教练在一次招募新人旅途中迷了路,他向一个年轻健壮的庄稼汉问路。这个庄稼汉正好就是纳戈斯基,他当时没有用马匹,自己在耕地,单手握着犁耙向教练指明方向。

这个故事可能不完全真实,但可以证实的是纳戈斯基靠实力证明了自己是大学时期的主力队员。1926-1930年间,他就读于明尼苏达大学,成为美国历史上首位同年获得全美明星"进攻后卫"和"截锋"两个荣誉称号的大学运动员。有了纳戈斯基,明尼苏达大学金地鼠队拥有18胜4平2负的骄人成绩,他们赢得了1927年的"十大联盟"奖。1928年和1929年,该队获得6胜2负的成绩,四场比赛中只丢了5分。1930年,他与芝加哥熊队老板乔治·哈拉斯签订合同,成为该队队员。

职业生涯

那个时代,大多数截锋体重都在175至190磅,纳戈斯基身高6英尺2英寸,体重225磅,他成为球场上最高大的运动员之一。他以公牛般的跑速而著名,但是他在拦截和擒抱方面都很强大。不用说,他在进攻和防守两个领域都非常引人注目,是名出色的进攻后卫和防守截锋。纳戈斯基是公认的完美球员。在效力于芝加哥熊队时,他证明了自己是最早的"中途岛恶魔"之一。有一个比较夸张的故事:小熊队主场瑞格利球场的一次比赛中,他在

exaggerated, during a game at Wrigley Field, while charging down the field he broke a player's shoulder and knocked another one out before reportedly running into the brick wall and cracking it. He managed to score the game–winning touchdown with that impressive, if somewhat embellished, run. When he came back to the bench he remarked to Bear's coach, George Hallas, "That last guy gave me quite a lick! "

On December 18, 1932, Nagurski led the Bears to a 9–0 win against the Portsmouth Spartans for the championship title. That game, which took place inside of the Chicago Stadium on an 80–yard field, was the first NFL championship to be played indoors. Nagurski won the game when he used his signature move against rival Red Grange with a two–yard touchdown jump pass. That famous pass was very effective not only in the 1932 championship game but in many other games, as he would fake a plunge before stepping back one or two yards to jump and lob a pass. Nagurski's skills prompted the NFL to change its rule on the forward pass, making it legal anywhere behind the line of scrimmage instead of at least five yards back from the line.

The following year, Nagurski carried his team all the way to the NFL's first official championship game on December 17th. He passed for two touchdowns, including the one that clinched the Bears' 23–21 victory over the New York Giants. Nagurski was named All–Professional fullback 3 years in a row, from 1932–1934, and he was also named a first– or second–team All–NFL in 7 of his first 8 seasons. When the Bears refused to give him a raise to $6,500 in 1938, he retired from football and became a professional wrestler until 1958. After wrestling, he opened a service station in International Falls until 1978 when he retired again at the age of 70.

Nagurski's retirement lasted for 5 years until he rejoined the Bears for one more season as a tackle in 1943 due to their lack of players during World War II. He switched to fullback late in the season when the team was behind in a must–win game. His line plunges first pushed a drive to the touchdown that tied the game and then made way for the winning score. One week later, on December 26th at Wrigley Field, the Bears competed against the Washington Redskins in the NFL championship game. Nagurski scored what would be the final touchdown of his career and helped put his team in the lead for good. The Bears won the game 41–21. During his career, Nagurski gained 4,301 yards, scored 242 points and completed 38 of 80 passes.

Nagurski's No. 3 jersey has been retired by the Bears and his University of Minnesota jersery No. 72, was retired in 1979, and he became a charter member of the College Football Hall of Fame in 1951. Also, the Bronko Nagurski Museum in International Falls was opened in 1993 and was the first museum ever to be dedicated to an individual football player. Among these and other honors, Nagurski was:

· All–American from 1927–1929 and the first college athlete to be honored as an
· All–American at two positions, fullback and tackle, in the same year.
· All–Pro fullback 3 consecutive years (1932–34)
· The movie called Hearts in Atlantis is a fictionalized version of Nagurski's 1943 comeback game.
· 2–time NWA World Heavyweight Champion
· 1–time NWA World Tag Team Champion with Verne Gagne (1957)
· Pro Football Hall of Fame as a Charter member (September 7, 1963)

About the Man Himself

During the 1944 season, Nagurski coached the football team at the University of California,

撞击过程中,使一名球员肩膀断裂,撞晕了另一名球员,随后自己冲撞到砖墙,导致墙面碎裂。即使这个故事有所加工,但他以这个令人难忘的跑撞,让球队取得了决胜的一记触地得分。当他回到座位上时,对熊队教练乔治·哈拉斯说:"最后那个家伙着实给了我一次机会!"

1932年12月18日,纳戈斯基率领熊队以9:0的比分战胜普茨茅斯斯巴达人队,摘得桂冠。这次比赛是在长度80码的芝加哥室内体育场举行,也是国家橄榄球联盟首次举办的室内比赛。纳戈斯基以其标志性的动作对抗对手瑞德·格朗奇,并以两码的跳传触地得分,让球队获胜。这个著名的传球非常有效,不仅在1932年冠军赛中有名,而且在许多其他比赛中也广为流传,因为他在后退一两码之前会有假跳,然后再高弧度地抛出。纳戈斯基的精湛球技让国家橄榄球联盟改变了向前传球规则,规定在争球线后任何地方都有效,以此取代至少5码线外的规则。

次年12月17日,纳戈斯基带领球队直闯国家橄榄球联盟的首次正式冠军赛。他两次触地得分,包括以23:21的比分战胜纽约巨人队时至关重要的一分。纳戈斯基在1932-1934年,连续3年获得"全职进攻后卫"称号,8个赛季中有7次都入选国家橄榄球联盟全明星第一或第二阵容队。1938年,熊队拒绝给他加薪至6500美元,于是他退役,并于1958年成为职业摔跤手。结束摔跤运动后,他在国际瀑布建立了一个服务站,一直管理到1978年70岁再次退役之时。

纳戈斯基从橄榄球赛场退出的时间就维持了5年,1943年,由于第二次世界大战,熊队缺乏队员,他再次以截锋身份复出,重新效力熊队一个赛季。该队输球后,他在赛季末一场必须取胜的比赛中担任了进攻后卫。他突破防线,首先获得一个触地得分将比分扳平,随后拿下决胜分数。一周后的12月26日,在瑞格利球场,熊队战胜了华盛顿红人队,终于夺得国家橄榄球联盟冠军。纳戈斯基获得了职业生涯中最后一个触地得分,帮助熊队成为永恒的球队之王。熊队最终以41胜21负赢得比赛。在纳戈斯基的职业生涯中,他获得总码数4301码,得分242分,80个传球中就有38次成功传球。

纳戈斯基的3号球衣被熊队永久封存,他在明尼苏达大学的72号球衣也在1979年退役,1951年他成为大学橄榄球名人堂创始会员。布罗科·纳戈斯基博物馆也于1993年在国际瀑布开业,这是史上首个专门为橄榄球运动员个人创办的博物馆。除此之外,纳戈斯基获得其他荣誉包括:
·1927-1929年,被评为"全美明星",在同一年获得全美明星"进攻后卫"和"截锋"两个荣誉称号的大学运动员
·3年蝉联"全职进攻后卫"称号(1932-1934)
·电影《亚特兰蒂斯之心》就是以纳戈斯基1943年重出江湖为故事背景拍摄的
·两次获得国家摔跤联盟"世界重量级冠军"称号
·与Verne Gagne一起获得国家摔跤联盟"世界双打冠军"称号(1957)
·成为职业橄榄球名人堂会员 (1963年9月7日)

关于此人
在1944年赛季中,纳戈斯基担当加州大学洛杉矶分校橄榄球队教练。1935-1958年,

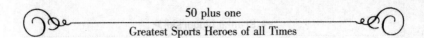
Los Angeles (UCLA). He wrestled professionally from 1935–1958 and was managed for most of that time by Tony Stecher, brother and manager of former National Wrestling Alliance (NWA) World champion, Joe Stecher. Nagurski's best years were during the late 1930s and early 1940s when he captured the NWA World title two times.

Nagurski married his childhood sweetheart, Eileen Kane in December of 1936. They had the first of their six children on Christmas Day the following year. That son was named after Nagurski and ended up playing with the Hamilton Ti–Cats of the Canadian Football league for 8 seasons. Nagurski, died on January 7, 1990, very much out of the public eye. However, even in death, he has been honored in various ways.

- NFL 75th Anniversary All–Time Team (1994)
- Seventh Greatest Player of All–Time, *College Football News*
- Since 1993, the Bronko Nagurski Trophy has been awarded annually to the College Defensive Player of the Year, and the Bronko Nagurski Scholarships are also awarded each year to two graduating seniors from Falls High School in International Falls.
- One of the 101 Best Athletes of the 20th Century, Associated Press
- John Madden's All–Madden All–Millenium Team.
- Associated Press named him as one of the 101 best athletes of the 20th century.
- In August of 2003, the United States Postal Service issued a stamp honoring Nagurski. Earlier that year.

It is obvious, and then, that Bronko Nagurski's name will continue to live on in the hearts of many fans–of football, wrestling and sports in general.

他是职业摔跤手,很长一段时间,他的经纪人都是国家摔跤联盟前世界冠军乔·施特歇尔的哥哥兼经纪人托尼·施特歇尔。纳戈斯基巅峰时期是在30年代末至40年代初,在此期间获得过两次国家摔跤联盟世界冠军头衔。

1936年12月,纳戈斯基与童年时代青梅竹马的艾琳·肯结婚。第二年圣诞节,他们6个孩子中的老大诞生了。儿子名字随了父亲纳戈斯基,他为加拿大橄榄球联盟的哈密尔顿猫队效力了8个赛季。1990年1月7日,纳戈斯基与世长辞,从此淡出公众视线。然而,他逝世后,仍获得许多荣誉:
·入选国家橄榄球联盟75周年全明星队 (1994)
·被《大学体育新闻》评为"史上第七最伟大球员"
·从1993年起,布罗科·纳戈斯基奖每年都颁发给大学最佳防守运动员,布罗科·纳戈斯基奖学金每年都奖励给国际瀑布高中的两个毕业生。
·被美联社评为"20世纪最出色101位运动员之一"
·入选约翰·麦登千年之队
·美联社评价他为"20世纪最出色101位运动员之一"
·2003年8月,全美邮政管理局发行了一版邮票,以此向纳戈斯基早年所作的贡献表示尊敬。
显而易见,布罗科·纳戈斯基的名字将永远铭记在众多橄榄球迷、摔跤迷及其他运动迷的心中。

Twenty-nine

Joe Namath

Why He is Among the 50 plus one Greatest Sports Heroes

Broadway Joe Namath was one of the most famous and controversial football players of his time and one of the most popular, yet often disliked, bad boys in the history of the game. In spite of a nagging knee injury and his reputation for being a rebel, he always managed to deliver on the football field. He led his team to victory in Super Bowl III, at the same time becoming a symbol of the legitimacy of the American Football League (AFL) in a National Football League–dominated world. Namath's powerful presence, no matter how conflicting, has earned him a spot among the greatest sports legends of all time.

On the Way Up

Joseph William Namath was born on May 31, 1943 in Beaver Falls, Pennsylvania, a suburb of Pittsburgh. He and his three brothers and adopted sister, were raised in the Lower End in Beaver Falls. Although his parents were divorced, Namath remained close to both of them as he was growing up.

Namath attended Beaver Falls High School, where he was a star football, baseball and basketball player. By the time he graduated, he had received offers to sign with six Major League Baseball teams. The Chicago Cubs had even reportedly offered him a $50,000 bonus, but Namath decided to go the college route instead. He wanted to attend the University of Maryland, but his college board scores were not high enough, so he ended up at the University of Alabama. Namath played on the Crimson Tide football team for legendary coach Paul W. "Bear" Bryant, who later said that Namath was the greatest athlete he had ever worked with.

During his sophomore year, Namath carried his senior–dominated team to a 10–1 record by completing 76 of 146 passes for 1,192 yards and 12 touchdowns. He broke curfew near the end of his junior year, which forced Bryant to bench him during the last regular–season game as well as the Sugar Bowl.

In his senior year, during a game against North Carolina State University, Namath suffered the first of his many right knee injuries. He injured it again 2 weeks later, and a third time while practicing for the 1965 Orange Bowl. Namath was not expected to be able to play in the bowl against the University of Texas Longhorns, but when Alabama started losing, he was put in the game to try and defend the honor of his No. 1 and undefeated team. Namath was named the game's Most Valuable Player, but his valiant efforts did not prevent the Crimson Tide from losing to the Longhorns 21–17. However, he was still able to bring his team to two Associated Press National Championships in 1964 and 1965 with records of 10–1–0 and 9–1–1, respectively.

The day after the Orange Bowl, on January 2, 1965, Namath signed a 3–year contract with the AFL's New York Jets as the No. 1 draft pick. Although he had been dismissed by the NFL as being too expensive, Sonny Werblin, owner of the team, saw more than just Namath's passing arm, he also recognized his star quality.

乔·纳玛什

他为何入选《50+1位最闪耀的体育巨星》

外号"百老汇"的乔·纳玛什是当代最著名、最有争议的橄榄球运动员之一,他广受欢迎、却常常褒贬不一,也被看成是橄榄球历史上的坏孩子。尽管常受膝盖受伤的困扰,还背负着"叛逆分子"的名声,他在橄榄球场上仍然努力成功。他带领球队赢得第三代超级碗冠军,同时成为美国国家橄榄球联盟主要体系——美国橄榄球联盟的合法代表队员。纳玛什强大的战斗力无论有多危险,已经为他在万古体坛英雄中赢得盛名。

成长之路

1943年5月31日,约瑟夫·威廉·纳玛什出生于宾夕法尼亚州匹兹堡的郊区——比弗福尔斯。他与3个兄弟和一个被收养的妹妹在比弗福尔斯的Lower End长大。虽然纳玛什的父母离异,他在成长过程中仍与兄弟妹们亲密无间。

纳玛什就读于比弗福尔斯高中时就是橄榄球、棒球、篮球明星运动员。毕业时,他应邀与6个大联盟棒球队签约。据说,芝加哥小熊队将给纳玛什5万美元的奖金,但是他决定走学院路线。他想进入马里兰州大学,但是他的大学入学考试成绩不够高,所以只能进入阿拉巴马大学。纳玛什效力于红潮风暴橄榄球队,教练是传奇人物保尔·W.布莱恩特,他后来评价说纳玛什是与他合作过的最好的运动员。

大二时,纳玛什带领大四学生为主力的校队获得10胜1负的成绩,146个传球中成功76个,码数为1192码,12个触地得分。他在大三快结束时打破禁令,迫使布莱恩特在最后一次常规赛和"糖碗"大赛中禁止他上场。

大四时,纳玛什在与北卡罗来纳州立大学的一场比赛中,第一次遭受右膝受伤。两周后右膝再次受伤,第三次受伤是在迎战1965年"橙子碗"大赛的练习中。纳玛什没什么希望能够参加与德州大学长角牛队的对抗赛,但是当阿拉巴马大学开始丢分时,他被换上场,试着为排名第一的卫冕校队捍卫荣誉。纳玛什被评为这次比赛的"最具价值球员",但是他的英勇奋战并没有帮助红潮风暴队,该队17:21不敌长角牛队。然而,他仍于1964年和1965年为球队赢得两次美联社国家冠军,成绩分别为10胜1平0负和9胜1平1负。

1965年1月2日,恰逢"橙子碗"大赛的第二天,纳玛什作为选秀大会第一名与美国橄榄球联盟的纽约喷汽机队签订3年合约。虽然后来他由于薪酬太贵而未被国家橄榄球联盟录用,球队创始人索尼·维布林认为纳玛什具有明星素质,而不仅仅传球出色。

Professional Career

Namath's knee injury plagued him throughout his entire career as a professional football player. His knee often became swollen with fluid and sometimes had to be drained during halftime in order for him to continue playing in a game. In fact, once his playing days were over, he had replacement surgery on both knees. Despite his injuries, Namath found success with the Jets. He became the team's starting quarterback halfway through his rookie year, and then in 1967, he passed for 26 touchdowns and 4,007 yards. This made him the first professional quarterback to pass for 4,000 yards in a single 14-game season.

The following year, Namath, led the Jets to the AFL's Eastern Division title. He threw three touchdown passes during the championship game and his six-yard touchdown pass to Don Maynard in the fourth quarter turned the game around for the Jets, who were losing 23-20. Thanks to Namath, they ended up with a 27-23 victory over the Oakland Raiders.

On January 12, 1969, during Super Bowl III, Namath and his Jets were pitted against the NFL's Baltimore Colts, who had a 16-1 record that season and had been dubbed The Greatest Football Team in History. There was a lot of hype surrounding the game, due to the question of whether the AFL was good enough to merge with the NFL. The first two Super Bowls had ended in sweeping wins for the NFL's Green Bay Packers, and this third game was being treated as a defining moment in the history of football. Three days before the game, Namath responded to a heckler and famously guaranteed that the Jets would win that Sunday.

Namath backed up his guarantee with pure performance. He completed 17 of 28 passes for 206 yards and led an offensive attack that bullied the Colts and forced interceptions. Namath and his team defeated their NFL opponents 16-7. Namath was credited as being the leading individual in the AFL and as a respectable and competitive force in the professional football arena.

After his successful season, Namath and fellow pro football players opened up an Upper East Side bar in New York City called Bachelors Ⅲ. Gamblers soon started hanging around the establishment, leading the commissioner of the NFL, Pete Rozelle, to order Namath to sell his share of the bar so that the league's reputation would remain in tact. In response, Namath chose to retire in June of 1969 but his retirement was brief. He finally sold his share of Bachelors Ⅲ and resumed playing for the Jets.

During Namath's first 5 years in the AFL, he did not miss a single game due but injuries plagued him between 1970-1973 and he played only 28 of 58 games. During those years, Namath's frequent absence was very apparent in the Jets' seasonal records of 4-10, 6-8, 7-7 and 4-10. In 1974, he was again healthy and the Jets won each of their last six games. The brief NFL strike seemed to affect the team and the Jets finished with measly 3-11 records in both the 1975 and 1976 seasons, losing in many blow-outs during which Namath suffered a number of hard sacks.

In May of 1977, the Los Angeles Rams signed Namath. By that time, he was plagued by knee injuries and a bad hamstring, among other aches and pains related to his many years as a football player. After only four games, Namath was hammered by the Chicago Bears and was out for the rest of the season.

Namath retired from professional football soon after with a career record of 77 wins, 108 losses and three ties. During his 12 seasons with the Jets, he completed 1,886 passes totaling more than 27,000 yards and 173 touchdowns, including 21 games with more than 300 yards and three with 400 or more. Along with his jersey No. 12 being retired by the Jets; he was named the Dodge Man of the Year; and presented with the George Halas Award for the Most Courageous Athlete. Namath has received many other honors for his team-leading achievements, including being:

职业生涯

纳玛什的膝盖受伤让他整个职业生涯都饱受煎熬。他的膝盖经常鼓脓，有时候为了继续比赛，必须在半场时就化脓。事实上，只要他的参赛日一结束，双膝就要接受修复手术。

尽管饱受伤痛，纳玛什在喷汽机队找到了成功。他作为新秀的第一年中途就成为球队四分卫，然后在1967年，他传球26次触地得分，码数为4007码。这使他成为首位在14场比赛的单个赛季中获得4000多码的职业四分卫。

第二年，纳玛什带领喷汽机队挺进美国橄榄球联盟东部赛区大赛。在冠军争夺赛中，他获得3个触地得分，在第四节时，以6码距离传球给唐·麦纳德，为当时以20:23比分落后的喷汽机队扭转了比赛局面。多亏了纳玛什，他们最终以27:23的比分战胜了奥克兰袭击者队。

1969年1月12日，在第三代超级碗大赛中，纳玛什和他的喷汽机队对抗国家橄榄球联盟的巴尔的摩小马队，而该队在那个赛季有过16胜1负的纪录，曾被评为"史上最佳橄榄球队"。在这次比赛中有不少质疑，因为大家质疑美国橄榄球联盟与国家橄榄球联盟结合是否有好处。前两次超级碗大赛都是彻底战胜国家橄榄球联盟的绿湾包装工，这个第三次的大赛被看做是橄榄球历史上的关键时刻。就在比赛前三天，纳玛什回答了一个激烈的质问者问题，向他保证喷汽机队一定能赢得周日的比赛。

纳玛什用行动证明了他的承诺。他成功地完成了28个传球中的17个，码数为206码，帮助球队发起进攻，威胁了小马队，并进行截球。纳玛什和队友以16:7战胜对手。纳玛什成为著名的美国橄榄球联盟领军人物，也是职业橄榄球赛场上受人尊重的中坚力量。

在纳玛什的成功赛季之后，他和职业橄榄球运动员朋友们在纽约市上东城开了一家酒吧，名叫"单身汉三号"。赌博很快就开始蔓延，国家橄榄球联盟主任彼得·罗泽尔命令纳玛什卖掉酒吧股份，这样才能保住联盟声誉。纳玛什选择于1969年6月退役作为对此事的回应，但是他的退役时间很短暂。他最终卖掉了"单身汉三号"的股份，重返喷汽机队。

纳玛什在美国橄榄球联盟的头五年，他从未错过一场正式比赛，但是1970–1973年间他受伤痛困扰，只参加了58场比赛中的28场。在那段岁月中，纳玛什的缺赛很明显导致了喷汽机队赛季4:10, 6:8, 7:7和4:10的败绩。1974年，他恢复健康，喷汽机队在后六场比赛中场场皆赢。国家橄榄球联盟大赛的短暂挫败似乎打击了喷汽机队，他们在1975和1976两个赛季中都以惨淡的3胜11负成绩收场，在此之中，本可以轻易得分，但纳玛什受到对手强硬的擒抱而接连丢分。

1977年5月，纳玛什与洛杉矶公羊队签约。那时，他受到膝盖和肌腱伤痛折磨，而他整个橄榄球职业生涯中受到过无数的伤痛。仅仅参赛4场后，芝加哥熊队使纳玛什惨败，他退出了赛季的剩余比赛。

不久，纳玛什退役，他的职业生涯纪录为77胜108负3平。在效力于喷汽机队的12个赛季中，他成功传球1886个，码数超过27000码，173个触地得分，包括21场比赛中的300多码的码数，还有3场比赛码数达到400或400多码。纳玛什的12号球衣被喷汽机队退役时，他获得"年度道奇人物"称号，乔治·哈拉斯"最勇敢运动员"奖也颁发给了他。纳玛什是球队的领军人物，他的成功也为他赢得了其他荣誉，包括：

· Rookie of the Year, AFL (1965)
· Four All−Star Games, AFL (1965 and 1967−1969)
· Most Valuable Player, AFL (1968−1969)
· Hickock Belt for Professional Athlete of the Year (1968)
· Most Valuable Player of Super Bowl III (1968)
· All−Time Team, AFL (1969)
· AFC−NFC Pro Bowl (1972)
· NFL Comeback Player of the Year (1974)
· Pro Football Hall of Fame (1985)

About the Man Himself

With the fame of Super Bowl III victory, Namath appeared in commercial advertisements as a sex symbol. He showed up wearing panty−hose in one commercial and shaved off his mustache with an electric razor during a Remington commercial.

Namath started a minor acting career with a few movies and starred in a shortlived television series called The Waverly Wonders (1978). He has guest−starred on many shows, including *The Brady Bunch*, *The Flip Wilson Show*, *The Dean Martin Show*, *The Simpsons*, and the *John Laroquette Show*. Namath also guesthosted for the Tonight Show with Johnny Carson a few times and co−hosted his own show with Dick Shaap in 1969, called The Joe Namath Show. He served for a time as a color analyst on NFL game broadcasts, including the 1985 season of *Monday Night Football*.

Namath has authored and co−authored a number of books, including: *American Football: A Complete Guide to Playing the Game; A Matter of Style;* and the controversial *I Can't Wait Until Tomorrow...'Cuz I Get Better−Looking Every Day*. He has also written an autobiography entitled *Namath*, which was released in October of 2006.

Deborah Lynn Mays and Joe Namath were married November of 1984 but later divorced in 1999. The couple has two daughters.

Namath is a member of its Arthritis Huddle Program, which offers doctors, patients and communities nationwide access to advanced osteoarthritis treatment techniques and educational programs.

While it is arguable whether Namath's rebel image helped or hindered his reputation, his fantastic football feats and charismatic personality make him legendary.

- 美国橄榄球联盟年度新人奖 (1965)
- 四次入选美国橄榄球联盟全明星赛(1965、1967–1969)
- 美国橄榄球联盟"最具价值球员" (1968–1969)
- 被授予"年度职业运动员"希考克腰带(1968)
- 第三代超级碗大赛"最具价值球员"称号(1968)
- 入选美国橄榄球联盟全明星队(1969)
- 美国橄榄球协会——国家橄榄球协会职业碗 (1972)
- 国家橄榄球联盟"年度东山再起球员" (1974)
- 职业橄榄球名人堂 (1985)

关于此人

纳玛什在第三代超级碗大赛中一举成名，他开始以男性形象代表出现在商业广告中。在一则广告中，他身穿紧身衣裤，还在雷明顿电动剃须刀广告中剃掉了胡子。

纳玛什开始在一些电影上扮演小配角，还主演过一部短期的电视连续剧The Waverly Wonders(1978年)。他曾在不少节目中担任嘉宾，包括：情景喜剧《布雷迪家庭》(《脱线家族》)、《菲利普威尔森秀》、《迪恩·马丁秀》、《辛普森一家》、《约翰·拉洛奎特秀》。还有几次，纳玛什作为嘉宾主持与强尼·卡森一起主持《今夜秀》，1969年他与迪克·夏普一起主持自己的节目《乔·纳玛什秀》。他曾担任过国家橄榄球联盟比赛的现场解说员，包括《周一橄榄球之夜》1985年的赛季比赛。

纳玛什自己写书，也与人合写过几本书，包括：《美国橄榄球：完全入门指导》、《风格问题》，还有辩论话题《我等不到明天，因为我每天都看到更好的前景》。他还写了一本名为《纳玛什》的自传，此书于2006年出版发行。

1984年，德普拉·林恩·梅丝嫁给乔·纳玛什，但是他们1999年离婚了。两人有两个女儿。

纳玛什是Arthritis Huddle Program活动成员，这个活动向全国的医生、病人和团体提供高级骨关节炎治疗技术和教育课程。

纳玛什的叛逆形象到底让他名扬四海还是声名狼藉，大家对此褒贬不一，他精湛的球技和极富魅力的个性让他成为传奇运动员。

Thirty

Jack Nicklaus

Why He is Among the 50 plus one Greatest Sports Heroes

Jack Nicklaus was named the 1888–1988 Golfer of the Century by Golf Magazine and was named Golfer of the Century or Millennium by virtually every major golf publication worldwide. During his career, he won six Masters, four U.S. Open and five Professional Golfer's Association (PGA) tournaments and he is either the sole owner of or tied for the most wins record in each one. Nicklaus should be, and is, considered one of the legendary athletes of all time.

On the Way Up

Jack William Nicklaus was born on January 21, 1940 in Columbus, Ohio. He started golfing at an early age and won the first of his two consecutive Scioto Club Juvenile Trophies when he was 10 years old. In 1952, he clinched the Ohio State Junior Championship, a victory that he would repeat for the next 4 years as well. He played in his first national tournament when he was 13 and won his first national title at age 17 in the U.S. National Jaycees Championship.

In 1957, Nicklaus qualified at the U.S. Open for the first time, but missed the cut. The following year, he qualified again and this time made the cut. He ended up finishing tied for 41st place. Then, at Cherry Hills in 1960, he came in second behind another legendary golfer, Arnold Palmer, and established a record 282 for an amateur entry. Nicklaus' final U.S. Open appearance as an amateur came in 1961 when he finished tied for fourth. Also during his time at Ohio State University, he captured the U.S. Amateur title in 1959 and 1961 as well as an NCAA Championship in 1961.

Professional Career

The man they called Golden Bear turned pro in 1962. By then, he had already developed a determined attitude embodied by a true poker face, enabling him to intimidate his opponents into making mistakes. In a career that lasted more than 40 years, he set a record for holding the most major championship titles, consisting of six Masters in 1963, 1965–1966, 1972, 1975 and 1986, five PGA Championships in 1963, 1971, 1973, 1975 and 1980, four U.S. Opens in 1962, 1967, 1972 and 1980 and three British Opens in 1966, 1970 and 1978. Nicklaus is tied with Ben Hogan, Bobby Jones and Willie Anderson for most U.S. Open wins and is also tied with Walter Hagen for most PGA Championship wins. He owns the record for most Masters wins and finished as a runner–up on a record four separate occasions.

Nicklaus was ranked No. 1 in lowest scoring average eight times, from 1964–1965 and 1971–1976. He holds many other records in the world of professional golf, including most World Series of Golf victories with five, most Tournament of Champion wins with five, most Players Championship victories with three and most birdies in a row to win a PGA Tour event with five in 1978 at the Jackie Gleason Inverarry Classic. Nicklaus is also tied with Arnold Palmer for most consecutive years winning at least one tournament with 17, which occurred from 1962–1978. He

杰克·尼克劳斯

他为何入选《50+1位最闪耀的体育巨星》

杰克·尼克劳斯被《高尔夫》杂志评为"1888–1998世纪高尔夫球手",基本上全世界每个主要的高尔夫刊物都把他称为"百年或千年高尔夫运动员"。在他的职业生涯中,共赢得六次名人赛、四次美国公开赛、五次职业高尔夫协会锦标赛,每次比赛他要么是最大的赢家,要么成绩与别人打平。毫无疑问,尼克劳斯是历史上公认的传奇运动员之一。

成长之路

1940年1月21日,杰克·威廉·尼克劳斯出生于俄亥俄州哥伦布市。他很早就开始打高尔夫球,10岁就首次获得蝉联两次的赛欧托俱乐部青少年奖杯。1952年,他赢得俄亥俄州青少年冠军,在随后的四年里,他一直获此殊荣。13岁时,他首次参加全国锦标赛,17岁时,他在美国国家青年商会冠军赛中生平第一次赢得国家级大奖。

1957年,尼克劳斯首次获得参加美国公开赛资格,但是没有晋级。第二年,他再次获得资格并成功晋级。最后他获得并列第41名的成绩。1960年,在樱桃山比赛中,他落后于另一位传奇运动员阿诺·帕玛,排名第二,而且创造了业余选手得分282的纪录。尼克劳斯作为业余选手的最后一次美国公开赛亮相于1961年,之前他的成绩是并列第四。在就读于俄亥俄州立大学时,他获得1959和1961年"美国业余选手"称号,同样在1961年,他还获得全国大学体育协会冠军头衔。

职业生涯

1962年,被誉为"金熊"的尼克劳斯成为职业运动员。那时,他的决心已在那张毫无表情、不露声色的脸上表现出来,成功地威胁对手、让其犯错。在四十多年的职业生涯中,他是重要冠军大赛冠军头衔最多纪录保持者,包括1963、1965–1966、1972、1975和1986年的六次名人赛冠军;1963、1971、1973、1975和1980年的五次职业高尔夫球协会大赛冠军;1962、1967、1972和1980年的四次美国公开赛冠军;1966、1970和1978年英国公开赛的三次冠军。尼克劳斯在众多美国公开赛中的纪录都与本·哈根、波比·琼斯和威利·安德森持平,他的职业高尔夫球协会大赛纪录也与沃特·哈根持平。他是名人赛冠军纪录保持者,并分别获得过四次亚军。

1964–1965和1971–1976年间,尼克劳斯八次都以平均最低击中分数排名第一。在职业高尔夫世界,他还是其他最高纪录的保持者,包括五次获得世界高尔夫联赛冠军,五次锦标赛冠军,三次选手锦标赛冠军,在职业高尔夫协会巡回赛和1978年艾文拉利精英赛中,他都以连续三击入穴最多次数获胜。1962–1978年间,尼克劳斯每年至少赢得一次锦

owns the record for most consecutive years on the Top 10 money list with 17 from 1962–1978 as well as for most years ranked No.1 in the final money standings with eight in 1964–1965, 1967, 1971–1973 and 1975–1976.

Nicklaus was also a member of the U.S. teams that beat Great Britain in the Ryder Cup in 1971, 1973, 1975, 1977 and 1981, and that tied with Great Britain in 1969. He became the non-playing captain of the 1983 U.S. team, which won, and the 1987 U.S. team, which lost. Nicklaus joined the Senior PGA Tour, now called the Champions Tour, in 1990. In 1996, he set yet another record by becoming the first golfer in PGA history to win the same Tour event four times. By the end of his career, Nicklaus had garnered 113 wins, 73 of which were on the PGA Tour, 10 of which were on the Champions Tour and 30 of which came from unofficial or international events. He officially retired from professional golf after the British Open in July of 2005.

Nicklaus will be remembered for his record–setting victories and significant rivalry with Palmer and for the way he arranged his schedule so that he could play in all of the majors. Many, in fact most, pro golfers have since taken on the same committed attitude and it is clear that Nicklaus should be accredited for heightening the intensity around the major title competitions.

About the Man Himself

Nicklaus is more than just a former professional golf player. He continues to stay connected to the game through the work of his company, Nicklaus Design, the largest golf design practice in the world, which has had its hand in the development of hundreds of renowned golf courses all over the world. Nicklaus has been designing courses since 1973 and his sons and son–in–law have also acquired solid reputations as designers. By the time 2005 had rolled around, 77 Nicklaus golf courses had hosted nearly 500 professional tournaments or national amateur championships.

In another path related to his golf career, Nicklaus has either written or co–written several golf instructional books as well as a book about his golf courses called *Nicklaus by Design*. He also wrote an autobiography that is simply entitled *Jack Nicklaus*.

Besides his lifelong passion for golf, Nicklaus has been able to carry out another of his missions through the Nicklaus Children's Health Care Foundation. The non–profit organization aids in the advancement of the ways in which childhood diseases and disorders are diagnosed, treated and prevented. It also helps notfor–profit programs that focus on pediatric health care. Nicklaus and his wife, Barbara, with whom he has five children (and 17 grandchildren), also make charitable donations of time and money to junior golf, children's hospitals and scholarship foundations, among other events and groups.

Nicklaus has been the recipient of awards that are related not only to his achievements as a golfer, but also to his achievements as a person. His family was named Golf Family of the Year by the National Golf Foundation in 1985 and they were also named Family of the Year by the Metropolitan Golf Writers Association in 1992. On an individual basis, Nicklaus was presented with the Father of the Year Award by the Minority Golf Association of America in 1999.

Jack Nicklaus made great strides to improve competitiveness in the world of professional golf and he continues to make great strides in other endeavors both inside and outside of that world. He is considered one of the greatest sports heroes of all times.

标赛,蝉联十七年夺冠的纪录与阿诺·帕玛创下的纪录持平。他从1962至1978年,连续17年登上排名前十的富人榜,在1964-1965、1967、1971-1973和1975-1976年间的年终薪酬排行榜中,八次蝉联第一名。

尼克劳斯还是美国队队员,该队于1971、1973、1975、1977和1981年的莱德杯大赛中战胜了英国队,1969年与英国队打平。他是1983年和1987年美国队的"不上场队长",1983年美国队获胜,但是1987年输了。1990年,尼克劳斯参加了"职业高尔夫协会高级巡回赛",即冠军巡回赛前身。1996年,他再次创下一个纪录,成为职业高尔夫协会历史上第一位在同一巡回赛中四次获胜的高尔夫运动员。尼克劳斯的职业生涯尾声,他共赢得113次冠军,其中73次职业高尔夫协会巡回赛冠军,10次是冠军巡回赛,30次的非正式比赛或国际大赛的冠军。2005年7月英国公开赛后,他正式退役。

尼克劳斯创造的纪录以及与帕玛之间的竞争将被人们记住,他为了参加所有重要大赛而制定的训练计划也会被人们记住。事实上绝大多数职业高尔夫运动员从那以后都开始同样敬业,显然,大家对主要大奖赛的热情高涨,这应归功于尼克劳斯。

关于此人

尼克劳斯不只是前职业高尔夫运动员。他通过自己的"尼克劳斯设计"公司,继续涉足此运动,这个公司是世界上最大的高尔夫练习设计公司,开发了全球众多知名的高尔夫练习场地。自从1973年起,尼克劳斯一直设计课程,他的儿子和女婿同样是知名的设计师。过了2005年,已经有77家尼克劳斯高尔夫球场举办过将近500次职业锦标赛或全国业余冠军赛。

与其高尔夫生涯密切相关的另一方面,就是他自己写过或与人合写过几本介绍高尔夫运动的书籍,包括一本关于高尔夫训练的《尼克劳斯设计》。他还写过一本自传,题目很简单,就叫《杰克·尼克劳斯》。

除了对高尔夫运动的终生热爱,尼克劳斯还实现了另一项任务:建立尼克劳斯儿童保健基金会。这个非赢利性组织改善了儿童疾病和功能失调的诊断、治疗及预防措施。它同样帮助非赢利性活动关注儿童健康保健。尼克劳斯和妻子芭芭拉共有5个孩子(17个孙子、孙女),他们也把时间和金钱花在慈善事业中,比如青少年高尔夫、儿童医院和奖学金基金会及其他赛事和团体中。

尼克劳斯获得的奖项不仅与他在高尔夫运动中的成就有关,还与他的个人贡献有关。1985年他的家庭被国家高尔夫基金会组织评为"年度高尔夫之家",1992年被大都市高尔夫作家协会评为"年度家庭"。个人方面,尼克劳斯于1999年被美国少数民族高尔夫协会评为"年度最佳父亲"。

杰克·尼克劳斯为提高世界职业高尔夫运动的竞技性作出了巨大贡献,他仍在高尔夫赛场内外的事业中鞠躬尽瘁。他是公认的一名50+1位最闪耀的体育巨星。

Thirty-one

Bobby Orr

Why He is Among the 50 plus one Greatest Sports Heroes

When asked to name the greatest hockey player of all time, many fans of the sport will name Bobby Orr without flinching and they would have good reason for believing it to be true. During his time on the ice, Orr was a defenseman unlike any other. Instead of staying at the point and never charging the net, he played defense with an aggressively offensive flair. He became famous for his speed, his skating skills and his end-to-end rushing, which helped him to score effectively while still doing his job on defense. Setting practically every hockey record that a defenseman could set, Orr changed the game and his team forever, thus placing him in the ranks among the best athletes in history.

On the Way Up

Robert Gordon Orr was born on March 20, 1948 in Parry Sound, Ontario, Canada. The middle of five children, doctors said that due to a dif.cult birth, there was a risk that Orr would not survive. Proving them wrong, the young boy inherited his father, Doug's skillful and speedy playing abilities and began skating when he was only 4 years old. He mostly played pick-up hockey, or shinny, on the frozen Seguin River. In kindergarten, Orr began playing organized hockey in the Parry Sound Minor Squirt Hockey League. When he was 9, he won the MVP in the Pee-Wee Division and he continued to progress so rapidly that he was playing against 16-year-olds by the time he was 12.

Also at the age of 12, Boston Bruins' scout, Wren Blair, signed Orr. The professional franchise made a small investment in Orr's Peewee team, which bound him to the Bruins once he reached the legal playing age of 18. In the meantime, he started playing for the Oshawa Generals in the junior league Ontario Hockey Association (OHA) when he was 14, going up against players as old as 20. In his third season with the Generals, Orr led them to the OHA championship and he averaged two points per game during his final season.

Professional Career

After his lawyer, Alan Eagleson, negotiated his first contract with the Bruins in the fall of 1966, Orr became the highest-paid player in the NHL's history at that time. He had his work cut out for him as the team had not made it to the playoffs since the 1958–1959 season. In his first year, Orr won the Calder Memorial Trophy as outstanding rookie even though he missed nine games due to a knee injury. But the Bruins still managed to finish dead last.

The true power of Orr's dominating defensive skills did not take hold of the Bruins until his second season. But when that did happen, it was as if the team had been struck by a bolt of lightning. Despite the fact that Orr played only 46 out of 74 games due to knee injuries during the 1967–1968 season, he led the Bruins to the first of the 29 straight seasons that they made it to the playoffs. During Orr's 10 years with the Bruins, he carried them to their first Stanley Cup in 29

波比·奥尔

他为何入选《50+1位最闪耀的体育巨星》

如果被问到谁是历史上最伟大的冰上曲棍球运动员,许多球迷都会毫不犹豫、异口同声地说出波比·奥尔的名字,他们有足够的理由相信所言极是。在奥尔的职业生涯中,他是与众不同的防守员。他并非只待在防守区从不冲撞到网上,而是在防守的同时带有强大的攻势。他的速度、滑冰技巧及流畅的冲滑步伐让他举世闻名,这些优点帮他在防守的同时成功得分。奥尔作为防守员,用实际行动创造了曲棍球纪录,并且改变了这项运动,当之无愧地成为50+1位最闪耀的体育巨星之一。

成长之路

1948年3月20日,罗伯特·戈登·奥尔出生于加拿大安大略省帕里湾。作为五个孩子的"中间儿",医生说奥尔由于难产,有无法存活的危险。但是他们都错了,小家伙继承了父亲道格教练而快速的运动能力,他在4岁时就开始滑冰。他主要是玩非比赛性的曲棍球或在结冰的塞甘河上玩简化曲棍球。上幼儿园时,奥尔开始在帕里湾小曲棍球联盟比赛。他9岁时,就赢得了儿童分赛区"最具价值球员"称号,他继续努力并取得长足进步,12岁时的对手就都是16岁的青少年。

同样在12岁那年,波士顿熊队球探雷恩·布莱尔发现奥尔并与其签约。这个职业球队在奥尔的少年队做了投资,他一旦到了18岁法定年龄,就要听从熊队管束。14岁时,他开始效力于安大略曲棍球协会青少年联盟的奥沙华将军队,与20岁的年轻人比赛。在将军队的第三个赛季,奥尔带领球队挺进安大略曲棍球联盟冠军赛,在最后一个赛季时,他平均每场比赛都拿下两分。

职业生涯

1966年秋,奥尔的律师阿兰·伊格尔森与熊队签订了第一份合同,他成为那时国家曲棍球联盟薪酬最高的运动员。1958-1959年赛季,该队未能闯进季后赛,他的比赛也突然结束。奥尔的新秀之年,虽然他因膝盖受伤错过了9场比赛,他仍作为杰出新人而获得卡尔德尔纪念杯。但是熊队最终仍渡过难关。

奥尔主要的防守技能力量强大,直到第二个赛季才运用到熊队。但是当他真正发挥时,熊队仿佛遭到闪电猛击。尽管1967-1968赛季中由于膝盖受伤,奥尔只在74场比赛中上场46次,他带领熊队首次冲进蝉联29个赛季的季后赛。奥尔为熊队效力的十年中,他率领球队于1970年5月10日捧回29年中的首个"斯坦利杯",1972年再次捧杯。

years on May 10, 1970 and again in 1972.

After that second championship win, Orr's knee injuries began to affect him more and more. Despite those injuries, though, he continued to dominate the NHL and led the Bruins to a first place league finish and the Stanley Cup finals in 1974. In 1976, even though several knee operations caused him to play in severe pain, Orr was honored as the most valuable player in the Canada Cup international competition, during which he played for Team Canada.

Orr's knee injuries sidelined him during the 1975–1976 season, when he played only 10 games. His contract with the Bruins was up at the end of that season and the franchise offered him a new, more lucrative contract that included an 18 percent ownership of the organization. However, Eagleson, Orr's lawyer–turned–agent, told him that the Chicago Blackhawks had offered him a better deal, leaving out the part about the Bruin's offer to make him part owner. Consequently, Orr signed with the Blackhawks as a free agent in 1976 even though his professional hockey career was quickly sliding toward a premature end. Over the 3 seasons that Orr was with Chicago, he played in only 26 games.

Orr retired in 1979 after more than a dozen knee surgeries and, at the age of 31, he was the youngest player to be enshrined in the Hockey Hall of Fame. He was among a group of only 10 players who got inducted without having to wait the mandatory 3 years after retirement. Also in 1979, Orr was made an Officer of the Order of Canada and was voted the greatest athlete in Boston history in a poll of New Englanders done by the Boston Globe newspaper. He beat out Ted Williams, Bill Russell, Carl Yastrzemski and Bob Cousy.

Perhaps the most emotional day of Orr's career was January 9, 1979, when the Bruins held Bobby Orr Night. The fans stood up and cheered for 11 straight minutes once he was introduced. Then, as a hush fell over the crowd, Orr's No. 4, was raised to the rafters, after which he made a brief but heartfelt speech about the love and gratitude that he felt for Boston and its fans.

Even though his career was cut short, Orr accomplished so much in so little time. He scored a total of 270 goals and 645 assists in 657 games, adding 953 penalty minutes. He played in the NHL All–Star Game from 1968–1973 and again in 1975. He was the NHL Plus/Minus Leader from 1969–1972 and from 1974–1975. When he retired, Orr was the leading defenseman in NHL history in goals, assists and points, and he was 10th overall in assists, 19th in points. Only Wayne Gretzky, Mario Lemieux and Mike Bossy have scored more points per game.

The following are the records that Orr set during his NHL career with the Bruins:

· Most points in one NHL season by a defenseman (139) (1970–1971)

· Most assists in one NHL season by a defenseman (102, broken by Wayne Gretzky in 1982) (1970–1971)

· Most goals in one NHL season by a defenseman (37, broken by Orr himself in 1975 with 46,broken by Paul Coffey in 1986) (1970–1971)

· Highest plus/minus in one NHL season (+124) (1970–1971)

· Most assists in one NHL game by a defenseman (6, tied with Babe Pratt, Pat Stapleton, Ron Stackhouse, Paul Coffey and Gary Suter)

Because of Orr's powerful abilities as an aggressive defenseman, there was some debate about whether or not to create a separate regular season award for the old–school defenseman. NHL officials were afraid that the new breed of offensive defensemen would sweep the Norris Trophy every year, but Rod Langway, a traditional rearguard player won it in 1983 and 1984 and the debate was put to rest. Since Orr won the trophy 8 years in a row, it is easy to see why the question arose in the first place. His accomplishments include winning the Norris Trophy, Art Ross

第二次夺冠后，奥尔的膝盖伤痛周而复始地折磨着他。尽管忍受伤痛，他继续主宰着国家曲棍球联盟，带领球队荣登联盟排名榜首，成为1974年斯坦利杯决赛冠军。1976年，虽然几次膝盖手术让奥尔在比赛时疼痛难忍，他仍效力于加拿大队，并被加拿大杯国际比赛授予"最具价值球员"称号。

奥尔在1975-1976赛季只出场了10次，他的膝盖伤痛迫使他提前退赛。他与熊队的合同也在赛季结束时终止，联盟分会又提供给他一个新的、更赚钱的机会，让他签订合同并获得球队18%的所有权。然而，奥尔的律师伊格尔森告诉他，芝加哥夜鹰队会给他更大的利润，不用去考虑熊队提出让他拥有部分所有权的条件。结果，1976年奥尔作为自由球员与夜鹰队签订合同，他的职业生涯不知不觉地将提早结束。奥尔为芝加哥效力的三个多赛季中，他参加了26场比赛。

1979年，在接受了不止12次的膝部手术后，31岁的奥尔退役，他是曲棍球名人堂里最年轻的运动员。球员退役后规定三年才能入选名人堂，他是仅有的10名无须等待三年便入选的球员之一。同样在1979年，奥尔担任加拿大治安长官，并且在《波士顿全球报》的"新英格兰人"投票选举活动中被评为"波士顿历史上最伟大运动员"。在此次选举中，他击败了泰德·威廉、比尔·拉塞尔、卡尔·亚斯特詹斯基和鲍勃·库西。

也许最感人的那天就是1979年的1月9日，熊队举办了"波比·奥尔之夜"。当介绍他的时候，球迷起立，连续欢呼11分钟。然后，当人群安静下来，奥尔的4号球衣升上缘木，之后他做了一个简短却真诚的演讲，向波士顿和球迷们衷心地表达自己的爱与感谢之情。

虽然奥尔的职业生涯缩短了，他仍在如此短暂的岁月中获得无数成功。在657场比赛中，他共进球270个，助攻645次，罚球时间为953分钟。1968-1973年，他入选国家曲棍球联盟全明星队，1975年再次参赛。1969-1972年和1974-1975年，他是国家曲棍球联盟正/负分数最高的队员。

以下是奥尔在国家曲棍球联盟生涯中效力于熊队所获得的荣誉：
·国家曲棍球联盟单个赛季得分最高的防守队员 (139) (1970-1971)
·国家曲棍球联盟单个赛季助攻最多的防守队员 (102, 1982年此纪录被韦恩·格雷茨基打破) (1970-1971)
·国家曲棍球联盟单个赛季进球最多的防守队员 (37, 1975年，奥尔本人以46个进球数打破此纪录；1986年此纪录被保尔·考菲打破) (1970-1971)
·国家曲棍球联盟单个赛季正/负分数最高的队员 (+124) (1970-1971)
·国家曲棍球联盟单场比赛助攻最多的防守队员 (6, 与贝比·布拉特、帕特·斯泰普莱顿、罗恩·斯塔克豪斯、保尔·考菲和盖瑞·舒特持平)
由于奥尔强大的攻势和进攻能力，大家对是否要对防守员增设单个正规赛季奖项而争论不休。国家曲棍球联盟官员生怕这种新的进攻性防守员每年都会捧走诺里斯纪念杯，但是罗德·朗威这名传统后卫在1983和1984年将诺里斯纪念杯揽入囊中，这才平息了这场争论。
为什么大家的疑问会首先出现，原因很简单，因为奥尔连续8次捧回了诺里斯纪念

Trophy, Hart Trophy and Conn Smythe Trophy in 1970, making him the only player to win four major NHL awards in one season. Other honors include:

- Calder Memorial Trophy (1967) · NHL Second All–Star Team (1967)
- NHL First All–Star Team (1968–1975) · NHL All–Star Game (1968–1973, 1975)
- James Norris Trophy (1968–1975) · NHL Plus/Minus Leade3r (1969–1972, 1974–1975)
- Art Ross Trophy (1970 and 1975) · Hart Memorial Trophy (1970–1972)
- Conn Smythe Trophy (1970 and 1972) · Stanley Cup (1970, 1972)
- Lester B. Pearson Award (1975) · Canada Cup Tournament MVP (1976)
- Lester Patrick Trophy (1979)
- Sportsman of the Year Award from Sports Illustrated magazine (1970)
- Voted Second Greatest Hockey Player of All Time by The Hockey News (1997)

About the Man Himself

Because of his continuing injuries Orr never cashed a paycheck during his 3 seasons with the Blackhawks. His belief was that he would only accept a salary if he played and since he did not play due to injuries he would not collect his salary. That in itself was a memorable act and showed how humble and honest he was. After retirement, Orr stayed close to the game. He worked for a brief time as an assistant coach for Chicago and later served as consultant to the NHL and the Hartford Whalers at various times. Although he did spend many years as a bank executive in the Boston area, he currently works as a player–agent in the city, helping young players understand the business side of hockey. Orr also coaches a team of top Central Hockey League (CHL) players against another team coached by Don Cherry in the annual CHL Top Prospects Game, and he continues to promote the game of hockey on a grassroots level.

Although Orr was tough on the ice, getting into his share of fights, he is a more humble and quiet man than his hockey player persona ever let on. He prefers to keep his family life and charity work pretty much under wraps. He and his wife, Peggy, were married in September of 1973 and have two sons. The couple recently celebrated their 30th anniversary. As for his charitable donations, Orr participates in such events as golf tournaments, dinners, carnivals and hockey games in order to raise money for organizations that support a wide range of causes. Some of the people that Orr has helped out through his charity work over the years are individuals with spinal cord injuries, firefighters and pediatric and adult cancer patients. With all of his extra activities, Bobby Orr has certainly proven that life does not end after 30, rather, it is just getting started.

杯。他的成就包括1970年赢得诺里斯纪念杯、阿瑟·罗斯杯、哈特杯和康恩·斯迈思杯,这让他成为首位同一赛季赢得4个国家曲棍球联盟大奖的运动员。其他荣誉奖项包括:
- 卡尔德尔纪念杯(1967)
- 国家曲棍球联盟第二全明星阵容队 (1967)
- 国家曲棍球联盟第一全明星阵容队(1968–1975)
- 入选国家曲棍球联盟全明星赛 (1968–1973, 1975)
- 詹姆斯·诺里斯纪念杯(1968–1975)
- 国家曲棍球联盟正/负分数最高的队员(1969–1972, 1974–1975)
- 阿瑟·罗斯杯(1970和1975)
- 哈特纪念杯(1970–1972)
- 卡尔德尔纪念杯(1970 和1972)
- 斯坦利杯 (1970, 1972)
- 莱斯特·B·皮尔森奖(1975)
- 加拿大杯锦标赛"最具价值球员" (1976)
- 莱斯特·帕特里克杯(1979)
- 被《体育画报》评为"年度体育人物"(1970)
- 被《曲棍球新闻》评选为"历史上排名第二的最伟大曲棍球运动员" (1997)

由于接二连三的受伤,奥尔效力于夜鹰队的三个赛季中从没有接受薪金。他认为只有参赛才能获得薪水;他由于受伤未能参赛,因此不能接受任何薪酬。此举令人记忆犹新,表明了他性格谦卑、诚实。退役后,奥尔仍密切关注曲棍球。他短暂地担任过芝加哥队的副教练,后来又有几次担任国家曲棍球联盟和哈特福特捕鲸者队的顾问。虽然在波士顿地区担任了几年银行经理,但他目前是该市的运动员经纪人,帮助年轻运动员了解曲棍球运动的商业方面。奥尔还是中央曲棍球联盟顶尖队员的教练,他们的球队在一年一度的"中央曲棍球联盟顶级展望赛"中,与教练唐·奇瑞率领的球队竞赛,他继续把曲棍球运动发扬光大。

虽然奥尔在运动时坚韧、粗犷,他在赛场外却分外谦卑、安静。他宁愿与家人一起共度时光,做很多慈善活动都不留名。他和妻子贝奇于1973年9月结婚,有两个儿子。夫妻俩最近庆祝了30周年结婚纪念日。关于奥尔慈善捐款方面,他出席了诸如高尔夫锦标赛、晚宴、狂欢节和曲棍球比赛的众多盛事,以此为支持慈善事业的广大机构筹集资金。奥尔通过慈善活动帮助过的人包括患脊髓炎的病人、消防员和癌症儿童及成人。波比·奥尔体坛之外的工作证明了一个真理:人到三十,人生并未结束,相反,恰恰刚刚开始。

Thirty-two

Arnold Palmer

Why He is Among the 50 plus one Greatest Sports Heroes

During his career, Arnold Palmer received almost every national award that exists in professional golf. And he was also recently named one of the 100 most influential student–athletes to participate in NCAA events during their college years. Needless to say, Palmer is guaranteed a spot among the highest ranking sports legends.

On the Way Up

Arnold Daniel Palmer was born on September 10, 1929 in Latrobe, Pennsylvania. His father, Milfred J. Palmer worked at the Latrobe Country Club for 55 years as a golf professional and the course superintendent. When little Arnie was 4 years old, Milfred cut down a set of clubs and gave it to his young son. Soon, the boy was playing better than most of the club's older caddies, and he started caddying at the age of 11. He eventually became somewhat of a jack–of–all trades at the club, working at almost every job that was available.

During high school, Palmer focused mainly on his golf game. He won the Pennsylvania high school championship twice and won the first of his five West Penn Amateur Championships when he was only 17. He also competed with great success in national junior events. Palmer later attended Wake Forest College, now Wake Forest University, where he developed into the team's best player and one of the top collegiate players of that time. He withdrew from the school during his senior year after one of his good friends and fellow classmen died in a car accident.

After leaving Wake Forest, Palmer served in the Coast Guard for 3 years and fought in the Korean Conflict. When he was discharged, he re–enrolled for a short time at Wake Forest, but then moved to Cleveland, where he had last been stationed. While in Cleveland, he worked in sales and began playing amateur golf. He won two Ohio Amateurs before going on to win the U.S. Amateur in 1954.

Around that same time, Palmer met his soon–to–be wife, Winifred Walzer, at an Eastern Pennsylvania tournament. 1954 was a celebratory year for Palmer, he turned professional in the fall and he and Winnie wed.

Professional Career

During his career as a professional golfer, Palmer clinched 92 championships of both national and international status. A whopping 62 of these wins came while he was on the U.S. PGA Tour, beginning with the Canadian Open in 1955. He also won the Masters Tournament in 1958, 1960, 1962 and 1964 as well as the U.S. Open in 1960 and the British Open in 1961 and 1962. It is not difficult to see, then, why some of Palmer's fans addressed him simply as The King.

As is befitting true royalty, Palmer received numerous honors for his outstanding leadership in the kingdom of golf during the 1960s through the 1990s. The following are the awards that he acquired during the first 2 decades:

阿诺·帕玛

他为何入选《50+1位最闪耀的体育巨星》

阿诺·帕玛在职业生涯中，几乎包揽了职业高尔夫球赛的所有国家级大奖。最近他参加了美国国家大学体育联盟的体育赛事，被评为"100名最具影响力大学生运动员之一"。毋庸置疑，帕玛在体育传奇人物中榜上有名。

成长之路

1929年9月10日，阿诺·丹尼尔·帕玛出生于宾夕法尼亚州拉乔伯市。他的父亲米尔弗瑞德在拉乔伯乡村俱乐部工作了55年，在那里担任职业高尔夫球教练及球场主管。小阿尼4岁时，米尔弗瑞德减少了一些俱乐部，把它们分给自己的小儿子。不久，小男孩就比俱乐部其他年长的球童打得更好，他11岁开始就成为高尔夫球手。最后，他在俱乐部什么都干，只要手边有活做。

高中时期，帕玛主要精力都花在高尔夫球上。他两次赢得宾夕法尼亚州高中冠军，17岁时是他5次"西部宾州业余冠军"的初次胜利。在国家青少年赛事中，他也取得出色成绩。帕玛随后就读于韦克·福雷斯特学院，即现在的韦克·福雷斯特大学，成为球队最优秀的球员，也那时大学顶尖运动员之一。大四时，他的好友亦是同班同学，在一场车祸中不幸丧生，于是他辍学了。

离开韦克·福雷斯特大学之后，帕玛在海岸护卫队效力3年，还参加了朝鲜战争。辍学后，他短暂地重返韦克·福雷斯特大学，但是又转至克利夫兰，最后才安置下来。在克利夫兰时，他做销售，并开始成为业余高尔夫球手。他两次赢得俄亥俄州业余选手大赛冠军，1954年又赢得了美国业余选手大赛冠军。

就在那时，帕玛在"东部宾州锦标赛"上遇到了妻子威妮弗蕾德·沃尔泽，并很快结婚。1954年对于帕玛来说是值得庆祝的一年，这年秋天他成为职业运动员，并且与威妮结婚。

职业生涯

在高尔夫运动员的职业生涯中，帕玛赢得92次全国和国际大赛的冠军。这些胜利中有62场是美国巡回赛，始于1955年的加拿大公开赛。他还于1958年、1960年、1962年和1964年获得名人赛的胜利，并赢得1960年美国公开赛和1961、1962年的英国公开赛。显而易见，当时帕玛的球迷称他为"王"是有道理的。

帕玛是高尔夫王国名副其实的王者，在60年代至90年代的岁月中，他因卓越的领袖才能而获得无数荣誉。以下是前20年获得的奖项：

• Gold Tee Award, Metropolitan (NY) Golf Writers Association (1965)
• William D. Richardson Award, Golf Writers Association of America (1969)
• Bob Jones Award, U.S. Golf Association (1971)
• Charter member, World Golf Hall of Fame (1974)
• Golf Digest "Man of Silver Era" (1975)
• Charles Bartlett Award, Golf Writers Association of America (1976)
• Herb Graffis Award, National Golf Foundation (1978)

During the 1980s, the awards that Palmer won reflected his developing maturity in the game and his respected status among professional golfers nationwide.

• PGA Hall of Fame (1980)
• Old Tom Morris Award, Golf Course Superintendent Association of America (1983)
• Man of the Year, All–American Collegiate Golf Hall of Fame (1984)
• Golfer of the Century, New York Athletic Club (1985)
• Commemorative Honoree, Golf Digest Commemorative Seniors Tournament (1987)
• Golfer of Decade for 1958–1967, Centennial of Golf, Golf Magazine (1989)
• American Senior Golf Association National Award (1989)
• Chicago District Golf Association Distinguished Service Award (1989)

Palmer's accolades in golf kept on coming even into the 1990s and beyond. They include but are not limited to the:

• Ambassador of Golf Award, World Series of Golf (1991)
• Bing Crosby Award, Metropolitan Golf Writers Association (1992)
• Memorial Honoree, Memorial Tournament (1993)
• Distinguished Service Award, PGA of America (1994)
• Centennial Award, Golf Associations of Philadelphia (1996)
• Lifetime Achievement Award, PGA Tour (1998)
• Golf Newsmaker of the Century, Golf World (1999)
• Ike Grainger Award, USGA (2000)
• Tri–State PGA Hall of Fame (2002)
• 50th Anniversary Atlantic Coast Conference golf team (2003)

Besides being awarded for all of his many accomplishments in golf specifically, Palmer was also crowned repeatedly for his performance as an athlete in general. These glorifying moments have occurred over a more than 40–year span. They include the:

• Hickok Professional Athlete of the Year (1960)
• Sportsman of the Year, *Sports Illustrated* magazine (1960)
• Dapper Dan Award, Pittsburgh (1960)
• Associated Press Athlete of the Decade (1960–1969)
• Sports Appreciation Trophy, Atlanta A.C. C.C.(1990)
• National Sports Award, Washington D.C. (1993)
• Sports Legends Award, Junior Diabetes Foundation (1993)
• Roy Firestone Award, Los Angeles (2004)

About the Man Himself

Many of Palmer's fans do not just consider him to be the king of golf, but also the king of pretty much everything else. His genuinely charming personality as well as his overwhelmingly kind and caring attitude toward everyone he meets reaches out to people so much so that Palmer's

- 大都会(纽约)高尔夫作家协会颁发的"金球座奖"(1965)
- 美国高尔夫作家协会颁发的"威廉·D·里查德森奖"(1969)
- 美国高尔夫协会颁发的"鲍勃·琼斯奖"(1971)
- 入选世界高尔夫球名人堂创始会员(1974)
- 被《高尔夫文摘》评为"银色年代人物"(1975)
- 美国高尔夫作家协会颁发的"查理·巴特利特奖"(1976)
- 国家高尔夫基金会颁发的"赫伯·格拉菲斯"(1978)

80年代,帕玛获得的奖项体现了他在高尔夫运动中逐渐成熟,也表明他在全国职业高尔夫球手中的受敬佩程度。

- 入选美国职业高尔夫协会名人堂(1980)
- 美国高尔夫球场管理协会颁发的"老汤姆莫里斯奖"(1983)
- 全美大学高尔夫名人堂"年度人物"(1984)
- 纽约体育俱乐部"世纪高尔夫球手"(1985)
- 高尔夫读者老手纪念荣誉锦标赛纪念人 (1987)
- 被《高尔夫》杂志"高尔夫百年"评为"1958–1967年代高尔夫球手"(1989)
- 美国老年高尔夫球协会国家奖(1989)
- 芝加哥地区高尔夫球协会杰出贡献奖(1989)

进入90年代之后,帕玛仍然获得许多高尔夫大奖。以下是部分获奖项目:

- 高尔夫世界联赛"高尔夫大使"(1991)
- 大都会高尔夫作家协会颁发的"宾·克劳斯贝奖"(1992)
- 纪念锦标赛纪念人 (1993)
- 美国职业高尔夫球协会"杰出贡献奖"(1994)
- 费城高尔夫球协会"世纪奖"(1996)
- 美国职业高尔夫球协会巡回赛"终生成就奖"(1998)
- 被《高尔夫世界》评为"世纪高尔夫新闻人物"(1999)
- USGA"埃克·格兰杰奖"(2000)
- 入选美国职业高尔夫球协会三州名人堂(2002)
- 入选亚特兰大沿岸会议50周年纪念日高尔夫球队(2003)

除了因高尔夫球方面的成功而获得无数奖项以外,帕玛作为普通运动员,表现也出类拔萃。在40多载的岁月中,他频频获奖,这些荣誉奖项包括:

- 希考克年度职业运动员奖(1960)
- 《体育画报》"年度体育人物" (1960)
- 匹兹堡"戴普·丹奖"(1960)
- 被美联社评为"时代运动员"(1960–1969)
- 亚特兰大华人基督教会"体育欣赏奖" (1990)
- 华盛顿特区"国家体育奖"(1993)
- 青少年糖尿病基金会"体育传奇人物奖"(1993)
- 洛杉矶"罗伊·菲尔斯通" (2004)

关于此人

帕玛的很多球迷不仅仅把他看成高尔夫球王,还认为他是所有领域的王者。他充满魅力的个性,友善以及关爱让每个与他接触的人都禁不住要喜欢上他。因此在全世界的

worldwide connections are sometimes collectively called Arnie's Army.

Palmer's king–sized heart led him to become involved in an inspiring amount of charitable endeavors. He served as a 20–year honorary national chairman of the March of Dimes Birth Defects Foundation and led the fund–raising drive that helped form Orlando's Arnold Palmer Hospital for Children and Women in the 1980s. He also held a major golf fundraiser for 6 years for Latrobe Area Hospital, of which he was a prominent member of the board of directors. This fundraiser eventually led to the creation of the Latrobe Area Hospital Charitable Foundation.

The humanitarian efforts of The King have not gone unnoticed. He has received awards from all over the country for his work, which include the:

· Arthur J. Rooney Award, Pittsburgh Catholic Youth Association (1977)
· Distinguished Pennsylvanian (1980)
· Gold Medal, Pennsylvania Association of Broadcasters (1988)
· Outstanding American Award, Los Angeles Philanthropic Foundation (1992)
· Humanitarian Award, Variety Club International (1993)
· "Good Guy" Award, American Legion of National Commanders (1993)
· Reagan Distinguished American Award, Jonathon Club, Los Angeles (1996)
· Lifetime Achievement Award, March of Dimes (1998)
· Spirit of Hope Award, University of Pittsburgh Cancer Institute (1998)
· Great Ones Award, Jim Murray Memorial Foundation, Los Angeles (2001)
· Presidential Medal of Freedom, George W. Bush (2004)

One of Palmer's major interests outside of his golf kingdom is business. This interest began during the 1960s and skyrocketed due to his determination, the help of his business manager and, of course, his widespread network. He is the principal owner of a car dealership in Latrobe and president of Cleveland–based Arnold Palmer Enterprises. The King has been active in automobile and aviation service firms throughout the years. In 1999, his contributions to aviation and his Western Pennsylvania community were honored when the Westmoreland County Airport underwent a name change. It is now known as the Arnold Palmer Regional Airport.

Palmer has managed to connect his passions for business and golf by becoming involved in both golf course design and ownership. He is president of the Palmer Golf Course Design Company, which got its start in the mid–1960s and has influenced the design of more than 200 new courses throughout the world. On the ownership side, Palmer has been president and sole owner of Latrobe Country Club since 1971. A year before that, he became president and principal owner of the Bay Hill Club and Lodge in Orlando, which hosts the annual Mastercardpresented Bay Hill Invitational on the PGA Tour. Almost 3 decades later, in 1999, Palmer and a group of investors bought the popular Pebble Beach golf complex on the coast of California.

Amongst all of his efforts in the humanitarian and business worlds, Palmer also manages to spend time with his family. He and his wife, Winifred, have two daughters and seven grandchildren. After 45 years of marriage, Winifred died of cancer in November of 1999. In January of 2005, Palmer married Kathleen Gawthrop, who has three children of her own.

Palmer has residences in Latrobe, Orlando and La Quinta, California. His restaurant, Arnold Palmer's, is located in La Quinta and he is working with Luna Vineyards to expand his portfolio of privately branded wine selections that will include Arnold Palmer Wines.

Palmer also has a knack for writing, in which he combines his love for golf with his all–around passion for life and helping others. He has written various books, including *Play Great Golf, Playing by the Rules, Arnold Palmer: Memories, Stories and Memorabilia,* and *A Golfer's Life.*

球迷汇聚成了一支军队——"阿尼军队"。

帕玛具有王者风范,参加了大量的鼓舞人心的慈善活动。他担任优生优育基金会二十年的荣誉主席,广筹资金,在80年代成立了奥兰多阿诺·帕玛妇女儿童医院。他还担任了拉乔伯地区医院6年的主要高尔夫资金筹集者,也是董事会永久成员。这个筹集资金的活动最终帮助成立了拉乔伯地区医院慈善基金会。

"王者"的人道主义行为受人关注。他的努力工作让全国各地都为他颁奖,这些荣誉奖项包括:
· 匹兹堡天主教青年协会"阿瑟·J.鲁尼奖" (1977)
· 杰出的宾夕法尼亚人 (1980)
· 宾夕法尼亚州广播工作者协会颁发的"金牌" (1988)
· 洛杉矶慈善家基金会颁发的"杰出美国人奖"(1992)
· 国际多种俱乐部"人道主义奖" (1993)
· 美国退伍将军协会颁发的"好人奖"(1993)
· 洛杉矶乔纳森俱乐部"里根杰出美国人奖" (1996)
· "新生儿缺陷基金会"颁发的终生成就奖 (1998)
· 匹兹堡大学癌症研究所颁发的"希望精神奖"(1998)
· 洛杉矶吉姆·默里纪念基金会"伟大人物奖" (2001)
· 乔治·W·布什颁发的"总统自由勋章" (2004)

高尔夫王国之外,帕码主要兴趣之一就是商业。这个兴趣是从60年代发展起来的,由于他的雄心壮志、经理的帮助以及广泛的关系网,他的事业突飞猛进。他是拉乔伯汽车特许经销处的老板,也是克利夫兰当地的阿诺·帕玛公司总裁。"王者"积极投身于汽车及航空公司的工作。由于对航空事业及他的西部宾夕法尼亚社团贡献突出,1999年,他获得一项殊荣,威斯特摩兰县机场的名字改朝换代,改为"阿诺·帕玛地区机场"。

帕玛把热情投入商业及高尔夫球运动,将两者成功结合,他担任起高尔夫球场设计,并且成为拥有者。他是"帕玛高尔夫球场设计公司"的总经理,这个公司在60年代中期起步,全球200多家新球场都靠它来设计。在所有制方面,帕玛自从1971年就担任拉乔伯乡村俱乐部的总经理及独家负责人。在这之前的一年,他是海湾山俱乐部及奥兰多旅馆的总经理兼主要负责人,每年组织"万事达"承办的美国高尔夫球协会巡回赛"海湾山名人邀请赛"。差不多过了30年,到了1999年,帕玛和一群投资者买下了加利福尼亚海岸著名的圆石滩高尔夫球综合企业。

在帕玛所有慈善活动和商业活动中,他没有忘记与家人度时光。他和妻子威妮弗蕾德共有两个女儿,7个孙子、孙女。威妮弗蕾德于1999年11月死于癌症,45年的婚姻也宣告结束。2005年1月,帕玛与凯瑟琳·高斯罗普结婚,她本人有3个孩子。

帕玛在拉乔伯、奥兰多和加利福尼亚的La Quinta都有住宅。他的阿诺·帕玛饭店坐落在La Quinta,他与露娜酒厂合作,以此扩大个人品牌的酒类精选品投资,包括阿诺·帕玛酒。

帕玛的文笔也不错,他把对高尔夫运动的热爱与对生活及助人为乐的热情相结合。写作的书籍包括:《打好高尔夫球》、《打球的规则》、《阿诺·帕玛:回忆录》、《故事及大事记》、《高尔夫球手的生活》。

Thirty-three

Walter Payton

Why He is Among the 50 plus one Greatest Sports Heroes

Walter Payton was much more than just a running back. He was an aggressive and tenacious player whose supreme balance, leg strength and stiff-legged gain made it more than difficult for his opponents to tackle him; he made it downright painful. Unlike many of his fellow running backs, Payton rarely finished a play by running out of bounds. Instead, he always looked for an extra yard or two and would try to take down with him anyone who got in his way. Although he played on mostly mediocre Chicago Bears teams during his NFL career, Payton himself could never in a million years be described as mediocre, either in football or in life. He is, indeed, one of the greatest sports heroes of all times.

On the Way Up

Walter Jerry Payton was born the youngest of three children on July 25, 1954 in Columbia, Mississippi into an athletic family. His older brother, Eddie, would later become a player in both the NFL and the Canadian Football League. Despite the family's love of sports, Payton's mother, Alyne, did not allow him to play high school football until he was a junior at Jefferson High. The following year, Payton transferred to Columbia High and became an instant starter. After leading the team to an 8-2 record, he was named All-State.

Upon graduating from high school, Payton decided to attend Jackson State University, where he joined his brother on the football field. Walter made the starting lineup his first year and by the time his last season rolled around in 1974, he had been named a two-time Little All-American after setting nine school records, scoring 66 touchdowns and rushing for 3,563 yards. Walter graduated with a BA in communications and finished his college football career with 464 points, an NCAA Division II scoring record that remained unbroken for 24 years. Despite the fact Jackson State was a small school, Payton was considered for the Heisman Trophy.

Professional Career

Drafted by the Chicago Bears in the first round, 5 foot 10 inch, 200-pound Payton was the first running back selected in the 1975 draft, and fourth pick overall. He would play with the team for the length of his professional career, which would last through1987. Payton missed only one game the entire 13 years and started in 186 consecutive games after that. Payton attributed his consistent playing ability to his off-season training routine, which included his legendary weight-lifting regimen and daily runs through sandy beaches; up steep hills near the Pearl River in Mississippi and up the steep mound of dirt near his South Barrington, Illinois home. His distinctive stiff-legged, high-stepping running style was adopted in a effort to avoid knee and leg injury.

The only game Payton missed was during his rookie year, and he missed it only because the Bear's rookie coach forced him to sit out due to a bruised thigh. The fact that Payton had not wanted to miss the game but was held out is a shining example of what a hard-working and tough

沃特·佩顿

他为何入选《50+1位最闪耀的体育巨星》

沃特·佩顿不只是个跑卫。他是个好胜、顽强的运动员,有着惊人的平衡力、腿力及直腿进攻,让对手望而生畏,不敢阻截,这着实令对手痛苦。与其他跑卫队友不同,佩顿很少在一场比赛中犯规跑出界外。相反,他总是瞄准一两码外,只要有人阻截他,他就会下潜抱摔。虽然佩顿在国家橄榄球联盟的职业生涯中,主要是为芝加哥熊队这个普普通通的球队效力,但是他本人在橄榄球体坛内外绝对不是平庸之辈。他是体坛中名副其实的英雄之一。

成长之路

1954年7月5日,沃特·杰瑞·佩顿生于密西西比哥伦比亚的体育世家,是三个孩子中最小的。他的哥哥艾迪后来成为了国家橄榄球联盟和加拿大橄榄球联盟的运动员。尽管佩顿的家庭钟爱体育,但是他的母亲艾琳直到他在杰佛森高中三年级时,才同意他打橄榄球。次年,佩顿转学至哥伦比亚高中,迅速成为首发大前锋。带领球队创下8:2的纪录后,人们开始称他为"全州明星"。

高中毕业时,佩顿决定选择杰克逊州立大学,在那里他与哥哥一起驰骋于橄榄球球场。第一年,沃特成为先发球员,到了1974年最后一个赛季时,他两次被评为"全美小明星",之前他创下了九个学校纪录,包括66个触地得分,3563码的跑码数。沃特毕业时获得传播学学士学位,整个大学橄榄球生涯中共拿下464分,这是大学联赛二区的总分纪录,24年无人能打破。虽然杰克逊州立大学规模不大,但是大家认为可以为佩顿颁发"海斯曼奖"。

职业生涯

在芝加哥熊队的第一轮选秀大会中,身高5英尺10英寸、体重200磅的佩顿在1975年的选秀中被选为"第一跑锋",排名第四顺位。直到1987年,他的整个职业生涯都在为该队效力。整整13个春秋,佩顿只错过一场比赛,之后连续在186场比赛中亮相。佩顿认为季后赛的日常训练成就了他贵在坚持的品质,包括他传奇式的举重强化训练、每天在沙滩上练习跑步、跑上密西西比珍珠河边陡峭的山地,以及伊利诺斯南巴林顿家附近高低不平的土墩。他与众不同的直腿和高抬腿的跑姿,帮他免受膝盖和腿部之伤。

佩顿错过的唯一一场比赛就是在新秀那年,只因为大腿撞伤,熊队新人的教练命令他坐在场外。事实上,佩顿不想错失比赛,坚持看完球赛,这也极好地证明了他是一个努力坚强的运动员。这种品质让他成功地立足于国家橄榄球联盟。由于性情温和,他的队友

player he was. That was what made him so successful in the NFL. Nicknamed Sweetness by his teammates for his gentle disposition, it was ironic that his theory on the field was that it was better to explode into any player who tried to tackle him than to let that player get an easy shot at him.

To prove how tough Payton really was, his most impressive individual performance of his career came only 2 days after he had been bed-ridden with the flu. On November 20, 1977, he ran for 77 yards in the first quarter against the Minnesota Vikings. He just kept on going as the minutes ticked on, reaching 144 yards by halftime and going further by the end of the third quarter with 192. After a 58-yard off-tackle dash in the last quarter, Payton closed the game with 275 yards, breaking O.J. Simpson's record by two yards.

Payton set other awe-inspiring records during his time in the NFL. He:
- NFL rushing record for most yards gained, game (275) (November 20, 1977)
- NFL rushing record for most games with 100 yards or more, career (77)
- NFL record for most attempts, combined net yards, career (4,368)
- NFL record for most yards, combined net yards, career (21,803)
- Shares the NFL rushing record for most seasons with 1,000 or more yards (10) (1976–1981 and 1983–1986)
- Shares the NFL rushing record for most consecutive seasons leading league in attempts (4) (1976–1979)
- Former NFL rushing record holder for most yards, career (16,726)
- Former NFL rushing record holder for most attempts, career (3,838)

With all of the records that Payton set, it would seem only fitting his team would win the Super Bowl at least once during his career. They did, and that has been, in fact, Chicago's only Super Bowl win to-date. The team that finally pulled through to the end was the 1985 Bears that included an interesting mix of characters so dubbed the Grabowski's by Coach Ditka. Payton led his teammates, including Punky-QB quarterback Jim McMahon and William (Refrigerator) Perry, to an 18-1 record that year and eventually to win over the New England Patriots 46-10 in Super Bowl XX on January 26, 1986.

The season following the big Super Bowl win proved to be Payton's recordbreaking year. That was the year he reached 1,000 yards rushing for the 10th time in his career and became the first player ever to hit a career total of 20,000 combined net yards. Feeling his age and the pang of various injuries, Payton decided the time was right to retire. In 1987, he announced that he was competing in his final season. Before the start of Chicago's last regular-season home game, Payton's No. 34, was retired.

Throughout his professional career Payton had recorded 125 total touchdowns scored, 110 of them in rushing and 15 of them in receiving. He had passed for a total of 34 times for 331 yards and eight touchdowns, and had played in nine Pro Bowl games throughout his career. The following are awards and honors that were bestowed upon Payton both during and after his fantastic run in the NFL:
- NFL Player of the Year Award (1977, 1985)
- NFL Most Valuable Player Award (1977, 1985)
- NFL Offensive Player of the Year Award (1977)
- NFC Player of the Year Award, The Sporting News (1976–1977)
- Pro Football Hall of Fame (1993)
- NFL's 75th Anniversary Team (1994)
- Most Valuable Player, Associated Press (1977)

给他起了个昵称叫"可爱先生",但是这个称呼却不适合他的球场理论,他认为当任何运动员要阻截他时,最好先发制人,不要让对方有机可乘、轻易攻击到他。

有一次比赛可以证明佩顿是多么顽强,他令人难忘的个人表演是在一次流感卧病在床后的两天。1977年11月20日,在对抗明尼苏达维京人队的第一节中,他就跑了77码。时间流逝,他只顾着继续跑,半场时跑了144码,更远的是在第三节快结束时,跑了192码。最后一节中,佩顿以58码的冲撞摆脱了阻截队员,最终以275码结束比赛,以两码的优势打破了O.J.辛普森创下的纪录。

在国家橄榄球联盟的那段岁月中,佩顿还创造了其他令人叹服的纪录,包括:
·NFL比赛中最多的跑码数纪录(275) (1977年11月20日)
·NFL生涯中跑码数为100或100多码的最多比赛场数纪录(77)
·NFL生涯中最高综合跑码数纪录(4,368)
·NFL生涯中最高综合跑码数比纪录(21,803)
·共享NFL跑码数为1000或1000多码的最多赛季纪录(10)(1976–1981和1983–1986)
·共享NFL传球最多的连续赛季纪录 (4) (1976–1979)
·前NFL生涯跑码数最高纪录保持者(16,726)
·前 NFL生涯传球最多的纪录保持者 (3,838)

佩顿创下的纪录似乎应该让他在职业生涯中为球队至少赢得一次"超级碗"。他们成功了,事实上,那是芝加哥队迄今的唯一一次"超级碗"之胜。那是在1985年,熊队最终渡过危机,当时熊队有趣地集中了各种不同风格的队员,被教练迪特卡称为"格拉鲍夫斯基"。那年,佩顿带领队友,包括"朋克"四分卫吉姆·麦克马洪和威廉·派瑞,拿下18:1的成绩,在1986年1月26日,他们最终以46:10战胜新英格兰爱国者队,捧回"超级碗XX"。

"超级碗"大获全胜后的下个赛季,是佩顿"破纪录之年"。那一年,他创下了职业生涯中第十次跑码超过1000码的纪录,成为第一位职业生涯中总共创下20000码数的运动员。佩顿感到年龄的增长、再加上大大小小的伤痛困扰,他决定是时候宣布退役了。1987年,他宣布参加最后一个赛季。在芝加哥最后一场常规赛主场比赛之前,佩顿的34号球衣也被退役。

佩顿整个职业生涯中,共有125个触地得分,其中110个冲球、15个接球丢球。他传球34次的码数为331码,8个触地得分,职业生涯中共9次参加"职业碗"大赛。以下是佩顿在国家橄榄球联盟职业生涯内外获得的奖项和荣誉:

·NFL 年度运动员奖(1977, 1985)
·NFL最具价值球员奖 (1977, 1985)
·NFL年度进攻球员奖 (1977)
·《体育新闻》国家橄榄球协会年度球员奖 (1976–1977)
·职业橄榄球名人堂 (1993)
·入选国家橄榄球联盟75周年全明星队(1994)
·被美联社评为最具价值球员(1977)
·入选美联社"全职队" (1976–1977, 1984–1986)

- All–Pro Team, Associated Press (1976–1977, 1984–1986)
- Offensive Player of the Year, Associated Press (1977)
- Most Valuable Player, Professional Football Writers of America (1977)
- All–League Selection, Professional Football Writers of America (1976–1978, 1984)

About The Man Himself

The end of his football career by no means meant the end for Payton. Instead, it proved to be a chance for him to pursue new interests and activities for which he had not had time as a professional athlete. After retirement, he took up auto racing and survived an almost tragic collision while racing at Elkhart Lake in 1993. He formed a racing team the next year with former driver Dale Coyne, making him the only African American team owner for a period of time. Payton Coyne Racing's top achievement was when one driver came in 3rd at the 1996 U.S. 500.

Payton also joined a group of investors who wanted to bring an NFL team back to St. Louis, but that venture eventually failed. Proving to be more of a success was his company, Walter Payton Power Equipment LLC., which remains one of the premier providers of heavy industrial and construction equipment both locally and nationally. In 1996, Payton opened up Walter Payton's Roundhouse Complex, a restaurant and brewery in Aurora, Illinois that is still open today.

In 1998, Payton started what was perhaps his life's greatest ambition with the Walter Payton Foundation, which worked to provide support for neglected, abused and underprivileged children in the state of Illinois. Tragically, Payton died the following year, on November 1, 1999, after being diagnosed with cancer. He was only 45–years old. His wife, Connie, whom he had married in July of 1976, continues to carry out his mission. The foundation was renamed the Walter and Connie Payton Foundation and is still in operation today, working closely with the Department of Children and Family Services in Illinois. Connie also started the Walter Payton Cancer Fund in honor of her husband and to help find a cure for cancer, and Brittany, their daughter, is one of the founding members of an educational campaign called Youth for Life: Remembering Walter Payton. The campaign encourages organ donations from young adults. His son, Jarrett, is currently an NFL running back.

Upon finding out about his illness, Payton worked hard to finish up the autobiography he had started. Named for one of his favorite sayings as a football player, *Never Die Easy: The Autobiography of Walter Payton*, published in 2000. Even in death, Walter Payton has proven unstoppable.

·被美联社评为"年度进攻球员"(1977)
·被美国职业橄榄球作家协会评为"最具价值球员" (1977)
·被美国职业橄榄球作家协会评为"全联盟选手" (1976–1978, 1984)

关于此人

橄榄球职业生涯的结束对于佩顿来说,绝不意味着人生就此结束。相反,他有机会追求新的兴趣和活动,这些是作为职业选手时无暇顾及的。退役后,他开始赛车,还于1993年埃克哈特湖镇赛车碰撞事故中幸免于难。次年,他与前赛车手戴尔·科因共同组建车队,成为当时赛车队第一位美国黑人老板。"佩顿科因"车队最大的胜利就是在1996年美国500英里大赛中,一位赛车手排名第三。

佩顿还加入一个投资群体,他们想把国家橄榄球联盟带回圣路易斯,但是这个冒险商业并未成功。佩顿的公司经营得比较成功,沃特·佩顿电力设备公司至今仍是全国各地重工业及建设设备的主要供应商。1996年,佩顿创办了沃特·佩顿圆屋综合企业,这是坐落在伊利诺斯州奥罗拉的饭店和酿酒厂,至今仍在营业。

1998年,佩顿创办了有可能是他此生最大的事业:沃特·佩顿基金会,服务于伊利诺斯州那些无人问津的、受虐的或贫困的儿童们。不幸的是,佩顿被诊断患有癌症后,于次年1999年的11月1日溘然长逝,年仅45岁。与他在1976年7月结婚的妻子科妮继续着他的慈善事业。基金会改名为"沃特·科妮·佩顿基金会",至今仍服务于社会,并与伊利诺斯州家庭及儿童服务机构密切合作。科妮以她丈夫的名义创办了"沃特·佩顿癌症基金",帮助找寻癌症治疗方法,他们的女儿布瑞特妮是一项教育活动"生命的青春:纪念沃特·佩顿"的创办者之一。这项活动旨在鼓励年轻的成年人捐赠器官。他的儿子杰瑞特现在是国家橄榄球联盟的一名跑卫。

被查出癌症后,佩顿加倍努力完成刚刚提笔的自传。自传的题目以他作为橄榄球运动员的名言命名:《永不言败:沃特·佩顿自传》,这本书于2000年出版。虽然佩顿已经与世长辞,但是他永远活在人们心中。

Thirty-four

Richard Petty

Why He is Among the 50 plus one Greatest Sports Heroes

Many racing fans and experts agree that Richard Petty was, and still is, one of the major reasons that NASCAR racing has become so popular in the United States. During his driving career, Petty captured victories in the Winston Cup and the Daytona 500 a total of seven times each and was named Most Popular Driver nine times. He owns the race team, Petty Enterprises, which has allows him to continue his constant presence in the NASCAR world. Petty is the king of car racing and, by extension, considered one of the greatest athletic in history.

On the Way Up

Richard Lee Petty was born on July 2, 1937 in Level Cross, North Carolina. He and his brother grew up watching their father, Lee, race stock cars and eventually become the Grand National Champion three times. A love of racing coursed through Petty's veins, but Lee did not allow him to race until he turned 21. When the time .nally came, he did not waste a second. Petty's first race took place in 1958, just a few days after his 21st birthday, and marked the beginning of a successful NASCAR career.

Professional Career

Petty, who competed against his father in his early racing years, was named NASCAR Rookie of the Year in 1959 after a season of nine Top 10 finishes and six Top 5 finishes. The following year, he came in second at the NASCAR Grand National Points Race, but would not achieve his first major victory until 1964. That was the year that he won his first Daytona 500, leading 184 of the 200 laps in his Plymouth, which was hooked up with a new Hemi engine. He also won his first Grand National Championship that year, earning more than $114,000 and nine victories.

After that amazing year, other racing teams began to complain that the engines built for Petty by the Chrysler Corporation were too powerful. In response, NASCAR banned the Hemi engine in 1965 and Chrysler boycotted the season, forcing Petty to temporarily switch to drag racing. But that decision proved to be a fatal one when, on February 28th, Petty's car suffered damage and zoomed into the crowd, killing an 8–year old boy. The incident deeply affected Petty.

In 1966, Petty returned to NASCAR and, on February 27th, he became the first driver ever to win the Daytona 500 twice. The following year was one of the most memorable of his career. He won 27 of the 48 races that he entered, including a record 10 straight, which took place between August 12th and October 1st. That year, he also finished in the Top 5 in 11 other races and went on to win his second Grand National Championship. Petty, who had also broken his father's career wins record with his 55th victory in less than 10 years on the circuit, earned the nickname King Richard after his many stellar performances that season.

Petty switched to Ford in 1969 because he believed that Plymouths were not competitive enough for the NASCAR world. He won 10 races and finished second in points before switching

理查德·佩蒂

Richard Petty

他为何入选《50+1位最闪耀的体育巨星》

至今仍有许多赛车迷和专家认为,纳斯卡(全国赛车联合会)车赛之所以风靡美国主要原因之一是因为有理查德·佩蒂。在佩蒂的赛车生涯中,他分别七次赢得温斯顿杯和戴通纳500英里赛,九次被评为"最受欢迎赛车手"。他拥有自己的车队——佩蒂公司,这样就可以让他继续驰骋于纳斯卡赛车世界。佩蒂是赛车之王,也是名不虚传的50+1位最闪耀的体育巨星之一。

成长之路

1937年7月2日,理查德·李·佩蒂出生在北卡罗来纳州Level Cross。他和弟弟从小看着父亲李开改装赛车,最后三次获得全国大奖赛冠军。佩蒂耳濡目染,对赛车的热爱油然而生,但是李直到他21岁才同意他开赛车。年龄一到,他便迫不及待。佩蒂的首次车赛是在1958年,正好是他21岁生日后几天,标志着他成功的纳斯卡生涯即将开始。

职业生涯

佩蒂在职业生涯早期号称是父亲的竞争者,1959年他被评为"纳斯卡年度新人",在之前的赛季他已九次排名前十、六次排名前五。次年,他在纳斯卡全国大奖赛中获得第二名,直到1964年才是生平的首战告捷。那一年他首次赢得戴通纳500英里赛冠军,赛车用上了新型Hemi发动机,他在普利茅斯的200圈行程中的第184圈先行到达。同样在那年,他首次赢得全国大奖赛冠军,赚了11万4千美元,还有其他九次大获全胜。

过了那个令人叹服的一年,其他车队开始抱怨克莱斯勒公司为佩蒂制造的发动机马力太大。作为对此事的回应,纳斯卡于1965年决定禁用Hemi发动机,克莱斯勒公司在那个赛季不再与佩蒂合作,他不得不短暂地参加短程高速车赛。这个决定仿佛是命中注定,2月28日,佩蒂的车坏了,冲向人群,轧死了一个8岁的男孩。这出悲剧对佩蒂影响颇深。

1966年,佩蒂重返纳斯卡,2月27日,他成为第一位两度获得戴通纳500英里赛冠军的车手。第二年是他职业生涯中最令人难忘的一年。他参加了48场比赛,27次夺冠,包括从8月12日至10月1日蝉联10次冠军的纪录。那年他在其他11次比赛中都是排名前五,接着又赢得了第二个全国大奖赛冠军。佩蒂在不到10年的时间里赢得55个冠军,这也打破了他父亲职业生涯的纪录,那个赛季无数的杰出表现为他赢来了"理查德王"的昵称。

佩蒂认为普利茅斯的竞争氛围不够强,不适合纳斯卡的世界,于是他在1969年转至福特。他获得10次冠军,1970年开着流线型新"超级鸟"重返普利茅斯之前的排名是第二。

back to Plymouth and its streamlined new Superbird in 1970. The following year proved to be another big one for Petty. On February 14, 1971, he made history twice more by becoming the only driver to win the Daytona 500 three times and the first one to earn more than $1 million in career earnings. He also captured his third and last Grand National Championship that year.

In 1972, Petty garnered eight wins as well as 28 Top 10 finishes and 25 Top 5 finishes. Sponsored by STP, he picked up his fourth Winston Cup championship. The next year, he won his fourth Daytona 500 and the year after that, he won his fifth, which became known as the Daytona 450 because the race had been shortened due to an energy crisis. Also in 1974, Petty clinched his fifth Winston Cup championship, having won the first four in 1964, 1967 and 1971–1972.

Petty won the World 600 for the first time in 1975, while also capturing his sixth Winston Cup. Those two victories made up a total of 13 in 1 season, which is a NASCAR record for the modern era (1972 to present). Jeff Gordon tied the record in 1998. In 1976, Petty failed to win the Daytona 500, in what would become one of the most talked–about finishes in the history of NASCAR. He and his rival, David Pearson, were running bumper to bumper on the last lap out of turn 4 when they collided into each other. The impact sent both of them spinning into the front stretch wall and even though Petty's car stopped only yards away from the finish line, his engine stalled and refused to start up again. This allowed Pearson, whose engine was still running, to roll past Petty on the infield grass and make it across the finish line to win the race. Petty was given credit for second place.

In December of 1978, Petty underwent surgery to have a substantial amount of his stomach removed due to ulcer problems. Two months later, he won his sixth Daytona 500 after a 45–race drought, and the victory would become part of his seventh and final Winston Cup championship. Then, in 1981, Petty also captured what turned out to be his seventh and last Daytona 500 win. Three years later, he broke yet another record by clinching his 200th career win on July 4, 1984 at the Firecracker 400 held at Daytona International Speedway.

Petty's 200th victory proved to be the last one of his career. After participating in a 29–race fan appreciation tour, he retired officially as a driver in 1992. During his last race at the Hooters 500 in Atlanta, Petty's outstanding career achievements were honored when he paced the field on a pace lap. He finished his career with 200 wins, 712 Top 10 finishes and 123 poles.

Petty's long list of honors for his successful driving career include being:
- Rookie of the Year, NASCAR (1959)
- Most Popular Winston Cup Driver (1962, 1964, 1968, 1970, 1974–1978)
- Meyers Brothers Award, National Motorsports Press Association (1964, 1967, 1971, 1992)
- Driver of the Year, NASCAR (1971)
- North Carolina Athletic Hall of Fame (1973)
- Driver of the Year, National Motorsports Press Association (1974–1975)
- International Motorsports Hall of Fame (1997)
- One of NASCAR's 50 Greatest Drivers (1998)

About the Man Himself

Richard Petty, even today, is still a driving force in the world of NASCAR racing. His father formed Petty Engineering in 1949, and 20 years later, it became Petty Enterprises, which, under Petty's steady hand, now has two Winston Cup teams and a NASCAR Craftsman Truck Series race truck. Just as Petty himself raced for Petty Enterprises, so now does his son Kyle. Kyle's son, Adam, was the fourth generation driver to continue the family's racing legacy, but his career and

就在第二年，对于佩蒂来说又是大获全胜的一年。1971年2月14日，他又两次获得戴通纳500英里赛冠军，成为首位三度夺冠的车手，也是第一位职业生涯中薪金超过100万美元的车手。那一年，他还获得了第三个、也是最后一个全国大奖赛的冠军。

1972年，佩蒂又获得8次冠军，28次排名前十、25次排名前五。受STP赞助，他又参加了他的第四次温斯顿杯冠军赛。次年，他第四次获得戴通纳500英里赛冠军，下一年又获得第五个，但是由于能源危机，赛程缩短，因此被称为"戴通纳450英里赛"。同样，在1974年，佩蒂获得了他的第五个温斯顿杯，前四次冠军分别于1964、1967、和1971-1972年获得。

1975年，佩蒂首次获得世界600英里大赛冠军，还获得了他的第六个温斯顿杯。这两次胜利使他创下了同一赛季总共13次夺冠的纪录，这也是当代和现代的纳斯卡纪录(1972年至今)。杰夫·戈登于1998年创下了持平的纪录。1976年，佩蒂没能赢得戴通纳500英里赛冠军，这成为纳斯卡历史中议论最多的话题之一。他和对手戴维·皮尔森在最后一圈第四个转弯处紧挨着飙车，互相碰撞。结果两辆车打转，撞到前墙，虽然佩蒂的车在离终点线只有几码的距离时停下来，他的发动机熄火，再也没发动起来。这让皮尔森有机可乘，他的发动机仍能照常运转，他的车从内场草地转离佩蒂，最终开过终点线赢得比赛。佩蒂居居第二。

1978年12月，佩蒂由于胃溃疡，接受了胃部分切除手术。两个月后，在缺赛45次之后，他赢得了自己的第六次戴通纳500英里赛冠军，这包含在他第七次即最后一次温斯顿杯胜利之中。然后，在1981年，佩蒂获得了自己第七次也是最后一次戴通纳500英里赛的冠军。三年后的1984年7月4日，他在戴通纳国际赛道上的Firecracker 400英里赛中摘得桂冠，以第200次夺冠刷新了纪录。

第200次的胜利是佩蒂职业生涯中的最后一次胜利。参加完29场车迷欣赏巡回赛后，他于1992年正式宣布退役。亚特兰大Hooters 500英里大赛是佩蒂最后一场比赛，当他开在预驶图时，他出色的生涯成就也一目了然了：他总共赢得200次冠军，712次排名前十，123次竿位(决赛起跑最前面的排位)。

佩蒂获得的荣誉及奖项包括：

·纳斯卡年度新人奖(1959)
·最受欢迎温斯顿杯车手(1962, 1964, 1968, 1970, 1974-1978)
·全国汽车运动新闻协会颁发的"梅尔兄弟奖" (1964, 1967, 1971, 1992)
·纳斯卡年度赛车手(1971)
·北卡罗来纳州体育名人堂(1973)
·全国汽车运动新闻协会颁发的"年度赛车手奖" (1974-1975)
·国际汽车运动名人堂(1997)
·纳斯卡50位最优秀车手之一(1998)

关于此人

理查德·佩蒂至今仍是纳斯卡赛车世界的核心人物。1949年，他的父亲创办了佩蒂工程设计，20年后，改为佩蒂公司，靠着佩蒂踏实的工作，公司现在已有"温斯顿杯车队"和纳斯卡卡车系列联赛的专用赛车。正如佩蒂本人为佩蒂公司参赛一样，他的儿子凯乐也参加了车赛。凯乐的儿子亚当是他们家族第四代赛车手，但是他的职业生涯和生命都很

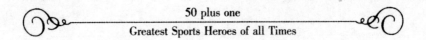
life were cut short in May of 2000 in a tragic accident during practice at New Hampshire Motor Speedway.

Petty Enterprises also currently maintains two companies under its umbrella: The Victory Junction Gang Camp in North Carolina and Richard Petty Driving Experience. The camp is a summer camp for children with illnesses in an effort to help them make good friends and memories. The other company offers racing fans a chance to either drive or ride along in a NASCAR–style stock car at more than 20 different tracks.

Petty had prostate cancer surgery in 1995 and a year later, the Republican Party selected him as its candidate for North Carolina's Secretary of State. That was one race that Petty lost, showing that perhaps he was meant more for the track than for politics. However, he has received some distinguished awards for his achievements not only as a racer, but also as an upstanding citizen and humanitarian, including the Medal of Freedom, which is the highest civilian award, in 1992 and the American Auto Racing Writers & Broadcasters Association's Man of the Year Award in 1995.

Petty's No. 43 car is on display at the Smithsonian in Washington D.C., and his career is showcased at the Richard Petty Museum in Level Cross. He has written several books including two autobiographies, the most recent is *King Richard I: The Autobiography of America's Greatest Racer*. Besides his son, Kyle, Petty had three daughters with his wife, Lynda, whom he married in 1958.

Even though he has been retired as a driver for almost 15 years, Richard Petty still reigns as king in the NASCAR world, and his accomplishments will reign in the memories of sports fans forever.

短暂，因为2000年5月新汉普夏郡汽车大赛练习中，他在一场车祸惨剧中不幸丧生。

如今，佩蒂公司旗下还有两个公司：北卡罗来纳州的"胜利路口电子阵营"和"理查德·佩蒂驾驶经验"。这个阵营是为患有疾病的儿童开设的夏令营，帮助他们结交朋友，留下美好的回忆。另一个公司为赛车迷提供了机会，他们可以沿着20多种不同的轨道，驾驶着或坐着纳斯卡型的改装赛车。

1995年，佩蒂接受了前列腺癌症手术，一年后，共和党选举他为北卡罗来纳州部长候选人。佩蒂竞选失败，也许正好说明他更适合驰骋于赛车世界，而非政治领域。然而，他不仅因为出色的赛车而受嘉奖，而且还作为正直的市民和慈善家而获殊荣，包括1992年最高平民奖项的"自由勋章"和1995年美国赛车作家及广播者协会颁发的"年度人物奖"。

佩蒂的43号赛车陈列在华盛顿史密斯松宁博物馆，他的职业生涯情况也能在Level Cross的理查德·佩蒂博物馆里看到。他写了几本书，包括两本自传，最近的一本书名为《理查德I世：美国最伟大的赛车手自传》。佩蒂1958年与妻子琳达结婚，除了儿子凯乐，还有3个女儿。

虽然理查德·佩蒂退出车坛已有15年，他仍被誉为纳斯卡世界之王，所有体育迷都将永远记住他的卓越成就。

Thirty-five

Jackie Robinson

Why He is Among the 50 plus one Greatest Sports Heroes

Jackie Robinson changed the face of baseball, literally, when he became the first African American to play in the major leagues. Although he was up against harsh, racist treatment by baseball fans, opposing players and even his own teammates, Robinson remained strong and came out on top as a true champion. His team won six pennants during his 10 seasons with them and he was inducted into the National Baseball Hall of Fame in 1962. Because of his heroic efforts, generations of African American and other minority athletes to make strides in the professional world of sports. Robinson's groundbreaking efforts make his an appropriate choice as one of the greatest sports heroes of all times.

On the Way Up

Jack Roosevelt Robinson was born on January 31, 1919 in Cairo, Georgia. His mother, Mallie, eventually moved the family to Pasadena, California. Robinson and his four older siblings grew up in a working-class neighborhood where racial prejudice was not uncommon. As a child, he was most comfortable playing sports and tried his hand at just about anything: baseball, basketball, dodge ball, football, golf, marbles, soccer and tennis.

Starting in 1939, Robinson attended the University of California, Los Angeles (UCLA) after excelling in sports at Pasadena Junior College. He continued his athletic success at UCLA, where he was a star player on the football, basketball, track and baseball teams. Robinson was the first athlete in the university's history to letter in four different sports. Robinson's accomplishments earned him letters as the highest scorer in basketball's Pacific Coast Conference for 2 years; nationalchampion long jumper; All-American football halfback; and All-American varsity baseball shortstop.

Robinson left school his junior year in 1941 due to financial difficulties and enlisted in the United States Army during World War II. His battalion, the U.S.761st Tank Battalion, was a segregated one, and although he was at first refused admission to Officer Candidate School, the strong-willed Robinson was finally accepted, graduating as a first lieutenant. One day, while he was training at Fort Hood, Texas, he pulled a Rosa Parks before she herself had even done so by refusing to sit in the back of a public bus. Robinson was court-martialed for insubordination, never making it to Europe with his unit. All charges were eventually dismissed and he received an honorable discharge from the Army in 1944.

In 1944, Robinson played shortstop for the Kansas City Monarchs in the Negro American League. It was during this time that he caught the attention of a scout who worked for Branch Rickey, the Brooklyn Dodgers' president and general manager. Rickey soon decided that Robinson had the strength, courage and, of course, skills to become the first African American professional baseball player. In 1946, Robinson was assigned to play for the Montreal Royals, the top minor league af.liate of the Dodgers. He played second baseman and lead the International

杰克·罗宾逊

他为何入选《50+1位最闪耀的体育巨星》

当杰克·罗宾逊成为棒球大联盟中第一位美国黑人运动员时，我们可以毫不夸张地说，他已经改变了棒球运动的面貌。尽管要面对棒球迷、对手、甚至自己队友严酷的种族歧视，罗宾逊依旧顽强，成为首屈一指、名副其实的冠军。他为球队效力的10个赛季中，球队赢得6次锦标赛冠军，1962年他入选国家棒球名人堂。罗宾逊英勇无畏，他的努力让更多的美国黑人及其他少数民族运动员积极投身于体坛。罗宾逊开辟了新的天地，理应在万古体坛中享有一席之地。

成长之路

1919年1月31日，杰克·罗斯福·罗宾逊出生在佐治亚州开罗。他的母亲玛丽后来携家搬到加利福尼亚的帕萨迪那。罗宾逊与他4个哥哥姐姐们从小在工薪阶层的环境中长大，经常受到种族歧视。孩提时，体育运动总让他很舒服，他什么都玩过：棒球、篮球、躲球游戏、橄榄球、高尔夫球、弹子、足球和网球。

1939年，在帕萨迪那初级学院有着出色体育成绩的罗宾逊选择在加州大学洛杉矶分校读书。他在大学时，体育仍然出类拔萃，在橄榄球队、篮球队、田径队和棒球队都是明星。罗宾逊是大学历史上第一个在4项运动中被授予校名首字母奖励的运动员。罗宾逊出色的表现，让他连续两年成为太平洋海岸联盟篮球最高分得主；他是全国跳远冠军、全美足球前卫、全美大学棒球第一代表队游击手，这些成就都让他获得了校名首字母的奖励。

由于经济困难，1941年，大三时的罗宾逊辍学了，并在二战期间加入美国陆军。他所在的美国761坦克营实行种族隔离制，虽然起初他被拒绝进入候补军官学校，但是意志顽强的罗宾逊最后还是被录取了，并作为第一位中尉毕业。有一天，在得克萨斯州胡得堡训练时，他推着一位"罗莎·帕克"（黑人女性），不让她坐到公共汽车后面的座位上，而她本人还没有这么做。罗宾逊因违抗规定而被告上军事法庭，他所在的部队也被禁止进入欧洲。所有的指控最终被取消，美国军部于1944年撤销了他的罪名。

1944年，罗宾逊担任美国黑人联盟的堪萨斯国王队游击手。就是在这段时间，他吸引了一位球探的注意，此人是为布鲁克林道奇队总裁兼总经理布里奇·瑞基工作的。不久，瑞基认定罗宾逊是位力量与勇气兼具的球员，当然，还有精湛的技术，一定能成为第一位美国黑人职棒运动员。1946年，罗宾逊与道奇队隶属的最顶尖的小联盟蒙特利尔皇家队签约。作为二垒手，他为国际联盟创下了平均349的打击率、40个偷垒的成绩，带领球队挺进"小世界冠军锦标赛"。罗宾逊在蒙特利尔逗留期间，球队以及球迷几乎疯狂地崇拜他、

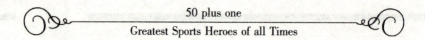
League with a .349 batting average, while also stealing 40 bases and carrying the team to the Little World Series championship. The team as well as the fans in Montreal respected and welcomed Robinson almost overwhelmingly during his stay in their city. But that kind of support would soon come to an end for him, for a while anyways.

Professional Career

Robinson made his major league debut as the Dodgers' first baseman on April 15, 1947 at Ebbets Field in Brooklyn. That game has been called one of baseball's most highly anticipated events as well as one of the most significant happenings in the history of the U.S. civil rights movement. Robinson was harassed by players and fans throughout that entire first season, having to put up with such occurrences as pitchers throwing at his head, base runners attempting to injure him with their sharp cleats and black cats being thrown onto the field. He took verbal abuse not only from players on other teams, but also from his very own teammates, some of who staged an unsuccessful rebellion. The St. Louis Cardinals even threatened to go on strike.

An aggressive man by nature, one of the motivating factors behind Robinson's unusually quiet strength in the face of such blatant prejudice was the understanding between him and Rickey that he was chosen to integrate baseball in part because he had promised to be able to practice self-control even when times got hard. So, rather than let his machismo get the best of him, Robinson let his game performances do the work. By the end of his first season, he had achieved a batting average of .297 in 151 games, and he led the league with 29 stolen bases. He was named the league's Rookie of the Year, a sign that he was quickly gaining the respect of fans and other players. In fact, other major league teams soon followed the Dodgers' lead and started hiring African American players.

In 1949, Robinson was named the National League's Most Valuable Player after completing a fantastic season. He led the league both in hitting with .342 and steals with 37, all while batting in a career-high of 124 runs. Although he played his rookie season with the Dodgers as a first baseman, he spent most of his career at second base and also played many games as a third baseman and an outfielder. Throughout his 10 seasons with Brooklyn, Robinson saw the team win six National League pennants in 1947, 1949, 1952–1953 and 1955–1956. The Dodgers also won the World Series in 1955 against their long-time rival, the New York Yankees. Robinson played in the last game of his professional career on September 30, 1956. He finished his career with a batting average of .311, 137 home runs, 734 runs batted in and 19 steals home.

In 1997, 50 years after Robinson's first season with the Dodgers, Major League Baseball (MLB) permanently retired his uniform No. 42 from all of its teams. And in 2004, it named April 15th Jackie Robinson Day, to be celebrated each year in every league ballpark. Some of the other honors that have been bestowed upon Robinson include him being:

· Rookie of the Year, MLB (1947)
· Most Valuable Player, National League (1949)
· All-Star Team, MLB (1949–1954)
· National Baseball Hall of Fame (1962)
· No. 44 out of the 100 Greatest Baseball Players, The Sporting News (2000)
· Major League Baseball All-Century Team (2000)
· No. 1 out of the 100 Most In.uential Student-Athletes, NCAA (2006)

欢迎他。但是这样的支持很快便出现了短暂的停止。

职业生涯

1947年4月15日，罗宾逊作为道奇队第一垒手首次在布鲁克林艾伯特体育场亮相。那场比赛堪称棒球史上期待最高的赛事，也是美国民权运动史上意义最重大的事件。罗宾逊全部第一个赛季都不断受到运动员和球迷的侮辱、折磨，他不得不忍受着，把这些痛苦当做是投手把球扔到他头上、穿着尖锐钉鞋的跑垒运动员试图撞伤他、霉运降临到赛场上。不仅其他球队的队员辱骂他，就连自己的队友也对他进行言语攻击，有些人表现在并未成功的反抗上。圣路易红雀队甚至威胁要罢工。

罗宾逊本质上争强好斗，面对这种公然的歧视，他的脸上异常的平静是有原因的，他与瑞基之间达成协议：由于他答应在时局最困难的时代也要试着控制好自己的脾气，瑞基才选择他作为棒球队一员。因此，罗宾逊只让自己的大男子气概表现在球场上。第一个赛季结束时，他在151场比赛中创下了297的平均打击率，带领联盟成功偷垒29次。

他被评为联盟"年度新人"，这个荣誉让他很快得到了球迷和其他运动员的尊重。实际上，其他大联盟球队也依照道奇队老板的做法，开始招募美国黑人运动员。

1949年，罗宾逊创造了成绩辉煌的赛季，并被评为"国家联盟最具价值球员"。他带领联盟创下了平均342的安打率和37个偷垒纪录，同时创造了124分的生涯高分。尽管在新秀赛季中，他作为第一垒手效力于道奇队，他职业生涯的绝大多数时间还是担任二垒手，也在许多比赛中担任三垒手和外野手。为布鲁克林效力的10个赛季中，罗宾逊与球队共同分享了1947、1949、1952-1953和1955-1956年间的六次国家联盟锦标赛冠军。道奇队在1955年还战胜了夙敌纽约扬基队，获得世界联赛冠军。1956年9月30日，罗宾逊参加了职业生涯中的最后一场比赛。他创下了平均311的打击率、137个本垒打、734次得分、19次盗本垒的成绩。

1997年，距离罗宾逊亮相道奇队的首个赛季，已时隔50年，棒球大联盟永久退役了他在所有球队中的42号队服。2004年的4月15日被定为"杰克·罗宾逊日"，今后每年的这个日期，所有棒球场都会举行庆祝活动。罗宾逊还获得过以下殊荣：
· 棒球大联盟"年度新人奖"(1947)
· 国家联盟"最具价值球员" (1949)
· 入选棒球大联盟全明星阵容队(1949–1954)
· 入选国家棒球名人堂 (1962)
· 被《体育新闻》评为"百名最伟大棒球运动员第44位" (2000)
· 入选棒球大联盟世纪之队(2000)
· NCAA 大学联赛百名最具影响的学生运动员第1名 (2006)

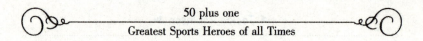
About the Man Himself

In February of 1946, Robinson married his college sweetheart and girlfriend of 5 years, Rachel Islum. The couple had two sons and one daughter and led a full family life. After his retirement from professional baseball, Robinson ventured into the business world. From 1956–1964, he was the vice president of Chock Full O' Nuts, which is still a beloved café and coffee company in New York City. He also co–founded Freedom National Bank of Harlem and a construction company that focused on helping black Americans become homeowners.

Robinson became involved in political endeavors as well. He served on the campaign of Governor Nelson Rockefeller before becoming special assistant to him, and also campaigned for Hubert Humphrey during the 1968 presidential elections. Robinson was very much into helping with the civil rights movement in any way that he could. He met Dr. Martin Luther King, Jr. on more than one occasion and lent his time, money and presence to the cause of racial injustice by speaking out against it at churches and at rallies. He was a board member of the National Association for the Advancement of Colored People (NAACP) and was also on the board of advisors for the Harlem YMCA. In 1956, Robinson was awarded the Spingarn Medal, which is given yearly by the NAACP to an African American who performs acts of distinguished merit and achievement. He appeared as himself in the 1950 movie *The Jackie Robinson Story*, and wrote an autobiography called *I Never Had It Made: An Autobiography of Jackie Robinson (1972).*

Robinson died on October 24, 1972. Shortly before his death, he was asked to throw out the first pitch at that year's World Series. That same year, Rachel started the Jackie Robinson Development Corporation, which builds low– and moderateincome housing. In 1973, she founded the Jackie Robinson Foundation, which is a public, not–for–profit national organization. The Foundation continues to strive to help deserving underprivileged minority youths by providing them with 4–year scholarships for higher education and access to an extensive mentoring program. In October of 2002, Robinson was posthumously awarded the Congressional Gold Medal of Honor, which Rachel accepted in a ceremony in the Capitol Rotunda. Robinson, who also received the Presidential Medal of Freedom by Ronald Reagan in 1984, is only the second baseball player to receive the Congressional Gold Medal.

Jackie Robinson's legend continues through his family as well as through his memorable performances on the field of baseball and in the field of life. Jackie Robinson is one of the greatest sports athletes of all times.

关于此人

　　1946年2月,罗宾逊与大学时相恋5年的女友拉结·伊斯拉姆结婚。他们有两个儿子、一个女儿,一家人幸福美满。罗宾逊退役后,他闯进了商业世界。从1956年至1964年,他担任Chock Full O' Nuts咖啡公司的副总裁,这个品牌至今仍风靡纽约市。他参与创建哈莱姆自由国家银行和建设公司,主要帮助美国黑人拥有自己的产业。

　　罗宾逊还积极投身于政坛活动。他为纳尔逊·洛克菲勒州长的竞选活动效力,后来成为他的助手,在1968年总统选举中,他还服务于休伯特·汉弗莱的竞选活动。罗宾逊为民权运动竭尽所能。他不只一次地会见小马丁·路德·金,把时间、金钱奉献于抵制种族歧视的事业中,在教堂和集会发表演说,批判不平等待遇。他是全国有色人种促进协会董事会成员之一,还担任哈莱姆基督教青年会顾问。1956年,罗宾逊被授予"史宾岗奖",该奖每年由全国有色人种促进协会颁发给辛勤努力、贡献杰出的美国黑人。1950年,他在电影《杰克·罗宾逊的故事》中扮演自己,写过自传《我从没有成功把握:杰克·罗宾逊自传》(1972)。

　　1972年10月24日,罗宾逊逝世。就在他逝世之前,他受邀在当年世界联赛中扔出第一球。同年,拉结开办了杰克·罗宾逊开发公司,房屋建造主要面向中低收入人群。1973年,她创立了杰克·罗宾逊基金会,这是公益的非盈利性慈善机构。此基金会继续帮助少数民族的贫困青年,为他们的深造资助4年奖学金,并设立私人教师辅导活动。2002年10月,罗宾逊获得身后的"国会金质奖章",拉结在国会大厦圆形大厅举行的授奖仪式中代授此奖。1984年,罗纳德·里根为罗宾逊颁发了"总统自由勋章",他是第二位获得国会金质奖章的棒球运动员。

　　杰克·罗宾逊的传奇故事在他的家庭继续着,大家不会忘记他在棒球场内外令人难忘的生活。杰克·罗宾逊不愧是一名50+1位史上绝顶运动员。

Thirty-six

Sugar Ray Robinson

Why He is Among the 50 plus one Greatest Sports Heroes

Sugar Ray Robinson boxed professionally for almost a quarter of a century, which during that time he won 125 consecutive fights and fought 18 world champions. He was a world welterweight and five-time middleweight champion, bringing such grace and power to the ring that fellow legendary boxer Muhammad Ali reverently called him the king, the master, my idol. While Ali may consider himself to be the greatest heavyweight fighter, he has admitted without hesitation that Robinson was the greatest fighter of all time. This only begins to explain why Robinson is considered one of the top athletes in history.

On the Way Up

Walker Smith, Jr. was born on May 3, 1921 in Ailey, Georgia. Leila moved Smith and his two older sisters to New York City where Smith began taking tap dancing lessons. He helped his mother out financially by working as a shoe-shine boy, a window cleaner and a meat and vegetable delivery boy, among other things. Smith and some of his friends also made extra money by dancing in front of Broadway theatres in the evenings.

The family moved to Harlem a few years later. When he was 15, he was invited to a gym that was operated by George Gainford, one of his classmate's uncles. Gainford would become Smith's trainer throughout his entire professional boxing career.

At first, though, Smith was still too young to fight in official amateur competitions. Gainford came to the rescue by giving him the Amateur Athletic Union identification card of a former boxer named Ray Robinson. With the go-ahead to fight under his new name, Smith won two New York Golden Gloves championships, as a featherweight in 1938 and as a lightweight in 1939. Around that time, a sportswriter for a Waterton, New York newspaper described Robinson's technique sweet as sugar, and the name Sugar Ray Robinson was born. He closed his amateur career with an 89–0 record, including 69 knockouts, 40 of them occurring in the first round.

Professional Career

Robinson's professional career began in 1940 when he knocked out Joe Echevarria in two rounds. He worked hard at achieving an undefeated record of 40 wins, but in a 1943 rematch against Jake LaMotta at Detroit's Olympic Stadium, Robinson suffered his first professional loss by decision in a 10-round bout. However, that would prove to be the only one of the six fights between him and LaMotta that he would lose, and after that initial fall, Robinson would not lose again for another 8 years. On December 20, 1946 in New York City, he beat Tommy Bell by a 15-round decision to win the vacant world welterweight title.

In 1947, before a fight against Jimmy Doyle, Robinson dreamt that he was going to kill the other fighter in the ring. Deeply disturbed by the dream, he decided to pull out of the fight, but a priest convinced him that it was okay to carry on. So, Robinson defended his title for the first time

舒格·雷·罗宾逊

他为何入选《50+1位最闪耀的体育巨星》

舒格·雷·罗宾逊在职业拳坛差不多打了25年，在那段岁月中，他蝉联过125次冠军，参加过18次世界冠军大赛。他是世界次中量级拳击冠军，5次获得中量级冠军，如此辉煌的战绩让另一名传奇拳王穆罕默德·阿里都称赞他为"拳王"、"大师"、"我的偶像"。虽然阿里自认为是最出色的重量级拳王，但是他毫不犹豫地说罗宾逊一直是拳坛最伟大的拳击手。这才刚开始说明为什么罗宾逊能屹立在万古体坛之中。

成长之路

1921年5月3日，小沃克·史密斯出生于佐治亚州艾雷。母亲雷拉带着史密斯和他两个姐姐搬家到纽约市，在那里，史密斯开始学习踢踏舞。他擦皮鞋、擦窗户、运送肉和蔬菜，帮助母亲减轻经济负担。晚上，史密斯还和他的朋友在百老汇剧院靠跳舞赚钱。

几年后，全家搬到了哈莱姆。15岁时，他应邀加入了同学叔叔乔治·甘福特开办的体操馆。甘福特在史密斯的整个职业生涯中一直担任他的教练。

虽然史密斯最初因为太小，而无法参加正式业余赛。甘福特帮他从前拳手雷·罗宾逊那儿拿到了业余体育联合会证。获得"通行证"后，史密斯就以这个名字打拳击，他两次在纽约金手套冠军大赛中夺冠，一次是1938年的次轻量级比赛，另一次是1939年的轻量级比赛。就在那时，纽约沃特顿报的一名体育新闻记者形容罗宾逊的战术仿佛糖一样甜蜜，舒格(糖)·雷·罗宾逊的名字应运而生。他以89胜0负的记录结束了业余生涯，包括69次击倒对手，其中40次发生在第一回合中。

职业生涯

罗宾逊的职业生涯始于1940年的那场比赛，他用两个回合就击倒了乔·埃切圭里。他努力练习，成功卫冕自己的40个冠军，但是在1943年底特律奥林匹克体育场进行的比赛中，罗宾逊败给了杰克·拉莫特，这是他头一次在职业赛的10回合较量中以点数战败给对手。然而，这是他与拉莫特6次较量中唯一失败的一次，头一回受挫后，罗宾逊在接下来的8年中再也没有失败过。1946年12月20日，在纽约市，他与汤米·贝尔的比赛中，以15回合点数胜出，弥补了世界次中量级冠军头衔的空缺。

1947年，在与吉米·戴乐比赛前夕，罗宾逊梦见自己将在拳场打死对手。受到这个梦的困扰，他决定退出比赛，但是一个牧师说服了他，告诉他继续比赛没有问题。因此，罗宾

against Jimmy Doyle and knocked him out in the eighth round. It was as if Robinson was psychic because Doyle died soon after from the injuries that he had sustained during the fight.

Robinson fought five times in 1948, but only one was in defense of his title. In 1950, though, he almost quadrupled that number by fighting 19 times. He defended the welterweight title against Charley Fusari and won the world middleweight championship by defeating Robert Villemain. While defending his newly acquired title on August 25, 1950, Robinson beat Jose Basora with a 50-second knockout that set a 38-year-long record.

Robinson fought LaMotta for the sixth and final time on February 14, 1951. He won the undisputed world middleweight title by technical knockout in the 13th round. After that fight, which became known as The St. Valentine's Day Massacre, Robinson left for his first European tour.

In 1952, Robinson challenged the world light-heavyweight champion, Joey Maxim, at Yankee Stadium in New York City. He was ahead for much of the fight until the 140-degree temperature started to slow him down. Robinson eventually collapsed at the end of the 13th round and was unable to answer the bell for the next round. That would prove to be the only knockout of his career.

Robinson retired after that fight with a record of 131-3-1-1, but he could not stay away for long, returning to the ring in 1955. He won five fights and lost one before going on to defeat Carl Olson for the world middleweight title, which he would then lose in 1957 against Gene Fullmer. However, a persistent Robinson challenged Fullmer to a rematch and won the title back for a fourth time by knocking the other fighter out in five rounds. The left-hook to the chin with which he knocked out Fullmer became known as The Perfect Punch by boxing critics. Robinson lost the title again later that year to Carmen Basilio, but he won it back for a record fifth time by beating the champion in points during a 1958 fight in Chicago, Illinois.

Paul Pender took the title away from Robinson in January of 1960 and Robinson's attempt to get it back for a sixth time later that year was unsuccessful. In December, he challenged Fullmer for the National Boxing Association middleweight world title, but the fight ended in a draw after 15 rounds.

Robinson went up against Fullmer for the fourth and final time in March of 1961 for the World Boxing Association middleweight title, but he lost by a unanimous decision in what ended up being his last title fight. During his remaining years as a professional boxer, Robinson fought 10-round bouts, beating future world champion Denny Moyer and losing to former world champion Joey Giardello.

In 1965, at age 44, Robinson retired for a second time after 25 years in the ring—this time permanently—with a record of 174-19-6-2, including 109 knockouts,in 201 total professional fights. With those numbers, he sits among the most productive knockout winners in boxing history. Sugar Ray lost only 19 fights out of 201.

Robinson has received various honors for his superb runs in the ring, including:
- Boxing Hall of Fame (1967)
- Fighter of the Year, International Boxing Hall of Fame (1942)
- Edward J. Neil Trophy, Boxing Writers' Association of America (1950)
- Fighter of the Year, International Boxing Hall of Fame (1951)
- International Boxing Hall of Fame (1990)
- 11th All-Time Greatest Puncher, *Ring Magazine* (2003)
- United States postage stamp (2006)
- No. 24 North American athletes of the 20th century, ESPN's SportsCentury

逊首次击败吉米·戴乐,卫冕成功,并在第八回合中将其击倒在地。罗宾逊似乎有超能力,因为不久后,戴乐确实死于比赛中受伤后遗症。

1948年,罗宾逊参加了五次比赛,但是只有一次是卫冕赛。1950年,19次比赛几乎是他参赛数的四倍。他击败对手查理·福塞瑞,成功卫冕次中量级冠军,又击败罗伯特·威利曼,赢得世界中量级冠军。1950年8月25日,罗宾逊击败对手乔斯·巴塞拉,卫冕自己新创的冠军头衔,并创下了38年来以50秒击倒对方的最快纪录。

1951年2月14日,罗宾逊第六次也是最后一次与拉莫特争夺冠军。在第13回合,他以一记技术击倒,毫无争议地摘下了世界中量级桂冠。这次比赛号称"情人节大屠杀",之后,罗宾逊开始了自己的首次欧洲巡回赛。

1952年,在纽约市扬基体育场,罗宾逊向世界轻重量级拳王乔伊·马克西姆发起挑战。在比赛中他一直领先,直到华氏140度的温度开始减慢他的速度。罗宾逊最终在第13回合倒下了,没有站起来进入下个回合。这是他职业生涯中唯一一次被击倒以失败告终。

这次比赛之后,罗宾逊退役,成绩为131-3-1-1,但是他不可能离开拳坛很久,1955年,他重返拳坛。在世界中量级拳王争霸赛战胜卡尔·奥森之前,他胜过五次,输过一次,1957年的世界中量级拳王争霸赛中,他败给了吉尼·福尔曼。然而,顽强的罗宾逊再次向福尔曼挑战,重新夺得冠军,并且是第四次仅在五局中就将对手击倒。他用左勾拳将福尔曼击倒在地,这次击倒被拳击评论家们称为"完美的一击"。那年末,罗宾逊败给卡门·巴西略,再次丢掉了这个头衔,但是在1958年伊利诺斯州芝加哥比赛中,他又一次赢回了冠军,并且创下了第五次以点数击败对手的纪录。

1960年1月,保尔·潘德夺走了罗宾逊的世界中量级拳王称号,为了夺回冠军,罗宾逊尝试了几次,但在那年末的第六次挑战中还是没有成功。12月,他挑战福尔曼,争夺国家拳击协会中量级世界冠军,但是这场比赛在15个回合后以平局告终。

1961年3月,罗宾逊第四次也是最后一次挑战福尔曼,争夺世界拳击协会的中量级冠军,但是他以毫无争议的点数战败,从此结束了拳王争霸的比赛生涯。职业拳击手的剩余岁月中,罗宾逊参加了10回合比赛,打败了未来的世界冠军丹尼·摩尔,但是输给了前世界冠军乔伊·吉戴罗。

1965年,44岁的罗宾逊第二次宣布退役,退出25年的拳坛生涯——这次是永远正式退役,职业生涯纪录为174-19-6-2,201场职业拳击比赛中共有109次击倒对手。这些数据足以让他在拳坛击倒数纪录中独占鳌头。在201场比赛中,舒格·雷仅输过19场。

罗宾逊在拳坛上的卓越表现为他赢得了无数荣誉,包括:
·入选拳击名人堂 (1967)
·国际拳击名人堂"年度拳击手"(1942)
·美国拳击作家协会颁发的"爱德华J.奈尔奖"(1950)
·国际拳击名人堂"年度拳击手"(1951)
·入选国际拳击名人堂 (1990)
·《拳击》杂志"史上最优秀拳击手第11名" (2003)
·美国专题邮票 (2006)
·被《ESPN体育世纪》评为"20世纪北美运动员第24名"

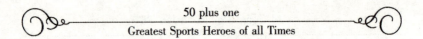

About the Man Himself

After Robinson's first, temporary retirement from professional boxing in the early 1950s, he began a dancing career, getting gigs in Las Vegas and even touring parts of Europe. He also concentrated on his business, Ray Robinson Enterprises, an entire city block of buildings that housed a café, a cleaners, a barber shop and his second wife's lingerie shop. While touring in Paris, France, Robinson received an urgent telegram forcing him to return home. He soon discovered money missing from his accounts, his buildings in foreclosure the Internal Revenue Service was making inquiries. These were the main reasons that he returned to boxing in 1955.

In 1969 Robinson founded the Sugar Ray Robinson Youth Foundation. This Los Angeles-based organization helped young people who lived in the inner city build their self-esteem through the development of skills in sports, fine arts and the performing arts. The foundation accomplished this through its after-school sports program, weekend sports competitions, tutoring program, arts and crafts courses and cultural enrichment activities, among other services and annual events. Many of the children who started out at the foundation grew up to be nationally prominent adults, including Olympic gold medalist Florence Griffith-Joyner.

Along with his charity work, Robinson picked up minor roles in movies and on television. He appeared on episodes of such television shows as *Mission:Impossible*, *The Mod Squad* and *Fantasy Island*. He also played small parts in movies such as *The Detective*, starring Frank Sinatra, and *The Todd Killings*. He even performed on a show called *Omnibus*, which was on the air from 1952–1961 and described as television's first showcase for the creative and performing arts.

During his early years, Robinson wrote an autobiography called Sugar Ray: The Sugar Robinson Story and in 1994, he co-wrote another one simply titled Sugar Ray. He married three times. His second marriage to dancer Edna Mae lasted 18 years until their divorce in 1962. Robinson and his third wife, Millie, were together until his death on April 12, 1989 in Culver City, California after years of suffering from Alzheimer's disease and diabetes.

Sugar Ray Robinson may have finished out his life in a quiet manner, out of the public eye, but his dedication to introducing sports to children, his powerful charisma and his astonishing career will forever be celebrated by boxing fans and sports enthusiasts everywhere.

关于此人

罗宾逊在50年代早期第一次短暂告别拳坛后,他开始了舞蹈生涯,在拉斯维加斯表演,甚至去过欧洲国家巡回演出。他还致力于商业,他经营的雷·罗宾逊公司涵盖了整个街区的商业店,包括咖啡店、干洗店、理发店和他第二任妻子的内衣店。在法国巴黎旅游时,罗宾逊接到了加急电报催促他赶快回家。很快他发现银行账户上的钱少了,原来美国国内税务署开始催促他的楼盘抵押贷款。这就是他在1955年重返拳坛的主要原因。

1969年罗宾逊建立了舒格·雷·罗宾逊青年基金会。这个洛杉矶机构主要帮助那些居住在市中心贫民区的年轻人通过体育、艺术和表演,重新审视自己获得自信。这个机构开办了课后体育活动、周末体育比赛、教育活动、艺术及工艺课程、文化活动等各种服务及年度赛事。很多在这里成长的孩子长大后都成为全国杰出运动员,包括奥运会金牌得主弗洛伦斯·格里菲斯·乔依娜。

除了慈善工作以外,罗宾逊还在电影和电视中扮演配角。他出演过电视剧《谍中谍》、《卧底侦缉队》和《幻想岛》。他还在一些电影中扮演小角色,比如弗兰克·辛纳屈主演的《侦探》及电影《The Todd Killings》。他还在1952-1961年间播出的"公共汽车"秀节目中有出色表演,他独创的表演艺术风格让该节目收视率第一。

罗宾逊前半生写过一本名为《舒格糖·雷:舒格·罗宾逊的故事》的自传,1994年他与人合著出书,题目很简单,就叫《舒格·雷》。他结过三次婚。他与第二任妻子——舞蹈演员艾德娜·梅的婚姻持续了18年,直到1962年离婚。罗宾逊与第三任妻子米丽的婚姻一直持续到他离开人世,1989年4月12日,罗宾逊经历了阿尔茨海默氏病和糖尿病的长期折磨之后,在加利福尼亚考佛市逝世。

舒格·雷·罗宾逊安静地结束了自己的生命,淡出了人们的视线,但是他把体育传递给了儿童,他的个人魅力以及令人惊叹的拳坛成就,会让全世界的拳击迷和运动迷们永远赞颂。

Thirty-seven

Babe Ruth

Why He is Among the 50 plus one Greatest Sports Heroes

It has been said that Babe Ruth revolutionized the game of baseball, turning the spotlight off of the pitcher and on to the home run–hitting batter. During his career, he led the American League in home runs for a total of 12 seasons. Upon his retirement, he led the league in numerous categories, and he still owns a few of those records today. Through his accomplishments, Ruth brought baseball to its status as a national pastime. For that, he deserves to sit with sports history's greatest kings.

On the Way Up

George Herman Ruth, Jr. was born on February 6, 1895 in Baltimore, Maryland. His parents, George and Kate, had a total of eight children, but Ruth and one sister were the only two to survive beyond infancy. While growing up he was often left alone to care for himself and would get into trouble. When he was 7 years old, his father took him to an orphanage called St. Mary's Industrial School for Boys, where he signed custody of Ruth over to the Catholic missionaries who operated the school.

Ruth spent the next 12 years at St. Mary's with little contact from his family. He became known as being a wild and uncontrollable student, but soon found a mentor in Brother Matthias, St. Mary's prefect of discipline. Brother Matthias was an athletic man who introduced Ruth to baseball.

While at St. Mary's, Ruth played the positions of catcher and then pitcher. Once it became apparent that he was talented at the position, he alternated between pitching and catching on the school's varsity team. At 19, he attracted the attention of Jack Dunn, the owner and manager of the Baltimore Orioles, a minor league affiliate of the Boston Red Sox. When the other players saw the left–handed Ruth, they began calling him Jack's newest babe. The nickname, the Babe, stuck. After spending only 5 months in the minors, Ruth was called up to the Red Sox as a pitcher in 1914. However, because the team had a stable of left–handed pitchers, he sat on the bench with a 1–1 record for a few weeks before they sent him to play with the Providence Grays, a minor league team in Providence, Rhode Island. Ruth helped the Grays win the pennant with his pitching when the Red Sox's called him up to the majors.

Professional Career

Ruth secured a starting position as pitcher for the Red Sox during spring training in 1915. The team won the pennant that year. During the season, Ruth maintained an 18–8 record as well as a .315 batting average. He also hit four home runs. The Red Sox defeated the Philadelphia Phillies for the 1915 World Series title.

Ruth would prove himself as one of the best pitchers in the American League (AL) during the 1916 season when he was 23–12 with a 1.75 earned runs average (ERA) and nine shutouts. He

贝贝·鲁斯

他为何入选《50+1位最闪耀的体育巨星》

据说，贝贝·鲁斯掀起了棒球运动的革命浪潮，棒球投手在本垒打球员光环的笼罩之下相形见绌。在他的职业生涯中，他带领美国联盟整整12个赛季都获得了本垒打。到退役时，他已为联盟创造了无数纪录，其中一些至今仍无人能打破。鲁斯成功地提高了棒球运动的地位，让它成为全国普及的娱乐活动。因此，他被称为"50+1位最闪耀的体育巨星"也是理所当然。

成长之路

1895年2月6日，小乔治·赫曼·鲁斯出生在马里兰州巴尔的摩。他的父亲乔治和母亲凯特共生了八个孩子，但是只有鲁斯和他的一个姐姐是没有夭折的两个。小时候，他经常独处照顾自己，老是惹是生非。7岁时，父亲把他送到名为"圣玛丽男子劳动学校"的收容所，在那里，父亲把监护人名字改为鲁斯，把他交给了办学的天主教传教士们看管。

鲁斯在圣玛丽学校呆了整整12年，几乎不与家人来往。他是出了名的难以控制的野小子，但是很快找到了良师益友，即圣玛丽的治安官马提亚。马提亚爱好体育，是他让鲁斯接触到了棒球。

在圣玛丽学校时，鲁斯先做接手，后来又做投手。当他在这两个位置中都显示出才华时，他便在校队接手和投手的位置频频交换角色。19岁时，他吸引了巴尔的摩金莺队老板兼经理杰克·唐的注意，该队是隶属波士顿红袜队的小联盟球队。当其他球员看见"左撇子"的鲁斯时，他们开始叫他"杰克的最新宝贝"。从此有了"贝贝"的昵称。

在小联盟仅呆了5个月，鲁斯于1914年被调到红袜队做投手。然而，由于球队来了个左撇子投手，他坐冷板凳几周后，球队成绩为一胜一负，他们决定让他参加罗得岛州普罗维登斯的小联盟队普罗维登斯灰衫军队。当红袜队把鲁斯送进大联盟时，他以投手身份帮助灰衫队在锦标赛中获胜。

职业生涯

1915年春季训练中，鲁斯开始担任红袜队投手。那一年，该队获得锦标赛冠军。在赛季中，鲁斯保持着18:8的成绩，同时拥有平均打击率为315的纪录。他还有四个本垒打。红袜队击败费城人队，夺得1915年世界联赛冠军称号。

1916年赛季，鲁斯靠实力证明了自己是美国联盟最佳投手之一，成绩为23:12，防御率为1.75，9次胜投。他的美国联盟左手投手单赛季胜投纪录与如今的纪录持平。鲁斯在那个

still shares the single season shutout record for an AL left−handed pitcher to this day. Ruth's fine performance that season led the way for him to pitch in his first World Series game in 1916, when he set a still−standing record for the longest complete game in series history against the National League champion team, the Brooklyn Robins. Although Ruth gave up an early run in the first inning, his performance evened out and he went on to pitch 13 scoreless innings out of a total of 14 for the 2−1 victory. The Red Sox won the series, four games to one.

In 1917, Ruth continued his great pitching by completing a record of 24−13, and he also finished with a .325 batting average, even with limited at bats. After one of his teammates, Harry Hooper, made the suggestion that Ruth would be more useful as an everyday player rather than a pitcher, Ruth's playing time in the outfield and as a hitter started to grow while his time on the pitching mound diminished.

During the 1918 season, which was shortened signi.cantly due to World War I, Ruth maintained a batting average of .300 and led the AL with 11 home runs in 317 at bats. That was much higher than the average total for an everyday player. Ruth still kept up his strong performance as a pitcher with a 13−7 record and a 2.22 ERA, and carried the Red Sox in their 4−2 defeat of the Chicago Cubs in the 1918 World Series. In that series, Ruth's pitching brought him to a 2−0 record with a 1.06 ERA, and he reached a total of $29\frac{2}{3}$ scoreless World Series innings, a record that would remain unbroken for 43 years. As far as hitting went, Ruth only batted five times during the series because the Cubs kept their top left−handed pitchers in for almost every inning.

Ruth, who would become known as The Bambino and The Sultan of Swat, pitched in only 17 out of 130 games during the 1919 season, switched to a full−time outfielder. With 29 home runs, he set his first single−season home run record, as well as achieving a .322 batting average and 114 runs. By that time, Ruth's famously huge appetite had literally gone straight to his waistline, transforming his previously tall, athletic physique into what one would call rotund.

Despite his achievements as base runner and outfielder, Ruth was gaining a reputation as a late−night carouser. During the 1918 season, he quit the team for a few days after getting into a verbal argument with manager Ed Barrow and was fined $500 for threatening to punch Barrow in the nose. That was also the year that Ruth began refusing to pitch in his starting rotation turns, claiming injuries. In 1919, Ruth signed a $10,000−per year contract with the Red Sox, but by the end of the year, he threatened to sit out for the entire 1920 season if the franchise did not start paying him $20,000 a year.

In December of 1919, Red Sox owner Harry Frazee sold Ruth to the New York Yankees, in part due to the franchise's need for money as a result of the war, and the simple fact that Ruth had become difficult to coach. After the sale, Frazee told the press, "While Ruth is undoubtedly the greatest hitter the game has ever seen, he is likewise one of the most selfish and inconsiderate men ever to put on a baseball uniform." The trade proved to be a monumental mistake for the Red Sox's. They went on to be the worst team in the AL from 1920−1934, when they finished last 10 times; did not finish higher than fifth place; and never had a winning season. The team, which fans said had been put under the Curse of the Bambino, ended up suffering an 86−year drought, unable to win another World Series title until 2004.

The Yankees benefited from the trade; New York would go on to win 39 AL pennants and 26 World Series titles. In 1920, Ruth almost doubled his own previous home run record with 54 home runs, and fans were soon flocking to the field to see him swing. While the Yankees had been sharing the Polo grounds with the Giants, another major league New York team, Ruth and his crew

赛季的出色表现让他首次以投手身份参加了1916年的世界联赛,并且创造了联赛历史上至今未能打破的最长时间完整比赛纪录,对手是国家联盟冠军队——布鲁克林罗宾。虽然鲁斯在第一局中早早地错过了得分,但是他的得分率趋于稳定,在14局中共13局投球未失分,最后2:1获胜。红袜队以四胜一负的成绩赢得联赛冠军。

1917年,鲁斯继续成功投球,获得24:13的成绩,即使安打数极少,他还是拿下325平均打击率。鲁斯队友哈利·胡佩尔建议他可以做全能运动员,而不只是投手,听到这个建议后,鲁斯在外野担任击球手的生涯逐渐开始,告别了站在投球区土墩上投球的日子。

1918年的赛季由于第一次世界大战而大大缩短,鲁斯保持着300打击率的纪录,带领美国联盟在317个安打中获得11支本垒打。这比普通球员平均总数要高得多。鲁斯仍然发挥着出色投手的强势,成绩为13:7,平均2.22得分率,带领红袜队在1918年世界联赛中以4:2的比分击败芝加哥小熊队。在那次联赛,鲁斯的投球让他获得2:0的成绩、1.06的得分率,在世界联赛中的292局中只有三局投球失分,这个纪录保持了43年。在击球方面,鲁斯在联赛中只有五次安打,因为小熊队在每局比赛中都派出了最优秀的左手投手。

鲁斯以"小孩"和"斯瓦特魔鬼"著称,他在1919年赛季的130场比赛中,只担任了17次投手,大多数时间都转型为全职外野手。他创造了自己首次单个赛季29本垒打的纪录,还获得322打击率和114次得分的好成绩。到那时为止,著名的"大胃王"鲁斯腰围越来越大,原本高大的运动员体形转眼变成了圆胖形。

尽管鲁斯在跑垒和外野方面表现突出,他还是出名的"夜店王"。1918年赛季时,他与经理艾德·拜洛发生口角,由于往拜洛鼻子上打了一拳而被罚500元,之后的几天他离开了球队。同样是在这一年,鲁斯以受伤为由开始拒绝做轮换投手。1919年,鲁斯以年薪1万签约红袜队,但是到年底,他威胁球队如果不支付2万年薪,就不参加1920年整个赛季。

1919年12月,红袜队老板哈利·弗瑞兹将鲁斯转给纽约扬基队,有部分原因是因为战争使球队缺钱,还有个简单原因:鲁斯越来越难管。交易之后,弗瑞兹告诉媒体:"虽然鲁斯是球场上难得一见的最优秀击球手,但是他也是最自私、最不考虑别人的运动员之一,从来不穿棒球服。"这次交易注定是红袜队的严重错误。1920-1934年间,在最后十次比赛后,他们的成绩一落千丈成为美联最差球队;从没有排名前五位;从没有赛季胜利。球迷都说这是"贝贝·鲁斯的诅咒",球队最终遭受了86年从未再胜的命运,直到2004年才再次夺得世界联赛冠军。

扬基队从交易中获益匪浅;纽约继续赢得39次美国联盟锦标赛冠军和26次世界联赛冠军。1920年,鲁斯以54支本垒打成绩几乎让自己之前创下的纪录翻一倍,很快,球迷们蜂拥而至观看他的比赛。当扬基队与纽约另一大联盟队——巨人队共用马球球场时,鲁斯和队友们挣了不少钱,分会在1923年建成了扬基体育场(贝贝·鲁斯之屋),开场赛中他

brought in so much revenue that the franchise was able to open Yankee Stadium in 1923 (The House that Ruth Built), and he proceeded to knock out a home run on opening day. The Yankees defeated the Giants 4 games to 2 and won their first ever World Series title.

During the 1927 season, Ruth smashed a total of 60 home runs in 154 games. This record lasted until the Yankee's Roger Maris hit 61 in an expanded 162–game schedule.

After the Yankees manager, Miller Huggins, passed away in 1929, Ruth made it known that he wanted to manage the team. However, the franchise selected former Chicago Cubs manager, Joe McCarthy, for the position instead. But he continued to play, and in 1932, he was the source of one of the most famous occurrences in baseball. It was during game 3 against the Cubs in the World Series, when he cracked what is believed to be the longest home run ever to be hit out of Chicago's Wrigley Field. The home run was a spectacular feat in itself, but was turned into a legend after the story spread about how Ruth had supposedly pointed to the center field bleachers right before he smashed the ball directly above that spot. The Yankees proceeded to beat the Cubs for the Series title, making it their third sweep in 4 years.

In one of his last major league games, Ruth smashed three home runs against the Pirates in Pittsburgh. The third one proved to be the 714th and final home run of his career. Ruth announced his retirement as a player from professional baseball on June 2, 1935.

During his career, Ruth led his teams to seven World Series victories, and he finished with a lifetime batting average of .342. Among other records, he now ranks first in career slugging percentage with .690, second in career home runs with his 714 and runs batted in (RBIs) with 2, 213, and third in career runs scored with 2,174 and career walks with 2,062. Ruth led the AL in home runs 12 times, in slugging percentage 13 times, in runs scored eight times and in RBIs six times.

Ruth was the recipient of many awards both during and after his career. In 1947, April 27th was declared Babe Ruth Day for all organized baseball leagues in the United States and Japan.

About the Man Himself

Ruth had set his sites as manager of the Yankees but was offered a managing position instead with their minor league team, the Newark Bears. He refused the offer. In 1938 the Brooklyn Dodgers asked him to join them as their first base coach. Ruth coached for one year then left baseball altogether. Ruth spent the rest of his life making appearances at orphanages and hospitals, and giving talks on the radio. During World War II, he worked as a spokesperson for the United States War Bonds. He established and endowed the Babe Ruth Foundation for impoverished children in 1947. Ruth wrote several books, including *How to Play Baseball and Babe Ruth's Own Book of Baseball*. Ruth married Helen Woodford in October of 1914 and the couple adopted a daughter. They officially separated in 1925. Helen was killed in a house fire in 1929, following which Ruth married actress and model, Claire Hodgson, in April of that same year. They were married until Ruth died of throat cancer on August 16, 1948.

In major league baseball even today, heroic home runs are often called Ruthian, a signal that Babe Ruth will be remembered throughout sports history as a one-of-akind, leading legend.

就击中一支本垒打。扬基队以四胜二负击败巨人队,首次成为世界联赛霸主。

1927赛季中,鲁斯创造了154场比赛中60支本垒打的纪录。这个纪录一直保持着,直到扬基队的罗杰马里斯在162场比赛中打了61支本垒打。

1929年,扬基队总经理米勒·哈金斯去世后,大家都知道鲁斯想接管球队。然而,分会却选择了芝加哥小熊队前任经理乔·麦卡锡。但是鲁斯继续参赛,1932年,他创造了棒球史上最著名的奇迹。在世界联赛对抗小熊队的第三场比赛中,他打到了最长距离本垒打,球落到了芝加哥瑞格利球场外。这支本垒打本身十分引人注目,但是事情被传成了传奇故事,说鲁斯故意瞄准中央球场看台区,然后将球径直朝上击。洋基队连续在联赛中击败小熊队,四年中第三次横扫对手。

在最后的大联盟赛的一次比赛里,鲁斯在匹兹堡对战海盗队时,击中三支本垒打。第三支是他职业生涯的第714支,也是最后一支本垒打。1935年6月2日,鲁斯正式宣布退役。

鲁斯在职业生涯中七次带领球队获得世界联赛冠军,职业生涯平均打击率为342。在众多纪录中,他至今仍以690的长打率排名第一,以714支本垒打和2213次打者打点数排名第二,以2174次跑垒得分和2062次胜投数排名第三。鲁斯12次率领美联本垒打,13次获得长打率,8次跑垒得分,6次打者打点。

鲁斯职业生涯内外受到过无数嘉奖。1947年4月27日,所有美国和日本的棒球联盟组织都把这天定为"贝贝·鲁斯日"。

关于此人

鲁斯在扬基队终于获得了经理职位,但是他却被安排担任小联盟球队——纽华克熊队的经理。他拒绝担任此职。1938年布鲁克林道奇队邀请他担任第一教练。鲁斯做了一年的教练后离开了所有的棒球队。在后半生,他频频出现于孤儿收容所和医院,通过广播发表演说。在二战期间,他出任美国战争债券代言人。1947年他创办了贝贝·鲁斯基金会,资助贫困儿童。鲁斯写过几本书,包括:《怎样打棒球》和《贝贝·鲁斯自己的棒球书》。1914年10月他与海伦·伍德福特结婚,夫妻俩收养了一个女儿。1925年他们宣布离婚。1929年海伦家中起火被烧死,同年4月鲁斯宣布与演员兼模特克莱尔·霍奇森结婚。两人一直保持着婚姻关系,直到1948年8月16日鲁斯死于喉癌。

棒球大联盟迄今为止仍把出色的本垒打称为"鲁斯打",这表明贝贝·鲁斯这位传奇运动员将永远铭记在人们心中。

Thirty-eight

Nolan Ryan

Why He is Among the 50 plus one Greatest Sports Heroes

Nolan Ryan has been called the fastest pitcher in the history of professional baseball time and time again. The issue of who is the fastest pitcher probably will never be resolved, and so only the facts remain. It is a fact that on August 20, 1974, the Guinness Book of World Records clocked his fastball at 100.9 miles per hour during a game against the Chicago White Sox. It is also a fact that Ryan set 51 major league records during his 27-year career. And it is a fact that he is the only player in major league history to have his uniform number retired by three separate teams makes Ryan one of the greatest sports heroes.

On the Way Up

Lynn Nolan Ryan, Jr. was born on January 31, 1947 in Refugio, Texas but grew up in Alvin, a suburb of Houston. While playing on the baseball team at Alvin High School, where he developed his incredible fastball, Ryan was drafted by the New York Mets in 1965. The team promoted him to the major leagues late in the following year, but they sent him back a few times to play for a minor league team in Marion, Virginia because he could not seem to .nd the strike zone.

Professional Career

Ryan finally began playing with the Mets for real in 1968. He did not become a powerhouse right away because the team's existing pitching staff was so solid. But when it came time for the 1969 World Series, he was finally able to prove himself as a rising star. He entered game 3 against the Baltimore Orioles to relieve a starter and ended up shutting down the opposing team for almost three innings. Ryan's efforts paid off for the Mets, who won that game as well as the next two to beat the Orioles in five games.

Ryan played for the Mets for a few more years before being traded to the California Angels in 1972. Although the Angels were a sub-.500 team and would keep that kind of below-average record for most of his time with them, Ryan's pitching success blasted off in California. He started winning between 19 and 22 games per season on a consistent basis, and set his first record in 1973 when he struck out 383 batters in a single season. This respectable record was made even more so because he accomplished it during the first year that the American League (AL) put the designated hitter rule into effect. It has been speculated that if AL pitchers had still been allowed to bat, Ryan might have been able to total more than 400 strikeouts that season.

The 1970s turned out to be a decade .lled with records for The Ryan Express, as he was sometimes called by fans. From 1973–1975, he tied an existing record by throwing four no-hitters. In 1974, he tied a single-game record when he struck out 19 batters in each of two games. This record stood until 1986 when Roger Clemens struck out 20 batters in one game. Ryan also led the league in strikeouts for 7 seasons during the 1970s.

212

诺兰·莱恩

他为何入选《50+1位最闪耀的体育巨星》

诺兰·莱恩频频被称为"职棒史上速度最快的投手"。关于谁是最快的投手，这个问题可能永远无解，但是事实却永远存在：1974年8月20日，他与芝加哥白袜队比赛中以每小时100.9英里速度的快投被收入《吉尼斯世界纪录》。莱恩在27年职业生涯中共创造了51项大联盟纪录。他也是大联盟历史上唯一一位球衣被三个不同球队退役的运动员，这份殊荣足以让莱恩登上50+1位最闪耀的体育巨星榜。

成长之路

1947年1月31日，林恩·诺兰·莱恩出生在得克萨斯州里菲吉奥县，但是从小生长在休斯敦郊区的艾尔文。效力于艾尔文高中棒球校队时，莱恩练就了不可思议的快球本领，1965年他在纽约大都会选秀中脱颖而出。第二年年终，球队提升他为大联盟队员，但是，由于他似乎找不到好球区，他们几次又把他送到弗吉尼亚州马里恩球队。

职业生涯

1968年莱恩正式为大都会队出赛。他并没有立刻成为核心力量，因为该球队已有的投手阵容强大。但是当1969年世界联赛到来之时，他终于能够证明自己就是一颗冉冉升起的新星。在对抗巴尔的摩金莺队的第三场比赛中，莱恩上场先发球，最后几乎三局都让对方束手无策。莱恩的努力让大都会队大获全胜，他们赢得了比赛，并且在接下来两次比赛中都以五局战胜金莺队。

莱恩又为大都会队效力几年，之后于1972年交易至加州天使队。虽然天使队是排名低于500的球队，而且莱恩在该队的绝大多数时间，他们水平一直低于平均成绩，但是他成功的投球让加州队异军突起。他开始每赛季固定参加19至22次比赛，1973年，他在单赛季中创下了383个三振出局的纪录，这是他职业生涯的首个纪录。这项令人敬畏的纪录仍在第一年里被他继续改写，迫使美国联盟指定击球员规定生效。据推测，如果美联规定投手可以继续击球，莱恩可能在那个赛季创下400多个三振出局的纪录。

70年代尽是"特快车莱恩"创造的纪录，这个绰号是球迷起的。1973-1975年，他打平了四次无安打投球比赛纪录。1974年，他每两场比赛中就有19次三振出局，打平了单场比赛纪录。这个纪录一直保持着，直到1986年罗杰·克莱门斯创下了单场比赛20次三振出局的纪录。

Despite all of the love that Angels' fans poured upon Ryan, the team's general manager, Buzzie Bavasi did not seem to have any kind of affection for the player. Bavasi described Ryan as a flashy .500 pitcher, and when Ryan left for the Houston Astros in 1979, Bavasi said that all he needed to do in order to match Ryan's 16–14 record the previous season was to obtain two 8–7 pitchers.

In 1979, Ryan packed up his bags and moved to Houston after signing a contract with the Astros that made him the first player to get paid $1 million per year. He started his new team off that season by hitting a 3–run home run against the Los Angeles Dodgers on April 12, 1980. It was the first of the two home runs that he would hit in his career and it brought him three of the six RBIs that he would hit that year. The Astros made it to the playoffs that year, but they did not get to the World Series, falling short by one game.

Ryan finally broke the no–hitter record on September 26, 1981 when he threw his fifth no–hitter and became the third pitcher ever to throw a no–hitter in both the American and National leagues. He also won the National League ERA title that season with an impressive 1.69. After this, Ryan's performance as an Astro evened out as he continued to play seasons that were good enough, but not spectacular. He did have one more stellar moment on April 27, 1983 when he broke the alltime strikeout record with his 3,509th strikeout.

The 1987 season turned out to be quite strange for Ryan. At 40–years old, he was the most dominant pitcher in the National League, leading the way in ERA (2.76) and strikeouts (270), but due to a lack of solid support from the Astro's offense, he finished the season with a lowly record of 8–16.

After the 1988 season, Ryan moved out of Houston, but stayed in Texas following a contract dispute that caused him to join the Texas Rangers. The Rangers' better offensive support helped pump life into Ryan's record. During his first year with the team in 1989, he won 16 games and led the league with 301 strikeouts. And on August 22nd of that same year, he struck out Rickey Henderson of the Oakland

Athletics to become the first pitcher in history to make 5,000 career strikeouts. Ryan threw two more no–hitters in 1990 and 1991.

The following month proved to be Ryan's last as a professional pitcher. On September 22, 1993, he tore a tendon in his right arm during a game against the Seattle Mariners, which ended his career two starts earlier than he had originally planned. Ryan left the game as baseball's all–time strikeout leader with a record of seven no–hitters and 5,714 strikeouts and he finished with 324 wins while playing more seasons than any other major league player.

During and after his numerous seasons as a professional on the pitching mound, Ryan was the recipient of many awards including:
- All Star Player (1972–1973, 1975, 1977, 1979, 1981, 1985 and 1989)
- American League's Joe Cronin Award (1973, 1989)
- Texas Baseball Hall of Fame (1987)
- Man of the Year, *The Sporting News* (1990)
- Male Athlete of the Year, United Press International (1990)
- Pro Sportsman of the Year, United States Sports Academy/USA Today (1990)
- Peter J. McGovern Little League Museum Hall of Excellence (1991)
- National Baseball Hall of Fame, Baseball Writers Association of America (1999)
- All–Century Team, baseball fans of America (1999)

尽管天使队球迷疯狂追星,但是该队总经理巴兹·巴瓦西却对莱恩没有任何好感。巴瓦西认为莱恩平均500的投球数只是昙花一现,1979年莱恩转至休斯敦太空人队时,巴瓦西声称自己所要做的就是吸纳两名8:7投手,以赶上莱恩在前个赛季16:14的纪录。

1979年,与太空人队签订合同成为第一位年薪100万的球员后,莱恩背起行囊奔赴休斯敦。1980年4月12日是他首次亮相于新球队,在与洛杉矶道奇队比赛中,他击中一个三分本垒打。这是他职业生涯中两次三分本垒打的头一次,也让他得到了那年六个打点的其中三个。那年,太空人队闯进季后赛,但是他们没有挺进世界联赛,只因一场比赛错失机会。

1981年9月26日,莱恩投出了生涯第五场无安打比赛,打破了无安打比赛纪录,成为美国和国家两大联盟中第三位参加无安打比赛的投手。那个赛季他还以惊人的1.69防御率获得"国家联盟最高防御率球员"称号。在此之后,莱恩以太空人队员身份继续参加赛季比赛,表现不错,但非完美。1983年4月27日,他再次改写了历史,以自己第3509个三振出局打破了自己创造的纪录。

1987年赛季对于莱恩来说比较奇怪。40岁时,他仍是国家联盟投手中的中流砥柱,创下2.76防御率和270个三振出局,但是由于太空人队缺乏强大的进攻力量,他在赛季结束时成绩很低,仅为8:16。

1988年赛季后,莱恩离开休斯敦,但是由于合同问题,他必须待在得克萨斯州,为德州巡逻者队效力。巡逻者队更强的进攻为莱恩创造了更多纪录。1989年他在该队的第一年里,就赢得了16场比赛,率领联盟取得301次三振出局的成绩。同年8月22日,他把奥克兰运动家队的瑞奇·韩德森三振出局,成为史上第一位创造5000次三振出局的投手。1990年和1991年,莱恩再度投出了无安打比赛。

下个月是莱恩作为职业投手的最后时光。1993年9月22日,在与西雅图水手队比赛时,他的右臂腱拉伤,两个开场比赛后,他比预定计划提前结束了职业生涯。莱恩是棒球历史上的"三振王",他投出了七次五安打比赛,5714个三振出局,324次胜利,参加的赛季也多于任何大联盟球员。
作为职业投手的莱恩在赛季内外都获得了无数奖项:
· 全明星球员 (1972-1973, 1975, 1977, 1979, 1981, 1985 和1989)
· 美国联盟乔·克罗尼奖 (1973, 1989)
· 得克萨斯州棒球名人堂 (1987)
· 《体育新闻》"年度人物" (1990)
· 合众国际社"年度男运动员"奖(1990)
· 美国体育学院/《今日美国》"年度职业运动员"奖 (1990)
· 入选彼得·J·麦戈文小联盟博物馆杰出名人堂(1991)
· 被"美国棒球作家协会"选入国家棒球名人堂 (1999)
· 被美国棒球迷选入"世纪全明星队" (1999)

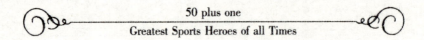
About the Man Himself

After Ryan retired from baseball, he ventured into the business world. He is the principal owner of The Express Bank of Texas in Round Rock, Texas and owns Nolan Ryan's Waterfront Restaurant near Three Rivers, Texas. He also owns and operates a number of cattle ranches in South Texas. In December of 1999, Ryan became a limited partner in Beefmaster Cattlemen, LP, which now markets Nolan Ryan Tender Aged Beef.

Ryan has remained close to the game of baseball. He is currently a consultant for the Houston Astros and is also credited with helping to bring a minor league baseball franchise to Central Texas. In May of 1998, Ryan, along with one of his sons and a group of investors, purchased the Double-A franchise, the Jackson Generals, from the Astros and moved them to Round Rock. The new team was called the Round Rock Express and played its debut home game on April 16, 2000. Then, in 2005, Round Rock purchased and relocated the Edmonton Trappers, a Canadian Triple-A team, and it also created a new Double-A team in Corpus Christi, Texas.

Ryan was appointed to 6-year term as a Commissioner with the Texas Parks and Wildlife Commission in 1995, and he has also served on the Board of Directors of such organizations as the Justin Cowboy Crisis Fund; the Natural Resources Foundation of Texas; the Texas Beef Council; the Alvin Community College Baseball Scholarship Fund; and his own Nolan Ryan Foundation. The Nolan Ryan Foundation was formed in Alvin, Texas in 1990 to provide resources for children, education and community development Its first project was the Nolan Ryan Center, the home of a continuing education department, was donated to Alvin Community College in the fall of 1996.

Ryan co-wrote two autobiographies, *Throwing Heat: The Autobiography of Nolan Ryan and Miracle Man: Nolan Ryan, The Autobiography.* Married to his wife, Ruth since 1967 they have raised two sons and one daughter.

Nolan Ryan will be remembered for his ripping fastball and his successful career as a major league pitcher and his dedication to his community, places Ryan as one of the greatest athletes of all times. No one can argue with that.

◀ Nolan Ryan ▶

关于此人

　　莱恩退役后闯入了商业世界。他是德州圆石市"德州运通银行"总裁,并在德州三河市附近经营"诺兰·莱恩水上餐厅"。1999年12月,莱恩成为Beefmaster Cattlemen, LP的有限合伙人,现在销售Nolan Ryan 的老牛嫩肉。

　　莱恩仍十分关注棒球运动。他现在担任休斯敦太空人队顾问,由于带领小联盟棒球分队进入中德州而成为极有声望的人物。1998年5月,莱恩携带儿子和一群投资者,买下了太空人队的"双A分队"——杰克逊将军队,搬到了圆石市。新队名字叫"圆石特快车队",于2000年4月16日第一次举行主场比赛。然后,在2005年,圆石队又买下并重新安置了一个加拿大"三A队"——埃德蒙顿捕猎者队,还在德州柯柏斯克里斯提创建了一个新的"双A队"。

　　1995年,莱恩签订6年期限的合同,担任德州公园与野生动物委员会委员,他还是众多机构组织的董事会成员,包括贾斯丁牛仔克里斯基金;德州自然资源基金会;德州牛肉联合会;艾尔文社区大学棒球奖学金基金;和他自己的诺兰·莱恩基金会。1990年,诺兰·莱恩基金会于德州艾尔文成立,为儿童、教育及社区发展提供资助。第一个项目是"再教育之家"——诺兰·莱恩中心,1996年秋,它被捐赠到艾尔文社区大学。

　　莱恩与人合作出过两本自传——《酷爱投掷:诺兰·莱恩自传》和《奇迹之人:诺兰·莱恩》。1967年他与妻子露丝结婚,育有两儿一女。

　　诺兰·莱恩快球出色,作为大联盟中的投手,他拥有成功的职业生涯,并且为自己的社区尽心尽力地作出贡献,他理应是万古体坛明星之一。这一点毋庸置疑。

Thirty-nine

Sam Snead

Why He is Among the 50 plus one Greatest Sports Heroes

Sam Snead is best known for his powerful athletic abilities and his graceful swing. In fact, fellow legendary golfer Jack Nicklaus once described Snead's swing "the most fluid motion ever to grace a golf course." That swing led him to 82 PGA Tour career victories, an impressive record that still stands today. Snead won seven major championships and is a member of the World Golf Hall of Fame. His smooth–swinging ways have earned him the right to be included as one of history's finest athletes.

On the Way Up

Samuel Jackson Snead was born on May 27, 1912 in Hot Springs, Virginia. He was the fifth and youngest son of a backwoods farmer, and grew up during the Great Depression. One of Snead's brothers used to practice his golf swing in the yard at the farm, which eventually sparked an interest in Snead himself. He started carving his own clubs out of tree limbs and used the balls that he had retrieved while caddying at the Homestead Hotel Golf Course. Yet, Snead focused on football, basketball and baseball during his years at Hot Springs' Valley High School. In fact, he dreamed of becoming a professional football player until an injury put an end to his dreams. Golf started looking very good to Snead right about then and he landed his first assistant pro job when he was 19. In 1935, he became the resident pro at the Greenbrier resort in White Sulphur Springs, Virginia before joining the PGA Tour the following year.

Professional Career

Snead, who was very outspoken, brought a certain kind of folksy spirit to the green with him. He wore a straw hat, sometimes played barefoot and possessed what some would call homespun wit. He was a natural athlete; his skills in golfing came just as easily to him as those in other sports. Perhaps that is what led to what some have called his relaxed, even lazy approach to golf. No matter how he played the game, though, no one can deny that Snead was highly successful on the golf course.

In 1937, his first year in the pros, Snead won a handful of tournaments. The fans noticed his long drives and nicknamed him Slammin' Sam and Slammer. The next year, he won eight times and walked away with the money title, which he would obtain twice more, in 1949 and 1950. He captured the first of his seven majors at the PGA Championship in 1942, and would go on to win the PGA two more times in 1949 and 1951. His remaining four majors consisted of three Masters in 1949, 1952 and 1954, and one British Open in 1946. The most memorable of those wins was probably the 1954 Masters when Snead, tied with Ben Hogan after 72 holes, triumphed in an 18–hole playoff, 70–71.

218

山姆·斯尼德

他为何入选《50+1位最闪耀的体育巨星》

山姆·斯尼德以其强大的运动能力和优雅的挥杆而著名。事实上，同样是高尔夫传奇运动员的杰克·尼古拉斯曾经这么描述过斯尼德的挥杆："这是高尔夫球场上最流畅优雅的动作。"

他的挥杆成就了高尔夫PGA巡回赛的82次生涯冠军，这个纪录令人印象深刻，保持至今。斯尼德共赢得7次大奖赛冠军，是世界高尔夫球名人堂成员。他如丝般平滑的挥杆让他荣登50+1位最闪耀的体育巨星榜。

成长之路

1912年5月27日，赛缪尔·杰克逊·斯尼德出生在弗吉尼亚温泉市。他成长于偏远山区的农民之家，在家中排行老五，也是最小的儿子，那时正赶上美国大萧条时代。斯尼德的一个哥哥经常在农场院子里练习高尔夫球挥杆，终于，斯尼德对高尔夫的兴趣也油然而生。他自己用树枝做球杆，高尔夫球就用在Homestead宾馆高尔夫球场捡来的球。但是，就读于温泉谷高中时期的斯尼德却专注于橄榄球、篮球和棒球。实际上，他曾梦想做个职业橄榄球运动员，但是一次意外受伤让这个梦想破灭。高尔夫球恰在此时是最适合斯尼德的运动，19岁时，他得到了职业助理球员的工作。1935年，他成为弗吉尼亚州白色硫黄温泉镇绿蔷薇度假村的常驻职业球员，第二年他便参加了高尔夫PGA巡回赛。

职业生涯

斯尼德很坦率，在他身上可以看到浓重的乡土气息。他戴着草帽，有时候赤脚打球、衣装简朴。他生来就是运动员，在高尔夫方面的天赋跟其他运动一样，对他来说都轻而易举。也许这造就了他打高尔夫球的风格，有时候被大家认为是一种轻松懒散的方式。无论他怎么打高尔夫，没有人能否认斯尼德是高尔夫球场上叱咤风云的王者。

1937年是斯尼德作为职业球员的第一年，他在锦标赛中满载而归。球迷看到了他的长打，从此"重击手山姆"的昵称不胫而走。次年，他赢了8次，巨额揽入囊中，又接着在1949年和1950年两年得到两次"最多薪金运动员"称号。1942年是他生平7个PGA锦标赛冠军的首次夺冠，1949年和1951年又两次赢得PGA冠军。其余大赛奖项分别是1949、1952、1954年的3次名人赛冠军和1946年英国公开赛冠军。最令人难忘的当属1954年名人赛，斯尼德创下了72杆进洞的纪录，与本·霍根打平，后来在18个洞的季后赛中以70:71胜出。

Despite his respectable seven–major win collection, Snead was never able to conquer the U. S. Open. He came in second a total of four times between 1937 and 1949, sometimes making what could be called absent–minded mistakes. For instance, during the1939 event, he thought that he needed a birdie on the 72nd hole to win, but he really only needed a par 5. He ended up making an eight to finish tied for fifth. In 1947, Snead missed a 30–inch putt on the final playoff hole, finishing second to Lew Worsham.

In 1950, Snead won 11 tournaments, thus becoming the last PGA Tour golfer to have a double–digit victory record in one season. During his career, he played on eight U.S. Rider Cup teams in 1937, 1939, 1941, 1947, 1949, 1951, 1953 and 1955, with an individual playing record of 10–2–1. He also captained the 1951, 1959 and 1969 Rider Cup teams. Snead holds the record for most career Top 10s with 358 and also holds the record for most PGA Tour victories in a single event, garnering eight wins at the Greater Greensboro Open in 1938, 1946, 1949–1950, 1955–1956, 1960 and 1965. It seemed that he got better with age, as he was competitive into his 60s. He became one of the best mature golfers in the history of the game. As a matter of fact, Snead was the oldest player to win a PGA Tour event when he came out on top at the 1965 Greater Greensboro Open at the age of 52 years, 10 months and 8 days. He was also the youngest PGA Tour player to shoot equal to and below his age. This momentous occasion took place in 1979 at the Quad Cities Open when a 67–year old Snead shot 67 and 66. That same year at the Manufacturers Hanover Westchester Classic, he became the oldest player to make a cut on the PGA Tour at 67 years, 2 months and 21 days old.

Snead retired from the Tour in 1979, but did not stray far from the golf course as he helped with the creation of the Seniors Tour a couple of years later. He went on to win six PGA Seniors titles and five World Seniors Championships. In 1983, Snead shot 60 at his old course, the Homestead Hotel, at the age of 71. Honors that have been bestowed upon him throughout the years are:

·Vardon Trophy, PGA Tour (1938, 1949–1950 and 1955)
·Player of the Year Award, PGA Tour (1949)
·World Golf Hall of Fame Induction (1974)
·Lifetime Achievement Award, PGA Tour (1998)

About the Man Himself

Snead married Audrey Karnes in 1940. They had two sons and were married until Audrey's death in 1990. He was forced to take a break from professional golf when he served in the United States Navy for a few years during World War II. Snead was a prolific writer. Not only did he co–write his autobiography, which was entitled *Slammin' Sam,* but he also authored and co–authored numerous instructional golf books. He wrote other books as well, two of which are *Golf Begins at Forty* and *The Game I Love*. Snead died of a stroke on May 23, 2002.

The legend of Sam Snead's superior swing and his dedication to the sport of golf makes Sam Snead one of the greatest athletes of all times.

尽管7次赢得大赛冠军令人敬佩，但是斯尼德从未赢过美国公开赛。1937至1949年间，他4次位居第二，有时还会犯些"开小差"的错误。比如，在1939年赛事中，他以为在第72洞以小鸟球(比标准杆少用一杆完成此洞)获胜，但是他只需要打帕(5杆)。最后他成绩为8杆，排名并列第五。1947年季后赛中，最后一个球离洞30英寸，斯尼德未能击中，输给了卢·沃尔山姆，获得亚军。

1950年，斯尼德11次赢得锦标赛冠军，成为PGA巡回赛中最后一位单赛季取得双位数胜利的球员。在他的职业生涯中，他于1937, 1939, 1941, 1947, 1949, 1951, 1953 和 1955年分别8次参加"美国莱德杯"大赛，创下了个人纪录10胜2平1负。他分别于1951、1959和1969年率领莱德杯队。斯尼德保持着生涯358次排名前十的纪录，还是PGA巡回赛单个赛事夺冠最多的球员，在1938、1946、1949-1950, 1955-1956、1960 和1965年，他八次赢得大格林斯伯洛公开赛。步入60岁时，他似乎越老越焕发出旺盛的斗志，成为高尔夫球历史上最年长的球员之一。实际上，斯尼德曾是赢得PGA巡回赛冠军中年龄最大的运动员，他在52岁10个月零8天的年龄时，赢得1965年大格林斯伯洛公开赛。他也是第一个打出与自身年龄数一样、或低于自身年龄杆数的球手。这一伟大时刻发生在1979年方庭市公开赛上，当时67岁的斯尼德取得了67与66杆的成绩。同年，在韦斯切斯特尔精英赛中，他以67岁2个月21天的高龄成为PGA巡回赛上年龄最大的球员。

1979年巡回赛后，斯尼德退役，但是仍然支持高尔夫事业，几年后，在他的帮助下创办了"常青巡回赛"。他继续赢得六个PGA常青巡回赛冠军和5个世界常青锦标赛冠军。1983年，斯尼德在他的Homestead宾馆老球场上取得了60杆的成绩，那时他已是70岁高龄。他获得的荣誉包括：
- PGA 巡回赛"沃尔登奖"(1938, 1949-1950 和1955年)
- PGA 巡回赛"年度球员奖"(1949年)
- 入选世界高尔夫球名人堂(1974年)
- PGA 巡回赛"终生成就奖"(1998年)

关于此人

1940年，斯尼德与奥戴丽·卡尼斯结婚。他们有两个儿子，婚姻一直到1990年奥戴丽逝世。二战期间，他效力于美国海军，被迫短暂退出职业高尔夫球坛。斯尼德还写了很多书。他不仅与人合写了自传《重击手山姆》，而且自己写或合写了一些高尔夫指导书籍。他也写过其他的书，比如其中两本《40岁开始打高尔夫》和《我喜爱的运动》。2002年5月23日，斯尼德因中风而与世长辞。

山姆·斯尼德出色的挥杆和对高尔夫运动的满腔热情，让他无愧于50+1位史上绝顶运动员称号。

Forty

Mark Spitz

Why He is Among the 50 plus one Greatest Sports Heroes

In 1972, Mark Spitz proved that he was the best swimmer the sport had ever seen. That was the year that he dominated the Summer Olympics in Munich, Germany by winning seven gold medals, a number that has yet to be topped by another Olympic athlete. Quite a feat in itself, Spitz did not just stop there. He also set new world records in each of those seven events. Besides the rest of his successful swimming career, the year 1972 is the main reason that Spitz is still considered one of the biggest fish in the ocean of sports history.

On the Way Up

Mark Andrew Spitz was born on February 10, 1950 in Modesto, California to Lenore and Arnold Spitz. From the time he was 2 years old, his father coached him to be a champion swimmer and ingrained in him the attitude of swimming is not everything, winning is. The Spitz family spent 4 years in Hawaii, which is where his father taught him to swim. When Spitz was 6, the family moved back to California, where he began his first competitive swimming lessons at the YMCA, and at the age of 9, he was swimming under the direction of Sherm Chavoor, a successful and popular coach. When Spitz's swimming and Hebrew School lesson schedules began to conflict, his father simply told the rabbi, "Even God likes a winner."

All of Spitz's early training started to pay off by the time he reached the tender age of 10. By then, he held 17 national age–group records and one world record, and was named the world's best 10–and–under swimmer. Despite having to drive more than 80 miles to work every day, his father moved the family to Santa Clara, California in 1964 so that Spitz could train with George Haines of the celebrated Santa Clara Swim Club. According to his father, it was now or never.

While still in high school, Spitz, otherwise known as Mark the Shark, was well on his way to becoming a world champion. He competed in his first international competition when he was 15 at the 1965 Maccabiah Games and, coupled with his return to Israel 4 years later, he won a total of 10 Maccabiah gold medals. When he was 16, he won the 100–meter butter.y, the sport's toughest stroke, at the National Amateur Athletic Union (AAU) Championships. A year later, Spitz swam away with five gold medals at the 1967 Pan–American Games in Winnipeg, Canada.

By the time he was 17, Spitz had set 10 world records, and by the time he was 18, he had 26 national and international titles under his belt and had broken 26 U.S. records. It is not difficult to see why his fans and experts of the sport had him pegged to win several individual gold medals at the 1968 Olympic Games in Mexico City. But Spitz made the mistake of announcing publicly that he would win six gold medals, which made him seem arrogant and would eventually come back to haunt him by the end of the competition. When it was all over, he had won two team gold medals in the 4×100–meter freestyle and the 4×200–meter freestyle relays, along with an individual silver medal in the 100–meter butterfly and an individual bronze medal in the 100–meter freestyle. Instead of being able to feel triumphant as many other athletes would after having won multiple

40

马克·斯皮兹

他为何入选《50+1位最闪耀的体育巨星》

1972年，马克·斯皮兹证明了自己是游泳史上最佳运动员。那一年，他参加了德国慕尼黑夏季奥运会，赢得七项赛事七枚金牌，另一名运动员至今仍保持此纪录。这项纪录简直是奇迹，斯皮兹却没有就此停止。他继续在七项赛事中创造新的世界纪录。除了职业生涯的其他成就以外，1972年的辉煌战绩仍是他荣登万古游泳体坛健儿榜的主要原因。

成长之路

1950年2月10日，马克·安得鲁·斯皮兹出生在加利福尼亚州孟德斯托，父亲是阿诺·斯皮兹，母亲是雷诺尔·斯皮兹。自从两岁起，他的父亲就开始训练他，目标是成为游泳冠军，他传授的游泳运动态度是：游泳并不是一切，胜利才是。斯皮兹一家在夏威夷住了四年，在那里他父亲教会他游泳。斯皮兹6岁时，全家又搬回加利福尼亚，他便在基督教青年会开始了第一节游泳比赛课程，9岁时，他在成功的著名教练Sherm Chavoor指导下学习游泳。当斯皮兹的游泳课程与希伯来学校课程发生冲突时，他的父亲坦率地跟老师说："连上帝都喜欢赢家。"

10岁时，斯皮兹童年时代的所有训练都初见成效。那时，他已拥有17项全国年龄组纪录和1项世界纪录，被誉为"10岁以内世界最佳游泳运动员"。尽管每天要开80多英里的路程去工作，他的父亲在1964年把全家搬到加州圣他克拉，在那里，斯皮兹可以接受圣他克拉游泳俱乐部著名教练乔治·海因斯的培训。在父亲看来，成败在此一举，否则将来没有机会。

高中时的斯皮兹有着"马克鲨鱼"的绰号，那时他已稳步走在通往世界冠军之路。15岁时，他生平第一次参加国际大赛——1965年马卡比游泳运动会，四年后他再回以色列，已经拥有10枚马卡比赛金牌了。16岁时，他在业余体育联盟锦标赛中赢得最难的100米蝶泳冠军。一年后，斯皮兹在1967年加拿大温尼伯举办的泛美运动会中赢得五枚金牌。

到了17岁，斯皮兹已经创下了10项世界纪录，18岁时，他已拥有26个全国及国际大赛的奖项，并且打破26项美国纪录。难怪他的追星族和体育专家们认定他能得到1968年墨西哥城奥运会的个人金牌，这让他骄傲自大，直到比赛接近尾声，他一直很自负。当比赛全部结束时，他赢得两枚团体金牌：4 x 100米自由泳和4 x 200米自由泳，在个人项目中，他获得100米蝶泳银牌和100米自由泳铜牌。

其他运动员在获得这么多奥运奖牌后一定会得意洋洋，斯皮兹却因为赛前趾高气扬、最终并未获得个人金牌而倍感失望、尴尬。幸运的是，当斯皮兹作为预备牙科学生就读于印第安纳州布鲁明顿诺的印第安纳大学时，他把在墨西哥城的那些消极态度化为更

medals at the Olympics, Spitz struggled with disappointment and embarrassment due to the cocky prediction he had made prior to the games.

Fortunately, Spitz turned the negative feelings from Mexico City into a more positive direction once he started attending Indiana University (IU) in Bloomington, Indiana as a pre–dental student. There, he trained with famed coach, Doc Counsilman, who had also been his coach during the Olympics. While at the university, Spitz won eight individual U.S. National Collegiate Athletic Association titles and by the time he graduated in 1972, he had won a total of 31 U.S. National Amateur Athletic Union titles since 1965. He also set 33 world records between 1965 and 1972, which was the year he graduated from IU. Spitz was named World Swimmer of the Year in 1969 and 1971–1972. He also became the first Jewish recipient of the James E. Sullivan Award in 1971 for his top U.S. amateur athlete status.

His Career

When the Munich, Germany Olympic Games rolled around in 1972, Spitz was more pumped up to win than he had ever been. Even though he dodged questions from the media about how many gold medals he was going to take home, he made a silent prediction of six. He had learned the hard lesson of not speaking too soon.

Spitz performed even better than his prediction. He won not six, but seven gold medals–four individual and three team–and set world records in every one of those seven events.

Until that time, no other Olympian had finished with such awe–inspiring results. Spitz swam the third leg of the 200–meter freestyle and 100–meter medley relays, and the final leg of the 100–meter freestyle relay.

1968 Olympic medals include:
- Gold 4 x 100–meter Freestyle Relay (3:31.7)
- Gold 4 x 200–meter Freestyle Relay (7:52.3)
- Silver 100–meter Butter.y (56.4)
- Bronze 100–meter Freestyle (53.0)

1972 individual records include:
- Gold 100–meter Freestyle (51.22)
- Gold 200–meter Freestyle (1:52.78)
- Gold 100–meter Butterfly (54.27)
- Gold 200–meter Butterfly (2:00.70)

1972 team records include:
- Gold 4 x 100–meter Freestyle Relay (3:26.42)
- Gold 4 x 200–meter Freestyle Relay (7:35.78)
- Gold 4 x 100–meter Medley Relay (3:48.16)

Other awards include:
- World Swimmer of the Year in (1967, 1971–1972)
- James E. Sullivan Award (1971)
- No. 33 *Sports Illustrated* Top 100 Athletes of the 20th Century (2000)

About the Man Himself

He retired from swimming directly following the Munich Olympics at the age of only 22, at which time he decided against going to dental school and started trying to make sense of his many endorsement offers. His agent signed him as a spokesperson for numerous companies that made a

加积极的动力。在那里,他的教练是著名的道克·康希尔曼,道克也是他奥运会期间的教练。

　　斯皮兹在大学时曾八次获得美国国家大学体育协会个人奖项,自1965年到1972年大学毕业,他共获得业余体育联盟的31项大奖。1965年至1972年间,他还创下了33个世界纪录,正好1972年是他毕业的那一年。1969年和1971–1972年,斯皮兹获得"年度世界游泳运动员"称号。作为美国顶级业余运动员,他于1971年首次以犹太人身份获得"詹姆斯·E·沙利文奖"。

职业生涯

　　1972年,当德国慕尼黑迎来奥运会时,斯皮兹比其他任何时候更加斗志昂扬,决心拿冠军。虽然他被媒体追问准备拿多少金牌时沉默不语,但是他内心预期拿六枚。他已经得到教训:不要过早说大话。

　　斯皮兹比预期比赛得更出色。他获得的不是六枚,而是七枚金牌——四枚是个人赛事,三枚是团体赛,在这七项赛事中,每一项都是新的世界纪录。

　　那个年代,没有哪个奥运运动员能取得如此令人敬畏的成绩。斯皮兹在200米自由式接力和100米混合接力中处于第三棒,100米自由泳接力赛中是末棒选手。

1968年奥运会奖牌:
· 4×100米自由式接力赛金牌 (3:31.7)
· 4×200米自由式接力赛金牌 (7:52.3)
· 100米蝶泳银牌(56.4)
· 100米自由泳铜牌(53.0)

1972年个人赛事记录包括:
· 100米自由泳金牌 (51.22)
· 200米自由泳金牌 (1:52.78)
· 100米蝶泳金牌 (54.27)
· 200米蝶泳金牌 (2:00.70)

1972年团体赛事记录包括:
· 4×100米自由式接力赛金牌 (3:26.42)
· 4×200米自由式接力赛金牌(7:35.78)
· 4×100米混合接力赛金牌 (3:48.16)

其他奖项包括:
· 年度世界游泳运动员称号 (1967, 1971–1972)
· 詹姆斯·E·沙利文奖(1971)
· 《体育画报》"20世纪百名最优秀运动员第33名" (2000)

关于此人

　　22岁参加完慕尼黑奥运会后,他很快就退役了,那时,他决定不去牙科学校,而是开始接受很多商业活动的邀请。他的经纪人让他与许多公司签约做代言人。这些公司包括Speedo、Adidas、Schick公司和加利福尼亚牛奶顾问委员会。有个地方的海报上,斯皮兹只

variety of products. These companies included Speedo, Adidas, the Schick Company and the California Milk Advisory Board. At one point, a poster came out of Spitz wearing only his swimsuit and his seven gold medals, making him something of a sex symbol.

Spitz's agent also tried to break him onto the television scene while his name was still fresh on everyone's minds. Even though he appeared on such shows as *The Tonight Show with Johnny Carson, The Sonny and Cher Comedy Hour, the Dean Martin Show* and a Bob Hope special, his dull and uncomfortable on-screen performances quickly made Spitz and many others, including his previous commercial clients, realize that he was not cut out for show business. He kept on for some years as a broadcaster, but was soon out of the public eye almost permanently.

Spitz started sailing and eventually established a successful Beverly Hills real-estate company. But when he was 41-years old, he again caught the media's attention when he tried to make a comeback and qualify for the 1992 Barcelona Olympics. His determination was fueled by film maker Bud Greenspan's $1 million offer if he succeeded in qualifying. Even though he had been training since 1989, Spitz failed to qualify for the 100-meter butterfly with the necessary 55.59. His best time was only 58.03.

In 2005, Spitz was honored with being the .ag bearer for the U.S. Delegation in the 17th Maccabiah Games. He was also ranked 33rd among North America's top 100 athletes of the 20th Century by ESPN. Spitz now lives in Los Angeles with his wife and two sons. He still sails and travels, but no longer runs his real-estate business. He calls himself an entrepreneur and still does promotional work. In December of 2003, Spitz joined the board of directors at Novations, LLC, which manufactures aquatic exercise devices in Boca Raton, Florida, and he has worked to promote the devices as well as safe swimming techniques. He wrote an autobiography called Seven Golds: Mark Spitz Own Story, and co-authored a book called *The Mark Spitz Complete Book of Swimming.*

Over a period of eight days, Mark Spitz had entered seven events, won all seven and set a world record in every one. Spitz is the only person to win seven gold medals at one Olympics and he is one of only four athletes to earn nine career gold medals. This amazing accomplishment secures Mark Spitz's spot as one of the greatest sports athletes of all times.

穿泳裤,还展示了他的7枚金牌,让他成为性感代表。

斯皮兹的名字对大家来说还是比较陌生,他的经纪人就想方设法让他登上荧屏。虽然斯皮兹上过一些电视综艺节目, 比如与强尼·卡森的《今晚秀》、《The Sonny and Cher Comedy Hour》、《狄恩马汀秀》和特别节目《Bob Hope》,但是他乏味无聊的演技很快让自己和其他人,包括前广告委托人意识到他并不适合综艺节目。随后的几年,他又担任过播音员,但没过多久就永远地消失于公众视线。

斯皮兹开始帆船运动,最后还成功建立了"比佛利山房地产公司"。但是,当他41岁时,他重新抓住了媒体的眼球,因为他在1992年巴塞罗那奥运会中重出江湖、争取参赛资格。如果他得到参赛资格,电影制作人巴德格林斯潘就会为他提供100万赞助费。虽然斯皮兹从1989年开始训练,他在100米蝶泳中成绩低于规定的55.59而未能获得资格。他最好的成绩曾经达到58.03。

2005年,第17届马卡比游泳运动会上,斯皮兹被荣幸地选为美国代表团旗手。他被体育娱乐频道ESPN评为"20世纪北美最佳百名运动员第33名"。如今,斯皮兹与妻子和两个儿子住在洛杉矶。他仍然航海、旅游,但是不再经营他的房地产了。他称自己为创业者,仍然做着推广的工作。2003年12月,斯皮兹加入Novations, LLC董事会,这个公司在佛罗里达州博卡雷顿制造水上运动设备,他的工作是改进设备、提高安全游泳技术。他写了本自传《七块金牌:马克·斯皮兹的故事》,还与人合写了本书,名为《马克·斯皮兹游泳完全手册》。

在短短的8天之内,马克·斯皮兹参加了7大赛事,全部获胜,每项都创了新的世界纪录。斯皮兹是唯一一位在一届奥运会中获得7枚金牌的运动员,也是仅有的4位生涯中获得9枚奥运金牌的运动员之一。这惊人的成就保证了马克·斯皮兹在50+1位史上绝顶运动员中享有一席之地。

Forty-one

Johnny Unitas

Why He is Among the 50 plus one Greatest Sports Heroes

After being told that he was too small and not intelligent enough to be a quarterback, Johnny Unitas proved all of his doubters wrong. His determination and skill as well as his ability to seize an opportunity when he was offered one enabled him to go from underdog to top dog status almost overnight. During his years in the NFL, he led his team to two consecutive league titles and a Super Bowl victory, while being chosen to five all-league teams and being named Player of the Year three times. Unitas is the quintessential loser turned winner and for that he shall take his rightful place among the most legendary of athletes.

On the Way Up

John Constantine Unitas was born on May 7, 1933 in Pittsburgh, Pennsylvania. When John was 5 his father died leaving his mother to raise him and his three siblings by herself. The family lived in a working-class section of Pittsburgh and his mother worked two jobs in order to take care of her children. When he got older, Unitas attended a small Catholic high school named St. Justin's, where he joined the football team. At first, he played halfback and end, but then switched to quarterback after replacing the injured starter at that position in the beginning of his junior year.

By the time Unitas was a senior, colleges started paying attention to him, although they were not beating down his door. In fact, the back.eld coach for his dream team, the University of Notre Dame, said that at 6 feet and 138 pounds, Unitas was not heavy enough and would not gain the appropriate amount of weight in order to play college football. The University of Pittsburgh offered him a scholarship, but he failed the school's entrance exam.

Unitas finally decided to accept a scholarship from the University of Louisville, where he became a starter in the sixth game of his freshman year and led the Cardinals to four wins. During his first two seasons, he gained 40 pounds and threw for 21 touchdowns, while also playing safety. His final two seasons were not as impressive, mostly because of injuries and below-average teams and he finished his college playing years with a career total of 27 touchdown passes and 3,139 yards passing. His jersey, No. 16, is the only number ever retired by the football program at Louisville.

During the 1955 NFL Draft, Unitas made it into the ninth slot for the Pittsburgh Steelers, but after not playing him in the season's five exhibition games, they told him that they could not use him after all and Unitas was let go. He found work in construction and played quarterback and defensive back for a local semi-pro team called the Bloomfield Rams. The team played with old equipment on sandlot fields, which had to be sprinkled down with oil before every game in order to keep the dust under control.

Professional Career

Unitas finally got his big break in February of 1956. The Baltimore Colts had been watching

41

约翰尼·尤尼塔斯

他为何入选《50+1位最闪耀的体育巨星》

有人怀疑约翰尼·尤尼塔斯太瘦小、不够聪明，做不了四分卫，但是他向所有质疑者证明了他们判断错误。他的意志和技术以及抓住所有机会的能力，让他仿佛从默默无闻的无名小卒一夜成名。在国家橄榄球联盟的岁月中，他带领球队两次蝉联联盟冠军，获得一次"超级碗"冠军，曾入选5支全联盟球队，并3次被誉为"年度球员"。尤尼塔斯是失败者成功转型为胜利者的典范，这让他成为最传奇运动员之一。

成长之路

1933年5月7日，约翰尼·尤尼塔斯出生于宾夕法尼亚州匹兹堡。5岁时，他的父亲就去世了，母亲独自一人挑起重担，抚养他和其他3个兄弟姐妹。一家人住在匹兹堡工薪阶层地区，他的母亲干两份工作来养育孩子。尤尼塔斯长大后，就读与一所名叫圣贾斯汀的小天主教高中，并参加了橄榄球校队。起初，他担任半卫和端锋，但是他在三年级开学时替代了受伤的发球队员，从此便做了四分卫。

尤尼塔斯四年级时，一些大学开始注意到他，但是并没有来找他。实际上，他梦想中的球队——圣母大学球队的后场队员教练认为：尤尼塔斯身高6英尺，体重才138磅，体重太轻，没有达到大学橄榄球队队员标准。虽然匹兹堡大学向他提供了奖学金，但是他却没有通过入学考试。

最后，尤尼塔斯决定接受路易斯维尔大学奖学金，在大一时的第六场比赛中他以发球队员亮相，带领红雀队赢了4场比赛。前两个赛季中，他增肥40磅，掷了21个触地得分，同时获得安全得分。他的最后两个赛季并不怎么出色，主要因为受伤和低于平均水平的球队，他大学运动生涯中共有27次传出触地得分球，传球码数为3139码。他的16号球衣是路易斯维尔橄榄球活动组史上唯一永久退役球服。

1955年国家橄榄球联盟选秀大会中，他以第九顺位选入匹兹堡钢人队，但是他们在赛季的5场表演赛中都没有让他上场，之后被告知他们最终无法用他，尤尼塔斯被解雇了。他找到了建筑方面的工作，在当地一支名为布卢姆菲尔德公羊队的半职业球队担当四分卫和防守后卫。该队使用的是陈旧的空地球场，每次都要洒上点油来控制尘土。

职业生涯

尤尼塔斯在1956年2月获得绝佳机会。巴尔的摩小马队一直在关注他，他已经长成6

as his frame filled out to 6 foot, 1 inch and 190 pounds and they offered him a $17,000 contract, which he gladly accepted. He made his first appearance against the Chicago Bears during the fourth game of the season when he replaced injured George Shaw. Unitas did not make a great initial impression as his first pass was intercepted and returned for a touchdown. To make matters worse, he fumbled during a handoff on his very next play and the Bears recovered it. The Colts lost that game 58–27.

After that horrible first game, he began working even harder, ending his first season with nine touchdown passes and a rookie record of a 55.6 percent completion mark. The following season, Unitas led the Colts to a 7–5 record after throwing for 2,550 yards and 24 touchdowns.

In 1958, Unitas led the Colts to an NFL title against the New York Giants, but he was injured in the sixth game when his lung was punctured and three of his ribs were broken. Unitas was hospitalized, but returned just four games later to carry the Colts to another decisive victory, this time over the San Francisco 49ers. Unitas said that "that win was even greater than the championship" due to his comeback

from the injuries as well as the fact that the Colts had been down 27–7 at halftime and had ended up winning 35–27. But many ardent fans would disagree with him because the 1958 championship game has been called the greatest game ever played, and he was the star of that nationally–televised game. With two minutes left, the Giants were up 17–14, but then Unitas made seven straight passes that set up a field goal to tie the game with only 7 seconds left. Then, he proceeded to lead the Colts in an 80–yard drive to beat the Giants in overtime.

The next season, Unitas, nicknamed by the fans, the Golden Arm and Johnny U, threw for a total of 32 touchdowns and he pulled his team past the Giants yet again to beat them for the 1959 championship title. In 1963, he broke the NFL passing record when he passed for 3,481 yards. The following year, he came in first in yards per pass attempt with 9.26 and led the Colts to a record of 12–2, which was the NFL's best record at that point. In 1967, Unitas achieved an NFL record 58.5 completion percentage, passing for 3,248 yards and 20 touchdowns. He missed much of the 1968 season due to injury, but returned to lead the Colts on their sole scoring drive in 1969's Super Bowl III, which they ended up losing 16–7 to the New York Jets. But in January of 1971, the team saved face by beating the Dallas Cowboys in Super Bowl V. During this game, Unitas threw a pass to John Mackey for a 75–yard touchdown, but then suffered an injury right before halftime.

Unitas got benched the season after the Super Bowl victory, then was traded to the San Diego Chargers. He only played with the team for 1 year before retiring in 1973. During his career, Unitas played 211 games and established NFL records for most pass attempts with 5,186; most completions with 2,830; most total yards with 40,239; most touchdowns with 290; most 300–yard games with 26; and most consecutive games throwing touchdown passes with 47 (this record still stands).

During and after his remarkable career as a professional quarterback, Unitas' honors were in abundance, including being:
- Player of the Year (1959, 1964 and 1967)
- NFL Most Valuable Player (1964 and 1967)
- Player of the Decade (1960s)
- Selected for Ten Pro–Bowls
- Pro Football Hall of Fame (1979)
- Greatest Player in the First 50 Years of Pro Football

尺1寸的个子,体重达190磅,他们想以1万7千美元与他签约,他也欣然答应。他在一次赛季的第四场比赛中换下了受伤的乔治·肖,初次上场对抗芝加哥熊队。尤尼塔斯首次亮相并没有给人留下好印象,因为他的第一个传球被拦截了,让对手触地得分。更糟的是,就在下一场比赛中他在手递手传球中漏接球,让熊队起死回生。最后比分为27:58,小马队以失败告终。

糟糕的首次比赛之后,他更加努力,第一个赛季结束时共9次传出触地得分,新人得分成功率为55.6%。下个赛季,尤尼塔斯率领小马队夺得7胜5负的成绩,创下2550码数和24个触地得分。

1958年,尤尼塔斯带领小马队挺进国家橄榄球联盟锦标赛,对手是纽约巨人队,但是他在第六场比赛中受伤了,肺部刺破,3根肋骨断裂。尤尼塔斯住院接受治疗,但是4场比赛后他就归队,并率领小马队再次夺冠,这次是战胜旧金山49人队。尤尼塔斯说"这次胜利远比冠军赛重要",因为他是受伤后重返球队,而且比赛进行到一半时,小马队以27:7落后,最后以35:27获胜。但是许多热情的球迷并不这样认为,因为1958年冠军赛被称作"前所未有的最了不起的比赛",他成为全国电视直播的明星。在最后两分钟内,巨人队以17:14领先小马队,但是尤尼塔斯连续7次传球,在剩下的7秒钟内点球得分,把比分扳平。然后,他继续带领小马队在加时赛中总传球80码,战胜了巨人队。

下个赛季中,外号"金手臂"、"约翰尼·尤"的尤尼塔斯总共有32次触地得分,再次击败巨人队,夺得1959年锦标赛冠军头衔。1963年,他以传球3481码数打破了国家橄榄球联盟纪录。次年,他每次传球码数为9.26,排名第一,并率领小马队获得12胜2负的成绩,这是那时国家橄榄球联盟最好的成绩。1967年,尤尼塔斯达到国家橄榄球联盟纪录:58.5传球率、传球码数为3248,20个触地得分。由于受伤,他错过了1968年很多比赛,但是重返小马队并带领他们闯入1969年的"超级碗III",这是他们唯一一次晋级决赛,最终以7:16败给了纽约喷气机队。然而,在1971年1月,该队在"超级碗V"大赛中击败了达拉斯牛仔队,为自己挽回颜面。比赛中,尤尼塔斯将75码触地得分球传给约翰·迈基,但是他却在中场前受伤了。

超级碗大获全胜后的那个赛季,尤尼塔斯一直坐冷板凳,后来他被换到圣地亚哥闪电人队。他只为该队效力1年,1973年便退役了。在尤尼塔斯职业生涯中,他总共参赛211场,并创下了国家橄榄球联盟多项"最多数"纪录:5186次传球数;2830次成功传球数;40239码数;26次300码比赛;连续47次传出触地得分球(此纪录保持至今)。

作为一名卓越的职业四分卫球员,尤尼塔斯的生涯内外都获得无数荣誉奖项:
·年度球员 (1959, 1964 和 1967年)
·国家橄榄球联盟最具价值球员(1964 和1967年)
·年代最佳球员 (60年代)
·入选十大职业碗冠军赛
·入选职业橄榄球名人堂 (1979年)
·20世纪上半叶职业橄榄球最佳球员
·入选国家橄榄球联盟75周年全明星队 (1994年)

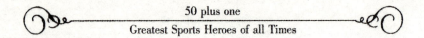

·Selected for the NFL's 75th Anniversary All–Time Team (1994)

About the Man Himself

After his football days, Unitas was involved in many charitable and civic groups. Some of those groups were the American Cancer Society, the American Legion, the Boy Scouts of America, the March of Dimes, The United Way and the American Foundation for Urologic Disease, Inc.

The Johnny Unitas Golden Arm Educational Foundation presented the first Johnny Unitas Golden Arm Award in 1987. Each year, the award goes to the best senior college quarterback in the United States.

In a somewhat ironic twist, although the foundation and award were named after Unitas' famous golden arm, his arm and the rest of his body were anything but golden in the years following his professional football career. In fact, due to the number of times he had broken his right hand, he had lost virtually total use of the hand near the end of his life. Unitas' struggle put a public spotlight on the plight of former professional football players who played in an era before padding and other safety equipment and who would later struggle with many different forms of permanent physical disabilities.

In a different kind of struggle, after the Colts moved from Baltimore to Indianapolis, Indiana, Unitas asked the Pro Football Hall of Fame to either list his display as belonging to the Baltimore Colts or remove it entirely. He did not want to have anything to do with Indiana, probably due to those long ago rejections by two Indiana college teams. Despite repeated requests from Unitas, the Hall of Fame never changed his display. He donated his Colts memorabilia to Baltimore's Babe Ruth Museum and it is currently on display in the Sports Museum at Camden Yards.

Unitas married Dorothy Jean Hoelle, in 1954 and, shortly after their divorce in 1972 he married Sandra Lemon. Unitas is the father of six sons and two daughters. He wrote several books, including his autobiography, *Johnny Unitas: The Johnny Unitas Story*. In 1993, Unitas underwent triple–bypass surgery, and on September 11, 2002, he died of a heart attack while exercising at a physical therapy center.

The story of Johnny Unitas' hard–working success as a professional football player and dedication to the sport of football, serves as an inspiration to all who aspire to greatness in anything they do. For this he is considered one of the greatest sports athletes of all times.

关于此人

结束橄榄球生涯后,尤尼塔斯加入了不少慈善及民事团体,比如:美国防癌协会,美国军团,美国童子军,美国优生优育基金会,美国联合慈善总会和美国泌尿系疾病基金会。

约翰尼·尤尼塔斯金手臂教育基金会于1987年第一次颁发了"约翰尼·尤尼塔斯金手臂奖"。每年,此奖项都会颁发给美国高级中学最佳四分卫。

有点讽刺的是,虽然基金会和奖项都以尤尼塔斯著名的"金手臂"命名,他的手臂和身体其他部分在职业橄榄球生涯后根本不能用"金"形容。事实是,由于他右手多次受伤,他的后半生基本不能使用这只手了。尤尼塔斯的痛苦反映了当时职业橄榄球运动员们的困境,他们那时没有护垫,也没有安全设备,很多人后来都有不同程度的永久性残疾。

另一种不同的困境出现了:小马队从巴尔的摩转成印第安纳州小马队后,尤尼塔斯要求职业橄榄球名人堂要么把他的所有展览资料归属巴尔的摩,要么全部撤销。他不想与印第安纳有任何关系,可能因为多年前曾遭两个印第安纳大学校队拒绝。虽然尤尼塔斯反复请求,但是名人堂从来没有改变过他的展览资料。他把他的小马队大事记捐给了巴尔的摩贝贝·鲁斯博物馆,如今被陈列在金莺球场体育博物馆。

1954年,尤尼塔斯与多拉丝·珍妮·荷艾勒结婚,1972年他们离婚后不久,他又娶了萨德拉·雷蒙。尤尼塔斯有六儿二女。他写过几本书,包括自传《约翰尼·尤尼塔斯的故事》。1993年,尤尼塔斯接受了3倍旁路手术,2002年9月11日,他在物理治疗中心锻炼时,因心脏病突发死亡。

约翰尼·尤尼塔斯是名努力而成功的职业橄榄球员,他辛勤致力于橄榄球运动,他的精神激励着无数有志者。这一点足以让他在50+1位最闪耀的体育巨星中享有一席之地。

Forty-two

Johnny Weissmuller

Why He is Among the 50 plus one Greatest Sports Heroes

Johnny Weissmuller did not lose one single official swimming competition throughout his entire career. Not a single one. What he did do, though, was win 52 U.S. National Championships and take home one bronze and five gold Olympic medals, while setting 67 world records. He may have been born in the early 1900s, but Weissmuller most definitely had game, and that is why he ranks amongst the greatest legends in sports history.

On the Way Up

János Weißmüller (Peter John Weissmuller) was born on June 2, 1904 in Freidorf, Austria–Hungary, or present–day Timisoara, Romania, to German–speaking Austrian parents, Petrus and Elisabeta. The family immigrated to the United States when Weissmuller was 7 months old, arriving in New York in January of 1905. After visiting relatives in Chicago, Illinois for a short while, they moved to Windber, a coal mining town in Pennsylvania. Several years passed before the family packed up their bags and moved to Chicago permanently.

Weissmuller and his younger brother, Peter, began spending their summer days swimming in Lake Michigan. They challenged each other aggressively as swimmers and soon, Weissmuller joined the Stanton Park pool, reigning victorious in all of the junior meets there. When he was 12 years old, he made the YMCA swim team and when he was 16, having dropped out of school after eighth grade, he began training at Chicago's Illinois Athletic Club under the highly successful coach, William (Big Bill) Bachrach. Weissmuller developed his unique high–riding front crawl (known as the six beat double Turdgen crawl stroke) during this time and his first official competition as an amateur took place on August 6, 1921, when he won his first Amateur Athletic Union race in the 50–yard freestyle. During the 1920s, he would go on to be a member of several of the club's championship relay and water–polo teams.

Weissmuller was a U.S. outdoor champion in individual freestyle swimming at 200 meters from 1921–1922; 400 meters from 1922–1923 and 1925–1928; 100 yards from 1922–1923 and 1925; 100 meters from 1926–1928; and 800 meters from 1925–1927. For the 100–yard and 400–meter events, it is likely the only reason he did not win in 1924 was because there were actually no competitions held in those events that particular year. Weissmuller also held the U.S. indoor titles in individual freestyle swimming for the 100–yard competition from 1922–1925 and from 1927–1928 as well as for the 220–yard event from 1922–1924 and from 1927–1928.

When it came time for the 1924 Summer Olympics, Weissmuller put down Windber, Pennsylvania as his birthplace as well as the birthdate of his younger brother in order to make sure that he was completely eligible to be a member of the United States Olympic team and to acquire a passport.

约翰尼·韦斯默勒

他为何入选《50+1位最闪耀的体育巨星》

约翰尼·韦斯默勒整个职业生涯没有输过一次正式游泳大赛。一次都没有。他真正做到的是52次赢得全美游泳锦标赛冠军,并夺得5枚奥运金牌和一枚铜牌,创下了67项世界纪录。

韦斯默勒虽然出生于20世纪初,但是他是最成功的体育明星,因此荣登50+1位最闪耀的体育巨星。

成长之路

1904年6月2日,约翰尼·韦斯默勒(彼得·约翰·韦斯默勒)出生于奥匈帝国Freidorf,即如今的罗马尼亚蒂米什瓦拉,他的父母是说德语的奥地利人。韦斯默勒7个月大时,全家移民至美国,于1905年1月搬到纽约。在伊利诺斯芝加哥亲戚家短暂逗留后,他们又搬到了宾夕法尼亚一个煤矿小镇——温博。几年后,全家搬迁至芝加哥,成为永久市民。

韦斯默勒和弟弟整个夏天都在密歇根湖游泳。他们之间展开激烈竞争,不久,韦斯默勒参加了斯坦顿公园游泳比赛,赢得了所有少年组冠军。12岁时,他入选YMCA游泳队,16岁时,他初二辍学,开始在芝加哥伊利诺斯体育俱乐部训练,教练是著名成功人士威廉(大比尔)·巴瑞奇。这段时间,韦斯默勒学会了独门爬泳(6次打水爬泳),第一次以业余选手身份正式参加了1921年8月6日的游泳比赛,并在50码自由泳中获得生平第一个业余体育联合会大赛冠军。20年代,他又陆续参加了俱乐部锦标赛接力队和水球队。

在室外自由泳个人赛事中,韦斯默勒是1921-1922年200米冠军;1922-1923、1925-1928年400米冠军;1922-1923和1925年100码冠军;1926-1928年100米冠军;1925-1927年800米冠军。在100码和400米赛事中,他没有获得1924年冠军,仅因那年没有举行这两项赛事比赛。韦斯默勒还多次获得美国室内自由泳个人赛事冠军,包括1922-1925、1927-1928年100码比赛;1922-1924、1927-1928年220码比赛。

到了1924年夏季奥运会,韦斯默勒把宾州温博当做自己的出生地,还换上弟弟的出生日期,以确保有资格作为奥运会美国队代表,并能够获得护照。

Professional Career

In 1924, Weissmuller did indeed get to travel to Paris, France with the U.S. Olympic team. Things would not have been the same without him. He beat another legendary swimmer, Duke Kahanamoku on February 24th to take the gold medal in the 100–meter freestyle event. This was expected as Weissmuller had broken Kahanamoku's world record back in 1922, swimming 100 meters in 58.6 seconds. During the 1924 Olympics, Weissmuller also brought home another individual gold medal for the 400–meter freestyle; a team gold medal in the 4 x 200–meter relay; and a team bronze medal as a member of the U.S. water–polo team. Then, at the 1928 Summer Olympics in Amsterdam, Weissmuller clinched two more gold medals in the 100–meter freestyle and 4 x 200–meter relay events.

Weissmuller, who won the Chicago Marathon twice and was a founding chairman of the International Swimming Hall of Fame in Fort Lauderdale, Florida, received many honors for his acheivements in swimming, most of them well after his career ended in 1929. Some of those honors are listed here:

· Greatest Swimmer of the First Half of the Century, sportswriters and sportscasters of America (1950)
· Helm's Hall of Fame medal (3 times)
· Sportsmen's World Award for Swimming (1968)
· American Patriot Award (1971)
· Awarded special sterling silver Olympic medals at the Munich Olympic Games (1972)
· Declared Sportsworld King (1972)
· Dewars Merit Award for Sports Immortal (1972)
· Declared an Undefeated King of Swimming, International Palace of Sports (1974)
· American Olympic Hall of Fame (1983)

About the Man Himself

Perhaps even more so than his swimming accomplishments, Weissmuller became famous through a highly successful movie career that began a few years after his retirement from the sports world. For the first couple of years after retirement, he also worked for BVD bathing suit company, representing their swimsuit line. He traveled around the country conducting swim shows, handing out BVD promotional pamphlets, signing his autograph and appearing on talk shows.

In 1929, Weissmuller made his motion picture debut with the movie Glorifying the American Girl, and he also played himself in the first of multiple Crystal Champions, a movie short that showcased different Olympic athletes. However, Metro–Goldwyn–Mayer (MGM) Studios was able to whisk Weissmuller away from his swimsuit job for good only after BVD got their way and photographed some of MGM's biggest names like Greta Garbo, Joan Crawford, Jean Harlow and Marie Dressler wearing BVD bathing suits.

Weissmuller did not hit it big in the movie industry until he signed a 7–year contract with MGM and played Tarzan in Tarzan the Ape Man (1932). Both the movie and Weissmuller experienced overnight success and Weissmuller went on to star in five more MGM Tarzan movies. Starting in 1942, he starred in six more Tarzan movies, this time with RKO Productions. Weissmuller earned an estimated $2 million total from those 12 movies, and to this day, he is the most famous of all the actors who have played Tarzan.

After leaving his beloved Tarzan role behind, Weissmuller starred in Columbia Pictures' Jungle Jim (1948), which was the first of 13 movies in which he would play the Jungle Jim

职业生涯

　　1924年,韦斯默勒的确入选美国队参加法国巴黎举办的奥运会。没有他,事情可能就不一样了。他在2月24日打败了传奇游泳名将杜克,才能摘得100米自由泳桂冠。这也是意料之中的,因为他在1922年以58.6秒成绩打破创下的100米世界纪录。1924年奥运会中,韦斯默勒又摘得一枚400米自由泳个人赛金牌、4×200米接力金牌,水球团体赛铜牌。在1928年阿姆斯特丹夏季奥运会上,韦斯默勒再次夺得两枚金牌:100米自由泳和4×200米接力。

　　韦斯默勒曾两度获得芝加哥马拉松赛冠军,也是佛州罗德岱尔国际游泳运动名人堂创始人,他因游泳事业的出色造诣获得无数荣誉,绝大多数是于1929年结束运动生涯后授予的。以下是部分获奖项目:
- 美国体育作家及体育广播协会"20世纪上半叶最伟大游泳运动员" (1950)
- Helm名人堂奖牌 (3 次)
- 游泳运动人物世界奖(1968)
- 美国爱国者奖 (1971)
- 慕尼黑奥运会特别银牌 (1972)
- 体育世界之王 (1972)
- Dewars 不朽运动员成绩奖(Dewars Merit Award for Sports Immortal) (1972)
- 国际体育宫殿"游泳卫冕冠军之王" (1974)
- 入选美国奥林匹克名人堂 (1983)

关于此人

　　韦斯默勒不仅游泳成绩卓越,在电影方面也造诣匪浅,他退役体坛几年后,成为一名著名而成功的电影人。退役后前几年,他还在BVD游泳衣公司工作,出任游泳衣形象代言人。他周游全国,组织游泳表演、分发宣传册、签名、上脱口秀节目。

　　韦斯默勒的荧屏处女秀是在1929年电影《伟大的美国女孩》中,并在最初的多个《水晶冠军》中出演自己,这个电影反映了不同的奥林匹克运动员。然而,自从BVD有了米高梅电影大腕们葛丽泰·嘉宝、琼·克劳夫德、让·哈洛 和玛莉·德莱索身穿泳衣的照片后,米高梅便终止了韦斯默勒为游泳衣代言的工作。

　　韦斯默勒直到与米高梅签订7年合同后,才真正成为电影界的巨星,他于1932年在电影《人猿泰山》中扮演泰山。电影和韦斯默勒都一夜成名,接着他又主演了5部米高梅公司的泰山系列电影。从1942年开始,他又演了6部泰山电影,这次是与RKO电影出品公司合作。韦斯默勒从12部电影中大约赚了200万美元,迄今为止,他仍是最著名的泰山扮演者。

　　告别自己最爱的泰山角色后,韦斯默勒又主演了1945年哥伦比亚影片公司的《密林吉姆》,这是他主演吉姆的13部影片中的第一部。1954年,就在结束那些电影拍摄后,他又

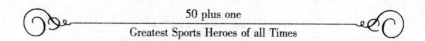

character. Right after he was .nished with those films in 1954, he appeared in three more jungle movies in which he played himself. The following year, he was the star in the *Jungle Jim* adventure television series for Screen Gems, which was a film subsidiary of Columbia. The show only ran for 26 episodes, but those episodes replayed time and time again on network and syndicated television for a long while.

Weissmuller eventually retired from his Hollywood career and moved back to Chicago in the late 1950s. He started a swimming pool company before retiring to Fort Lauderdale in 1965. In 1970, he was presented to Queen Elizabeth at the British Commonwealth Games in Jamaica and made a cameo appearance in The Phynx with Maureen O'Sullivan, who had played the character of Jane in some of his Tarzan movies.

Weissmuller continued to live in Fort Lauderdale until 1973, when he moved to Las Vegas, Nevada and briefly became a greeter at the MGM Grand Hotel. He broke his hip and leg in 1974 and learned that he had a serious heart condition. This probably came as a shock to Weissmuller who had exercised daily since birth.

In 1976, Weissmuller made his final motion picture appearance in *Won Ton Ton, the Dog Who Saved Hollywood*. He also made his final public appearance that same year after being inducted into the Body Building Guild Hall of Fame. The following year, he suffered multiple strokes, which slowed him down. He was a patient for a while in 1979 at the Motion Picture & Television Country House and Hospital in Woodland Hills, California, after which he moved to Acapulco, Mexico.

Weissmuller was married five times of which four ended in divorce. His wives included: band and club singer Bobbe Arnst, actress Lupe Velez, Beryl Scott, Allene Gates and Maria Bauman. He and Beryl had one son and two daughters, and his son, Johnny, Jr., has also been in his share of television shows and movies. Weissmuller died on January 20, 1984 of a pulmonary edema while at his Acapulco retirement home.

Weissmuller was a man of many talents and was able to transform his swimming talents to the big and small screen. Johnny Weissmuller's skills in swimming were Tarzan-sized making him one of the greatest athletes of all times.

主演了3部丛林片,扮演自己。次年,他出演了哥伦比亚旗下屏珍影业冒险电视剧《密林吉姆》。这个节目只播放了26集,却在美国网络和集团式电视中反复重播了很长时间。

韦斯默勒在好莱坞功成身退,于50年代末重回芝加哥。1965年从罗德岱堡退休后,他开办了游泳池公司。1970年,他在牙买加英帝国及联邦运动会中,受到伊丽莎白女皇的接见,并与泰山电影中珍妮的扮演者玛琳·奥沙利文在喜剧片The Phynx中精彩亮相。

韦斯默勒继续居住在罗德岱堡,直到1973年他搬到内华达州拉斯维加斯,曾短暂担任米高梅大酒店接待员。1974年他摔伤了臀部和大腿,并得知心脏有严重问题。这对于自出生起就一直锻炼的韦斯默勒来说,无疑是巨大打击。

1976年,韦斯默勒最后一次亮相于电影《好莱坞的救世主冯·顿顿》。入选健身名人堂后,他最后一次在那年出现于公众视线。次年,他好几次中风,导致行动缓慢。1979年,他在加州伍德兰德山电影及电视乡村疗养屋医院住过一段时间,后来他转到了墨西哥阿卡普尔科。

韦斯默勒结过5次婚,4次以离婚告终。他的几任妻子分别是:乐队及俱乐部歌手波比·安斯特,演员卢帕·维莱斯、白莉·司各特、阿兰妮·盖茨 以及玛莉亚·鲍曼。他和白莉育有一儿二女,儿子小约翰尼也上过他的电视节目和电影。1984年1月20日,韦斯默勒因肺水肿在阿卡普尔科的退休人士房屋中病逝。

韦斯默勒多才多艺,将游泳运动的成功造诣又转向了电视及电影业。约翰尼·韦斯默勒的游泳技能如同泰山的本领,这让他成为一名50+1位最闪耀的体育巨星。

Forty-three

Serena Williams

Why She is Among the 50 plus one Greatest Sports Heroes

Serena Williams, along with her older sister, Venus, has used her powerful playing abilities as well as her charismatic personality to bring worldwide public attention to the sport of tennis and to raise the bar substantially in women's tennis competition. She is the first black woman to win a Grand Slam event since 1958 and was ranked No. 1 in the World Tennis Association (WTA) tour at the end of her 2002 season. Her positive role model and outstanding contributions to worthy causes has added Serena Williams to the list of history's greatest sports heroes.

On the Way Up

Serena Jameka Williams was born on September 26, 1981 in Saginaw, Michigan. She and Venus, along with their three older half sisters, grew up in the Los Angeles suburb of Compton, California. Even though he had never played the sport himself, her father, Richard, dreamed of raising at least one tennis star. So, he picked up a book on how to play tennis and proceeded to teach Williams and her sister the basics of the game, bringing them to neighborhood tennis courts, where they trained. One of Richard's favorite ways to train the girls was to shoot hundreds of tennis balls at them in rapid-fire succession so that they would learn how to defend themselves with their rackets.

Williams began playing tennis when she was 5 years old, and before she had even reached the age of 10, she had won 46 out of 49 tournaments. There was a time when she took over her sister's spot as the No. 1 ranked tennis player aged 12 or under in California. In 1991, the family moved to Palm Beach Gardens, Florida so that Williams and her sister could train with Rick Macci, who had worked with other young stars like Jennifer Capriati. The two girls started winning even more tournaments and were soon the dominating forces in junior tennis competition. It was not long, however, until Richard took over as coach and promoter for his daughters and eventually pulled them out of the junior tennis circuit so that they could focus more on their education.

Professional Career

In 1994, Williams just beat the WTA rule change that prohibited 14-year-olds from competing in all tour events and she turned pro in October of that year. One year later, she played in her first professional non-WTA competition, the Bell Challenge in Vanier, Quebec. Williams did not have much individual success until 1997, when her ranking skyrocketed from No. 453 to 304. She beat Mary Pierce and Monica Seles at the Ameritech Cup in Chicago, making her No. 100 in the worldwide rankings. In July of 1998, Williams and her partner, Max Mirnyi, took home the mixed doubles title at Wimbledon, and she was ranked No. 21 by August.

In early 1999, Williams experienced her first WTA tour singles win at the Open Gaz de France in Paris. That season proved to be a great one. She won five singles titles in 48 matches, and defeated Martina Hingis for the U.S. Open championship in September. That victory made her

塞瑞娜·威廉姆斯

她为何入选《50+1位最闪耀的体育巨星》

　　塞瑞娜·威廉姆斯拥有超强的运动才能和魅力非凡的个性，她让全世界的目光都关注到网坛，改善了女子网球比赛的情况，她的姐姐是著名的网坛名将维纳斯。她是自1958年起唯一获得大满贯的黑人女运动员，2002年赛季末她在世界网球协会巡回赛中排名第一。她树立了积极向上的榜样，为高尚事业做出了杰出贡献，不愧是50+1位最闪耀的体育巨星中的一员。

成长之路

　　1981年9月26日，塞瑞娜·杰米卡·威廉姆斯生于密歇根萨吉诺谷。她和维纳斯以及3个同父(母)异母(父)的姐姐们成长在加利福尼亚州洛杉矶近郊康普顿市。虽然她的父亲理查德从未涉足过体坛，但是他梦想着培养出至少一名网球明星。因此，他开始读书了解如何打网球，教威廉姆斯和他姐姐基本技能，带她们去邻里网球场训练。理查德最喜爱的一种训练方法就是朝她们接二连三地发无数个球，这样她们就能学会如何用球拍保护自己免遭伤害。

　　威廉姆斯5岁开始打网球，还不到10岁就在49个锦标赛中获胜46次。在加州12岁以内网球运动员排名中，她取代了姐姐的位置，名列第一。1991年，全家搬到佛罗里达州棕榈滩花园，在那里，她和姐姐可以接受教练瑞克·马奇的培训，他也是诸如詹妮佛·卡普里亚蒂等其他小明星的教练。姐妹俩开始赢得更多的锦标赛，很快成为青少年网球比赛中的统治力量。然而，没过多久，理查德自己担任了女儿的教练兼赞助人，后来让她们离开了青少年网坛，这样可以把更多精力集中到学习中。

职业生涯

　　女子职业网球协会规定14岁少年不得参加任何巡回赛，但是1994年，威廉姆斯打破了这一常规，10月份成为职业球手。一年后，她参加了自己第一个职业性非女子职网协会的比赛——魁北克瓦涅举办的贝尔挑战赛。威廉姆斯直到1997年才取得了个人赛事的胜利，她的排名从第453名猛升到第304名。在芝加哥举办的Ameritech杯大赛中，她击败了玛丽·皮尔斯和莫尼卡·塞莱斯，在世界排名中直升为第100名。1998年7月，威廉姆斯和搭档马克斯·米尔尼捧回了温布尔登混双大奖，8月时，她已排名世界第21。

the first African–American woman to take home a Grand Slam singles title since Althea Gibson, who won five of them in the late 1950s. The day after her big win, Williams teamed up with her sister to capture the doubles title as well. Then, in October, Williams beat her sister for the very first time in the finals of the Grand Slam Cup in Munich, Germany. She ended that season among the top five ranked players worldwide and was the third–highest paid player in regards to prize money.

In 2000, Williams and her sister clinched both the Wimbledon and the U.S. Open doubles championships, and in the fall of that year, they won a gold medal and their 22nd consecutive doubles match in the finals at the Olympic Games in Sydney, Australia. They were the first sisters ever to win that event.

The next season was a bit of a roller–coaster ride for Williams, but she held her own at the U.S Open in September of 2001, beating Lindsay Davenport in the quarterfinals and Hingis in the semifinals. She ended up losing to her sister after two sets in the finals, but the two did make history together once again by being the first pair of sisters since 1884 to compete against each other in a grand slam final.

Williams came back stronger in 2002 and moved up to No. 1 in the WTA tour rankings after beating her sister in the finals of the French Open, Wimbledon and the U.S. Open. In 2003, she also beat her sister in the Australian Open, which was her fourth straight Grand Slam singles title. Williams was the ninth female tennis player to win all four Grand Slam events and only the sixth to hold all four of them during a 12–month time span. Despite winning her seventh Grand Slam event in the 2005 Australian Open singles, Williams' performance has dropped significantly due to a nagging left knee injury, which has forced her to withdraw from many competitions over the past few years. Some critics have questioned her commitment to the sport and have suggested that she has instead turned her attention to her fashion and acting careers. Williams denies any such claims.

For a list of Williams' professional wins so far, visit www.encouragementpress.com.

Throughout the years, Williams has received numerous awards for her grand accomplishments on the tennis court. Among other honors, she has been named:
- Most Impressive Newcomer, WTA Tour (1998)
- Rookie of the Year, TENNIS magazine and Rolex (1998)
- Most Improved Player, WTA Tour (1999)
- Player of the Year, TENNIS magazine (1999)
- Female Athlete of the Month, United States Olympic Committee (Sept. 1999)
- Doubles Team of the Year (with sister, Venus), WTA Tour (2000)
- Player of the Year, WTA Tour (2002)
- Best Female Athlete in the World, Associated Press (2002)
- One of the Sports Personalities of the Year, BBC (2002)
- Female Athlete of the Year, ESPY (2003)
- Female Tennis Player of the Year, ESPY (2003)
- President's Award (with sister, Venus), NAACP Image Awards (2003)
- Most Marketable Female Athlete, *Sports Business Daily* (2003)
- Third Most In.uential Minority in Sports, *Sports Illustrated* (2003)
- Comeback Player of the Year, WTA Tour (2004)
- Best Female Tennis Player, ESPY (2004)

　　1999年早期,威廉姆斯在法国巴黎室内公开赛上夺得了自己第一个女子职网协会巡回赛单打冠军。那个赛季她很了不起。她在48个比赛中赢得了5项单打冠军,9月份美国公开赛中,她打败了玛蒂娜·辛吉斯,获得冠军。这次胜利让她成为继阿尔西·吉布森之后第一位获得大满贯的美国黑人,阿尔西·吉布森曾在50年代末获得过5项。大获全胜后,威廉姆斯和姐姐组队双打。在10月份时,威廉姆斯第一次打败姐姐,赢得德国慕尼黑大满贯杯决赛。那个赛季结束时,她已是世界排名第五的选手,也是排名第三的获得高额奖金的运动员。

　　2000年,威廉姆斯和姐姐获得了温布尔登和美国公开赛两项双打冠军,那年秋天,姐妹俩在澳大利亚悉尼奥运会上赢得一枚金牌,也是第22次蝉联双打决赛冠军。她们是第一对赢得奥运会冠军的姐妹花。

　　下一个赛季对于威廉姆斯来说有点走下坡路,但是她在2001年9月的美国公开赛的四分之一决赛中击败了琳赛·达文波特,在半决赛中打败辛吉斯。在决赛中她输给姐姐两局,但是继1884年第一对在大满贯决赛中竞争冠军的姐妹花之后,她们再次书写了历史。

　　威廉姆斯2002年重返比赛时变得更厉害,她在法国公开赛、温布尔登和美国公开赛上打败姐姐后,排名在WTA巡回赛排名榜中晋升为第一。2003年,她在澳大利亚公开赛中再次打败姐姐,这是她第四次蝉联大满贯单打冠军。威廉姆斯是第九位赢得4项大满贯赛事的女运动员,也是6位保持四项大满贯的运动员中唯一在12个月内夺冠的球手。尽管威廉姆斯在2005澳大利亚公开赛单打决赛中赢了第七个大满贯赛事,她的表现因左膝受伤的困扰而明显不佳,这也使她不得不在接下来的几年内放弃很多比赛。有些评论家开始质疑她对体育的责任感,认为她已把注意力转到了时装和表演事业中。威廉姆斯对此坚决否认。

　　威廉姆斯至今取得的所有职业大赛冠军,请登录www.encouragementpress.com.
　·威廉姆斯在网坛职业生涯中因其出色成绩,获得了无数荣誉及奖项,包括:
　·WTA巡回赛"最突出新人奖" (1998)
　·被《网球》杂志及《劳力士》评为"年度新人" (1998)
　·WTA巡回赛"进步最快球手"(1999)
　·被《网球》杂志评为"年度运动员"(1999)
　·被美国奥委会评为"月份最佳女运动员" (Sept. 1999)
　·WTA巡回赛"年度双打队"(和姐姐维纳斯)(2000)
　·WTA巡回赛"年度最佳球手"(2002)
　·被美联社评为"世界最佳女运动员" (2002)
　·BBC年度国际体育人物奖 (2002)
　·ESPY年度女运动员 (2003)
　·ESPY年度网球女运动员 (2003)
　·有色人种民权促进协会总统奖(和姐姐维纳斯一起获得)(2003)
　·《体育商业日报》"最杰出女运动员" (2003)
　·《体育画报》"少数民族第三位最具影响力人物"(2003)
　·WTA巡回赛"年度最佳复出运动员" (2004)
　·ESPY年度最佳网球女运动员 (2004)

About the Woman Herself

As previously mentioned, Williams maintains a full and active life outside of tennis. She was home–schooled by her mother and received her high school diploma, and also attended the Art Institute of Florida where she studied fashion design. Showcasing her unique fashion sense both on and off the tennis court, Williams was included on the list of fashion trendsetters in the October 2002 issue of *People* magazine and was also one of the fashion icons in the January 2004 issue of *Vogue Italia.* She really hit it big in the fashion industry when her customdesigned Nike clothing line debuted in Paris in May of 2004.

Williams has also made her share of television and movie appearances, including a cameo appearance in Martin Lawrence's movie *Black Knight* and a small role as a school teacher in the sitcom *My Wife and Kids.* She has also appeared with her sister on the Late Show with David Letterman and her voice has been used in an episode of The Simpsons and on Disney Channel's *Higgleytown Heroes.* She was also in the *Do My Video,* which was by rapper Memphis Bleek and featured Jay–Z. Along with her sister, Williams has co–written two books so far. One is called *How to Play Tennis: Discover How to Play the Williams Sisters'* Way and the other is less of a tennis book and more of a life book. It is called *Venus and Serena: Serving from the Hip: 10 Rules for Living, Loving and Winning.*

Williams also makes charity work a priority. She hosts and participates in tennis clinics and makes appearances at schools and community organizations. For example, she visited the Challenger Boys and Girls Club of Downtown Los Angeles to give a motivational speech to more than 100 children and aspiring athletes as a part of a community event hosted by Bank of America. She has also donated $10,000 to Clarendon, South Carolina's School District 1, where tennis icon Althea Gibson was born.

In 2003, she was awarded with the Celebrity Role Model Award at the 3rd annual Avon Foundation awards event. She received another award in 2003 called the Young Heroes Award. Big Brothers Big Sisters of Greater Los Angeles and Inland presented her with the award because of her achievements as an exemplary role model in making a difference among the youth in the community. In 2004,

Williams was named that year's Player Who Makes a Difference by Family Circle magazine and Prudential Financial for her outstanding contributions to worthy causes.

Williams has proven at a young age that she can bring game to many aspects of life and, whether it be in tennis or something else entirely, only time can tell what she will accomplish next. The world will wait and watch as Serena William's star continues to rise.

关于此人

前面已经提到过威廉姆斯网坛内外的生活都很丰富多彩。她母亲在家教她读书，后来她获得高中文凭，进入佛罗里达州艺术学院主修服装设计。威廉姆斯在网坛内外都展示了自己独特的时尚理念，她在2002年10月的一期《人物》杂志上荣登引领潮流人物榜，也是2004年1月《时尚女装》(意大利)的时装偶像之一。2004年5月，她的"耐克"客户定制服装生产线开始登陆巴黎，标志着她已真正涉足时尚界。

威廉姆斯还出演了一些电视剧和电影，包括在马丁·劳伦斯的电影《黑骑士》中扮演小角色，还在情景喜剧《我的妻子和孩子》中扮演一名教师。她和姐姐上过大卫·莱特曼的《大卫深夜脱口秀》，她还为一集《辛普森一家》和迪斯尼频道的《喜乐镇英雄》配过音。她还上过Do My Video电台，这是两位说唱大将Memphis Bleek和Jay-Z的音乐在线电台。

威廉姆斯和姐姐写过两本书。一本是《怎样打网球：找到威廉姆斯姐妹的打球方法》，另一本书《维纳斯和塞瑞娜：生活、爱情和胜利的十大规则》没有过多涉及网球，而是更多关于生活。

威廉姆斯总是优先考虑慈善事业。他开办与参与网球诊所的工作，频频出现在学校及社区机构。比如，她参观了洛杉矶市中心的"挑战者男孩女孩俱乐部"，发表演讲、激励100多个儿童及有志运动员，这也是美国银行举办的一项社区活动。她还把1万美元捐赠给南卡罗林那第一学区所在地克莱仁登，这里是网球偶像阿尔西·吉布森的出生地。

2003年，她在第三届雅芳基金会颁奖大会中被授予"名人楷模奖"。同样在2003年她还获得"年轻英雄奖"。Big Brothers Big Sisters of Greater Los Angeles and Inland把她当做社区青年中的楷模而颁发此奖项。2004年，她因为慈善事业作出的杰出贡献而被《家庭圈》杂志和美国万全金融评为"年度最具影响力运动员"。

威廉姆斯在她年轻的时候就已证明她能将运动带入生活的各个方面，无论是网球运动还是其他，只有时间会告诉我们她接下来会有怎样的成就。全世界翘首以待，塞瑞娜·威廉姆斯这颗明星将继续升起。